PRINT NEWS AND RAISE HELL

The *Daily Tar Heel* and the Evolution of a Modern University

PRINT NEWS AND RAISE HELL

KENNETH JOEL ZOGRY

THE UNIVERSITY OF NORTH CAROLINA PRESS

Chapel Hill

This book was published with the assistance of the Blythe Family Fund of the University of North Carolina Press.

Designed by Richard Hendel
Set in Linoletter and Klavika types
by Tseng Information Systems, Inc.

The University of North Carolina Press has been
a member of the Green Press Initiative since 2003.

COVER ILLUSTRATION: Newspaper mastheads
courtesy of the *Daily Tar Heel*.

Library of Congress
Cataloging-in-Publication Data
Names: Zogry, Kenneth Joel, author.
Title: Print news and raise hell : the Daily Tar
Heel and the evolution of a modern university /
Kenneth Joel Zogry.
Description: Chapel Hill : The University of North
Carolina Press, [2018] | Includes bibliographical
references and index.
Identifiers: LCCN 2017037710| ISBN 9781469608297
(cloth : alk. paper) | ISBN 9781469669229
(pbk : alk. paper) | ISBN 9781469608303 (ebook)
Subjects: LCSH: Daily Tar Heel—History. | College
student newspapers and periodicals—North
Carolina—Chapel Hill. | University of North
Carolina at Chapel Hill—Periodicals. | Journalism—
Study and teaching—North Carolina—Chapel Hill.
Classification: LCC LH1.N7 D339 2018 |
DDC 378.1/989709756565—dc23
LC record available at https://lccn.loc
.gov/2017037710

The author dedicates this book to

WILLIAM CLYDE "BILL" FRIDAY (1920–2012)

A Great Tar Heel

CONTENTS

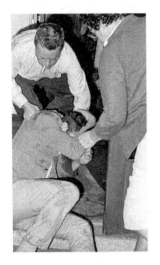

PRINT NEWS AND RAISE HELL

The job of a newspaper is to

print news and raise hell.

—Slogan under the masthead of the

Daily Tar Heel, *1966 (paraphrased*

from a quotation originally attributed

to Wilbur F. Storey, publisher of the

Chicago Times, *1861)*

INTRODUCTION

The *Daily Tar Heel* is the university's gyroscope.

—Bill Friday

In the year before his death at the age of ninety-two, Bill Friday sat down with me twice for interviews for this book. Because of his long and legendary career with the University of North Carolina system, Friday knew and worked with almost all of the *Daily Tar Heel* (*DTH*) editors and many other staff members over a remarkable five decades—almost half the paper's life—from the time he became Dean of Men at the University of North Carolina at Chapel Hill (UNC) in 1948, through his tenure as system president (1956–86), and then until his retirement as president of the William R. Kenan, Jr. Charitable Trust (1986–96). Friday's longevity and his understanding of college journalism (he served as sports editor of the *Technician* while an undergraduate at North Carolina State University) placed him in a unique position to reflect on the significance of the *DTH*. In his opinion, one of the most important contributions the student newspaper has made over the decades has been to "shine a bright light into the dark corners of the university, and, when necessary, hold it accountable." Friday deemed the *DTH*, past and present, a "first-rate" publication and referred to it as "the university's gyroscope." According to *Merriam-Webster*, a gyroscope is a "device used to maintain orientation during motion," an apt metaphor to describe a periodical that has both chronicled events at UNC and helped influence the direction of the evolving university since 1893. In researching and writing this book, I was encouraged by Friday to take a broad view of the paper's role on campus and across the state, advice I've followed.[1]

"News is the first rough draft of history," according to an oft-repeated quotation dating back more than a century. The *Daily Tar Heel*—which

has in essence been the social-media platform for UNC, long before digital communication was invented and the term coined—provides perhaps the best rough draft of the modern history of the nation's oldest public university. The fact that content is created by students, not faculty or administrators, allows for a wide range of perspectives that go beyond, and at times challenge, official policy. When this project began, the concept was to understand why the *DTH* has for many decades been considered among the best of college newspapers; what formative experiences on the UNC student paper led so many to go on to make important contributions in media and a variety of other fields and professions; and how

the *DTH* is weathering the challenges to print journalism in the early twenty-first century.[2]

All of these questions are explored in this book, within the broader framework of viewing the evolution of the modern University of North Carolina since 1893 through the paper's unique lens. The modern research university and the student newspaper are siblings; born and developing almost simultaneously as part of the post–Civil War generation which named itself the "New South." At times it is impossible to determine whether the growing pains of UNC drove changes at the *DTH*, or vice versa. Throughout its history a number of the school's most gifted students served on the paper's staff, where they were nurtured in an environment of free expression of ideas that complemented their classroom education. Unlike their classroom experiences, however, many an idealistic editor and staffer ran headlong into the limitations and consequences of free speech in the real-world setting of journalism. Working on the *DTH* was an intellectual and professional coming-of-age for generations of students, many of whom hailed from small southern towns and arrived in Chapel Hill with a limited worldview. Seasoned by their tenure on the paper, a remarkable number of these students went on to careers influencing and shaping the university's direction as faculty, administrators, trustees, or political leaders, thus completing the circle.

Another popular adage proclaims: "A free press is the cornerstone of democracy." The history of the University of North Carolina since its reopening and reconstitution in 1875, following the disruption of the Civil War and Reconstruction, can be characterized as a process of creeping democratization, slowly moving from a campus exclusively reserved for white men to the inclusion of all, regardless of gender, race, ethnicity, or sexual orientation. Despite the university's vaunted reputation for inclusion and liberalism, and the fact that it is publicly funded, achieving democratization has not always been a priority. In this regard the path followed by UNC reflects the broader social, cultural, and political evolution of North Carolina and the nation. Across the decades the university's student newspaper has been on hand to report events, serve as a public forum, criticize and prod authority, and, in its finest moments, actively work to effect change for the greater good.[3]

The evolution of the university, as well as of the editorial policy of the *Daily Tar Heel*, has been neither linear nor always consistent. North Carolina's modern history is different from that of most other southern states in that there has been a persistent strain of progressivism in a region steeped in "traditional" values and customs. The dynamic tension between progressivism and traditionalism—also characterized as liberalism and conservatism, respectively—has created a unique social and political climate. The University of North Carolina has often been cited as the epicenter of the progressive side of that schism in the state, and since the 1920s both the university and the *DTH* have been frequent targets of political and social conservatives. But, as the history of the *DTH* reveals, that characterization is overly simplistic, as both the school and the paper have also been strongly criticized at times for not being sufficiently progressive. Additionally, the UNC community has always maintained a strong core of conservatism among given groups of students, faculty and administrators, and alumni—many of whom served on governing boards or as elected state officials with oversight power and control over the university's purse strings. And though it can be legitimately argued that the paper's news coverage and editorial policy have historically tilted left of center, this book reveals that the voice of conservatives has also been well represented, often by students who later became prominent businesspeople and politicians.

Therefore, as this book reveals, it is not surprising that a significant portion of the paper's history is political; either in the small *p* sense of campus politics, or the capital *P* sense of state and national politics. And though the *Daily Tar Heel* did not begin routinely endorsing presidential and other candidates until 1960 (most students could not participate in elections until 1971, when the voting age was lowered from twenty-one to eighteen), the paper, along with the university, began to be involved in state politics as early as the 1920s. A reading of the paper since that time reveals frequent grappling with the concept of the limits of social and political rights in a constitutional democracy, and of achieving equilibrium in one sense or another—the proverbial gyroscope in motion. What is the proper balance between progressivism and traditionalism at a public university? What is the obligation of the university to preserve or expand the rights of any particular group? This debate is most clearly manifest in the tension over race, which has been a central moral and political issue at UNC from its founding, from slavery and emancipation to segregation and the struggle for equality in all forms.

Woven through the many news stories, editorials, and sketches of personalities that found their way into the *Daily Tar Heel* over the past century-and-a-quarter are three historical threads that tie the narrative of this book together. The first strings together the various strands of discussion and debate over the ideological direction of the university and the state since the late nineteenth century—the ongoing tug-of-war between progressivism and traditionalism (or conservatism). The second tracks issues and conflicts related to freedom of words and ideas: academic freedom in the classroom, freedom of speech on campus, and freedom of the press with regard to the *DTH* and other publications. The third and final thread follows the role of "big-time" athletics at a top-tier public research institution, a thread that begins in the

earliest issues of the paper, soon after intercollegiate sports first came to Carolina, and continues to this day.

Focusing on these often interwoven historical narratives while keeping the book a reasonable length was a daunting challenge. Nearly 20,000 editions of the paper have been issued since 1893, the number of student editors-in-chief approaching 150, and staff totaling somewhere in the thousands. Such is the nature of a collegiate publication, with a transient staff usually limited to four years' involvement, at most. Each issue of the paper contains a dozen or more stories that unfold as they happen, most often without context and always without knowledge of how the story ends. Sifting through the sea of articles and editorials was fascinating, but for a historian felt at times like slogging through wet cement—slow and opaque, without being able to see where your feet would land. Frequently the stories had to be pieced together and contextualized using additional sources, including other publications, oral history interviews, and materials now housed in the University Archives. Meeting these challenges meant employing the fine art of reduction. Every individual, every story, every controversy, every anecdote—and there are thousands—could not be recounted. Entire books could have been written on such topics as the student experience in the *DTH* office (which often eclipsed academic endeavors), Carolina sports coverage over the decades, the role of student cartoons, and the history of advertising in the paper—just to name a few other interesting areas. Although major developments in the paper's operation, management, and style are outlined, especially where relevant to the main themes, this book does not constitute an exhaustive institutional history of these complex subjects. For those readers interested in delving deeper into specific stories or learning more about particular individuals, additional resources exist, notably expanded "birthday" editions of the paper, including those published to mark the seventy-fifth, one-hundredth, and one-hundred-twentieth anniversaries of the publication of its inaugural edition.

In addition to the formidable challenges posed by the primary materials, little scholarship exists with regard to the history of the American collegiate press. Further, historical writing on the modern history of UNC is more limited than one might expect. This book attempts to add to the scholarship in both of these areas, in a manner accessible to a wide readership. In terms of mechanics the book's chapters are organized broadly in chronological order, divided within by topical sections. The chapter chronology follows the academic calendar, with years beginning in the fall and ending the following spring. For ease of reading, spelling, capitalization, punctuation, and in some instances style have been standardized.

Hopefully this book will contribute to scholarship in a variety of disciplines, and help those who care for the venerable *Tar Heel* to see the bigger picture, something very difficult during a limited four-year college experience, or even a multi-year professional career. Understanding the fundamentals of sound journalism—which haven't changed from the days of quill pens and hand-cranked presses to the present virtual world of the digital information age—and the principles of free speech, a free press, and academic freedom, will guide the paper forward for at least another 125 years.

1

OFFICIAL ORGAN OF THE ATHLETIC ASSOCIATION

1893–1923

BEGINNINGS

At first glance, the campus of the University of North Carolina in the early months of 1893 seemed an unlikely place for the birth of a newspaper. Especially one that would become an important voice for the school throughout the twentieth century and well into the twenty-first, and would help launch the careers of dozens of noted journalists and graduates in a wide range of professions. Despite the fact that the university was to celebrate its centennial that October—the 100th anniversary of the laying of the cornerstone of the first building, Old East—the campus retained a small, bucolic atmosphere. The student body was tiny, with 317 students and 23 members of the faculty. Year-round Chapel Hill residents could be counted in the hundreds, and the nearby cities of Raleigh and Durham had populations of about 13,000 and 5,800, respectively. The largest city in North Carolina at the time was Wilmington, with a population of just over 20,000 residents.[1]

Physically the campus looked little different in 1893 than it had on the eve of the Civil War. An alumnus of the class of 1860 returning more than three decades later would have found virtually everything familiar. There were ten principal buildings on campus, all of which, except the newer Memorial and Commons Halls (both now demolished), were antebellum structures. None of the buildings served a single school or department, as none were large enough at the time to require one. The school of medicine was less than 15 years old and offered only two years of instruction, no formal school of law yet existed, and the creation of a department of journalism was three decades in the future. The ante-

Old Well, 1892. The young man on the right is likely a member of the UNC baseball team, based on his cap. This is one of the earliest known images of the interlocking "NC" logo. (NCC)

bellum buildings had no central heating, electricity, or telephones. Plumbing was primitive at best: there were five "shower baths" in the basement of Smith Hall for the entire student body. The Old Well was not the iconic, symbolic structure it would later become; it was a rough-hewn wooden hut with a bucket that served as a source of water for students and horses. The small library was located in Smith Hall, and the majority of books were not owned by the university but by the Dialectic and Philanthropic Societies, the oldest student organizations on campus. A rudimentary baseball field with rickety wooden bleachers had been erected in the late 1880s, but no football stadium yet existed.[2]

It was an inauspicious setting for an independent, student-run weekly newspaper, published, as the editors announced in the first issue, "under the auspices of the University Athletic Association, devoted to the interests of the University at large." The paper had a bold and broad mission to "contain a summary of all occurrences in the University and village of Chapel Hill," and though primarily established to cover

Front page
of the
inaugural
issue of the
Tar Heel,
February 23,
1893. (NCC)

THE TAR HEEL.

VOL. I. UNIVERSITY OF NORTH CAROLINA, FEBRUARY 23, 1893. NO. 1.

The Tar Heel,
University of North Carolina.

EDITORS.

CHARLES BASKERVILLE,
WALTER MURPHY,
A. C. ELLIS,
W. P. WOOTEN.
PERRIN BUSBEE,
J. C. BIGGS,
A. H. McFADGUE.

Editor in Chief
    CHARLES BASKERVILLE,
Managing Editor,
    WALTER MURPHY,
Business Manager,
    A. H. McFADGUE.

THURSDAY, February 23, 1893.

CHURCH DIRECTORY.

Baptist Church.
REV. J. L. CARROLL, D. D.
Preaching every Sunday, morning and night. Sunday School at 9:30 a. m. Prayer meeting every Wednesday night.

Presbyterian Church.
REV. J. E. FOGARTIE.
Preaching every Sunday, morning and night; except the first Sunday in each month. Sunday School at 10:30 a. m. Prayer meeting every Wednesday night.

Methodist Church.
REV. N. M. WATSON.
Preaching every Sunday, morning and night Sunday School at 10:30 a. m. Prayer meeting every Wednesday night.

Episcopal Church.
REV. FREDERIC TOWERS.
Sunday services at 7, 11 and 7 o'clock. Weekly services at 4 p. Friday. Sunday School 4 p. m During Lent services daily at 4 p. m

UNIVERSITY DIRECTORY.

University Choir.
PROF. KARL P. HARRINGTON, Leader.
Organists, J. A. MAXWELL and CHAS. ROBERSON.

UNIVERSITY MAGAZINE,
SIX TIMES A YEAR.

EDITORS.

PHI.	DI.
W. P. Wooten,	W. P. M. Currie
J E. Ingle, Jr.,	J. M. Check,
A. H. Koonce,	T. J. Wilson.

Business Manager,
    Prof. Collier Cobb.

UNIVERSITY LIBRARY.

DR. EBEN ALEXANDER, Librarian,
F. L. WILCOX Student Librarian
Open every day except Sunday, from 11:30 to 1:30 and from 3 to 5. Open Sundays from 3 to 6 p. m.

University Reading Room
Open every day. Leading papers published in Union and State on file.

University Press Association.
H A. Rondthaler, president,
Dr. B Whitaker, Secretary.
Julian Engle Dr. B. Whitaker,
H. A. Rondthaler, Walter Murphey, Executive Committee.

Object is to further the disbursement of news relating to the University.
Meets at the call of the president.

University Athectic Association.
H. B. Shaw, president.
J. L Pugh, sec'y. and treas.
Meets regularly the second Saturday in September and January Other calls subject to the president

University Foot Ball Team.
Michael Hoke, captain,
Charles Baskerville, Manager.

University Base Ball Team.
Perrin Busbee, captain,
W. R. Kenon, manager.

University German Club.
J. C. Biggs, president,
C. R. Turner, sec'y. and treas.
Meets at the call of the president. Leader selected for each German.

University Glee Club.
E. Parson Willard, president and leader,
Charles Roberson, manager.
Prof. Karl P. Harrington, director.

Shakespere Club.
Dr. Thomas Hume, president,
J. M. Check, sec'y. and treas.
Meet in the Y. M. C. A. hall the third Tuesday night in each month. Library open one hour each day.

Elisha Mitchell Scientific Society.
Prof. J. A. Holmes, president,
Prof. J. W. Gore, vice-president,
Dr. F. P. Venable, secretary and treasurer.
Meets in Person hall second Tuesday night in each month.
Journal issued twice a year.

Historical Society.
Dr. Kemp Battle, president and corresponding secretary.
H. M. Thompson, secretary and treasurer.
Meets at the call of the president.

Philanthropic Society. (Secret)
Meets every Friday night in Phi. hall new east building.

Dialectic Society. (Secret)
Meets every Friday night and Saturday morning in Di. hall new west building.

The Order of Gim Ghoulds. (Secret) Junior.
The society meets in February. October. Banquet Thursday night of commencement.

Fraternities. (Secret)
Sigma Alpha Epsilon, Kappa Alpha, Zeta Psi Alpha San Amega, Sigma Nu, Phi Kappa Sigma, Phi Delta Theta, Phi Gamma Delta Sigma Phi. Beta Thata Pi Delta Kappa Epsilon, meet in their respective halls every Saturday night.

Y M. C. A.
F. C. Harding, president,
George Stephens, secretary and treasurer,
R. E Zachary, organist.
Meets four times a week in Y. M. C. A. hall. Members appointed to lead. Hand books issued every September.

Philological Society.
Dr. Eben Elexander, president.
Prof. Karl P. Harrington, secretary and treasurer,
Meets first Friday night in each month.

The Hellenian. (Annual)
Published by the Fraternities,

THE TAR HEEL.

A weekly paper published at the University of North Carolina, under the auspices of the University Athletic Association, devoted to the interest of the University at large.

Issued every Thursday morning. It will contain a summary of all occurrences in the University and village of Chapel Hill.

Space will be assigned for the thorough discussion of all points pertaining to the advancement and growth of the University.

A brief account each week of the occurrences in the amateur athletic world, with especial attention to our own athletic interests, and progress in Football, Baseball, Tennis, etc.

All society news, personals and every subject of interest both to the students and citizens of the village, will be treated each week.

The columns will be open to discussion on all appropriate subjects with an endeavor to do full justice to everyone. The chief and his assistants will decide as to appropriateness of articles—no anonymous articles will be accepted without autho, nam being known to the chief, which will be in confidence, if desired.

Advertisers will note that this is the *best, quickest,* and *surest,* means by which they can reach the students. For notes see or write "Business Manager of TAR HEEL" Chapel Hill N. C, or drop him a card and he will call.

Subscription one Dollar and a half per session. This spring 75cts.

SALUTATORY.

The growing demands of the University have shown the need of a weekly paper. The University Athletic Association regarding itself as the means by which such a need could be supplied, at a stated meeting elected a board of editors (chief and five subs.) and a business manager.

With this apology only, the first issue of the first volume of the TAR HEEL makes its appearance.

This new venture is necessarily entered upon by the present board with no little trepidation, nevertheless with a determination, to make a success which can only be done through the indulgence and assistance of our faculty and fellow-students. Therefore we invite honest criticism and any aid in the advancement of this new project will be thoroughly appreciated.

THE LEGISLATIVE COMMITTEE VISIT THE UNIVERSITY.

The following members of the legislature composing the visitation committee arrived at the University on a special train Friday morning, February 3rd:

Messrs. Battle, chairman; Cheek Aycoke, James, Pou, of the senate; and Messrs. Holt (chairman) Euse, Parker, Starnes, Walker, Ward, of the house.

After breakfasting, the regular chapel exercises were attended, then visits were made to the reading room, libraries and various lecture rooms where classes were assembled. The numerous laboratories were inspected as well as some of the students' rooms. In the afternoon meetings of both the societies were held and the gentlemen who were not alumni were made honorary members. Just after prayers the boys called repeatedly for speeches from our visitors, a majority of whom responded most felicitously and gave words of encouragement for the future outlook of the university, from a legislative appropriation standpoint. All saw the need of a sufficient appropriation to fully equip, this the most useful and important of all the State properties, and give to a university of whose past brilliant record and whose future prospects are such as would make any State in the union proud to be the possessor of such an heritage to hand to posterity, a sufficient appropriation to put the university on a financial basis equal to its rapid expansion and growth. When some of the committee expressed their deep regret at not having had an opportunity of receiving an education, in their youth, we could not but feel that it was a duty that was owed to future generations, and which has been due to those that have passed away, that the supreme law making power in the State, ought to make tuition at the university free to North Carolinians as is done at the University of Virginia to Virginians and the only way to do this is to appropriate a sufficient amount to keep the university up, until resources from outside States and the technical courses shall make itself sustaining, and, too, we could not but think what a shame and loss it was to North Carolina, that it had failed to open the doors of the university, in the past to such sterling manhood as represented the legislature on the committee. The body of the students were well pleased with our friends, if they are a fair sample of our legislators this year. North Carolina is in good hands. They know the needs of the University.

UNC athletics, "space will be assigned for the thorough discussion of all points pertaining to the advancement and growth of the University." Thus, on Thursday, February 23, 1893, "the *Tar Heel* first placed its tender foot to the ground and made its first print" (as an article in the *University Magazine* cleverly punned on the occasion of the paper's twentieth anniversary).[3]

The creation of what is today the *Daily Tar Heel* was rooted in two events: the reopening of the University of North Carolina in 1875, and the school's first intercollegiate football game in the fall of 1888. After struggling through both the Civil War and the political turmoil of Reconstruction, the university limped virtually lifeless into the 1870s. With the endowment spent and enrollment at a trickle, the trustees voted to close the school in February 1871. Over the next four years proponents wrangled over the possible new direction of the university, with Kemp Plummer Battle, an alumnus and trustee who had first proposed changes in the 1860s, leading the charge. The "Battle Plan," as it was known, was based on the so-called German model of higher education then gaining popularity in Europe and the United States. This model emphasized research over oratory, required faculty with earned graduate degrees, and implemented theses and examinations with a standardized grading scale as a means of assessing individual student performance. Research, not rote memorization of the classics and traditional scientific models, was central to this pedagogical approach, and the result was a revolution in higher education. The introduction of these practices at the newly reopened university in 1875 brought entirely new curricula in applied and social sciences, marking a sharp break from the antebellum classical education based primarily on the concept of preparing middle- and upper-class young men to take their place in a rigidly ordered society. This new educational structure was far more effective in preparing students to meet the challenges of the industrializing postwar South, and would become the basis of the modern research university in the twentieth and twenty-first centuries.[4]

The introduction and immediate popularity of intercollegiate football at UNC also played a key role in the creation of the *Tar Heel*. The sport was seen from the time of its inception not only as an extracurricular activity that built school spirit, but also as a source of "manly" vigor for the university and its students. It was the physical embodiment of a new academic culture, one based on individual achievement that contributed to the team's success. According to historian James Leloudis:

> Sports became a source of shared identity on a campus where students no longer studied a common curriculum or participated in campus-wide debating unions. Young men might view themselves as historians, chemists, economists, or philosophers during most of the week, but on game day, they were all united as "Tar Heels." Athletic competition also recapitulated the lessons of the classroom. On the gridiron, as in academic pursuits, success required the mastery of a specialized knowledge of plays and strategy, and the difference between winning and losing was measured by a cold numerical score. The victorious athlete, like the triumphant scholar, had to apply himself constantly to self-improvement, for at any moment he might

confront a rival who had been more resolute in his preparation.[5]

Significantly, football also quickly became the principal means of bringing alumni back to UNC on a regular basis—and their moral and financial support became increasingly important as the university pushed to modernize in the late nineteenth and early twentieth centuries. In the fall of 1892, four years after Carolina's first intercollegiate game (played against Wake Forest), the team won a much-celebrated victory over archrival the University of Virginia, giving the school an early regional title. After that victory the desire to follow training of the football team and chronicle its triumphs on the field became more widespread among both students and alumni, and resulted in the creation of the weekly *Tar Heel*.

The newspaper industry was dramatically expanding in the 1890s, both nationally and in North Carolina. Until development of commercial radio in the 1920s, newspapers were the primary source of daily news in the United States. As the nation's population began to move in earnest from the countryside to rapidly growing urban areas, the need for increased communication offered by newspapers grew proportionally. In addition, new technologies, including advances in typesetting and the development of photogravure and halftone photography processes, allowed newspapers to become larger and more visually appealing. In North Carolina these advances, coupled with a growing population, created a central role for newspapers in the state's seminal political battle of the 1890s, which pitted a biracial "fusion" coalition of black Republicans and white Populists against the Democrats, who ran on a platform of white supremacy. The fierce fighting played out in a half a dozen newspapers supporting one of the two sides and was led by Democrat and UNC alumnus Josephus Daniels, editor and publisher of the *Raleigh News and Observer*, who printed race-baiting editorials and front-page cartoons showing African American men as incompetent and lusting after white women. The most incendiary incident of the battle—literally—occurred in November 1898, when racial violence broke out in Wilmington following the publication of an editorial by African American Alexander Manly, editor and publisher of the Wilmington *Daily Record*. Manly turned the argument about black men lusting after white women on its ear, pointing out that in fact black women had suffered sexual violence at the hands of white men for centuries. The result was the torching of the *Daily Record* building by white supremacists infuriated by Manly's editorial, followed by the forceful removal of the city's duly elected officials—the only domestic coup d'etat in U.S. history. When the smoke cleared in 1900, the fusion coalition was broken. Victorious Democrats passed legislation instituting codified Jim Crow segregation and election reform effectively leading to political disfranchisement of African American men—all promoted in the pages of the *News and Observer* and other papers. Such was the importance and power of the newspaper industry in North Carolina in the last decade of the nineteenth century.[6]

The *Tar Heel* was born into this atmosphere and also followed a well-established tradition of college newspapers in the United States. The first edition of the *Dartmouth Gazette* appeared in 1799, with a poem and short story by famous nineteenth-century orator and statesman Daniel

This ca. 1900 photograph shows the small and almost rural appearance of the UNC campus at the time the *Tar Heel* began. From left to right, Old West, South Building, Gerrard Hall, and the original Memorial Hall, demolished in 1930 and replaced by the current structure. The gazebo is not the Old Well, but another water pump. (NCC)

Webster, then a student, published under the moniker "Icarus." An editorial in the *Tar Heel* in February 1907 erroneously called Webster "the legitimate father of 1,500 children," referring to the number of college newspapers in existence at the time. But Webster only wrote for the first edition of the Dartmouth paper; he did not found it. And before the Civil War, college newspapers numbered only some two-dozen in the United States, with honors for the first at a public university going to Miami University of Ohio in 1867,

some twenty-six years before the appearance of the *Tar Heel.* At UNC, student publications began in 1844 with the first issue of the *N. Carolina University Magazine,* a largely literary periodical that remains in print, despite numerous changes in name and format over the years. In 1890 the Athletic Association at Carolina made an initial attempt at a newspaper with the appearance of the *Chapel Hillian,* but that paper folded in 1892.[7]

Much of today's *Daily Tar Heel* can be seen evolving in the yellowed and brittle pages of

First staff of the *Tar Heel*, 1893.
Editor Charles Baskerville is seated on the right. (NCC)

early editions of the *Tar Heel*. Not only was the paper's format and style created during its first thirty years, more significantly, editorial policy was developed and journalistic integrity established that set the highest possible standards. From the very first issue, freedom of speech and freedom of the press were ferociously guarded. In addition, a number of the *Tar Heel*'s early editors and staff would go on to play key roles in creating and nurturing a nascent school of journalism at Carolina, and in building the modern university.

EARLY OPERATIONS

It is likely no coincidence that the first issue of the *Tar Heel* appeared in February 1893, the same month the university press opened its doors, as other options for local printing were limited. Established by five members of the faculty who represented the university's new academic direction, the purpose of the university press was to publish all manner of materials—scholarly, literary, and administrative—related to UNC. Its founders were among the most prominent and forward-thinking men on campus: Francis Venable, professor of chemistry and later UNC president whose research with students John Motley Morehead III and William Rand Kenan Jr. led to the practical development of calcium carbide and creation of the Union Carbide Corporation; John Manning, who created the university's modern school of law; Richard Whitehead, who is largely responsible for the early development of the school of medicine; Joshua Gore, who taught engineering and brought all manner of modern services to campus, including electricity, heating plants, and long-distance telephone service; and Collier Cobb, professor of geology, who served as the press's manager. Although the press was a private operation, the university sanctioned its creation by providing it a home on the first floor of the campus building known as New West. Over the next three decades it produced a range of student publications, including the monthly *University Magazine*, humor periodicals such as *Tar Baby*, and even for one year a rival newspaper, the *White and Blue*. In 1922, following establishment of the University of North Carolina Press, a full-service publishing house created to publish scholarly monographs, the university press moved off campus and was no longer officially associated with UNC. By that time, however, the *Tar Heel* had found a printing company in Durham.[8]

Getting out the *Tar Heel* in the early years

with a small staff and perpetually unstable financial resources was something of a hit-or-miss proposition. New issues of the paper usually appeared on Thursdays, though sometimes problems arose that caused it to appear a day or two late or even miss a week entirely. In October 1909 the paper began appearing twice a week, on Tuesdays and Fridays, but in 1911 it reverted to a weekly because of an inability to sustain the increased cost. Publication usually began in September of each year, following the academic calendar, and continued through graduation the following spring. In 1919, the year novelist-to-be Thomas Wolfe was editor, the first issue did not appear until October—one wonders if Wolfe was busy collecting his thoughts. Despite the late start, Wolfe succeeded in putting the paper on a semiweekly schedule again: first on Wednesdays and Saturdays, and then on Tuesdays and Fridays. Special editions were rare, consisting of two regular issues devoted to the YMCA, as well as annual commencement issues (including several year-end pictorial editions in the 1910s) and a 1916 edition put out to cover a statewide newspaper convention held on campus.[9]

Early issues of the *Tar Heel* were printed as a four-page periodical, 10" × 12" with four columns set in 11-point type. Modern headlines were unknown, and articles appeared with titling set either in bold print or in a slightly larger point size. Following late-nineteenth-century punctuation standards, titles of even one word were followed by a period, as was the banner until 1909. In fact, the style of font and size of the *Tar Heel* banner changed continuously over the years. A block print typeface of various styles was used from 1893 until 1923, when an Old English style was introduced (the word "heel" appeared with a lower case "h"). To celebrate a baseball victory over archrival Virginia, the entire issue of May 2, 1896, was printed in "Carolina blue" ink (several other issues were similarly printed in the 1890s, including one in red and blue ink); otherwise, the paper did not use color printing during this period. Early issues rarely contained illustrations, and photographs did not appear until 1901. The size of the paper was enlarged to a more standard 12½" × 19½" in 1895, and by 1918 it was divided into five 2¼" columns. In 1916 the editors announced the expansion of the paper to six pages, using an automobile analogy: "It has evolved this year from a four cylinder to a six. Whether the 1917 *Tar Heel* will be built on the old 1900 model, slow and heavy and uncomfortable, or whether it will be a supersix, serviceable, powerful, and beautiful no one can yet tell." A year later the paper reverted to four pages due to lack of funds, and it remained that size for the duration of World War I.[10]

As a self-supporting publication independent of the university, the *Tar Heel* was financed entirely through subscriptions and advertisements from 1893 to 1923. The first year, 231 sub-

THE TAR HEEL.

THE OFFICIAL ORGAN OF THE UNIVERSITY ATHLETIC ASSOCIATION.

Vol. 4.   UNIVERSITY OF NORTH CAROLINA, CHAPEL HILL, N. C., MAY, 2nd. 1896.   NO. 27.

CAROLINA FOREVER !!

We Win from Virginia by Superior Scientific Base Ball.

Umpiring Fair and Satisfactory.   Score 14 to 6.

Yackity-Yack,
Hooray! Hooray!
Yackity Yack,
Hooray! Hooray!
Carolina Varsity!
Boom Rah! Boom Rah!
Car—o—li—na.

The Carolinians were on top. They arrived in Danville on Friday, the 24th. at 1:40 and were in it from the start. That afternoon they put up a very pretty practice on the Danville Diamond where the great game was won.

The Virginians arrived on Friday night and at the sight of them, the Carolinians put on a more determined look and prepared to do or die. Saturday morning was dark and cloudy and it looked like more hard luck for Manager Carmichael. But the Fates were kind and about noon the clouds sailed away, giving us a pretty afternoon. The N. C. boys were also much grieved that their star first baseman was sick and in bed, but with the drifting of the clouds, he, too pulled round and came upon the field with grit enough to stick until the game was ended.

On the field, the Virginia team was first and they did good snappy work. But they were eclipsed in this too. The Carolinians were there to do their best and they did it. Manager Tilton, of Virginia, remarked, "If we could'nt beat that team, I'd take the boys right back to Charlottesville." Well, "he laughs best who laughs last."

The game with the exception of Virginia's fielding was superb, and was won by superior batting, fielding, and base running. The infield played a better game than the one against Yale, and the out field deserves much credit for their good snappy work. The battery work was fine and especially at critical moments that they work together. The game was worthy of the team whose record for the Spring of '96 will always be remembered.

field amid hurrahs from their many sympathizers.

Fred Pearsall smiled when the umpire called three balls and he smiled still more when McGuire sat down, out on strikes. Then Marshall gave Grex a "pod-up" and Dillard retires the side at first on Johnson's pretty throw.

Stanly came up from short and let an easy one hit him and ofcourse stole second. Winston flew out to Dillard and Gregory made a sacrifice hit advancing "Cap" to third. Bailey gave Hoxton a hot one which he threw wild to first, as Stanly crossed the plate, scoring our first run. Marshall caught Brem's foul fly.

E. C. GREGORY.

Second inning. Garnett goes out, Stanly to Winston and Hoxton hits a pop-fly to "Grex." Bonney drives it for three bases but dies at third when Stanly takes in McKim's fly.

Graham is out from McGuire to Cochran and Whitaker on a foul to Marshall. Johnson and Pearsall walk to first but Pearsall is out at second on Stanly's grounder.

Third inning. One, two, three for Virginia. Cochran and Kern pop up flies to Stanly and Johnson, and McGuire goes out easily on a grounder to Winston.

ger to right. Bailey bunts safely putting Gregory on third and then steals second. Brem gets first on attempt to put Gregory out at home.

Graham's two bagger to left sends Bailey over the plate and Brem and Graham follow him on Whitaker's hit. Johnson flies out to Dillard and Pearsall strikes out. *Fourth inning.* Marshall got a safe one to third but goes out at second on Dillard's grounder. Dillard steals second, goes to third on Garnett's out at first, and scores on Hoxton's hit. Bonney ends the inning with a grounder to Gregory. Stanly is out from Hoxton to Cochran. Winston gives Garnett a fly. Gregory makes a hit but dies at second on Bailey's grounder.

S. H. HILL.

Fifth inning. McKim hits safely to left but he and Cochran succumb to a pretty double play from Stanly to Winston. Kern gets first on Carolina's only error. Johnson's wild throw to first,but McGuire retires the side with a drive to Graham.

Brem is out by a beautiful catch of a foul fly by Garnett Graham lets four bad ones go by and steals second. Whitaker's hit puts him on third. Whiaker is out at second on Johnson's grounder. Johnson steals second and Pearsall walks to first. Three men on bases, but Stanly has hard luck and is out on a foul. *Sixth inning.* Marshall hits safe. Dillard's grounder to Pearsall retires him. Garnett gets to first on a hit to center and Hoxton gets first by a ball in the ribs. Bonney drove a long one to center but Whitaker pulls it down by a long run. Marshall scoring on the hit. McKim hits safely, scoring Garnett, and Cochran flies out to Gregory.

Winston gets hit with the ball and Gregory forces him to second with a base on balls. And then the slaughter began. Bailey hits safely and fills up the bases. Brem makes a sacrifice, sending Winston

ver the plate and "Grex" and "Fletch" follow him when Graham puts one over second. Graham goes to third on Whitaker's hit and scores when Marshall makes a poor throw to catch Whitaker. Johnson hits safely. Whitaker scores and Johnson lands on second. Hill takes Pearsall's time at the bat and flies out to Kern. Stanly's two bagger sends Johnson home with the sixth run and Winston retires the side by a grounder to short. *Seventh inning.* Kern. McGuire and Marshall can not do more than give three flies to Gregory. Whitaker and Hill.

F. L. PEARSALL.

McGuire goes to right field and puts Lockett in the box. But he gets poor support and is rather wild. Gregory starts off with a fly to Lockett. Bailey draws a base on balls. Brem hits to Garnett who throws wild to second, advancing Bailey to third and Brem to second. Cochran's error puts Graham on first, Bailey scoring. Graham steals second and Brem scores on Marshall's passed ball. Whitaker goes out from McKim to Cochran, but Johnson hits safely, scoring Graham. Hoxton throws Hill out at first.

J. D. WHITAKER.

Eighth inning. Dillard flies out to Gregory, Garnett hits safely and Hoxton gets first on an attempt to catch Garnett at second. Bonney hits safely, scoring Garnett. Mc-

(Continued on fourth page.)

CAPT R. E. STANLY.

At 4:10 Umpire Heydler called the game and the Carolinians took the

F. H. BAILEY.

But Carolina is in it. Winston can't find the ball. Gregory gets Carolina's first base hit, a two-bag-

scriptions were sold, some number of them to alumni and townspeople. The paper initially sold for an annual price of $1.50, which remained unchanged until after World War I, when it increased first to $2, then to $2.50. Collecting that fee was a constant challenge on a small college campus. Many students were perpetually short of funds, and single copies of issues were passed around residence halls and classrooms. The problem of collecting subscription fees vexed the paper's business managers, who at times resorted to running dire (though humorous) announcements in bold banner-sized type with headlines that shouted "LAST CHANCE," "PLEASE STEAL ALL THE MONEY YOU CAN GET," and "DANGER! There is a danger that you will forget to pay your subscription if you don't do it NOW. That is a bad habit for you and lots of worry and trouble for us." The paper's other source of revenue for the first thirty years was the sale of advertisements. Placement of ads began slowly, but from an early date businesses in Raleigh and Durham, as well as Chapel Hill, bought space, attesting to the *Tar Heel*'s wide exposure among students and townsfolk. The range of advertising is quite fascinating: among the expected ads for books, school supplies, rooming houses, and clothiers are ads for tonsorial parlors (barbershops), diversions and amusements of all descriptions, firearms and ammunition, and men's and later women's underwear (complete with illustrations).[11]

The *Tar Heel*'s first office was temporary, consisting of an upstairs storeroom in a house next to the Methodist Church on Rosemary Street. In essence, the paper was homeless for fourteen years, which caused a variety of problems. In an October 1904 front-page response to a letter from

PLEASE STEAL

the time to pay your subscription to The Tar Heel. The Business Manager needs

ALL THE MONEY

that is owed him. So please take a bracer and pay him up on the first opportunity.

YOU CAN GET

an alumnus who complained of having to write each year to renew his subscription, the editor lamented the lack of adequate offices in which to conduct business. "The paper has no centre [*sic*], no base which is permanent," the editor wrote, and acknowledged that "the accounts are kept largely in the nature of personal accounts of the business manager." In addition he complained that "the editorial department suffers also from having no place where the board can meet and discuss the policy of the paper." The *Tar Heel* needed a permanent office, he concluded, "to reach its best growth." As late as February 1906, students were asked to place news items in a desk drawer in the faculty room in Alumni Hall.[12]

It was construction of the new campus YMCA building that finally provided the *Tar Heel* its first permanent home. The paper excitedly announced in October 1906 that it would be moving into a room on the second floor of the building, which was to be furnished by an alumnus, Dr. W. W. Craven, class of 1901, who was then on the medical staff of the South & Western Railroad and was a former UNC athlete. The Y was completed in January 1907, and on the last day of the month the editor announced: "the *Tar Heel* office has ceased to be a myth." It was located over the entrance to the building and handsomely furnished with "a desk, office chairs and a table of oak, finished in mahogany, and chairs of Austrian bent work, also finished in mahogany." The paper's close relationship with the campus Y (which served as an ad hoc student union before Graham Memorial opened in 1931) made its location in the new structure a natural fit. The *Tar Heel* offices were housed in several locations in the Y building for the next fourteen years, until relocating to New West in 1921. New West served as a barracks during World War I, and following the war it was the home of the Reserve Officers' Training Corps (ROTC); thus upon the move the editor noted that "the click of the automatic rifle would [soon] give way to the more monotonous, swifter click of the typewriter."[13]

EARLY ATHLETIC COVERAGE

The *Tar Heel* was founded and its stature grew "simultaneously with that of athletics at the University," as editor Charles Tennent noted in a 1918 article marking the paper's twenty-fifth anniversary. Sports coverage and commentary constituted about one-quarter of the paper's content in the years before World War I (the balance being news stories, editorials, and advertisements). In the early 1890s athletics at Carolina consisted of football, baseball, tennis, and track and field, at both the intramural and intercollegiate levels. The Athletic Association, a student organization formed in 1888, supported, managed, and promoted the teams, including hiring the coaches and paying their salaries (which came from ticket sales and association dues). Like the sports themselves, the structure of American collegiate athletic management was a work in progress in the late nineteenth century. The Athletic Association was first put under the direction of the campus YMCA, which was an autonomous entity, but it became quickly evident that some official university oversight was required. As a result, in 1890 the administration created both a student-run Athletic Council and the Faculty Athletic Council as governing bodies.[14]

Intercollegiate athletics in the United States kicked off in 1869 with a football game between Yale and Rutgers. Carolina began playing other schools in the fall of 1888, with a game against Wake Forest held at the North Carolina State Fairgrounds in Raleigh (Carolina lost, 6–4). The UNC trustees banned intercollegiate play in 1890 as the result of "controversies and disorders"— a sign of things to come—but the ban was lifted following a "vigorous and manly" petition by several alumni. Almost immediately, football became Carolina's preeminent spectator sport, as well as the best means of keeping alumni connected to the school. The sport evolved over the next half century, and those early games would look considerably different to fans of modern football. Along with lack of standardization of everything from the length of the field to the shape of the ball, the game in the late nineteenth century involved considerably more brute force than it would by the 1920s. Protective headgear was unknown, and uniform padding was minimal. Teams moved the ball down the field by sheer muscle, with plays including "the wedge" in which men would link arms together and push forward heads-down in a phalanx formation.[15]

Edward Kidder Graham, who served as editor of the *Tar Heel* in his senior year—and would later be credited with teaching the first class in journalism at UNC in 1909, and go on to serve as the school's president—defended the brutality of the game in a November 1897 editorial, following the death of a Georgia fullback on the field:

> We have no disposition to argue the question of the abolition of football by the colleges or the state. We grant that it is a rough game; perhaps, at times, a brutal game. But its immense popularity is final evidence of the fact that it is a natural game; [and fills] a place in the life of healthy people. We haven't yet gotten past the point where we demand rough amusement, and must have it. If it were not football it would be something else; we want men in hand to hand conflict and the desire will find expression in our games. It cannot be suppressed, but should of course be directed. Very few people go to see a tennis match[—] the balls are too soft. At the present stage of civilization a bit of hair or blood is not objectionable.[16]

The roughness of football was celebrated as an admirable masculine quality in the late nineteenth century, and the *Tar Heel* often referred to the sport's "manly" nature. In a world where the majority of men still earned a living through physical labor and the sweat of their brows, obtaining a college education carried a bit of a stigma as being effete. Proving oneself as manly was a desirable quality during the era, and by fielding a burly football team the university could project a more muscular, virile public image. Football also supported the popular notion of "muscular Christianity," which seamlessly melded the close relationship of both the Athletic Association and the *Tar Heel* with the campus YMCA. But questions soon arose about the game's role at the university and its moral challenges, especially with the emphasis on winning at any cost and amid allegations of irregularities and the ineligibility of certain players.[17]

Football coverage has always been an important part of the paper—both of action on and off the playing field. Given the *Tar Heel*'s role as the official organ of the Athletic Association, it is not surprising that gridiron reporting during the paper's first thirty years was front-page news. It may be more surprising to modern readers, however, that, since the first issues appeared in 1893, there has been ongoing discussion and debate about both the positive and negative aspects of the game and the ever-increasing role of intercollegiate athletics at the university. In the early days this created a complicated journalistic relationship, as the paper's first editor, Charles Baskerville, was also captain of the football team. But even with such close ties to the game, ethical issues involving players, coaches, and alumni were periodically debated in editorial columns. Baskerville was in fact a young member of the faculty working on his PhD, and after his playing days became chairman of the Faculty Athletic Council (he was something of a Renaissance man: a brilliant chemist, gifted athlete, and ama-

teur actor, among other accomplishments). Fielding faculty players was controversial, but the practice continued until banned in the early twentieth century. Another prominent faculty player was Edward Vernon Howell, a professor of pharmacy (for whom that department's building would later be named), who ran the winning play in the 1898 game against the University of Virginia. The relationship between rival teams and faculty was actually somewhat incestuous in the early days: Baskerville had played for Virginia before coming to Carolina to do graduate work and teach; and both Edward Howell and

Francis Venable, chemistry professor and president of the university from 1900 to 1914 as well as a major proponent of athletics at UNC, had played on the Wake Forest team.[18]

To be fair, rules of eligibility and of the game itself were still fluid in the last years of the nineteenth century, and the paper followed the formation and evolution of the Southern Intercollegiate Athletic Association (SIAA) in 1893 and other authoritative bodies in subsequent years (UNC joined the SIAA for a brief period and then resigned). On March 30, 1893—scarcely one month after the inaugural issue was published—

the first editorial about athletics appeared on the front page of the paper, primarily addressing football. "College athletics, as at present managed, have been the subject of attack in certain quarters of late," the editorial's author conceded, but he took the position that "physical training and honest, manly sport" was needed at the university. He fired back at critics who "harp on the evils of inter-collegiate contests and railroad travel" as being uninformed (those "evils" included the potential for drinking and gambling on games). He concluded that Carolina athletics had been through periods of "absolute freedom, prohibition, and license … and no one acquainted with the fact can fail to see that license is best." That license included the handling of team money by either an alumnus or a faculty member and a series of restrictions on players imposed by the university administration, including limiting absence from classes and benching any student who was on probation or "reported by the professors as delinquent in his studies."[19]

Along with concerns over drinking, gambling, and lack of attention to academics by students, there were issues of eligibility and the amateur status of players. In October 1893 editor Baskerville published an open letter to H. W. Ayers of the North Carolina State Fair, where the annual game with Wake Forest was to be played, calling for a list "stating that every player is a *bona fide* student pursuing a regular course of study and receiving no remuneration for playing.... Neither Umpire nor Referee shall be connected with either institution as either teacher, student, or alumnus." Clearly such problems were occurring at the time, but ironically Professor Baskerville considered his playing for Carolina

to be within the bounds of the regulations, apparently because he was simultaneously working on his PhD.[20]

When a new set of national intercollegiate football rules was published in the fall of 1894, the *Tar Heel* noted with pride that "at last our University is beginning to gain the reputation it deserves in college athletics," citing the inclusion of a picture of the team's captain, D. A. Kirkpatrick (the article also proudly noted that the UNC tennis team was invited by Yale to play that season). But the pride soon turned to shame and repudiation in March 1895, when Carolina was accused of employing a paid player on the team. The problem was compounded the following February, when a campus-wide meeting was held with university president George Tayloe Winston amid allegations that T. C. "Doggie" Trenchard, the football coach, was a drunkard and a gambler. (Trenchard subsequently left UNC, but in an interesting twist to the story returned to coach the team in 1913.) These stains on the team's reputation made national news in April 1896 when a leading periodical of the day, *Harper's Weekly*, reported that Carolina and Virginia refused to rejoin the SIAA, adding that "deplorably enough, these two are among the most important educational institutions in the South, and the gravest offenders in college sport. … Neither has shown any desire to cleanse its athletics." Despite the harsh tone of the article, the *Tar Heel* reprinted the damning allegations, signaling its dual position of loyally supporting the team but expecting rules and standards of good sportsmanship to be practiced. Following a housecleaning of the football program, the *Tar Heel*'s editor William A. Graham declared, "Our Athletics are safe.... The very evils which caused our troubles have been supplanted by advantages.... The air of professionalism has been removed and we have in its place a purer spirit. Men will no longer come to college for athletic honors but these will come as a result of a healthy life while doing college work."[21]

Graham continued both his support for the game and strong opposition to its potential abuses in the pages of the *Tar Heel* through the fall of 1896. In a front-page editorial in September, he proclaimed that football at UNC was now marked by "manliness of conduct and strict conformity to the rules of sobriety," and that alumni who had played the sport "departed these classic walls in the full glory of manhood, and [are] doing their part in the battle of life, better prepared to face the turmoils and struggles of this world from accepting the athletic and educational advantages afforded them at this institution." Graham conceded that "foot-ball is beset with many evils and has its objectionable features," but at Carolina "professionalism is shunned, intemperance is never permitted; and gentlemanly conduct at all times characterize our athletics in every department." Despite all of this coverage, some students and alumni criticized the paper for not devoting enough space to athletics. Graham responded that the editors felt such criticism was "without foundation," and though as an organ of the Athletic Association it "is our duty to lay stress upon athletics ... there are other interests as vital as athletics it is our duty to emphasize. Athletics alone would make our life dwarfed and one-sided. The plain duty of the *Tar Heel* is to make this life well-rounded and harmonious."[22]

In line with the university's new mission, and perhaps in response to some of the problems that beset the program, the Carolina team soon adopted what was known as "scientific football," in which plays were developed that emphasized strategy over sheer muscle and girth. One of these developments, which also reduced the game's brutality, was the introduction of the forward pass, and Carolina is often credited with an early use of the play in an intercollegiate game against the University of Georgia in 1895. When the team won a victory over a rival using "scientific" methods, the paper was quick to praise the effort. But the lure of winning at any cost remained strong: in 1898 Carolina was accused of importing a professional player from a northern team.[23]

Football continued to be a hot topic during the first quarter of the twentieth century, though the scandals subsided. In 1900 UNC rejoined—then resigned from—the Southern Intercollegiate Athletic Association, preferring to police its teams internally. An October 1902 editorial sided with the university in this action, citing opposition to the rule that forbade transfer students and others from playing on the team unless they had been enrolled for a full year (the so-called one-year rule). A national debate in 1905 about the appropriateness and roughness of football on college campuses brought even President Theodore Roosevelt into the discussion, and caused much ink to flow in the *Tar Heel*. In the midst of this debate the question was raised again about the purpose of the paper, to which editor Victor Stephenson responded: "What should the paper be? A mirror reflecting the doings of all those who fall within our sphere? Yes. A means of communication which shall bind the distant alumnus to the scenes of his alma mater? Yes. But more than these. A conservator

of all that is truest in University traditions, an influence ... on every question touching our life in
this college world—that is our ideal."[24]

But the debate was not always carried on in
such a serious tone. Stephenson, ever the prank-
ster and editorial gadfly, is probably responsible for a facetious front-page story that ran
in February 1906 under the headline "Football
Made Humane—A Few Suggestions Regarding Proposed Changes in the Rules—Extreme
Roughness Eliminated." Faculty, according to
the author, should select the team, and no student "should be eligible unless he is up in his
class work and has a reputation for piety." The
qualifications for captain should be "the highest
grade in Greek Mythology." Upon entrance onto
the field each team should greet the other "with
the Chautauqua salute, which consists of waving the handkerchief," and after "a few friendly
chats concerning books and writers" determina-

tion of which side will get the ball will not occur
by coin toss, but rather "the two captains shall
be called upon to extract a cube root of a number, provided by the professor of mathematics....
[The] first to hand in the correct solution gets the
ball." The ball was not to be advanced by runs
and passes, but rather would be moved forward
by the answers to questions about a fossil shown
on the field by the geology professor—two yards
for the fossil's correct period, and five yards for
its correct scientific name. After several more
suggestions in this vein, the article concluded by
stating the rules of conduct during the game: "No
pushing, scuffling, or boisterous conversation
will be permitted. Both players and spectators
must maintain absolute silence during the mental tests."[25]

Humor aside, throughout the first two decades of the twentieth century the faculty and
administration worked to balance the inter-

ests of the university, amateur athletes, and the desire to win by students and alumni alike. Rules about academic eligibility and amateur status were strengthened periodically. Generally the *Tar Heel* continued to take the position of head campus cheerleader and promoter for all sports, especially football. For example, Frank Porter Graham, the paper's editor in 1908 (also a cousin of Edward Kidder Graham and later president of the university), wrote an open letter to the team the week before the final game of the season, reminding the men that "all of you are representatives of the students and … centered in you are the past traditions and present ideals of the University." Yet editors also kept a watchful eye not only on the possible abuses intercollegiate football tended to create, but also on the game's ever-increasing role in university life. Graham's successor, O. W. Hyman (who later went on to become dean of the University of Tennessee's College of Medicine), was less of a booster, and penned a sharp editorial in November 1909 questioning the hero worship of football players on campus. Hyman lamented the fact that players received more acknowledgment than student magazine editors or scholars, pointedly noting that lettered football sweaters were more conspicuous on campus than Phi Beta Kappa keys. "Such a state of affairs is bound to bring its own ruin unless stopped," Hyman warned. "The athletic plant has already grown until very little nourishment and sunlight is available for anything else and it bids fair soon to freeze out competitors. We have got to look about and wake up to our danger and do it quickly."[26]

The push-pull over intercollegiate athletics continued throughout the decade of the 1910s, with different editors of the *Tar Heel* sometimes coming down on different sides of the issue. In December 1912 the paper reported that "the most significant step that has been taken in Carolina Athletics in years was made Monday night when representative Alumni in conference with the Faculty and students demanded a share in the running of athletics." The paper voiced support for recommendations that resulted from the meeting, including alumni involvement in all aspects of athletics, even "procuring coaches." Following the First World War, however, the paper took a different stance, because of what it saw as too much alumni involvement including, apparently, the presence of professional players. In a February 1919 editorial entitled "Circumstances Alter Cases," the question was asked, "What is the purpose and aim of college athletics?"

Is it to advertise the collegiate institution, to build up tradition and a practice of college spirit, to furnish excitement for the alumni and the public as well as for the student body? Or is it to endow the individual members of the student body with health and strength? At Carolina both of these objectives are aimed at, but the *benefit* of the individual *student* is *paramount*. Paying men to come to college to play on the various teams, encouraging the tramp athlete to drift to the institution in order that athletic prestige might be made powerful; these are some of the [recent] evils."[27]

THE *WHITE AND BLUE* CHALLENGE

The fledgling *Tar Heel* was challenged soon after its one-year anniversary by a rival publication put out by a handful of students on a crusade — a holy war, as they saw it, to kill the rising influence of fraternities and return campus life to the intellectual activities offered by the college's original two student organizations, the Dialectic and Philanthropic Societies. Under the masthead of "America Means Freedom, and Freedom Means Equality and Opportunity," the first issue of the *White and Blue* appeared on March 8, 1894. "As the name imports"—referring to the colors of each organization, which were to become adopted as the official university standards— "the chief objective of this paper is to help revive those societies, the Dialectic and Philanthropic, in which so many of our distinguished alumni, in former days, received that training so essential to public success.... Sad to relate, they are now almost completely neglected by a class of students." The culprits, as the staff of the *White and Blue* saw it, were fraternities. "This paper is not a mere college newspaper. The painful necessities of the present hour forbid this. There are subjects of far greater importance than mere news. ... Fraternities are detrimental to the best interests of the student-body and of the University ... and the evil should be immediately uprooted."[28]

The actual roots of the "evil" dated back several decades. The two societies were formed in the earliest days of the university, and were the primary student institutions on campus before the Civil War. Every student was required to join one body or the other, and by tradition students from the western part of North Carolina joined the Dialectic Society, while students from the east joined the Philanthropic Society. The two organizations held debates that helped students build oratorical skills many would use after graduation when they took their place in broader society, especially as public officials, lawyers, and clergymen. The societies regulated stu-

dent behavior and meted out discipline, serving in essence as the university's governing bodies before establishment of a formal student government, and they built and operated libraries that served in the absence of a central university facility. In the late antebellum era, the societies released juniors and seniors from membership because the numbers of freshmen and sophomores had increased and filled their ranks. The upperclassmen, desiring some sort of social organization, began forming fraternities and aligning themselves with chapters on other campuses, even though these groups were not sanctioned by the university. When UNC reopened in 1875, fraternities were officially banned in the new charter, but this provision was overturned in 1885, with the conditions that each organization submit a list of its members to the faculty and pledge "not to use intoxicating liquors." By the mid-1890s it was clear that the socially oriented fraternities, which were growing in popularity among students, were a better fit for the new modern university than the two literary and debating societies, whose mission had become somewhat outdated. Seeing the growth of fraternities and under some pressure from the societies, which were beginning to suffer declining membership, the Faculty Council in 1885 reiterated the rule that all students were required to join one or the other of the societies, or they would not be afforded certain university privileges. However, by the mid-1890s the societies themselves, facing the inevitable, ended this requirement.[29]

Dwindling membership also meant dwindling resources, and in March 1894 the societies turned over control of their libraries to the university. Interestingly, there may have been a connection between this event and the appearance of the *White and Blue*. In the same issue of the *Tar Heel* announcing the change in library management, an editorial was published citing establishment of the forthcoming paper as "the result of the refusal of the *Tar Heel* to print certain articles submitted to it." Further, "The present board of editors wish to reiterate that so long as they have control of this paper, the columns shall not be used as a medium for the airing before the people of the State the petty jealousies or spites one person, or party may have against another person or clique." This statement set the stage for a showdown between the nascent *Tar Heel* and the upstart *White and Blue*. Though some later sources speculate that creation of the *White and Blue* was solely the result of a belief that the *Tar Heel* was not only an organ of the Athletic Association, but also a tool of the fraternities, the reasons for its formation are somewhat more complex. "The statement has been going the rounds of the press, that the *White and Blue* is in opposition to the *Tar Heel*. This is not true," an editorial on the front page of the first issue stated. "The *Tar Heel* only touches one phase of University life [athletics] and so far we heartily cooperate with it. The *White and Blue* covers a broader field and its columns are open to the discussion of all subjects pertaining to the University." All subjects primarily meant, as stated in italics, to "*abolish fraternities forever*." In stating the paper's mission, the editors gave four reasons for banning fraternities from campus: "Firstly we believe that they are the chief cause of the present sad decadence of those once glorious institutions the Dialectic and Philanthropic societies; secondly because they are destructive to the college spirit; thirdly because they have a tendency to be

hurtful to athletics ... [and] lastly because they are opposed to the free and democratic spirit which above all, ought to characterize a state institution, and are, therefore, un American."[30]

Actually, the number of fraternity men on campus was still relatively low in the late nineteenth century. According to university historian and librarian Louis Round Wilson, in 1900 only 18 percent of the student body (93 of 512 students) belonged to fraternities. And though a number of fraternity men did belong to the Athletic Association and could be found on the *Tar Heel* staff, they did not exclusively control either organization. In fact, there is surprisingly little coverage of fraternity events in the *Tar Heel* during this era, and all of the early editors of the paper reiterated their commitment to covering "all points pertaining to the advancement and growth of the University," as Charles Baskerville wrote in the inaugural edition's mission statement. So the *White and Blue*'s charge that the *Tar Heel* was "a publication controlled exclusively by fraternity men" was an overstatement. The *Tar Heel* editors took umbrage at the accusation, replying, "We have never, nor would we now, injure the feelings of any man, wears he the [fraternity] badge or not." The deeper issues that created the rival newspaper were twofold: a socioeconomic divide between students that was more pronounced than it had been before the Civil War; and the new direction of the university, which had the unintended consequence of making the literary and debating societies increasingly obsolete. Regarding the first issue, historian Wilson notes, "Many of the students of the immediate antebellum period, when the South was at the peak of its economic development, came from well-to-do families. But the war had materially

changed that situation, and attendance at the University for three-fourths of the students now called for hard struggle and self-denial by parents and students alike." The editor of the *White and Blue* saw this change as creating a significant divide in the student body, outwardly expressed in sartorial terms:

> The fight is really one of town against country. The town boy, because he has generally had superior advantages both social and educational, and because as a rule he dresses somewhat more stylishly than the average country boy, who less favored by environment has not had these advantages, often presumes a superiority.... [This feeling] is perpetuated and magnified by the fraternity system that puts a premium on these very qualities of show and dress, forgetting that moral and intellectual worth should be the only badge of superiority in college life, forgetting that whereas they assiduously solicit membership from the sons of distinguished men, they coldly pass by many who stand head and shoulders about them, [who] are to be distinguished men themselves.[31]

The editorials over the course of the paper's yearlong run became increasingly strident in the cause of abolishing fraternities, and on one hand can be viewed simply as sniping by less affluent students who were snubbed by wealthier fraternity members. But there is another dimension to it; in this debate can be clearly seen the growth—and the growing pains—of the University and North Carolina in the last quarter of the nineteenth century, as both took their respective places in the post–Civil War "New South." The *Tar Heel* was thus put in the position of representing the modern university and its new direction, a position it would embrace and that would come to define it in the twentieth century. This New South–Old South dichotomy is made clear in an eloquent letter to the *White and Blue* by Thomas Bailey Lee, editor of the *Tar Heel* in 1894, and published on the front page of the rival newspaper on March 15 of that year, along with a lengthy rebuttal. Under the title "The Societies Decline: What Has Caused It?" Lee pointed out that the shrinking of the Dialectic and Philanthropic Societies was the result not of the rise of fraternities, but of three other factors: the coming of intercollegiate athletics; the rise of technical departments in the curriculum and establishment of societies for original research; and the "requirement of theses, abstracts, and essays in the course[s]." Lee also pointed out that participation in athletics was much higher than it had been before the Civil War and took a more organized form, consuming an increased amount of the students' free time. Regarding the second and third points:

> With the amount of work and original research here required, a man has little time or desire to prepare himself for society performance. Southern oratory and debate [are] no longer universal. They cannot be. We, with the progressive majority [,] have become scientists, specialists in our quest for bread and butter. The time once devoted to the literary society is now spent in the laboratory and dissecting room.... We must accept the fact of the earth's rotation and govern ourselves accordingly. Our whole civilization is now in the midst of a transition. We have left the oration and the poem for fact and formula. To retrace our steps is an impossibility.[32]

Throughout this debate, even as the rhetoric grew more heated and increasingly ugly, the editors of the *Tar Heel* took the high road and generally chose not to respond in print. The author of a 1913 *University Magazine* article about the history of the *Tar Heel* speculated that this tact was "due more to better editorial policy than to better manners." By simply ignoring the ranting of the *White and Blue*, the *Tar Heel* treated it as nothing more than the buzzing of an annoying insect, and simply waited for its rival to fly away. In reality, the threat to the *Tar Heel* was somewhat more serious. The battle divided the student body to a certain extent, and with only a few hundred potential subscribers between them, the two papers competed for much needed revenue. Talks of a merger began, and the Faculty Council got involved and mediated a settlement. Though the Athletic Association accepted conditions of the merger that would have included changing the name to something neutral such as the *Varsity*, and election of the editorial staff by subscribers (the first time voting for editors is ever mentioned), in the end the weaker *White and Blue* ceased publication without requiring these changes to the *Tar Heel*. The conclusion of this battle marked the last time the *Tar Heel* would be seriously challenged as the university's primary newspaper.[33]

The debating society members behind the creation of the *White and Blue* did succeed in gaining two concessions from the faculty. First, though they were not able to abolish fraternities, they were able to have a rule instituted that prevented freshmen from pledging. Second, and of longer-term significance to the growth of the university, a new type of student organization called "county clubs" was created. The idea for the county clubs was first proposed in January 1895, the concept being that students from the same geographic area would organize to "materially promote their own interests and well being and be indirectly of great service in increasing the favor of the university, by extending to new comers from their respective counties a cordial welcome, and by rendering kindnesses in manifold ways such as would command their lasting good-will and gratitude." Ironically, rather than building membership in the debating societies, as they were no doubt intended to do, the county clubs evolved in the first half of the twentieth century to epitomize the direction and broader mission of the modern University of North Carolina.[34]

Though the *White and Blue* challenge may seem like a historical footnote more than a century after the heated rivalry, it was a critical event for the university in several ways. First, it marked decline of the influence of the Dialectic and Philanthropic Societies, and a recognition and acceptance by the student body of the new mission and academic structure of the univer-

sity. Second, the weakness of the societies led to the takeover of their libraries by the faculty, and within a few years the creation of a student government, primarily to administer the university's honor code. Third, it created the county clubs, which would come to define the modern university on the public stage in the first half of the twentieth century. Editors of the *Tar Heel* during the period enthusiastically supported all of these outcomes. In addition, the *Tar Heel* saw the competition from the *White and Blue* as healthy, showing if nothing else the need on campus for a school of journalism. When the rival paper first appeared, the *Tar Heel* quipped that its presence should stimulate more students to "shove the quill," and "if properly conducted, this should be but the beginning of a school of journalism ... and we will congratulate our contemporary for augmenting the progressiveness of our university."[35]

THE YMCA, THE *TAR HEEL*, AND THE INTRODUCTION OF BASKETBALL TO CAROLINA

Despite early accusations that the *Tar Heel* promoted only athletics and fraternity interests, the institution the paper covered and supported most vigorously during its first thirty years was the university's YMCA. The Y was the center of campus social and spiritual life during the late nineteenth and early twentieth centuries and served as the student union before Graham Memorial was opened in 1931. Founded in 1860, the Y at UNC oversaw the social as well as religious "soul" of the students, assuring that they behaved in a (Protestant) Christian manner and didn't fall victim to temptations that might sidetrack them, including drinking and gambling.

Though the centrality of an overtly religious institution on a public university campus is foreign to twenty-first-century sensibilities, it was accepted during this period.

Scarcely a week went by when the paper didn't include articles about activities and lectures at the Y, most—but not all—of a religious or moral nature. As an example of a secular activity, in February 1908 the *Tar Heel* announced, "Fear is expressed on all sides that staid old Chapel Hill is about to have forced upon it a reign of terror in the way of citified doin's, for O Sacrilege, a moving picture show has come to town and, horror of horrors, the exhibitions are being given in the chapel of the Y.M.C.A. building." The writer also quipped that the "faces of olduns wear a gloom black as night, but—the younguns go to see it." The following week the paper reviewed the show (actually a series of film shorts), making it the first movie review to appear in Chapel Hill. The reviewer declared it "a hit ... the best show for money that has visited these parts in years. Some of the scenes were excruciatingly funny and kept the hall in an uproar of laughter. And natural, so natural that no flight of vivid imagination was required to put words into the mouths of the pantomimic actors."[36]

The relationship between the Y and the *Tar Heel* was so close that at times they seemed indistinguishable. When the Y announced plans to build its own permanent facility on campus, the *Tar Heel* promoted the project heavily, devoting two special editions to the Y's mission and fundraising efforts on behalf of the new building. When the castellated Gothic Revival structure was completed in January 1907, one of its second-floor offices became the *Tar Heel*'s first permanent home, further cementing the relationship between the two organizations. Several editors of the paper were also associated with the Y, including cousins Edward Kidder Graham and Frank Porter Graham, both of whom would later serve notable terms as president of the university and continue to support the Y in that capacity. Frank Graham actually held the positions of editor of the *Tar Heel*, president of the senior class, and president of the Y simultaneously in the fall of his senior year (along with managing the baseball team and other extracurricular activities). Apparently even the famously energetic Graham was overcommitted, as the paper announced his resignation as editor in January 1909. "The cause for his decision was over work and weak eyes," the paper reported. "It was with profound regret the whole student body saw Frank give up the *Tar Heel*, but it was known that the physicians had so ordered."[37]

The YMCA's connection to sports dates to the earliest days of intercollegiate athletics at UNC. The newly formed Athletic Association—

eventual parent of the *Tar Heel*—operated under the direction of the Y for its first two years. The national Y also fostered the concept of "muscular Christianity," encouraging members to participate in athletics as a means of promoting a healthy lifestyle and of enticing young men to embrace religion. The university was closely aligned with the national Y organization in several ways. Thomas Hume, who helped found the first college YMCA while a student at the University of Virginia, and who throughout his life maintained a close relationship with the national organization, came to UNC as professor of English in 1885. In 1889, at the suggestion of John R. Mott, national secretary of the YMCA, the university hired Lacy Little as the first athletic director and to serve as captain of the football team. Little had received athletic training at the Y-sponsored School for Christian Workers in Springfield, Massachusetts, where the game of basketball would be created two years later.[38]

The campus Y and its strong ties to the national organization, student interest in expanding college athletics, and the efforts of the *Tar Heel* all converged to create a groundswell of support for bringing basketball to Carolina. The fascinating early origins of what was to become UNC's nationally preeminent sport can be seen emerging in the pages of the *Tar Heel* in the late 1890s. Though Carolina's first intercollegiate basketball game was played against Virginia Christian in Bynum Gymnasium in January 1911, the roots of the sport at UNC go back more than a dozen years earlier. The first mention of the game in the *Tar Heel* occurs in a January 1898 article entitled "Basket Ball: Why Has It Not Been Introduced?" The paper made a strong argument that as basketball was an indoor sport with a winter season, it made perfect sense to play the game between the fall football and spring baseball seasons.[39]

The origins of basketball at Carolina may actually date back to 1896—and, more significantly, the concept of it was likely brought to campus by someone who learned the game from its creator, James Naismith. On April 25, 1896, a small article in the *Tar Heel* reported that a Mr. H. E. Mechling had been hired as the university's physical instructor and noted that Mechling, like Lacy Little before him, came to UNC from the School for Christian Workers in Springfield, Massachusetts. A subsequent article stated that Mechling was a graduate of that school and had also served there for three years as the assistant physical instructor. That puts Mechling at the school in 1891, the year Naismith first mounted two peach baskets on poles—without holes, as early on players had to retrieve the balls from the baskets—and invented basketball. In 1941, on the fiftieth anniversary of the game, a news-paper in Louisville, Kentucky, ran an interview with the elderly Mechling (who had moved there after leaving UNC in 1898), in which he reminisced about being on Naismith's first basketball team. No records survive that verify Mechling's story about being on the first team, but certainly he learned the sport directly from Naismith. At Carolina, Mechling served not only as physical instructor but was a medical student and captain of the medical and pharmaceutical student's intramural football team.[40]

Basketball was first played at UNC in mid-November of 1898. It seems Mechling set the wheels in motion before leaving for Louisville at the end of the previous spring term, and his successor, J. W. Calder (who also likely knew basketball from his YMCA training in New York), oversaw the first games. A *Tar Heel* article on November 1, under the headline "Improvement in the Gymnasium," reported that "apparatus [has been] ordered" and that one of "the most attractive features of [the improvements] will be basket ball, an enormously popular sport.... Basket ball has come to stay." Two weeks later the paper noted: "Basket Ball is progressing. It seems to have come for good. The intense interest shown in the sport just at this time in the midst of the most exciting period of the foot-ball season, speaks well for it the new game—Push it." In December 1901 the rules of the game were published in the *Tar Heel*, and the accompanying article reported that an "attempt is being made to arrange a basket-ball schedule." Regular intramural games between students in different classes and graduate programs commenced in early 1903.[41]

Interest in basketball ebbed and flowed during the first decade of the twentieth century,

Medical and pharmacy student intramural football team, 1897. The captain, in the center holding the ball, is H. E. Mechling, who likely introduced basketball to UNC in his position as athletic director. (NCC/*Hellenian*)

though the *Tar Heel* pushed and prodded it along relentlessly. The game was first played in the original Memorial Hall, an immense and foreboding Gothic Revival structure built in 1885, dedicated in part to the university's Confederate dead, and patterned after a similar building at Harvard dedicated to that school's fallen Union soldiers. The cavernous open interior with its maze of exposed and darkly stained wooden trusses was the logical place for the game, as the freestanding benches could be moved against the walls, and rudimentary portable baskets set up. In 1904 Bynum Gymnasium was completed, and soon after the paper noted that "basketballs and racks" were provided for students. How often the game was played in Bynum in the early years

UNC's first intercollegiate basketball team, 1911. The team was so new that they did not have uniforms yet and wore sashes emblazoned "Carolina" for the photograph. (NCC)

remains in question, however, as the university's physical instructor frowned on it because of the scratches the players' fast movement in leather bottomed-shoes made on his shiny new wood floors.[42]

In hopes of moving the creation of an intercollegiate basketball team forward, former *Tar Heel* editor and football captain Charles Baskerville wrote a letter to the paper in January 1908, which was reprinted in its entirety. "The *Tar Heel* is right in urging the introduction of basketball into our athletics," Baskerville declared. The following October a front-page story reported that "Basket Ball Men Organize," along with a strong

editorial likely written by Frank Porter Graham: "Often has an editor, having scratched his head in vain for news either real or imaginary, turned to the devoted subject of basketball. But the men who gathered together Friday night, once and for all, removed the subject of basketball from the number of those subjects which have been often and so unsteadily go to make up the editors' disputed repertoire." In January 1911, a Carolina team first took the court against another school. From these humble beginnings, few could have imagined that the University of North Carolina's men's varsity basketball program would one day stand atop the sport nationally.[43]

THE ANTI-HAZING CAMPAIGN
AND EDITORIAL FREEDOM

One of the most important campus social issues the *Tar Heel* took up in the first years of the twentieth century was that of hazing. This was not fraternity hazing per se, though apparently fraternity men participated in some numbers. This type of hazing involved sophomores terrorizing freshmen in a variety of ways, the most notorious being "blacking," a ritual that involved ambushing unsuspecting first-year students and covering their faces and hands with printer's ink, kerosene, lampblack, or some other dark substance. Aside from the difficulty in removing these dyes from the skin, blacking also carried obvious racial overtones during the early years of Jim Crow segregation in the South. Over an eight-year period, from 1904 to 1912, the paper consistently and strongly condemned hazing, publishing editorials and articles that employed various approaches—including humor, cajoling, appealing to student honor, and even outrage—in an effort to end the practice. The first anti-hazing editorial appeared in February 1904, with a campaign begun by Charles Phillips Russell (known as Phillips), a third-generation member of a family with deep roots at the university, who would later become a highly influential professor in the School of Journalism. "We are sorry to see some of the hazing spirit showing itself around campus again," Russell wrote. "We had entertained hopes that we had outgrown this sort of thing. All the leading colleges have done away with the practice and it seems childish and medieval to have it in our midst again." Russell called hazing an act of "pitiful cowardice" and "small and contemptible," though he made clear that "we are not denouncing hazing so much for

treating freshmen roughly. Life is not a bed of roses and a little rough treatment is not going to hurt the right kind of man." He nonetheless concluded the editorial by stating that "hazing is not a square and manly thing."[44]

Freshman hazing—or the threat of it—became increasingly dangerous as the first decade of the twentieth century progressed. In late September 1906 the *Tar Heel* reported that "a Freshman, surprised the night before last on a shaded pathway on the campus by a party of Sophomores, and believing that he was to be hazed, fired at one of his assailants and came near to ending his life." The editor at the time, Quincy Mills—who would to die himself from gunfire on a World War I battlefield in 1918—strongly condemned the incident, noting with irony that less than six hours before the near-fatal shooting the sophomore class had passed a resolution banning hazing, which obviously proved futile, as "resolutions amount to nothing, and the majority of the class has not endeavored to control the minority as it should have done." Although the sophomores involved in the incident apparently were not intent on hazing the freshman, Mills noted the practice was so prevalent that the student thought hazing was their intent, and "as hazing it will be interpreted throughout the state and used to the injury of the University." The small number of university co-eds jumped into the fray, as reported in October, with suggestions that any upperclassman appearing on campus after 7:30 P.M. be expelled, and that "Freshmen be permitted to range at large after that hour only when heavily armed." The next edition of the paper included an editorial that wryly proposed "to furnish each Freshman, along with his registration card, with a six shooter and a commission empowering him to hunt down every Sophomore on the Hill.... [This] plan pleases us simply because it would furnish the otherwise homesick Freshman with so much harmless sport and diversion."[45]

The practice of students carrying firearms on campus was apparently widespread in the late nineteenth and early twentieth centuries, despite an 1882 rule forbidding "any pistol or dangerous weapon." Another shooting involving a freshman who believed he was about to be hazed occurred in 1910. In a front-page article, the *Tar Heel* reported that one S. I. Parker accidentally shot his roommate, Henry Fairly, at their rooming house. Hearing a group of rowdy students coming up the stairs and assuming them to be sophomores intent on hazing, Parker, a freshman, fired down the stairs and hit Fairly. Fortunately the wound was not fatal. Along with editorials aimed at efforts to stop hazing, occasional small items would appear in the paper asking students not to shoot at birds, outdoor light fixtures, or windows. Perhaps even more surprising than the prevalence of guns on campus was the paper's complicity in the practice, as it ran numerous ads for firearms and ammunition. In fact, firearms and ammunition ads were among the largest and most fully illustrated to appear in the paper during the period before World War I.[46]

The fight to end hazing resulted in the *Tar Heel*'s first real challenge to editorial freedom in 1908. In September 1907, at the beginning of the academic year, a student-organized anti-hazing conference was held at the university that received front-page coverage. The following April a so-called blind editorial appeared lambasting a "blacking crowd" in Carr Hall, stating that some of the perpetrators were "of a known fraternity" but publishing no names. The author was

Herbert Gunter, the paper's editor in chief, who had been managing editor under Quincy Mills during the hazing controversy two years earlier. A firestorm erupted when some fraternity members on campus took umbrage at the blind article and demanded through the Athletic Council that Gunter either prove the accusation by naming those involved, apologize for running the article, or resign his post. Gunter refused, "insomuch as we had sufficient evidence to substantiate our statements." A campus-wide debate ensued regarding whether or not Gunter was under obligation to reveal sources and information and, if not, whether he should be subject to a recall election. This incident is fascinating not only because it raises the question of editorial freedom, but also because it illustrates the broader role the *Tar Heel*, still an independent entity, played at the university by the turn of the twentieth century. In addition it offers a curious clue about the selection of early editors. Despite the fact that all other sources indicate that the Athletic Association chose editors before 1923 (the year paper became an official student publication), Gunter cryptically stated that he was beholden to the entire student body, and not just to the membership of the Athletic Association. "We deny that the Athletic Association, as now constituted, has the power to dictate to us," he wrote. "We were elected under the old regime and cannot see where eighty-five men have the right to put us out." What the "old regime" was is not clear, however what is clear is that arbitration was suggested to settle the matter and Gunter refused, arguing that he "was elected by the student body and was answerable only to the student body."[47]

After ten tense days of accusations and recriminations, the president of the senior class called a meeting of the student body, and a recall election was held—without Gunter ever revealing his sources or naming names—and he received an overwhelming vote of confidence. According to a report in the *Tar Heel*, "Circumstantial evidence was ... produced to the effect that some fraternitymen saw the blacking and knew who composed the blacking crowd. By a vote of about 300 to 8 the student body voted that the editorial was warranted." Following the vote the paper printed an editorial stating that "as the matter now stands, we feel we have been vindicated by the student body. The student body, as we see it, is supreme in the matter, and as it has declared that we are warranted in making the statements, we are satisfied." What this means remains a mystery; perhaps there had been a one- or two-year experiment in electing the *Tar Heel* editors by the entire student body, but by 1910 control of the process was firmly back in the hands of the Athletic Association.[48]

Its editorial freedom vindicated, the *Tar Heel* kept up pressure to end ritualistic hazing. Its position was prescient, as the practice became increasingly violent. In March 1912 the paper reported that following a sophomore banquet, some of the attendees "came up on campus singing, giving blood curdling yells [and] shooting guns." The rowdy group then decided to go to a nearby rooming house where four freshmen were sleeping, with the intent of hazing the unsuspecting students. Standing outside the building the sophomore mob began yelling for the freshmen to come out, and when the young men did not comply, the rabble "threw rocks, brick bats and missiles of every other description." The barrage broke blinds, window sash and glass, and when this action still failed to smoke out the terrorized freshmen, five or six shots were fired into their darkened room.[49]

Despite the escalation in violence associated with hazing, it was not a bullet that would finally end the practice, but a piece of glass. In the early hours of September 13, 1912, a small group of sophomores roused two freshmen from their beds and marched them out to the athletic field. There they were made to dance on a barrel, and Isaac Rand of Smithfield, North Carolina, slipped and fell, cutting his jugular vein on a piece of broken glass that was lying in the grass. At first the other students didn't realize the severity of the situation, and by the time they did and tried to get him medical attention, Rand was dead. The incident made state and national news, and the university's reputation, according to the paper, was "crippled and mangled." President Venable expelled the four sophomores involved, and three were later convicted of manslaughter by an Orange County court (they did not serve prison time, however, as they were remanded to the custody of their fathers). Following the trial, the *Tar Heel* commented, "Now that the tragic inevitable has happened there is no need for sermons and editorials.... It is the final chapter in what began as a frolic and ended as a tragedy that was sent broad-cast over the state and nation and was commented upon and discussed everywhere." But the editor couldn't resist commenting on the irony of the location of the tragedy, managing to make both a religious and a football analogy by stating that Rand's death "was deemed necessary to the fulfillment of His Purposes by Him who is behind the big game."[50]

The *Tar Heel*'s anti-hazing campaign of 1904–12 was a critical test of the paper's journalistic independence—both in terms of the Athletic Association and the university at large, as well as of the mettle of its editors and staff. At the beginning of the campaign President Venable called Phillips Russell into his office and instructed him to submit all editorials for review before they were published. The quick-thinking Russell agreed—with the stipulation that President Venable come to the *Tar Heel* office to read them. Russell knew the formal Venable would not assent to appearing in a student office, and as a result he never read an editorial before it appeared in print.[51]

The effects of the anti-hazing campaign and the lessons learned would reverberate in the university's institutional memory into the third quarter of the twentieth century, as several of the student editors who worked on the *Tar Heel* during the period later went on to careers as faculty members and administrators at UNC. Phillips Russell would serve on the faculties of the Department of English and School of Journalism; Frank Porter Graham as professor of history and then university president; and Oscar Coffin as professor and later dean of the School of Journalism (in addition, Russell and Coffin each served terms as faculty advisor to the student staff of the

paper). The anti-hazing campaign also coincided with the creation of a structured student government at UNC, to replace the role once played by the Dialectic and Philanthropic Societies. Discussions about establishment of an officially sanctioned student government first appeared in the pages of the *Tar Heel* in 1895 (perhaps not coincidentally about the same time as the demise of the *White and Blue*), and for nearly a decade the editorial staff consistently championed its development. Finally, in 1904, the same year the paper's anti-hazing campaign began, the administration approved establishment of the University Council, which became the Student Council in 1910. Its primary functions were to monitor the school's honor code and investigate and discipline incidents of hazing. "The student body," the paper proclaimed in 1910, "has shown decidedly that it wants a student council at the head of the honor system." Regarding hazing, an editorial declared that the Student Council would be more effective than the UNC faculty in rooting out those responsible and administering discipline, as "the faculty won't know until next week sometime, that a blacking crowd did a handsome job on some fifteen or twenty freshmen," and, in addition, "there is hardly a culprit in the University that fears punishment from the faculty."[52]

CREATION OF THE TWENTIETH-CENTURY UNIVERSITY

Though the modern academic structure of the University of North Carolina was put into place in 1875, other institutional elements developed at various paces over the following half-century. To achieve national standing in the twentieth century, UNC would need to grow both conceptually and physically. The *Tar Heel* chronicled and assisted that development, and often played a significant role in helping the institution evolve into a fully modern university.

The relationship between the *Tar Heel* and the faculty and administration was somewhat formal and distant during the first two decades of the paper's history. Writing about George Tayloe Winston, who was president of the university at the time the paper was founded, the author of an early editorial proclaimed that Winston's work "will not cease until he has placed [the university] on that plane of supremacy which it adorned in Ante Bellum days.... It will be what it formerly was, the centre of learning and education in the South." Occasional letters from the next two presidents, Edwin Alderman and Francis Venable, were published in the paper, along with summations of their speeches to students, but little else. The *Tar Heel* staff, however, enthusiastically supported the work of these three men to expand and modernize the university. Growth required money, and in a debate that continues to resonate more than a century later, constant battle was waged with the North Carolina General Assembly for adequate funding. "The storm has burst at last," an editorial declared in April 1894. "A series of articles aimed directly at the State appropriation for the University has appeared. An institution so illustriously venerable as the University of North Carolina will suffer naught so long as its existence depends upon a citizenship as deliberate as that constituted by the conservative people of the state."[53]

The editors were particularly pointed in comments aimed at retaining the best professors. "the *Tar Heel* desires to publish a record of the work done by the faculty and students in the way of original research," the paper announced in December 1909. "The faculty here does more research work of the kind than any other in the South. We are proud of the fact and we think the alumni who read the college paper should be acquainted with it." A run of resignations by faculty for better-paying positions around the same time caused consternation and outcry. "Going, Going Gone"—the cry of an auctioneer—was the title of an article following the loss of three prominent professors in 1910: "We have got to put a stop to this wholesale loss of prominent educators." Another editorial proclaimed, "Some day we hope the legislature of North Carolina will wake up to the fact that they are cutting their own throats by letting these men go when they could retain them by a small raise in salary. The allowance permitted the University annually is entirely too small. If we are to keep the University efficient we've got to keep efficient professors here."[54]

Although Presidents Winston, Alderman, and Venable all worked toward modernizing the university, it was Edward Kidder Graham who would greatly expand UNC's mission beyond its campus borders and set the school's philosophical direction for the new century. "We hope to make the campus co-extensive with the boundaries of the State," Graham famously declared in 1914. In his inaugural address of 1915, Graham laid out his vision. The university, he stated, is "an organism at the heart of the living democratic state, interpreting its life, not by parts, nor a summary of parts, but wholly fusing them all into a new culture center, giving birth to a new humanism." The *Tar Heel* staff embraced the selection of Graham with pride, not only because he was a former editor and thus one of their own, but as a man of unique vision who would

Edward Kidder Graham, 1897–98 editor of the *Tar Heel*, later professor of English and university president. Graham taught the first course in journalism at UNC. (NCC)

build a modern university of national stature. At the opening of the school year in September 1914, an editorial ran expressing the students' wholehearted support. "President Graham, we are behind you to help fulfill your hopes that ... '[we have a] great opportunity to mold a University, and a University standard, and a University student-citizenship that will not only command the admiration of our own people, but will set a standard for the colleges of the whole nation.'"[55]

That the university attracted nationally known speakers to campus in the decade preceding America's entry into the First World War attests to its growing reputation. Future U.S. president Woodrow Wilson spoke at UNC in January 1909 (as president of Princeton University) and gave the baccalaureate speech in May 1911 (as governor of New Jersey), former president and Supreme Court Chief Justice William Howard Taft in March 1915, and perennial presidential candidate and noted orator William Jennings Bryan in November 1915. Also in 1915

national YMCA leader John R. Mott, noted educator John Dewey, and English poet Alfred Noyes all made their way to Chapel Hill to speak to the students.[56]

In terms of the future of the university, the most important visitor to campus during this period was economist Eugene C. Branson, a North Carolina native then on the faculty of the State Normal School of Georgia. A leading proponent of New South ideology, Branson epitomized Graham's vision for the expansion of the university to extend to every corner of the state, but he also held somewhat progressive views on race (within the framework of the prevailing white supremacy of the day). On October 7, 1913, Branson delivered a talk on the "Negro problem" in the South, at the invitation of the YMCA. The *Tar Heel* covered the lecture at some length, summarizing Branson's main points. During the first two decades of the twentieth century, African Americans were leaving the South in large numbers and relocating to the North for better opportunities, in what was known as the Great Migration. White southerners became alarmed that their low-paid workforce was leaving, and there was much discussion about how to stem the tide. Branson pointed out that the African Americans who remained were buying up small tracts of rural land and earning a sparse living as poor farmers. He suggested that for the benefit of southern society, "industrial training will make [the Negro] a good citizen," and that better overall treatment was required, stating that "the rule to be applied in working with the [Negro] must be that of the ten commandments." The article noted that after the lecture the YMCA announced a six-week course to "study the negro problem," and more than seventy students, inspired by Branson, enthusiastically registered.[57]

Given the impact of Branson's appearance on campus, it was no surprise that one of Edward Kidder Graham's first acts as president in 1914 was to bring him from Georgia to join the faculty at UNC. The *Tar Heel* was ebullient in its praise for this hire. In an editorial entitled "A New Kind of Professor," the paper gushed about Branson and his importance to UNC:

Those men who see the University of North Carolina as a state university in the deepest significance of the term have cause for rejoicing in the news of Professor E. C. Branson's coming to Chapel Hill. To the men here who did not know of Professor Branson before his visit last fall, his work was a revelation; to the men who did know of the work, the man himself was a revelation and an inspiration. He is a personality that grips even in the shortest acquaintance, and he is bound to be a progressive force on this campus. But his work overshadows and dominates the man. Professor of Applied Economics and Rural Sociology they will call him, we see him as a Professor of the People of North Carolina.[58]

Soon after his arrival on campus Branson established the North Carolina Club, with the goal of sending students to conduct economic and social surveys in each of the state's counties, in order to identify problems and areas needing improvement. Known as "extension work," the county surveys put into practice President Graham's objective to make the campus "coextensive with the boundaries of the state." The county clubs, established nearly two decades

earlier as one of the conditions of the cessation of the rival *White and Blue*, became absorbed into this effort. The week following Branson's initial 1913 lecture at UNC, the *Tar Heel* published a glowing editorial about the Johnston County Club, holding it up as an example to follow. "To present," the editorial declared, "the University and its unparalleled opportunities for securing a higher education for the people of Johnston County, and to bring them to realize that, as a state university it is their University. To unite the Public, the Public High, and the Graded schools of [the] county in one great educational system." The next month another editorial was published carrying this relationship further, linking the county clubs to UNC, current and future students, and alumni. The paper wholeheartedly supported these efforts, and summed up their importance in October 1914:

Extension is the center of interest and attention throughout this university. Professor Branson's work is the best known and probably the most important of all of the features of extension. The doing of the work will educate the University to the importance of extension. The finished work will educate the State to the value of extension.... At this moment the University is enjoying wider publicity and more intelligent support than at any other time in her history. Work will find a quicker and larger result if expanded in the North Carolina club than in any other student activity.[59]

The *Tar Heel*'s enthusiastic endorsement of Branson was by no means a foregone conclusion; he could have been seen as an outsider and a troublemaker during this era. The paper's embrace of Branson's efforts—the embodiment of what Edward Kidder Graham wanted to accomplish at UNC—was likely critical to the wider acceptance of his work among students and alumni. In fact, the *Tar Heel* supported Branson's efforts and those of the county clubs to such an extent that it offered to send copies of the paper at discounted rates to various schools and organizations across the state in the counties where clubs were operating. The work of Eugene C. Branson marked a seminal moment in the history of the development of the modern university; it paved the way in succeeding decades for faculty in a number of fields to push the envelope and focus harsh light on the economic, social, and racial inequalities of the South. These efforts would earn the institution a reputation for being aggressively progressive or "liberal" and would lead to a series of battles with conservative alumni, industrialists, and state religious and political leaders who would attempt to clamp down on what they viewed as radical teaching, the ideological brainwashing of young minds, and meddling in affairs beyond the university's scope.[60]

CAMPUS ATTITUDES TOWARD WOMEN AND AFRICAN AMERICANS

The University of North Carolina had been a bastion of white male exclusivity for the first century of its existence. As the question of whether to admit women students began to be discussed in the mid-1890s, the *Tar Heel* editors treaded lightly. Edwin Alderman, who had been among the founding faculty of the all-female State Normal and Industrial School in Greensboro (present-day UNC–Greensboro), became president of UNC in 1896 and called for the admission of women in his inaugural address. An editorial in the paper in February 1897 expressed hope that women would be admitted to all departments, to "stimulate a desire for outward polish" among the male students. Later that year women were admitted to UNC for graduate study in small numbers—in fact one of the first female students, Mary McRae, joined the *Tar Heel* as literary editor in 1898, and a photograph of the staff taken at that time shows her seated in the center. Over the years a few more women could be found in the *Tar Heel* office. "Girls were in the newsroom in the 1920s," according to J. Maryon "Spike" Saunders, the paper's editor in chief in 1924–25 (and later longtime leader of the General Alumni Association). "We had some female reporters. They didn't cover the type of stuff the men covered, but they were reporters."[61]

In the early twentieth century the university began allowing women to transfer in as juniors from other schools, notably from the State Normal and Industrial School. But immediately following World War I, when the university was pushing for greater legislative funding (and not coincidentally during the last years of the fight for women's suffrage), a movement grew to enroll women in larger numbers. Predictably the discussion of more women on campus brought journalistic winks and nods from the predominately young male newspaper staff. But as the issue was discussed more seriously, the sophomoric humor turned into pointed debate. In March 1923, the topic reached a crescendo in the pages of the *Tar Heel* when an "extra" edition was put out regarding construction of the first dormitory exclusively for women. Intending to sensationalize the story, the paper featured full front-page head-

Staff of the *Tar Heel*, 1898, showing the first female student at Carolina, Mary McRae (seated center), who was literary editor. R. D. W. Connor, later the first archivist of the United States, stands in the back row, second from the right. (NCC/*Hellenian*)

lines declaring overwhelming student opposition to larger numbers of women on campus, as well as editorials historian Louis Round Wilson termed "none-too-gallant," such as one titled in 1920s clipped parlance: "Shaves and Cigs, But Not Rats and Rouge" (the latter terms referencing a popular women's hairstyle of the day, and makeup).[62]

The *Tar Heel* called for a student vote on the matter, and the results ran in boxes on either side of the banner: "The Students Say . . . No 937, Yes 173." At the heart of the matter was what historian Wilson characterizes as a misunderstanding by the students. Campus leaders, and even some alumni and state legislators, were apparently under the impression that the money appropriated for the women's dormitory would be taken from funds already allocated for the existing male students, and they believed this action signaled an attempt to begin to admit equal numbers of women and men as undergraduates. The editions of the *Tar Heel* covering the story in such a sensational manner were seen across the state, to the extent that university president Harry Woodburn Chase was compelled to issue three statements (including one that ran in the *Greensboro Daily News*) denying that either funds were being diverted for the women's dormitory or that the admittance policy for women was changing.[63]

The status of African Americans as citizens in the South—the region's most significant social issue during the century following the Civil War—was another topic debated at the university and in the pages of the *Tar Heel*. During the first quarter century of the *Tar Heel*'s existence the attitudes of the young white college men who wrote for and edited the paper predictably mirrored those of their parents and southern society at large. A front-page article in October 1893 mocking the presence of an African American player on Harvard's football squad was typical: "Harvard's centre rush is a Negro, and he is said to be a fine player; if some one would hit him on the shins he would be no good. We people down here in the South know you cannot hurt a Negro by punching his head, but it is quite to the contrary if you tackle his other end."[64]

Following the state elections of 1894, the paper, which rarely commented on politics before World War I, lamented that North Carolina had been "corrupted by the allied [biracial] forces of the Populists and Republicans. . . . The result was democracy's loss and fusion's gain." And despite the dramatic achievements of many African Americans in North Carolina during the last quarter of the nineteenth century, including some political success, racial stereotypes persisted among many southern whites. In March 1895, for example, the *Tar Heel* reviewed a speech given on campus by one Polk Miller of Richmond, Virginia, entitled "The Old Plantation Negro," in which he told "amusing" stories of "faithful and affectionate servants," concluding that "the Negro was infinitely better off before the war than now." After initial victories by the state's Democratic Party in November 1898 on a white supremacist platform, an article from the *North Carolina Magazine* was reprinted in the *Tar Heel* that read in part, "The Negro as a race is shown to be unfit for the burdensome duty and high responsibility of citizenship. . . . Disfranchisement of the ignorant mass of Negro voters is the only solution." Following the Democrats' successful wresting of control from the Populists and Republicans in the election of 1900, both po-

litical disfranchisement and Jim Crow segregation were legalized and instituted throughout the
state. The university was eager during this era to
show that it was in accord with these practices,
so much so that the paper reported in November 1910 that Professor Kemp Plummer Battle
had begun a lecture on the history of the campus
"by declaring that he wished to contradict the
widespread rumor than Negro students had ever
been at the University."[65]

The University of North Carolina was deeply
rooted in the culture of the Old South and "Lost
Cause" sentimentality of the Confederacy well
into the twentieth century. The *Tar Heel* annually carried stories and occasional editorials
about festivities to mark Robert E. Lee's birthday. When the minister and former state legislator Thomas Dixon spoke on campus in 1896,
the paper crowned him the "orator of the age"
and declared that he "deserves [our] tribute."
His book *The Clansman* would be published in
1905, and was later turned into the controversial
motion picture *Birth of a Nation*. In one of the
earliest movie advertisements in the *Tar Heel*,
a 1921 screening was announced at the Pickwick Theater on Franklin Street, in which the
paper touted the film as an "American Institution.... Truthful—Thrilling—Tremendous ...
With an Orchestral Accompaniment of the Original Score." The Lost Cause was also enshrined
on the campus landscape; in April 1911, on the
occasion of the fiftieth anniversary of the start of
the Civil War, the *Tar Heel* ran a front-page picture of a proposed new monument to the university's Confederate soldiers. The romanticized
sculpture of a student-turned-soldier (later nicknamed "Silent Sam") was purposefully sited to
face north and the oncoming invaders. "Standing

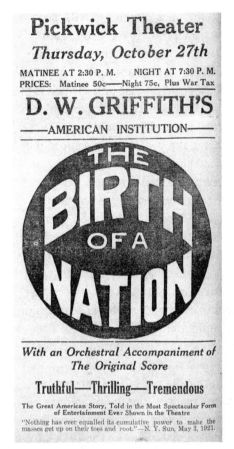

Pickwick Theater
Thursday, October 27th

MATINEE AT 2:30 P. M.   NIGHT AT 7:30 P. M.
PRICES: Matinee 50c—Night 75c, Plus War Tax

D. W. GRIFFITH'S
——AMERICAN INSTITUTION——

THE BIRTH OF A NATION

With an Orchestral Accompaniment of
The Original Score

Truthful—Thrilling—Tremendous

The Great American Story, Told in the Most Spectacular Form
of Entertainment Ever Shown in the Theatre
"Nothing has ever equalled its cumulative power to make the
masses get up on their toes and root."—N. Y. Sun, May 3, 1921.

on campus for all time the monument will ever
be to all future generations an object lesson of
service rendered and duty performed, and it will
impress upon them their obligation to be faithful
to the record of the past," the paper proclaimed.[66]

As the university evolved during the early decades of the twentieth century, attitudes of contempt and superiority toward African Americans
gave way to paternalistic concern, and the *Tar
Heel* chronicled this transition. In February 1916,
Eugene Branson hosted an academic conference
at UNC on race in the South, and the paper reported on the proceedings under the title "Col-

lege Men Urged to Check Lynching Evil." The attendees drew up a letter strongly condemning the increase in racially motivated lynchings across the South in recent years, calling the practice "a contagious social disease and as such is of deep concern to every American citizen and to every lover of civilization." In a bold pronouncement, Branson and the conference declared that college men could and should do something to stop these unlawful and barbaric acts: "Herein lies the college man's opportunity to serve his fellows: interpose deliberation between impulses and actions and in that way control both. Society has a right to expect college men to help in molding opinion and shaping conduct in matters of this sort; it is their privilege and duty to cooperate with others in leading crusades against crime and mob rule and for law and civilization. The college man belongs in the front rank of those fighting for moral and social progress."[67]

The following October, the *Tar Heel* carried a story informing readers that the university YMCA "resumes work in Negro night schools." First established in 1915, and apparently inspired by Eugene Branson's philosophy, the instruction consisted of forty-five-minute lessons five nights a week in arithmetic, history, English, debating, and hygiene, taught by faculty with the assistance of students. The article also noted that this was a collaborative effort, as the African American YMCA "gave an oyster supper and 'possum stew' Thursday night to pay expenses this fall." A year later, in October 1917, an article entitled "Negro Night School Promising" noted the continued educational work of the Y in the black community and listed Frank Porter Graham as one of the instructors. Both of these very public activities—hosting a conference on race de-

Y. M. C. A. RESUMES WORK IN NEGRO NIGHT SCHOOLS

The negro work carried on by the Y. M. C. A. here began Monday night with the first meeting of the negro night school at the colored Y. M. C. A. on Cameron Avenue. Brief meetings lasting about forty-five minutes are now held every night except Saturday and Sunday. The subjects taught are arithmetic, history, English, debating and hygiene. The following students are assisting in the teaching: Alfred Lindau, Theodore Rondthaler, William Boyd, Parkhill Jarvis, Roland McClamrock, Herman Stephenson and Robert Wunsch.

The negro Y. M. C. A. gave an oyster supper and " 'possum stew" Thursday night to pay expenses this fall.

nouncing lynching and actively working with African Americans to improve educational opportunities in their communities—were bold acts at a state-funded institution in the South during the early years of Jim Crow segregation, and would lay the foundation for criticism of the school's "liberalism" on racial issues in years to come.[68]

THE GREAT WAR

The expansion of the university's horizons was also reflected by the *Tar Heel*'s coverage of the Great War between 1914 and 1919, which was the first time in its history the paper devoted substantive space on a regular basis to a national news story that reached far beyond the school's borders. The expanded coverage was the natural result of the worldwide effects of the war, which transformed the university community as it did the nation. In many ways the coverage surrounding World War I marked the beginning of the journalistic maturation of the paper—a process that continued into the early 1930s—as from that point forward the *Tar Heel* was far less provincial in its reporting.

The *Tar Heel* followed the emerging crisis from all angles, but eventually came down editorially on the side of "making the world safe for democracy." In November 1915, William Jennings Bryan gave a rousing pacifist speech on campus attacking the warmongering of newspaper editors, which the *Tar Heel* covered in detail. "If the dogs in Europe won't stop fighting, don't let us get hydrophobia over here," Bryan declared. "If we ever have a war I think that the jingo editors ought to be put on the front line and be allowed the glory of dying before anyone else. You can no more judge the sentiments of a peace loving nation by the ravings of the jingo editors than you can measure the depth of the ocean by the foam on its wave."[69]

At first, the paper's coverage of the war was sympathetic and patriotic—if not jingoistic—as students marched around campus with wooden rifles and hung on every word of firsthand accounts such as that of Fredrick Palmer, a European newspaper correspondent who gave an illustrated lecture about trench warfare on the front lines to a packed audience in Memorial Hall in the spring of 1917. But as America's entry into combat became more likely, the paper and the administration grew increasingly alarmed at the number of young men who were overly eager to leave the university and enlist. Under the title "Democracy—The Task of the University," a February 1917 editorial emphasized the importance of maintaining high standards of education, even in wartime, by quoting from a report by President Graham. "The issue is but a new form of the ancient issue of slavery and freedom," Graham wrote. "An ignorant people are as truly in slavery, economic and intellectual, as if they were in physical bondage. An educated mind is the genius of democracy.... It is the only dictator that the freemen acknowledge and the only security that freemen desire. Without it there is no freedom."[70]

Following the country's entrance into the Great War in April of 1917, however, the university and the *Tar Heel* fully supported the effort. "The single thought of the University is to cooperate in every intelligent way with the government," the paper quoted Graham as saying in an address to the campus. "To this end it offered several weeks ago its all—every resource and equipment, means and men. It organized military training under competent instruction, and complied with the requirements for a Reserve Officers Training Corps.... Our larger task is peace; our immediate task is war. There is now no alternative for a Christian democracy." During the conflict the paper reported that students were "doing their best to crush Kaiserism," and cartoons and advertisements supporting the war effort appeared regularly. In the Thanksgiving edition an editorial put the campus sentiments this way:

> We give thanks that we are free to give and to fight for that which is best in the world; that we are not led by a ruthless government into a shameless struggle but that we unselfishly, may 'dedicate our lives and all that we have' to the greatest ideals—that we may lay down our lives and give our all for even the least of these in order that the world may at last become a better place in which to live and that all mankind may have the glorious privilege of peace, freedom, and justice, and that men may at last be brothers.[71]

Not only did students enlist in large numbers, but the campus became an official army training facility late in the war. Glenn Hutchinson, in an article in the *Carolina Magazine* in 1937, used issues of the *Tar Heel* from the era to write the following account of life at the university during its time under military occupation.

> The height of patriotic fervor was reached in the fall of 1918, when the University ceased to be a university and became a government camp, the Students Army Training Corps [SATC] taking over the campus, lock, stock and barrel. The 750 Carolina men in the Corps were part of 150,000 men in 500 American colleges who were inducted into the organization at the beginning of the fall term.
>
> When Lt. G. W. S. Stevens of the U. S. Army moved his military headquarters into the Sigma Chi fraternity house and took charge of the SATC, he really took charge of the University, for the student body and the SATC were

practically the same thing. Military terminology and regulations were the order of the day. The dormitories were referred to as barracks, Swain Hall was known as the mess hall, and Memorial Hall became the Armory. The old liberal arts curriculum was thrown out, class lines were abolished, and military training was the paramount consideration, with each student's course being arranged to fit him for some branch of the service. Students were grouped by ages instead of classes, and eleven hours of military training and three recitation hours in the study of the issues involved in the war were required. These classes in War Issues were the largest of any in the University.

> As a part of their realistic war training the student-soldiers dug trenches near the Raleigh road, complete with barbed wire, dug-outs and all the trimmings. There they practiced trench warfare, staged mock engagements, practiced bomb throwing and laid down barrages of artillery. They even had the local Red Cross chapter serving them coffee and doughnuts "up at the front." But the boys didn't stay in the trenches. The whole town of Chapel Hill was the scene of mock street fighting and military maneuvers on a grand scale. One of the "pitched battles" occurred in the arboretum late one evening, a fact that ought to emphasize how no phase of campus life was exempt from the impact of the war.[72]

Some 2,240 UNC alumni, students, and faculty served in the war. The university suffered a total of 56 casualties, including those who were wounded as well as those who died in battle or from disease. Though proportionally university

casualties were low, the *Tar Heel* family was particularly hard-hit. Quincy Sharpe Mills, who had been editor in 1906–7 during the anti-hazing campaign, was killed in an attack on German lines in 1918. Equally devastating to the carnage on the battlefields was a particularly deadly strain of influenza resistant to available treatments that quickly swept through Europe and the United States. Unlike most flus, which attack the very young, the elderly, and those with weakened immune systems, the strain which caused the influenza pandemic of 1918 struck healthy adults. The flu appeared in Chapel Hill in the fall of 1918, and the campus was placed under quarantine for three weeks in October. Several students died, and their names were printed in the paper in black-bordered boxes. The quarantine, along with the ongoing war effort, led to the absence of any festivities on October 12, traditionally celebrated as University Day to mark the anniversary of the 1793 laying of the cornerstone of Old East. Eleven days later the paper's headlines read "Influenza Situation Improving," but on October 26, President Edward Kidder

Front page memorial to the late Edward Kidder Graham,
October 1918. (NCC)

THE TAR HEEL

OFFICIAL ORGAN OF THE ATHLETIC ASSOCIATION OF THE UNIVERSITY OF NORTH CAROLINA

Volume XXVII.   CHAPEL HILL, N. C., WEDNESDAY, OCT. 30, 1918   Number 5

SQUAD PREPARES FOR WAKE FOREST ELEVEN

PIGSKIN HEROES GO THROUGH STIFF PRACTICE BEFORE GAME WITH BAPTISTS

GAME SCHEDULED FOR SATURDAY

Three Games are Assured in Five
Games Scheduled—Ancient Thanksgiving Classic Probable

With the past week of good weather
football has once more loomed up
large on the athletic horizon of Carolina. Coach Ritch has been putting
his men through a stiff practice, and
as a result, after only one week of
training, the squad is rapidly being
whipped into form and the coach believes he has the material for a team
which will not only more than hold
its own against opposing state college
teams but will duplicate the performance of the famous 1916 team, and
send the proud pigskin warriors from
Virginia once more under the yoke
in the annual Thanksgiving classic.

The only great difficulty in the
way of varsity athletics this year
is the lack of time for practice. While
every spare moment is being utilized
for the gridiron candidates, Coach
Ritch is badly handicapped. However,
all colleges are laboring under the
same disadvantage, and are practically on a par in respect to the time
at their disposal for football.

A full schedule has not been definitely arranged yet, but we are sure of
three games in a five game schedule.
The proposed schedule is as follows:
November 2—Wake Forest at Chapel Hill.
November 9—Washington and Lee
at Lynchburg, Va.
November 16—Davidson at Winston.
November 23—Open.
November 28—University of Virginia—pending.

The only difficulty that is holding
back the final arrangements between
Carolina and Virginia is the lack of
time for coaching and practicing the
teams. But in all probability the
great annual game will be staged, as
neither team's schedule would be complete without this traditional climax.
The game will most likely be played
on Emerson Field, thus giving the Tar
Heels an opportunity to enjoy the holiday treat which the Virginians have
had so long.

(Continued on Page 3)

NEW RIFLES RECEIVED BY MILITARY ORGANIZATION

200 ARRIVE—300 MORE ON WAY RIFLE RANGE TO BE MADE READY FOR PRACTICE

GENERAL ORDERS FOR SENTINELS

Will Walk Post During Drill Hours—
Battalion Passes in Review
Before Governor

With the arrival and distribution
of 200 Winchester rifles, alloted fifty
to the Company, the University S.
A. T. C. men are ready to begin a new
and more advanced phase of training,
the manual of arms. The drills for
the past week have been mostly in
platoons and companies, the school of
the soldier and squad having been
pretty thoroughly mastered by the
men of this command. Three hundred additional Russian Rifles are now
in transit to the University and with
their arrival each man in the Battalion will be equipped, ready to begin training in the handling, care and
operation of the weapon. A Rifle
Range will be fitted out and target
practice will soon be the order of the
day.

This week has also witnessed the
opening of another new chapter in
the martial life of the S. A. T. C.
Sentinel duty has begun. The twelve
general orders of the sentinel have
been printed in sufficient numbers so
that each man of the Battalion can
secure a copy. No Guard Mount at
night will be attempted yet, sentinel
duty being confined to the drill hours.

On the twenty-eighth, the Battalion
passed in review before Honorable
T. W. Bickett, Governor of the State,
who came over to attend the funeral
services of the late President Graham.
To comply fully with regulations, orders were issued from Military Headquarters for all men to wear canvas
leggins, except the Guard of Honor,
who were permitted to wear spirals.
All men wore their blouses, shirt col-
lars inside and no hat cords were
allowed. The entire organization did
its best and, considering the short
period of time it has been in training,
acquitted itself in a decidedly credi-
table manner. The Governor expressed himself as being very favorably
impressed with the discipline and sol-
dierly bearing of the men.

News of great interest to a
number of students at the University
has just been received at Military
Headquarters, to the effect that men
of other registrants prior to September 12th, 1918, and in Class 1 are now

DR. EDWARD KIDDER GRAHAM

Edward K. Graham, president of the University, died at his home
here Saturday, October 26, following an illness of five days from influenza and complications. Dr. Graham had been ill a few days when
pneumonia set in, and, although the student body was aware of the
serious nature of his illness, every hope was entertained for his recovery. The unexpected news of his death has overwhelmed the student body with a keen, personal grief and has brought sorrow to the
hearts of those who knew him.

The University has lost, by the death of President Graham, a great
leader—a virile young leader of the new era who brought the University he loved into a more intimate relationship with people all over
the state and at the same time placed it in the forefront as one of the
Universities of the nation alive to educational requirements of today. In
his inaugural address, delivered April 22, 1915, he characterized the
State University as "a living unity, an organism at the heart of the
living democratic state, interpreting its life, not by parts, nor a sum-

HUNDREDS ATTEND THE FUNERAL OF DR. GRAHAM

GOV. BICKETT AND OTHER WELL KNOWN MEN WERE PRESENT FROM ALL PARTS OF STATE

BATALLION ACTED AS ESCORT

Burial of President was marked by
Beautiful Simplicity of Funeral
Services

Edward Kidder Graham, President
of the University of North Carolina,
whose death from pneumonia occurred Saturday night, was buried
here this afternoon at 2 o'clock. The
services, marked with a simplicity
and beauty in complete harmony with
the life of President Graham, were
conducted at the grave by Dr. W. D.
Moss, the pastor of the local Presbyterian church.

The affecton and high esteem in
which President Graham was held
were evidenced by the presence of
hundreds of friends, former students
and alumni within and without the
state, by telegrams and messages
to members of the family and the
university faculty from every part of
the country, and by a profusion of
floral designs and autumn flowers of
unimagined beauty.

The following active and honorary
pallbearers were present:
Honorary: Governor Thomas W.
Bickett, Dr. J. Y. Joyner, Dr. Kemp
P. Battle, Dr. F. P. Venable, Mayor
W. S. Roberson, M. C. S. Noble,
Dr. H. H. Williams, Dr. W. D. Toy,
Major William Cain, George Pickard,
W. N. Everett; Active: Dr. W. D.
McNider, R. D. W. Connor, Dean M.
H. Stacy, Dr. A. H. Patterson, Dr. L.
R. Wilson, Dr. J. G. De Roulhac Ham-
ilton, Dr. Archibald Henderson,
Charles T. Woollen.

In the funeral procession leading
to the cemetery were the military
guard of honor, of 40 men, led by
Captain C. C. Helmer, Commandant
at the University; Trustees of the
University, representatives of other
Colleges and schools, directors and
Commandants of the S. A. T. C. College units in the state, the Faculty
of the University, the Alumni and
other visitors, and the student battalion.

Among the representatives of edu-
cational institutions were President
Wallace C. Riddick, of the State A.
& E. College; President J. I. Foust,

(Continued on Page 4)

Graham, class of 1898, former editor in chief of
the *Tar Heel*, and the first to teach a class in journalism at UNC, succumbed to the disease at the
age of forty-two.[73]

The *Tar Heel* served as the official university
mourner for President Graham. "We have suffered the loss of a loved friend, and our hearts

ache," the lead editorial read on the day after his
funeral. A black-bordered photograph of the late
president appeared on the front page, and the
paper eulogized him as "a product of the institution he was to lead so well, endowed with every
requisite for leadership, a great thinking, clean
minded young leader.... [At] the turning point

of the University's life ... a virile young leader of the new era who brought the University he loved into a more intimate relationship with people all over the state and at the same time placed it in the forefront as one of the Universities of the nation alive to educational requirements of today."[74]

EARLY EDITORS—AND MR. WOLFE

The editorial style of the paper predictably changed from year to year, reflecting the personality of the staff—particularly that of the editor in chief. The early staff of the *Tar Heel* numbered eight students each year. From the time of the first issue in 1893 until the paper became an official university publication in 1923, the Athletic Association chose the editor in chief annually (though sometimes more frequently; during those three decades a total of 44 men served in the position). The selection process evolved somewhat over time, but with the possible exception of one or two years around 1908, it is evident that the student body as a whole did not elect the editor in chief by popular vote until 1923. Apparently in the first few years a choice was made by members of the Athletic Council, the student governing body of the Athletic Association, though by 1898 an election was being held among all association members.[75]

The establishment of the first classes in journalism at the university in 1909, coupled with controversy surrounding the coverage and editorializing about hazing, put pressure on the Athletic Association to make the election of editors and staff more democratic and merit based. "The editorship of the *Tar Heel* is no honorary degree to be conferred upon some member of the senior class.... It is a responsible position to be filled by the ablest man in college," a 1910 editorial de-

clared. A series of amendments to the Athletic Association's constitution regarding the election of the editor in chief, selection of assistant editors, and compensation of the paper's staff were proposed and passed in both 1910 and 1913. The 1910 amendments expanded the staff to nine members, with the editor in chief being elected by members of the senior class, and the associate editor in chief by members of the junior class. The Athletic Council was charged with nominating two candidates for the position of editor in chief, with the winning candidate chosen through election by the entire membership of the Athletic Association. These candidates had to qualify for nomination by being seniors with at least one year of experience on the paper, and the elections were to be held the first Saturday in May. Any profits from the paper were to be split equally in thirds between the Athletic Association, the editor in chief, and the business manager. Kinks soon appeared in this system, however, and additional amendments were added to straighten them out in 1913. Meetings to select the editorial staff often dragged on for hours, the paper reported, and, in an apparent holdover from the battle with the *White and Blue*, fraternity men were pitted against non-fraternity men. "The old way has one other drawback—its political feature," an editorial noted. "In the past it has been a practically accepted understanding and custom that one of the assistant managers be a fraternity man, and one a non-fraternity man. This always provided the ammunition for a hot political debate in which much harm resulted and often the least efficient of perhaps two inefficient men was elected because of his political affiliation with one side or other."[76]

Of the first forty-four editors in chief who

served from 1893 to 1923, thirteen went on to successful careers in journalism, including: Ralph Graves (city editor for the *New York Evening Post* and Sunday editor of the *New York Times*), Charles Phillips Russell (reporter for the *Charlotte Observer* and professor of journalism at UNC), Victor Stephenson (reporter for the *New York Evening Post* and the *Charlotte Observer*, and editor of the *Winston-Salem Journal*), Herbert Gunter (city editor of the Raleigh *News and Observer* and editor of the *Winston-Salem Journal*), Oscar Coffin (reporter for the *Winston-Salem Journal*, news editor of the *Charlotte Observer*, columnist for the *Greensboro Daily News*, and professor of journalism at UNC); Lenoir Chambers (city and associate editor of the *Greensboro Daily News*, editor and publisher of the *Norfolk Virginian-Pilot* and Pulitzer Prize winner), Jonathan Daniels (editor of the Raleigh *News and Observer*), and Julius "Jake" Wade (sports editor of the *Charlotte Observer*, managing editor of the *Greensboro Record*, and director of UNC sports information). In addition, several of the first forty-four editors in chief went on to notable careers in other fields, including Edward Kidder Graham and Frank Porter Graham (presidents of UNC), J. C. B. Ehringhaus (governor of North Carolina), W. J. Brogden (North Carolina Supreme Court justice), and R. D. W. Connor (first archivist of the United States).[77]

Perhaps the most famous name associated with the paper in its early years is that of Thomas Wolfe. Before he became a celebrated novelist, Wolfe was a precocious and ambitious student from Asheville, arriving on campus in 1916 at the tender age of 15. Tall and gangly, Wolfe was quite a presence at UNC, and while his at-

tention to his studies was at times sporadic, he threw himself with a passion into a variety of mostly extracurricular literary pursuits, including writing for all of the campus publications (the *Tar Heel*, the *Carolina Magazine*, and the *Tar Baby*). His youthful energy was boundless; in addition to writing for these publications he wrote and performed plays for the newly formed Carolina Playmakers Theater group—and still found the time to frequent brothels in Durham. His name first appeared in the *Tar Heel* in a March 1918 review of the spring issue of the *Carolina Magazine*, to which he contributed a poem and a short story. It was also the first published criticism of his work. The reviewer was enthusiastic about Wolfe's writing, stating that his poem, "The Challenge," "perhaps sets the high water mark for this number. It is full of fire and its rhythm is well sustained.... The poem has many excellent lines and the dignity of true poetry." Regarding Wolfe's short story, "A Cullenden of Virginia," the reviewer wrote that it was "a good study in cowardice ... [and] many of the descriptive touches are good." Although the critic suggested that the short story's "denouement might have been handled a little more effectively, perhaps," he did predict the writer's success: "Mr. Wolfe's two contributions to this issue give promise that he is to do much excellent work in the future. He writes well and with much imaginative insight."[78]

Wolfe became assistant editor of the *Tar Heel* in 1918, and during that year he returned to Asheville to visit his beloved brother Ben, who contracted influenza during the pandemic and subsequently died, an episode the writer recounts in his seminal 1929 novel, *Look Homeward, Angel*. As the brief but intense period of

Thomas Wolfe, 1919–20 editor of the *Tar Heel*, later celebrated as one of America's greatest novelists. (*Yack*)

THE TAR HEEL

CAROLINA W...   A. AND E.

T.C. WOLFE
Editor-in-chief

the First World War ended, he was elected editor in chief of the paper for the 1919–20 academic year, a time of renewed optimism on campus. Wolfe's style was wrought in broad flourishes that often showcased his noted wit and budding literary talent. Breezy and sometimes cleverly alliterative headlines appeared, such as: "Capacity of Emerson Field Trebled Turkey Day; 5,000 Pilgrims Expected for Gridiron Classic," "About Donning the Denim" (a humorous editorial about the new fad of students wearing denim overalls and jeans on campus) and "Dialectic Disciples Hold Forth in Feed," which con-

tinued on page two under the title of "Diabetic Disciples Hold Forth in Feed"—with Wolfe, one is never sure if this was a typo or done on purpose. He made changes and additions to the paper, including starting a regular column titled "Ancient History," which quoted items of interest from the *Tar Heel* of years past. One of his most significant contributions was a lengthy editorial entitled "The Creative Movement in Writing," penned just a week after his election as editor in chief. Wolfe took this piece very seriously, forgoing his usual flippancy and signing the column with his name, still a rare occurrence in the *Tar Heel*. In the somewhat self-congratulatory column he credited the blossoming of creative writing at UNC to the recent efforts of Professor Frederick Koch who instituted "perhaps the most distinctive work that has been done in this line ... under the auspices of the newly-formed Carolina Playmakers Association—that most unique, but democratic organization."[79]

Wolfe also took particular interest in the aesthetic qualities of the campus. In the editorial "Is Modern Civilization to See a New Type of Architecture?" he managed to skewer both the original Memorial Hall and modern art:

To our more or less untutored architectural minds architecture in Chapel Hill, past and present, is characterized by a pleasurely unfitness that should joy the heart of almost any freak,—particularly a futurist painter. Let us consider that marvelous barn that we have erected as a housing place for numerous homeless benches. How sweetly doth it break the monotony of our architectural schemes. "Simple but appealing"—you know. Nor is this the only bid to fame. Every freshman is told with pride, "The largest unsupported roof in the South, sir."[80]

Wolfe's tenure as editor coincided with the realization of the physical expansion of the UNC campus initiated by Edward Kidder Graham, and continued by succeeding administrations. Landscape architect John Nolen, known for his work across the country including the original plan for the Myers Park neighborhood in Charlotte, first conceptualized a unified master plan for the university in 1917 that created the basic layout for the quadrangles evident on the main campus today. Following Graham's death a committee of trustees, led by J. Bryan Grimes in conjunction with President Harry Woodburn Chase, continued the plans for expansion. The celebrated New York firm of McKim, Mead & White was retained to fully develop the initial vision, and to oversee design and construction. The firm was renowned for work on important commissions such as the 1893 Columbian Exposition in Chicago, the second Madison Square Garden in New York City, the Boston Public Library, and both the redesign of the National Mall in Washington, D.C., and the major 1902 renovation of the White House under President Theodore Roosevelt. The hiring of McKim, Mead & White was a conscious effort to provide the UNC with a sophisticated campus that echoed in bricks and mortar the university's modern organizational structure, and, equally important, to embed the landscape with tangible references to the Old South and the early Republic. Elements of this first-quarter twentieth century expansion—including the naming of many buildings for prominent former slaveholding alumni and Confederate veterans, and the erection in 1913 of the Confederate Sol-

dier's monument near Franklin Street—would in later generations come under intense criticism as glorifying the racist, white supremacist roots of the state and the university.[81]

While the overall plan was thoroughly modern, the design of the new buildings harked back to the late eighteenth and early nineteenth centuries. The red-brick "colonial style" (as it was incorrectly termed) was the idiom chosen to visually organize and aesthetically unify the architecturally eclectic campus. Though not strictly authentic replicas of early American buildings, the formal Georgian and neoclassical details did create a cohesive appearance with many of the existing structures. This expansion unified McCorkle Place and created the dramatic Polk Place, along with the smaller adjacent quadrangles of classroom buildings and the regular groupings of dormitories east of the center of campus. Wolfe applauded the overall plan and design aesthetic in an editorial titled "Old Buildings and New" in January 1920:

> The builders of the University adopted a definite architectural scheme that gave a distinctiveness to the plan. The type of architecture we are referring to is typified by South, Old East, and Old West.... Roughly analyzed these old buildings are the hub around which the new University has and is being built up. The buildings are consistent; they are old but their age is found in the same clean, thoroughbred appearance.... We have no criticism to make in general of the newer buildings on campus. But the greatest material development of the University is to come and it's coming fast. And the architecture of our coming buildings ought to have the characteristic look of the old

buildings; our beautiful old campus ought to be adorned by buildings which harmonize and are consistent.[82]

Wolfe's highly developed literary and aesthetic sensibilities may have created good copy for the *Tar Heel*, but they did not enhance the bottom line. The paper's business manager at the time, Nathan Gooding, remembered Wolfe fondly half a century later, but reflected on his lack of savvy—or concern—for financial matters. Wolfe's boundless creativity resulted in "reams of copy," which were sent by bus to the Seeman print shop in Durham, where the paper was produced. The print shop would immediately set the articles, columns, and editorials in type, creating for each issue two to six galleys more than could be printed, creating cost overruns. Additionally, Wolfe on his weekly trips to Durham to oversee the final makeup of the paper, had the habit of cavalierly tossing out paying advertisements Gooding had secured and replacing them with copy he felt was more important. At the end of the year the *Tar Heel* was $400 in debt—a sum large enough to buy an automobile at the time—and Gooding quietly spent the year after his graduation working to pay off the obligation.[83]

Wolfe's successors as editor in chief were Daniel Grant and Jonathan Daniels (son of Josephus Daniels, and a member of the well-known publishing family who owned the state's most widely read newspaper, the Raleigh *News and Observer*). Both reined in the wittier elements of the *Tar Heel* characteristic of Wolfe, and instituted standards of professionalism such as bringing titling and format in line with the industry, and actively participating in the North Carolina Collegiate Press Association. And it was Daniels who would set the *Tar Heel* on a new course by proposing in 1921 that the paper cease to operate under the direction of the Athletic Association, and become part of the newly proposed Student Publications Union Board. When instituted in 1923, this change brought a new management and revenue structure to the paper, and made the *Tar Heel* for the first time in its history an official publication of the University of North Carolina.[84]

2
CRACK-BRAINED PROFESSORS AND BABY RADICALS

1923-1941

As the University of North Carolina rapidly expanded and modernized during the 1920s and 1930s, so did the *Tar Heel*. Over the short span of just nine years the paper matured and professionalized: in 1923 it became an official university publication supported by student fees with an editor elected annually by the entire student body; in 1929 it became a daily (published every day except Monday); and in 1932 an official stylebook, based on those employed at several of the nation's top newspapers, was published for internal use. In addition the paper's staff actively promoted and participated in both collegiate and professional journalism associations, as well as being a driving force behind the creation of the university's Department (later School) of Journalism in 1924. By the late 1920s UNC was recognized as one of the leading public universities in the nation, and by the late 1930s the banner under the masthead declared that the *Daily Tar Heel* was "The Only Daily College Newspaper in the South."

The structure that formally brought the independently published *Tar Heel* into the university in the spring of 1923 was the newly established Publications Union Board. Though the student-run Athletic Association created the *Tar Heel* in 1893, the fit between the organization and the newspaper had rarely been a comfortable one. Members of the association, nonmember students, and alumni routinely assailed editors on a variety of issues, including the extent of the paper's athletic coverage. Moreover, the editors and staff of the paper were no strangers to clashes with leadership of the association, whose influence on campus diminished by the 1910s as the university administration took increasing control of the athletic programs. But the issue that finally caused the *Tar Heel* to break with the Athletic Association was money. For three decades the paper's business staff begged and pleaded with students and alumni to buy subscriptions, and they scurried around Chapel Hill and as far as Greensboro and Raleigh selling advertising space. More than once the paper failed to appear because it lacked sufficient funds to publish, and attempts over the years at increasing its size or number of editions per week proved unsustainable. The paper's chronic financial problems were finally solved in large measure when it joined the new Publications Union Board (PUB), which was funded by student fees.[1]

The first mention of the paper potentially becoming part of the PUB appears in December 1921, in an op-ed piece by editor Jonathan Daniels (son of the Raleigh *News and Observer* publisher, Josephus Daniels). Discussions about the shift may have occurred earlier, as the banner "Organ of the Athletic Association" disappeared from under the masthead in June of that year. Sanctioned by the university, the PUB brought four previously independent student publications under its wing: the *Tar Heel, Yackety Yack* (the UNC yearbook), the *University Magazine* (a monthly literary journal) and the *Tar Baby* (a humor magazine). With two members of the faculty on the board, the arrangement was also supported by the university administration, which was able to exercise some degree of oversight over the publications if necessary. Creation of the PUB for a one-year trial period was put to a student vote and passed overwhelmingly, 876 to 141. On May 5, 1923, the *Tar Heel*, then thirty

years old, officially became a publication of the University of North Carolina. Two changes were immediate: the annual selection of the editor in chief became an election open to all students (as opposed to only those who were members of the Athletic Association); and the financial pressure to keep the paper afloat through subscriptions was eliminated, though advertising remained an important source of revenue. As a result of the infusion of student fees, the *Tar Heel* made a small profit the first year, but it was not an entirely easy transition. Over the next two decades the paper, now a sibling of the other three publications, would become periodically entangled in their problems—particularly those of the humor magazine.[2]

The creation of the PUB was followed by the realization of a dedicated department of journalism in September 1924, with a mission of both raising the tone and professional standards of journalism on campus, and supplying trained newsmen for the state's newspapers. The department had been thirty years in the making, and its formation was in part the result of efforts by the *Tar Heel* and its editors. During the battle with the rival *White and Blue* in March 1894, the *Tar Heel* ran an editorial welcoming its competitor, stating that hopefully the increased interest in the field would "be but the beginning of a school of journalism in the University," which would serve in "augmenting the progressiveness" of UNC. Fifteen years later, in 1909, former *Tar Heel* editor and then-English-professor Edward Kidder Graham offered the first course in journalism, and that same year the university awarded the first student prize in the field, the Preston Memorial Cup. After Graham became acting president of the university in 1913, em-

E. J. EVANS

W. D. PERRY
PRESIDENT

J. O. MARSHALL

Publications Union

J. M. LEAR
FACULTY ADVISOR

O. J. COFFIN
FACULTY ADVISOR

The Publications Union Board, 1927–28. Among the members are former *Tar Heel* editor Oscar J. Coffin, then on the faculty in the Department of Journalism, and E. J. Evans, later mayor of Durham, N.C. (NCC/*Yack*)

phasis on the teaching and practice of journalism increased, both because he saw it as a viable and expanding profession in the first decades of the twentieth century, and because he understood that UNC graduates could serve as clarions to sound the call of the new progressive agenda of the university throughout the state and beyond. Through the network of the county clubs in the mid-1910s, students were encouraged to serve as representatives to their county and town newspapers, giving them valuable practical experience and an opportunity to provide stories about the university and the work of its faculty.[3]

By 1916 the university's reputation for teaching journalism rose to the point that the North Carolina Newspaper Association's annual institute was held on campus, the first of many such statewide press gatherings at UNC. Former U.S. president William Howard Taft delivered the opening speech, and during the convention the *Tar Heel* published a four-page special edition put out by journalism students. Editor William Polk (who went on to a career with Winston-Salem's *Twin City Sentinel* and the *Greensboro Daily News*) wrote that the institute "shows that the State and the University realize perhaps as never before the great need of more efficient training in the fields of journalism. It shows another instance of how the state and its educational agent can co-operate in producing effective results." In his address to the institute, quoted extensively in the *Tar Heel*, President Graham emphasized not only the importance of journalism to the state and the role of the university in the expanding the profession, but also its broader meaning in a participatory democracy—and in achieving the mission of making "the boundaries of the campus co-extensive with

the boundaries of the state." It was just this expanded mission, set forth by Graham and championed by the *Tar Heel*, which was soon to put the university at the center of a series of important ideological controversies about the direction of the state. The University of North Carolina was, according to Graham:

An institution of the people for the people. The newspaper men are invited to come here, not to be taught by us, but that we may be a medium through which knowledge is spread, and given to the great bulk of the people which both newspaper and University try to reach. We may co-operate with each other in relieving and solving the great problems of the people in both prosperous and stunted communities. The country newspaper should do everything in its power to healthfully develop the community in which it is in. Just as the University is the product of the ideas and feelings of its own community, so it is with the newspaper.... Such meetings [as this institute] spread the true spirit of progress.[4]

Inspired by the North Carolina Newspaper Association, and as part of an ongoing effort to raise the *Tar Heel*'s professional standards, editor Daniel Grant (who would later become editor of the *Carolina Alumni Review*) became one of the founding members of the North Carolina Collegiate Newspaper Association in January 1921. Its first conference was held the following month, with the mission of bringing together editors from across the state so that "problems that present themselves to the different papers would be discussed and studied."[5]

Faculty support for journalism as a discipline and a potential career path for students also increased in the early 1920s, as shown by the appointment to the English Department in 1921 of the first full-time journalism professor, Louis Graves. Not only did Graves have substantial practical experience in the field—having worked at the *New York Times* and other newspapers—but his blood ran Carolina blue and his ties to the *Tar Heel* were strong. He had grown up on the edge of campus in a boardinghouse run by his mother (site of the present-day Carolina Inn), and graduated in the class of 1902. The *Tar Heel* described him as "a great football player, and probably the best tennis player in the university." His brother Ralph served as editor of the *Tar Heel* in 1897, and went on to become Sunday editor of the *New York Times*. Louis Graves also married Edward Kidder Graham's sister-in-law, and the couple raised Edward Kidder Graham Jr. (who would serve on the staff of the *Tar Heel* in the 1930s), following the early deaths of his parents. In January 1922, Professor Graves gave students in his advanced news writing class the assignment of writing articles and sending them to state newspapers for possible publication. "Professor Graves hopes to see the journalistic field at Carolina developed within the next two or three years until a department of journalism is founded," the *Tar Heel* reported, "and on that department he hopes to build a school of journalism that offers a degree." The author of the article then added a pointed jab sure to rile southern pride: "The lack of a school of this sort is keenly felt as men in North Carolina desiring training in this field are forced to leave the state to go north."[6]

The paper kept up a steady drumbeat for establishment of a department of journalism at the university, even though Graves's attention soon turned toward establishment of a town newspaper, the *Chapel Hill Weekly*. In September 1923, another strong editorial summing up the need for such a school appeared in the *Tar Heel*, prompted by Graves's cancellation of a journalism class that fall, leaving the twenty-seven registered students without a course to attend:

The University is the foremost training ground in the state for all walks of life, and offers a generous scope of course from rural economics to Einstein's theory of relativity, but neglects to furnish instruction in the most powerful influence on American thought and ideals, the Press. There are many young men in the University eager to make journalism their life work, if the proper inducements and training were offered them, and it is truly pitiful that they are not given the opportunity they desire. It is not only a serious handicap to them, but also to the state, for North Carolina has a crying need for thoroughly trained newspaper men.... There is a glowing chance for some energetic, experienced newspaper man to build up a strong school of journalism here. The classroom work could be collaborated with the student publications and practical instruction could be given in the mechanical side of editing a newspaper now that Chapel Hill boasts of a live printing office.[7]

Thus the formal establishment in 1924 of what later became the School of Journalism at UNC was the result, in no small measure, of thirty years of lobbying by the *Tar Heel*. And even though the paper and the department were never officially linked (as student newspapers

and journalism programs are at many universities), the *Tar Heel* would, through its alumni, exert a great deal of influence on the teaching of the discipline at the university for decades to follow. Edward Kidder Graham and Louis Graves taught for only a short time, but several other *Tar Heel* editors went on to long-term teaching and administrative careers in the School of Journalism, including Oscar Coffin (1926–53), Charles Phillips Russell (1931–56), and Walter Spearman (1935–84).[8]

HARRY WOODBURN CHASE: UNIVERSITY EXPANSION AND THE ANTIEVOLUTION DEBATE

The death of Edward Kidder Graham in the influenza pandemic of 1918 was a catastrophic event in the life of the university, and nowhere was it more keenly felt than among the *Tar Heel* family. Graham had not only been a beloved professor, president, and visionary for the university, he had also been an integral part of the *Tar Heel* and of the promotion of the teaching of journalism at UNC. Following Graham's death professor Marvin Hendrix Stacy was appointed as interim president, but he too succumbed to influenza less than a year later.[9]

Demoralized and rudderless in the aftermath of Graham and Stacy's deaths, and in the wake of World War I, the trustees pinned their hopes for the future of the university on a relative outsider, Harry Woodburn Chase. A Dartmouth graduate who held a PhD in psychology from Clark University, Chase arrived in Chapel Hill in 1910 to teach in the School of Education. Though he had been on campus for nearly a decade by the time of his appointment as president in 1919, his roots were not in southern soil. The student body was wary of Chase, and this attitude was reflected in the cautious and cool coverage he received in the *Tar Heel* during the first several years of his administration. Not only was he seen as an outsider, but his manner was not as familiar as Graham's. It took time, but gradually Chase earned the respect of students and alumni alike, and the university community came to realize how fortunate it was to have a man of his convictions and with his considerable managerial and organizational skills at the helm during the critical period of the 1920s.[10]

Chase's first order of business was to close the deal with the North Carolina legislature for the largest appropriation in state history to expand UNC along the lines of Graham's vision, and to meet the needs of the state's growing populace. This expansion was to be physical, organizational, and intellectual: enlargement of the physical plant to create a university with facilities that could be favorably compared with those on other major American college campuses; creation of an organizational plan based on business and corporate models; and expansion of the faculty in size and scope to allow the university to compete on the national level. Chase began the process to realize these goals by mounting a campaign with alumni in the fall of 1920 and spring of 1921 to lobby the legislature for adequate funding. Former *Tar Heel* editor Frank Porter Graham, now on the faculty, headed a key component of the campaign. The *Tar Heel* supported the effort by publishing editorials about the need for more dormitories, classroom buildings, and a modern library. On October 5, 1920, the paper reported that on four days' notice "the largest alumni meeting the University has ever had" convened, and those present "made up the most serious minded and loyal group of men who have ever come together for the purpose of discussing the University's growth and development."[11]

The brief but well-organized campaign was effective: in the spring of 1921 the legislature voted to approve the appropriation—$20 million, of which more than half, $11.5 million, was earmarked for UNC. Soon the sounds of construction echoed across campus. By January 1922, the *Tar Heel* reported that "accompanied by the sounds of clanking machinery operating late into the night beneath the full glare of high powered electric lamps the new dormitory quadrangle at the University is proceeding according to schedule." Chase worked with trustees to create the overall look of the campus, which was influenced by his familiarity with the best of American collegiate architecture. During the decade-long building campaign, the eclectic collection of university buildings of various architectural styles dating back to the 1790s was unified by a new master plan, creating the footprint of the main campus that remains familiar today.[12]

The crown jewel of the expansion was a new library that anchored the south end of newly created Polk Place, designed in a grand Beaux Arts style, and more grandiose than the simpler red-brick "Collegiate Colonial" style found in the new quads of classroom buildings and dormitories. Completed in 1929 and named in the 1950s for longtime librarian Louis Round Wilson, the library was a thoroughly modern facility that signified in solid marble, in the soaring expanse of its grand entrance portico, and in the beautiful domed rotunda of the main reading room, that UNC was now a research institution of national standing. In lauding the impending completion of the library, and noting the orientation of the new quad south of South Building, *Tar Heel* editor Glenn Holder penned a column titled "The University Goes South," in which he stated that the library "will in all probability become the real center of campus. In effect the University has followed in its program of expansion the example of modern industry and the advice of the successful business man to the younger generation: 'Go South young man, go South.'"[13]

In addition to the state-funded projects, privately funded construction added to the campus expansion in the 1920s and early 1930s. The staff of the *Tar Heel* actively promoted two of these projects, Memorial Hall and Graham Memorial, both of which honored alumni. The origi-

The building program of the 1920s followed a master plan to expand and unify the campus architecturally and created ordered groups of residence halls and classroom buildings. Shown here are Saunders (renamed Carolina Hall in 2015), Manning, and Murphey Halls soon after completion about 1922. (NCC)

nal Memorial Hall, built in 1885 to commemorate the school's Confederate dead and others, was a dark and cavernous Victorian Gothic structure at the height of fashion in its day, but hopelessly out of style by the 1920s. More than any other of the earlier buildings at UNC, it stuck out amid the studied uniformity of the new Georgian and Neoclassical revival campus architecture. A structural assessment of the building was made in 1929, with the conclusion (perhaps somewhat exaggerated) that the rafters were unsafe under the weight of the slate roof and that the build-

ing should be razed. Various writers and pundits at the *Tar Heel* had derided Memorial Hall for years—most famously Thomas Wolfe—and with the ammunition of the engineering report, the paper led the charge in 1929 for replacing it with a modern building in the new style. The paper also played a role in the creation and completion of Graham Memorial, on McCorkle Place. Initially conceived in 1919 to serve as the university's first student union, and as a fitting memorial to the late President Graham, fundraising and construction limped through the decade. By the late 1920s, the *Tar Heel* routinely published photographs of the partly constructed building and its great hall, pointing to its unfinished state as a campus embarrassment. A final fundraising push allowed the building to be completed in 1931, though in truncated form that omitted wings on either end (as shown in drawings published in the paper). Most significantly for the staff of the *Tar Heel*, the new building included a four-room suite of offices on the second floor for the paper, which it occupied until 1968.[14]

Along with expanding the campus physically, President Chase established efficiency and organizational integration at the university. In March 1924 an organizational flowchart entitled "University Life Unification Plan" was published on the front page of the paper showing the two principle components of the university, academics and administration, each divided into three sections. Student activities were to be overseen by a central council consisting of the editor of the *Tar Heel* and the presidents of the student body and senior class. The unification initiative followed corporate business models becoming widely used in the 1920s, and Chase's plan predated a similar strategy adopted by Governor O. Max Gardner for North Carolina's state government in the early 1930s.[15]

Chase created new departments and areas of research, increased the size of the faculty, and brought academics to the university who shared in the broader vision. Under Chase, departments of music, psychology, social welfare, and journalism were established, and the law and graduate schools were enlarged. But the most significant academic component he created was the Institute for Research in Social Science (IRSS), funded by the Rockefeller Foundation.

To head the new institute, Chase brought an old friend and graduate school classmate, sociologist Howard W. Odum, to UNC in 1920. Odum and his colleagues were soon to be at the center of a series of controversies about the ideological direction of the university and what should be taught at the state-supported school.[16]

Just getting approval for Odum to join the faculty was no easy task. According to historian Daniel Singal, some trustees "could not differentiate between a sociologist and a socialist." Odum staffed the IRSS with progressive-minded scholars, including Guy Johnson, Guion Griffis Johnson, Rupert Vance, and Arthur Raper. Soon after arriving Odum and the IRSS faculty became involved with several projects that raised the ire of certain legislators and business leaders, and thus began a battle for the soul of the university that continued through the twentieth century and into the twenty-first. To publicize their work they established the *Journal of Social Forces* in 1922, which pushed the envelope of social and economic change in the South, angering conservatives and leading industrialists. The ideas of this group were furthered by the establishment of the University of North Carolina Press (also in 1922) and by the support of its longtime director, William Terry Couch.[17]

Chase's philosophy about the mission of the university was summed up in his speech marking the opening of the academic year in September 1924, which was extensively quoted in the *Tar Heel*. In the speech, entitled "The University's Intellectual Responsibility," Chase declared that "the function of the University is to train the young men of the state for leadership in the south of the future," to provide "an intellectual life of high quality and sound standards with freedom to think and teach.... Through intellectual freedom lies the way to truth." Aware of rising concerns about communism and "Bolshevism" at institutions of higher learning in the wake of a national Red Scare, Chase defended an open and fertile educational environment, disagreeing with the precept that "it is the business of education to subjugate men's minds to authority, making them docile rather than independent."[18]

All of these factors—increased financial support from a more conservative legislature that now felt it also had an increased right of oversight, Chase's vision for the expanded university, and the hiring of progressive faculty—proved a volatile mixture and provided the ingredients for an explosive situation. The match that lit the fuse came in February 1925 with the introduction of what became known as the Poole bill, and the flames of ideological warfare lapped at the university's doorstep for much of the rest of the twentieth century. The *Tar Heel* found itself in the midst of this maelstrom, and its staff navigated it in different ways over the years, depending in part on the ideological bent of the editor in any given year and his willingness to engage in controversial social and political issues. Also bound up in the fight over the Poole bill were issues of academic freedom and free speech, central to the mission of the university and the paper.

On February 10, 1925, the state House Committee on Education began hearings on a bill introduced by Representative David Scott Poole to ban the teaching of biological evolution in public schools, including the university and state-funded colleges. Poole and his supporters declared that evolution was "a mere guess" and that teaching it was tantamount to putting "the

religion of the Lord Jesus ... on trial." The debate came several months before the famous Scopes "monkey" trial in Tennessee and in the midst of a wave of evangelicalism sweeping the nation, especially the South, during the 1920s. It didn't help that Dr. William Poteat, a faculty member at Wake Forest University who professed the belief that religion and evolutionary science were not mutually exclusive, was a frequent speaker at UNC. The potential harm to the university's academic sovereignty by passage of the Poole bill was immediately recognized. Frank Porter Graham, then a UNC faculty member on leave at the London School of Economics, cabled President Chase and likened the bill to acts of the Spanish Inquisition. Chase took up the cause and vigorously opposed the bill, cheered on by the staff of the *Tar Heel*. Along with the threat to academic freedom, he argued that its passage would remove individual freedom and human liberty from the university. In a powerful speech echoing Patrick Henry's stand against King George in 1773, Chase threw down the gauntlet: "If it be treason to oppose the bill offered in the name of tyranny over the mind ... I wish to stand here in the name of progress and make my protest." In a letter to a legislator urging defeat of the bill, Chase wrote: "The passage of the Poole Resolution would virtually set up a tribunal before which every teacher of science and related subjects would be badgered, worried, and disgraced. Good men will simply not teach in an environment of that sort.... It is an abridgement of the freedom of discussion and thought which will go a long way toward ruining the University, because it deals with the vital education process itself, of which the appropriations and buildings are simply the means to create."[19]

The *Tar Heel* carried detailed coverage of the fierce debate over the Poole bill, including Chase's speech on the matter to students on February 13. "If teaching is to be honest it must be free," Chase was quoted in the lead of the front-page article the following day. The news writer paraphrased Chase's objections to the bill by stating that "it is contrary to the essential ideas of education; it is an infringement on the liberty of thought and speech that is guaranteed by the constitution; and the University cannot feel that a discussion of the theory and facts of evolution is harmful to the religion and morals of intelligent men." The thoughtful and well-written column that day by editor J. Maryon "Spike" Saunders (who later became the longtime executive secretary of the UNC General Alumni Association) summed up the situation:

> Chase clearly and concretely defined the University's position on evolution. It matters not to the University whether or not a student or teacher may or may not have his own convictions as to the truthfulness of the doctrine that man is linked in blood relationship with some lower form of life.... [Following passage of the Poole bill] the University would be materially handicapped in biology and its related studies. Not only does the Poole bill remind one of the lists of prohibited books of the middle ages but it is directly in contrast with the spirit and in fact the letter of both the Constitution and that of the State. We believe that [many people] have jumped to the wrong conclusion in regard to the stand taken by the University. They have pictured the University as an out and out advocate of evolutionary principles and at the same time an enemy to those whose

opinions [differ].... The University does not seek to prohibit the teaching of contrary doctrines to the evolutionary theory, and it likewise cannot take a stand to prohibit the teaching of evolution. It does take a decided stand for the freedom of thought and liberty of conscience that is so vital a part of our national principles of individual freedom and liberty.[20]

Understanding the threat the bill posed not only to academic freedom but also to the state appropriations then supporting the campus expansion, another editorial several days later wryly reflected on the larger public relations problem for the university. "The debate on the Poole bill brought out some interesting sidelights on how some people must look on the University and its student body," the editorial commented, adding, "No, no, dear old state, we are not as much monkeys down here as some others we know."[21]

After a bitter fight, the Poole bill went down in defeat by a vote of 67–41. Chase had been able to rally the support of some alumni who were members of the legislature, including a young Sam Ervin (later U.S. senator and chair of the Watergate hearings). Though the university may have won the battle, the war was just beginning. The antievolution controversy was the first attempt to censor free speech on the UNC campus by the state legislature, but it would not be the last—it was the opening salvo in an ideological war that would continue for half a century. And the *Tar Heel*, "speaking the campus mind" (the title of an opinion column that appeared in the paper regularly during the era) was in the thick of each of these subsequent battles, both reporting and shaping the debates.

GROWING INTO ITS OWN: THE BIRTH OF THE *DAILY TAR HEEL* AND THE STANDARDIZATION OF STYLE

As the campus experienced growing pains between the two world wars, so did the *Tar Heel*. In addition to becoming an official student publication in 1923, the presence of the new Department of Journalism helped a succession of editors professionalize both the format and the content of the paper. During the 1920s the paper became more sophisticated in style and tone; for example, the first bylines appeared (though limited to columns not written by the editor and articles not written by staff), and in 1922 the now iconic Gothic banner font was used for the first time. Not all the changes were beneficial, however. In May 1924, apparently in a move to save money, an editorial announced that henceforth the *Tar Heel* would be "dressed more in the fashion of a regular newspaper," which meant a shift from "book print" paper to more standard newsprint. The change may have saved money, but it produced a noticeable difference in the longevity of the paper, as existing copies from this era have deteriorated more rapidly than those of earlier issues.[22]

Editorially, the *Tar Heel*, which had devoted very little space to stories beyond the campus borders until the outbreak of World War I, also increasingly adopted a broader worldview in the 1920s and 1930s. In a 1923 editorial entitled "Students and National Politics," the writer noted that "when one considers that the news of today is the history of tomorrow, he must be impressed with the peculiar state of conditions in which we students have hardly paid any attention to the turn of national affairs at present," adding however, that "there are signs of a deeper interest

being developed among the student element." Associate editor D. D. Carroll promoted national and state politics during the 1928 presidential campaign year, and in October the first campus mock election favored the Democratic nominee, Al Smith, 780–293.[23]

Perhaps the person most responsible for the professionalization of the *Tar Heel* in the 1920s was Walter Spearman, who, following graduation in 1929, worked for *The Charlotte News* and then returned to UNC as a respected professor of journalism, teaching from 1935 to 1984. In October 1927, as assistant editor of the *Tar Heel*, he began a column of short, pithy comments on campus life entitled "Random Thrusts," accompanied by a visual pun of his name—a graphic of a medieval knight on a horse wielding a jousting spear. But Spearman was not cut from the same cloth as some of the editors and staff of his generation, who were still outgrowing adolescent hijinks. He was serious minded and goal oriented, and following his election as editor in chief in the spring of 1928, instituted a series of style and format reforms that created the modern student paper at UNC, along with spearheading the move to daily publication. In October 1928, an editorial titled "the *Tar Heel*'s New Dress," introduced the new format: "Today we present the *Tar Heel* in its latest evolution. The progress of the paper from a little sheet issued irregularly by the athletic association to the present, tri-weekly considered by critics to be one of the best in the south has been one of constant growth.... The paper is interested in presenting attractive modern 'make-up' to aid its readers in the assimilation of its news, and in its slightly changed appearance is pleased to follow the splendid leadership of the very good commercial dailies of the state."[24]

In January 1929, Spearman was the official UNC representative to the fourth annual National Student Association of America conference, where he participated in a panel discussion on journalistic conduct with the coeditor of the *Harvard Crimson*. After returning to campus Spearman penned a column on editorial freedom, "To Whom Is the College Newspaper Responsible?": "When a college newspaper is subject to censorship by the faculty, it ceases to be a student enterprise and becomes an official bulletin. The college newspaper is the organ of the students. Its function is to provide them with the news and to express their viewpoint and opinions in all cases which may arise. The editor is elected by popular vote of the student body, not by faculty appointment or by board election.... To the student body then, belongs the final authority."[25]

During his tenure Spearman also proposed the increase in publication to six days a week, creating the *Daily Tar Heel*. The principle concern about this change, which required a vote by the student body, was the additional cost involved. A multi-part plan was put forward to reduce and consolidate the student publications, both for efficiency and to provide additional funding for a six-day-a-week newspaper. Through articles and editorials, the staff of the *Tar Heel* supported the entire plan, which would end publication of the humor magazine and incorporate the literary magazine into the *Tar Heel*. The student body voted to create the *Daily Tar Heel* but to retain the humor magazine and publish the literary magazine as a bimonthly supplement to the newspaper.[26]

Another key element in the maturation of the paper was publication of its first official stylebook in February 1932. A twenty-seven-page pamphlet, the stylebook includes a clear statement of the *Daily Tar Heel*'s purpose, as well as outlining the staff's responsibilities and operational structure, and providing technical specifications and guidelines regarding accuracy, sourcing, and journalistic fairness. Almost certainly the project was Walter Spearman's idea, though work began in December 1930, under the editorship of William Yarborough. Several factors likely contributed to the decision to create the manual, including the then-formalized teaching of journalism at UNC, and the realization that if the paper was going to engage with state dailies and journals on important issues of the day (such as it had on the debate over the Poole Bill, and as it was at that moment over organized labor in North Carolina), it needed to be viewed as a professional publication.[27]

The title page of the pamphlet includes a list of newspapers that agreed to share their style-books with the *Daily Tar Heel*: the *New York Times*, the *Los Angeles Times*, the *Sun* (Baltimore), the *Times-Picayune* (New Orleans), and *The World* (New York). Only one college newspaper is mentioned, the Massachusetts Institute of Technology's *Tech*. The pamphlet is laid out in four sections: "Organization," "News," "General Style," and "Heads and Their Writing." Duties of the editor—who it notes is "elected yearly by the student body, [and] is responsible only to it"— are enumerated, along with those of the managing editor and board chairs. The staff's interest in how the paper was perceived in the broader world is evident from the duties of the foreign news board chair, who had "charge of reading the exchange issues and clipping articles or editorials concerning the *Daily Tar Heel* or any branch of the University." The broad mission—now forged by four decades of publication, creation of the Publications Union Board, and expansion to a daily—is ambitiously stated under the heading "Aim of the Paper":

The *Daily Tar Heel* is a factor in University life. It aims, through news stories, through its well-written, accurate, and unbiased editorials, interviews and features, to cause its readers to have well-rounded interests; to stimulate them to a deeper appreciation of and knowledge of art, literature, music, and dancing; to present a full variety of sports; to offer facts about economic and political situations of the world; and to bring some realization of ethical and spiritual life. In addition to that, it is the aim of the *Daily Tar Heel* to foster open-minded and genuine liberality which will admit the possibility of two sides to every question. The *Daily Tar Heel* attempts to throw the weight of its influence toward those sides of questions of great moment which in the opinion of the editorial control are more nearly right. It also holds its columns open always to the other side, with the single reservation that only the truth must be spoken.[28]

On practical matters the stylebook informed staff that stories must be submitted typewritten and double-spaced, and that news meetings were held once a week on Sunday evenings. It advises reporters to get to know the men on their beat, and "quote your man accurately," as well as recommending that reporters read the stories clipped from other papers by the foreign news board chair. Under suggestions adapted from the *Los Angeles Times*:

Be brief. The day of the long story has passed.
Be direct. Cultivate simplicity of style.
Be accurate. Don't stretch or color the facts to get effects.
Be temperate. Preserve the judicial attitude. Never editorialize in a news story.
Be careful. Like a little knowledge, having a few facts is a dangerous thing.
Be helpful. Remember that the first business of a newspaper is to serve the public and that makes it the business of every member of the *Daily Tar Heel*.

rate, the paper was to be interesting, to contain pigment, a spark of life, readability. The *Tar Heel* was going to be produced for the student readers rather than for the files of the library." He concluded by noting that "the *Daily Tar Heel* has long been proud of its freedom from faculty control of any sort, and proud, as well, of the degree of organizational efficiency which permits a staff of its size and undergraduate sort to put out the 'only college daily in the South' on a midnight deadline."[30]

The stylebook would be published in subsequent editions and became a standard for *Daily Tar Heel* reporters for decades to come. It was considered so important to the consistency and quality of the paper that beginning in October 1932, reporters were required to pass a quiz on its contents. Along with publication of the stylebook, 1932 marked other significant milestones for the *Daily Tar Heel*. For the first time since becoming a daily in 1929, the paper turned a profit, and an Associated Press wire was added to the pressroom. In a front-page story in November, it was announced that the *DTH* was one of the five best-known college dailies in the United States, along with papers at Yale, Princeton, Columbia, and the University of Wisconsin.[29]

By the late 1930s the *Daily Tar Heel* had completed its maturation process, growing into a professional newspaper both in terms of style and content. In the 1938 *Yackety Yack*, editor in chief J. McNeill Smith wrote about the role of the paper at the university: "Actually it is the student newspaper, slid under every student's door each morning with its facts and opinions, that keeps the campus knit together and continuously aware of itself.... As well as being accu-

CRACK-BRAINED PROFESSORS AND BABY RADICALS

The increasing professionalization of the *Tar Heel* in the 1920s resulted in greater statewide visibility, and it came to be seen as the public voice of the university. As such it periodically became a target for other publications, especially when an idealistic editor in chief with a sharp pen was at the paper's helm. Among the most significant of these activist editors was Glenn Holder. A reporter his freshman and sophomore years, and associate and managing editor his junior year under Walter Spearman, Holder was rarely restrained when it came to putting his opinions in print. In the fall of 1928, the *Tar Heel* invited all presidential candidates to campus to speak, and the most prominent to accept, Norman Thomas of the Socialist Party, arrived in October. He spoke to a group of some 500 students, and Holder interviewed him for the paper. In a front-page story entitled "A Sociable Socialist," Holder stirred up trouble by presenting a favorable impression of Thomas, writing that those expecting a fire-breathing radical were disappointed: "They had expected a ranting, raving, long-haired prototype of Lenin and Trot-

sky—and lo! When he appeared he was only a smooth-faced middle-aged man of pleasing personality and gracious manners. He neither condemned the capitalists to the everlasting flames nor urged the extinction of all aristocrats. Not a word of blasphemy against organized government fell from his lips, nor did he urge the abolition of privately owned industry. In brief, he impressed us as the antithesis of commonly accepted ideas of what socialists are like."[31]

Holder noted that students favorably received Thomas as "logical and sensible," concluding that "Mr. Thomas convinced us that a good, sensible socialist is not a bad fellow to have around." Holder's words surely rankled the state's conservatives, but it was only a prelude to what followed. Soon after becoming editor in chief in the spring of 1929, Holder took the *Tar Heel* somewhere it had never been before, engaging directly in one of the most explosive social issues of the day: railing against deplorable and unfair working conditions in North Carolina's mills and calling for the organization of labor unions to fight for workers' rights. The fierce debate that ensued followed on the heels of the controversy over the Poole antievolution bill, and put the *Tar Heel* in the spotlight, resulting in a very public and increasingly nasty war of words between Holder and David Clark, editor and publisher of the influential *Southern Textile Bulletin*. The University of North Carolina, as represented by the *Tar Heel*, was now seen by the state's conservatives as un-Christian, pro-socialist, and pro-union—the antithesis of what they viewed as traditional values, and wholly inappropriate for North Carolina's publicly funded university. The heated print battle begun by Glenn Holder stoked the embers for a smoldering feud be-

tween David Clark and a succession of *Tar Heel* editors that flared up periodically into the early 1950s.[32]

The roots of the bitterness dated back to 1923, when UNC sociologist Howard Odum published an article in the *Journal of Social Forces* by Owen Lovejoy, an advocate for child labor laws—laws strongly opposed by David Clark. A fiercely loyal alumnus of North Carolina State College, Clark began in the textile industry sweeping up lint and eventually rose through the ranks to own his own mill operation, which failed in the Panic of 1907. In 1911 he began publication of the *South-*

ern Textile Bulletin, which he continued for four decades through two world wars and the Great Depression, until his death in 1955. The *Charlotte Observer* characterized Clark as "a volunteer spokesman for an ultra-conservative philosophy in business and educational matters" and "a stirrer-upper of no mean proportions." According to historian Hugh Hindman, he "did more to delay federal child labor legislation in America than any other single person." In 1916 and 1919, when Congress attempted to enact legislation to abolish child labor in mining and manufacturing, "Clark personally arranged the cases that resulted in the Supreme Court declaring the laws unconstitutional." When an amendment proposed to address to the issue of child labor was debated in the 1920s, Clark created the Farmers' States Rights League to oppose the efforts.[33]

The Lovejoy article was followed in 1925 by a study of textile mill conditions across the state undertaken by Odum and research associate Harriet Herring. Although Odum attempted to gather the support of mill owners first—textiles ranked second only to tobacco production in North Carolina at the time—the tactic backfired and stories about the project and the perceived dangers that the mill owners might face were soon splashed across the state's newspapers and periodicals. The most vociferous opponent of the study was David Clark, who fired back from the pages of the *Southern Textile Bulletin*.[34]

The activities of Howard Odum deepened the enmity Clark harbored for the University of North Carolina, which proved to be a problem as he served on the board of trustees of the consolidated university for many years. As a trustee he embodied the concerns and mistrust of the state's more conservative populace about the real and perceived radicalized "liberal" nature of UNC, and not surprisingly he was a thorn in the side of both President Harry Woodburn Chase and his successor, Frank Porter Graham. Five years after the controversial IRSS textile mill study, reaction in the university community to escalating labor disputes focused Clark's intense ire on the school and its mouthpiece, the *Daily Tar Heel*.

In April 1929, following a series of mill strikes in Piedmont North and South Carolina that led to violence, particularly in Gastonia and Charlotte, Glenn Holder wrote an impassioned editorial entitled "The Only Hope for Mill Workers." In it he stated that mill workers were "living under highly deplorable conditions," lamenting the fact that "from the very start the strikes in Gastonia and Charlotte were doomed to failure," in part because two acknowledged Communists represented the strikers and the men "prejudiced the people of the state against the workers." Holder concluded by emphatically stating: "the only hope for the millworker lies in organization." Three days later the front page of the paper featured a picture of history professor Frank Porter Graham in a framed box, pointing out that he "recently has done some notable work in connection with the passage of the Workmen's Compensation Act and with the cotton mill strikes." In fact, Graham had authored in essence a workers' bill of rights, the full text of which had previously run in the *Tar Heel*. As Clark and others began to object in their publications to meddling by UNC faculty and students, Holder wrote an editorial on publicity and censorship, noting that the University News Bureau vetted almost all stories, positive or negative, before they were released.[35]

But Holder's editorship was almost over before it began, the result of a sophomoric prank. At a baseball game with the University of Virginia on May 10, Holder and other members of the Sigma Upsilon literary fraternity distributed a sharp-edged humor tabloid entitled the *Yellow Journal*, which had appeared periodically at games previously in the 1920s. Not only were articles in the tabloid which referenced young women in the Chapel Hill community of questionable taste (and potentially libelous), the university administration had expressly forbidden publication of the sheet a year earlier after an issue with similar content was circulated. In a letter to the president of the General Faculty Council, nineteen professors resigned their membership in Sigma Upsilon, stating that the recent tabloid was "coarse, indecent, and libelous in reference to young girls all of whom are locally known." Holder and John Mebane, who was also on the *Tar Heel* staff and was the editor of the *Carolina Magazine*, issued a tepid apology that ran on the front page of the paper, but it wasn't enough, and the two men along with sixteen other students involved in the incident were suspended. "Temporary Change in *Tar Heel* Staff," a headline announced on May 14, as "pending investigation by the Student Council of the recent *Yellow Journal* affair, in which certain members of the *Tar Heel* staff are supposed to be implicated, the places of five editors and reporters are being temporarily filled by other men."[36]

Following the investigation, the Student Council reinstated six of the students, but Holder and Mebane were suspended for the remainder of the school year. The Dialectic Society debated the matter and voted for censorship of the *Yellow Journal* but not to disband Sigma Upsilon. The paper reported that "a wide range of argu-

ments were presented on both sides; ranging all the way from the statement that the last issue of the *Yellow Journal* was the most vile, diabolical, and indecent bit of slander that has ever been perpetuated on the honest and worthy citizens of Chapel Hill—to the argument that the *Yellow Journal* is a useful critic and that its suppression would be a suppression to the freedom of speech." A front-page editorial, likely penned by Walter Spearman, marked the incident as a "breach of good taste" and stated that "the campus has no place for Yellow Journals." In a fitting twist, Walter Spearman stepped back into the role of editor in chief for the suspended Glenn Holder during the last month of the academic year, and in that capacity he oversaw inauguration of the first issue of the *Daily Tar Heel*, which he had worked so diligently to establish.[37]

As soon as Holder returned as editor at the beginning of new academic year, he defiantly resumed his agenda of expanding liberalism at the university and supporting efforts to organize labor in the state. After a speech at the campus YMCA by British Labour Party leader Herbert Gray in November 1929, Holder wrote an editorial pushing for union organizing in North Carolina:

Evidently the forces of labor are preparing for a long war against the capitalists in this state. The bloody battles at Marion and Gastonia are but the opening skirmishes in the campaign. … A strong American labor party would do more than anything else to make governmental regulation of the critical situation existing in the south practicable. … We North Carolinians are in for it—there can be no doubt about that. All hell has already been a popping, to

December 1929 photograph of *DTH* editor Glenn Holder (third from right) and his custom-painted, early 1920s Ford Model T. It appears the automobile is painted "Carolina" blue with the letters "UNC" in white on the back. Also in the photo are other student journalists, including two female *DTH* reporters, all delegates to the North Carolina Collegiate Press Association.

University Delegates To Press Meeting

use the vulgar but expressive parlance, and it's agoin' to pop some more damn soon.... And practically our only hope ... is that a strong political organization representative of labor will arise to become a power in Washington.[38]

A month later, realizing that many of the next generation of the state's business and political leaders were likely at UNC, Holder went a step further by imploring students to understand the labor debate, and to become "liberal" in their thinking—a plea that surely raised the hackles of many conservatives and those opposed to unionization in North Carolina. Under the title "A Problem and A Duty for Undergraduates," he wrote: "As thinking men and future leaders of the nation, the present undergraduate generation

should familiarize themselves with the true state of affairs in this country, develop a liberal and rational attitude toward and knowledge of the fundamental problems underneath the ominous portents of national unrest which are sweeping the country, and prepare to cope with them. The problem of unequal distribution of wealth is, in our opinion, the basis of all our industrial unrest, and should merit the close attention of every college man."[39]

Holder's support of racial tolerance and equality in the midst of the Jim Crow era pushed the limits even further. In an editorial entitled "Liberalism and Tolerance on the University Campus," Holder pointed with pride to recent efforts at the university to understand African American culture, and initiatives to research and address social and economic inequalities between blacks and whites in the South. These efforts included programs sponsored by the YMCA such as the Human Relations Institute, and issues of the *Carolina Magazine* devoted to black authors, all of which, Holder wrote, were

enthusiastically received and heartily supported by the undergraduates. Racial and national antagonisms have been rare indeed on the University campus. At this time it is especially important that the University's reputation for liberality be maintained. Especially during the past few years has the reputation of the institution become nation-wide; a critical stage has been reached in the development of the University, and the intellectual eyes of the entire country are focused upon Chapel Hill. The University is on the borderline in culture, combining the literary and intellectual interests of the old South with the new culture of the modern era … [and it] approaches closely the ideal attitude combining liberalism and tolerance with ardent individualism.[40]

Holder's strong editorials put pressure on the university from some business leaders and social conservatives, and garnered national attention. Likely in response, articles began to appear in the *Daily Tar Heel* pointing out examples of universities where free speech was being curtailed. These included the University of Pittsburgh, where liberal speakers were not allowed and liberal students and professors were pressured to leave; and Howard University, where a professor was forced to resign because he stated that the Bible should not be taken literally. Other college newspapers took note of Holder's crusades. In

December 1929 Holder wrote a scathing editorial about Furman College's *The Hornet*, which had taken him to task for criticizing a minister who called for the public whipping of northern mill reformers. Holder pointed out not only that his statements were correct, but that his sentiments should have been even stronger. In response to the exchange with *The Hornet*, a number of student editors came to Holder's defense. A front-page article entitled "Holder Commended" reported that the *DTH* editor "has received several communications from editors of collegiate newspapers commending him for his stand on the unionization of the textile mill workers of North Carolina."[41]

Holder's editorials were the equivalent of a matador waving a red flag in front of a snorting bull—in this case, David Clark. Holder's ardent support of mill workers' rights (including the right to organize) challenged the hegemony of some of the state's richest and most powerful men, who were subscribers to and friends of the *Southern Textile Bulletin*. Not surprisingly, the publication's editor and publisher took on the role of publicly ridiculing the *Daily Tar Heel* and the academic environment at UNC, where he believed Holder's "radical" ideas were fostered. In one of his more infamous attacks, Clark described the university as being a hotbed of "crack-brained professors and baby radicals," calling the *Tar Heel* editors "twisted," and accused radical professors of manipulating their "plastic young minds." Though he later claimed that he was only opposed to "a small group of radicals whom I regard as a cancer upon the institution," Clark and his conservative allies saw faculty and students as challenging the triumvirate of traditional southern values: Christianity, white supremacy, and capitalism. "Everyone is proud of the University of North Carolina, and its able faculty," Clark wrote in 1930, "but it is well known that within this faculty is a small group of radicals who are in an insidious manner, eternally fighting that which they frantically call 'Capitalism.'"[42]

Glenn Holder responded in kind on the pages of the *Daily Tar Heel*, suggesting that when Clark used words like "socialist" and "radical," the state's average citizen thought of long-haired bomb throwers "advocating free love and anti-Christ" who wanted to nationalize private property, and he added that this perception could be "corrected by popular education and an enlightened press." "Enemy of labor," "crack-brained radical," "twister of plastic young minds," Holder charged, "are adjectives frequently employed by the *Bulletin* in its attempts to blacken the reputations of the professors who have incurred its enmity. The editors deny the fundamental rights of American labor, unionization and collective bargaining, and they are attempting to coerce institutions of higher learning into suppression of liberal thought."[43]

While Clark's attacks may have stung the university and the *Daily Tar Heel*, vindication of the school's direction was surely found in the words of Oswald G. Villard, editor of the influential *Nation*, who gave the keynote address at the annual North Carolina Newspaper Institute held at UNC in January 1930. "The liberalness and open-mindedness of the University of North Carolina is well recognized in the North and all over the country," the paper quoted Villard as saying. "Most colleges declare themselves aloof and apart from the communities in which they are situated, and the interest and study of vital prob-

lems of the vicinity on the part of the University of North Carolina is particularly interesting." Villard, the grandson of abolitionist William Lloyd Garrison, also "found the work done here in the field of the study of the Negro unusual," the *DTH* reported.[44]

By late January 1930, Holder grew weary of battling with Clark in print. In an editorial entitled "Not Worth a Truck-Driver's Damn, Anyway," Holder declared: "No more shall we inflict David Clark and the *Southern Textile Bulletin* upon *Daily Tar Heel* readers; we give our solemn promise. Already we have devoted far more space than they deserve, even in the *Tar Heel*, to Clark's insipid attacks upon certain University professors and to his puerile attempts to discredit labor's efforts for organization in the southern textile industry. But we were unable to resist one more opportunity for one parting shot at Mr. Clark."[45]

Holder may have imposed a moratorium on David Clark in the pages of the *Daily Tar Heel* during the remaining few months of his editorship, but Clark's battles with UNC and his opposition to its liberal leaders were only beginning, and they would soon escalate into a full-scale war with the school's next president, Frank Porter Graham.

FRANK PORTER GRAHAM: THE GREAT DEPRESSION AND THE GRAHAM PLAN

The grand dedication of the new university library in October 1929 came ten days before the stock market crash; the dedication ceremony was front-page banner-headline news in the *Daily Tar Heel*, while the economic collapse on Wall Street passed with barely a mention. Of course the long-range implications of the stock market

Front-page coverage of the inauguration of UNC president
Frank Porter Graham, November 1931.

The Daily Tar Heel

VOLUME XL   CHAPEL HILL, N. C., THURSDAY, NOVEMBER 12, 1931   NUMBER 46

Five Thousand See Graham's Inauguration

SESSIONS' BEGIN FOR UNIVERSITY GROUP MEETING

Association of American Universities Opens in Convention Here Today.

The American association of universities, "founded for the purpose of considering matters of common interest relating to graduate study," will convene here this afternoon at 3:00 o'clock, for its thirty-third annual meeting. The delegates from the leading universities of America to the inaugural yesterday will also represent their institutions in the executive sessions of the association, which is composed of twenty-nine institutions of America that are generally regarded as the foremost, the Universities of Virginia and Texas being the only other southern members.

Pierson Chairman

Dean W. Whatley Pierson, of the University's graduate school, who is chairman of the com-

PRESIDENT RECEIVING OATH OF OFFICE

W. J. Adams, associate justice of the North Carolina supreme court, in the left of this photograph, is administering a formal oath inducting Frank Porter Graham into the presidency of the University, yesterday morning. Immediately behind the president is Governor O. Max Gardner. Other dignitaries concerned with the occasion appear in the background.

Foremost Institutions Of America Are Represented

H. V. Wilson Greets Graham For Faculty

Dr. Henry Van Peters Wilson, speaking for the faculty at the inauguration, congratulated Mr. Graham upon his accession to the presidency by saying, "The faculty think it very fortunate that the direction of the University's affairs has been placed in your hands.

"Among schools and cultural institutions in general which make for happiness, none, I think, out-rival universities. We may say . . . that universities contribute to happiness in a particular way, in that they seek knowledge as well as seek to impart and diffuse it. Older students we call the faculty. And so Mr. President, to you as the foremost in this group of older students, we the other members of the faculty bring our salutations . . . and we promise you all of our support and affection."

EVENTS BROUGHT TO CLOSE WITH DINNER SESSION

Reception in Graham Memorial And Glee Club Recital Included in Day's Program.

Five thousand persons gathered at Chapel Hill yesterday morning to participate in and witness the inauguration of Frank Porter Graham as the eleventh president of the University of North Carolina. For fifteen minutes the South building bell called the divisions of the procession to their various stations. Promptly at 10:30 o'clock trumpets sounded a signal for a slow march to the north side of Kenan stadium which was especially amplified for the occasion.

First in the procession were representatives of the student body, followed by members of the class of 1909. The third division was composed of Uni-

---

crash were not immediately evident, and when the editors of the *Daily Tar Heel* did address it, they proved to not adequately understand its significance. An ill-informed editorial, "Stock Market Crash a Benefit to Public," appeared on October 30, with the premise being that the crash would weed out weak financial institutions and leave stronger ones. Of more immediate interest than the impending financial crisis to the university community that October was the appearance of a withering Carnegie Foundation report on collegiate athletics, which cited UNC as one of the schools violating both established rules and the spirit of amateur college sports. That embar-

rassing situation would be dealt with by Harry Chase's successor, Frank Porter Graham.[46]

By early 1930 President Chase had largely accomplished his goals for the university by thoroughly modernizing its operations, expanding its intellectual offerings, defending its academic freedom, and bringing it to national prominence. He had served as president of the National Association of State Universities, as a director of the Julius Rosenwald Fund, and on the Rockefeller Foundation's General Education Board (both established to improve public education in the South, particularly for African Americans). Perhaps most importantly, Chase had been able to secure for UNC the institutional presidency of the American Association of Universities—the first time the school had been accepted into that prestigious organization. As an example of his national recognition, the *Daily Tar Heel* reported in January 1930, "Chase Lunches with President Hoover." However, the years of fighting the likes of David Clark and dealing with pressure from some state business leaders and alumni had taken their toll, and by the late 1920s Chase had been forced to narrow the parameters of academic freedom at the university. Perhaps feeling increasingly boxed in philosophically, and facing the reality of battling for funds during the Depression, Chase finally accepted one of the numerous offers he had been receiving and left Chapel Hill in 1930 to become president of the University of Illinois. The *Daily Tar Heel* lamented Chase's departure, and summed up his achievements:

> A great leader, a man of remarkable personal charm and splendid executive ability, President Chase brought to the difficult office of the presidency of the University a combination of talents and abilities rarely witnessed in one man. He guided the University through a period of "growing pains," of rapid development and constantly increasing enrollment. There was grave danger that the institution would lose some of its finest heritage of liberalness and independent thought during this period, but Dr. Chase succeeded in retaining and even in increasing those intangible possessions which may be either the greatest attributes or the most objectionable features of an educational institution.[47]

The trustees began an internal search for a successor, and the *Daily Tar Heel* chimed in, running a student poll. Frank Graham won the poll, and the trustees offered him the position, but he wasn't particularly interested and had to be persuaded to accept (other candidates included another former *Tar Heel* editor, R. D. W. Connor, professor of history, who went on to become the first archivist of the United States). In the *DTH*, editor Glenn Holder wrote that "we believe that Frank Graham embodies an unusual combination of energetic leadership, traits of character which compel affection and respect, and wise, tolerant, but firm convictions." Graham was inaugurated on Armistice Day, November 11, 1931, and took the opportunity to give a major speech on peace, academic freedom, and democracy that was printed in its entirety in the *DTH*. Graham, who had served as editor of the *Tar Heel* as a student in 1908, was both rooted in North Carolina and educated on a more cosmopolitan level. After receiving undergraduate and law degrees at UNC, he did graduate work at Columbia, the London School of Economics, and the University of Chicago. He supported the work of progressive faculty, including sociologists Howard Odum and Arthur Raper, anthropologist Guy Johnson, economist Eugene Branson, dramatist Paul Green, and William Terry Couch, director of the UNC Press.[48]

Graham's research and efforts on behalf of labor rights in the 1920s led to a close relationship with President Franklin Roosevelt and First Lady Eleanor Roosevelt, and he served on several boards and commissions during the Roosevelt administration, including chairing the committee that created the Social Security system.

President Roosevelt delivered a speech on campus in December of 1938, and Eleanor Roosevelt made several trips to Chapel Hill in the 1930s, including one to deliver the commencement address in June of 1935. The close relationship between the president of the university and the president of the United States was to prove economically beneficial—perhaps vital—to UNC during the Great Depression and World War II.[49]

Graham, affectionately known as "Dr. Frank," had a personal magnetism and ideological perspective that profoundly influenced generations of students, including a generation of *DTH* editors during the 1930s and 1940s. Philip Hammer, editor in 1935–36, went on after graduation to be one of the first Rockefeller Fellows, earn a law degree at Harvard, and become a highly respected economist and city planner who helped to shape the post–World War II urban landscape of the South. Hammer remembered UNC as the place "where I learned something about being a public servant," and credited Graham as a "major inspiration.... [He] played a major role in setting my goals." Hammer later described being a product of this man and this era, of coming "out of the University under Frank Graham and the microcosm that was Chapel Hill in the thirties ... where 'liberal' meant being broadminded and having concern for one's fellow man. Dr. Frank was the inspiration.... He was a Christ-like man."[50]

As Graham took office, the effects of the Depression began to be felt in Chapel Hill. The staff of the *Daily Tar Heel*, some of whom were beginning to personally feel the sting of the economic collapse, saw that their lot was still far better than many in the community and organized an effort in 1930 to raise money for struggling families in Orange County. As the Depression deepened, the school's scholarship fund, which did not anticipate such a wide-ranging financial crisis, was pushed to its limits as more students requested aid. Pressure increased in 1931 when the state legislature began a series of draconian cuts in an effort to balance the state budget. The paper mounted a campaign against the cuts, supporting a January 1933 protest march in Raleigh that brought 5,000 people to the capital in opposition. As the legislation neared a vote in March, the paper ran a box on the front page every day for a week titled "Wire Home Immediately," urging students to contact their parents to lobby their state legislators against the proposed budget. The effort failed, and the 1933–34 state appropriation was 56 percent smaller than it had been four years earlier, even though enrollment was expected to be up some 15 percent from 1928–29. In an attempt to buffer the students from the worst of the crisis, Graham canceled spring break in 1933 (as many couldn't afford to go home) and arranged for them to have credit with local merchants.[51]

In the midst of the crippling effects of the Great Depression, the university's critics did not reduce their pressure on the school. In September 1932, L. A. Tatum of Belmont, North Carolina, presented Governor O. Max Gardner with a petition bearing the signatures of 300 citizens offended by the university's liberal and anti-Christian agenda. Known as the "Tatum petition," the document reopened the debate about academic freedom, freedom of speech, and the philosophical direction of the university. "Tatum Petition Recalls Struggle Arising from Poole Bill of 1925" a headline in the *Daily Tar Heel* declared. The paper went on to proclaim, "If the signers of the Tatum petition about the liberal policies of the university expected the institution to cower under their attack, they completely forgot the courage and spirit displayed in Chapel Hill under similar fire." President Graham wisely chose to indirectly respond publicly to the Tatum petition in a major speech on higher education and democracy at Columbia University, and the *DTH* applauded him, noting how he kept the ship afloat during the worst economic crisis in the nation's history. "A new era in education is opened to the people of North Carolina," the paper reported, and "President Graham is respected and loved by all who come in contact with him." It continued: "Dr. Graham with broad vision and dynamic personality set to work to advance still further the cause of education in the south and in the state through the means of this institution.... The University if not having progressed thus far during his incumbency at least has not regressed. Such a declaration at times when the greatest universities of the land are retrenching is a compliment worthy of the man who has guided the institution through the perils of depression."[52]

If David Clark was wary of Harry Chase, Frank Graham made him absolutely apoplectic. When the Consolidated University of North Carolina system was created in 1932—an attempt by state government to save money by streamlining operation of the three public university campuses in Chapel Hill, Raleigh, and Greensboro—a movement was mounted to make Graham president of the new entity. Graham and some members of the UNC community were wary of the consolidation plan, as there was concern it would negatively impact the larger Chapel Hill campus. David Clark was a trustee of the new system, and the *Daily Tar Heel* reported rumors that the "Clark-Tatum element" wanted Graham made president of all three schools in the hopes that it would leave him less time to exert as much influence on UNC. But even after Graham's appointment as president of the consolidated system, Clark kept up the pressure. In 1933 he offered a cash reward to anyone who could prove that Graham was a member of a radical organization—a shocking bounty offered by a sitting trustee of the greater university board.[53]

One of Graham's most difficult challenges did not come from David Clark or conservatives who didn't agree with him philosophically, however; it came instead from within the university family. Graham's attention early in his presidency had been focused on keeping the university afloat amid drastically reduced state appropriations during the first years of the Depression, but by 1935 he was able to address the issues raised in the 1929 Carnegie Report regarding the integrity of UNC's athletic program. The result, which

quickly became known as the "Graham Plan," was proposal of a series of rules and restrictions meant to keep intercollegiate athletics in the Southern Conference on a strictly amateur basis. No gifts or favors could be given or promised during recruiting, no scholarships were to be given except on academic merit, all players had to be students in good standing, and no one, including alumni, could subsidize players above or below the table. According to the *Yackety Yack*, "Alumni ... raised hell over the Graham Plan ... and newspapers waxed hotter."[54]

The principal argument against the Graham Plan at UNC was that other major schools "winked" at athletes being subsidized, and that if Carolina played "clean" the athletic program would suffer by being at a disadvantage. At first the *Daily Tar Heel*, under the editorship of Philip Hammer, took the side of the alumni and criticized the plan. However, following Graham's handling of the cheating scandal in early 1936 (discussed later in this chapter), the *DTH* made a public reversal of its position. In a front-page story entitled "Our Stand with Graham," Hammer wrote: "When one becomes cognizant of his misplaced belief in superficial aspects of a problem, then he has the moral right and duty to revise that belief, to alter it and bend it to the right interpretation, with the letter of the moral law beneath it. Our opinions crossed on the matter of letting alumni send athletes through school, as athletes PER SE. Thus our opposition has been directed in actuality against amateurism, the principle to which college athletics must be committed."[55]

Hammer was severely criticized by students and alumni alike for reversing position, and the situation waxed so hot for Graham that there

Front page of a *Tar Heel* supplement section celebrating the opening and dedication of Kenan Memorial Stadium, November 1927. Pictured are William Rand Kenan Jr., donor; Robert Fetzer, director of athletics; and Charles Woollen, UNC business manager. Though the supplement was touted as "color," it was actually printed in sepia tone.

were serious efforts to remove him as president. Though Graham retained his position, fallout from the plan continued for several years. In 1936 popular head football coach Carl Snavely accepted an offer at Cornell, ostensibly as the result of the Graham Plan (he would return to Carolina in the 1940s), and the "wrath of alumni boiled over and a sports writer said 'I told you so.'" In October 1937, the *Daily Tar Heel* broke the story that basketball and tennis star Ramsay Potts had resigned from both teams and left the university, after admitting that had lied on his athletic eligibility form by stating that he had not received outside funding, when in fact his tuition was provided by "an unrevealed source." Potts left voluntarily; he had not been caught by anything other than his own conscience. The paper praised his principled action, ran an editorial about "the million dollar business," and asked the university community: "Do you want to recognize athletics, especially football, as the big business that it is?" The *Daily Tar Heel* also ran a series of articles entitled "Let's Be Practical about Intercollegiate Athletics," and in the last of the series the reporter, Stuart Rabb, recounted a scary conversation with his barber. While Rabb was being shaved, the barber complained that the articles he was writing were "mighty foolish," adding that even if they were true, "how come you got to put it in the paper and make everybody mad?" "Well it would be a lot easier to let things alone," Rabb replied, noting that the barber "still had that razor open."[56]

Ultimately the Graham Plan was in effect a short four months, as other conference schools withdrew from promises of compliance. By 1938, President Graham turned his attention from athletics to securing one of the last large matching grants from the Public Works Administration (PWA)—the federal stimulus dollars of the era. The major building expansion of the 1920s had come to a halt in 1931, as the Depression forced the state legislature to reverse course on funding for the university, even as enrollment continued to increase. The sounds of machinery and hammering began to be heard across campus again beginning in 1938, however, largely as a result of Graham's connections to Washington, which allowed the university to continue its development even while the nation remained mired in the Depression. In total, PWA projects resulted in thirteen new buildings on campus, as well as additions and renovations to several others. The *Daily Tar Heel* carried detailed coverage of the construction projects during the late 1930s, and in 1939 published a map of campus showing the federal government's investment at UNC.[57]

THE LIMITS OF LIBERALISM

For more than a decade preceding America's entrance into the Second World War, the UNC faculty and students discussed, debated, and in some cases flirted with the ideas of socialism and communism, particularly in the context of labor organizing and combating the devastating economic and social effects of the Great Depression. In addition, the university community continued to struggle with the question of race, complicated by the involvement of a limited number of acknowledged socialists and communists on the issue. Some more conservative North Carolinians outside the university became increasingly wary of what was largely seen as a permissive if not radical atmosphere on campus, and as World War II drew closer pressure increased on UNC to disavow these philosophies. The tension became so acute by 1940 that President Graham had to go on the defensive and state that there was, in fact, no "Red Menace" on campus.

Arguments about radicalism and permissiveness on campus appeared in the pages of various state papers and journals, and the *Daily Tar Heel* responded in kind. Taken as a whole, the level of discourse penned by the young college students running the paper in response to older journalists and business and civic leaders is remarkably thoughtful and sophisticated. While the position of the paper, representing the students if not the faculty and administration, generally supported a progressive or "liberal" social, political, and academic agenda—as well as unfettered freedom of speech and of the press—there were at times dissenting and even conflicting internal opinions. The student body, including the paper's staff, was not uniformly liberal. This was particularly true when dealing with the subjects of race and the admission of African Americans to the state's flagship public university.

David Clark continued to lead the university's critics in the 1930s. In late October 1931, the paper published a front-page story about a speech Clark gave condemning the state public colleges, Duke University, and the *Daily Tar Heel* specifically, as "spreaders of radicalism and harbingers of extremists who taint the minds of boys and girls with insidious doctrines of free love and conversions to socialism and communism." After the appearance of the Tatum petition in 1932, *Daily Tar Heel* editor Charles Rose joined other student leaders to pen a letter to Governor O. Max Gardner (a UNC alumnus) strenuously objecting to the accusations leveled against the university. "In our opinion, the University has been misrepresented to its friends by un-

friendly agencies," the students wrote. The group found the university to have "a mentally wholesome and morally inspiring atmosphere," and after quoting from a pamphlet on student government and speeches by President Graham, the students stated: "We have found no reason to object to the University's policy as regards freedom of speech, publication, teaching and research. In our opinion this right is not abused by either the faculty or the students. There are no courses … that teach communism, atheism, free love or the doctrines of other subversive forces. … No official University publication or organization is in the hands of Socialists, Communists, or any other factional group." The letter continued by noting that out of a student body of some 3,000, only eight students were members of the socialist organization on campus, and the communist club boasted membership of exactly two. In summation they quoted President Graham: "We must have deeper spiritual faith than those who would have us strike down the freedom of speech and publication because [they believe] it has been abused."[58]

As the debate about "Reds on campus" raged on, editor Rose ran an editorial entitled "Mental Hygiene in High Places," in which he repeated accusations made by signers of the Tatum petition that the university consisted of "Reds and Socialists, Pacifists, and their college professor allies," who wished to let murderers go free, instill "subversive doctrines into the [students'] minds," and promote a "widespread assault on the sanctity of marriage and sacred family relations." In refuting these outlandish claims, Rose explained that "paganism and Communism are terms used vaguely and comprehensively to cover all forces which terrify and mystify because they are not understood. Clear truthful information will quickly dissipate the terrifying delusions which have come to exist in their brains. New students who come with preconceptions of Chapel Hill as being a vicious, terrifying, distorted place where insidious forces are at work playing upon their innocence will be quickly disappointed."[59]

Following an attack on UNC Press by Clark in early 1933, Don Shoemaker, chair of the paper's editorial board (and later editor of the *Asheville Citizen* and the *Miami Herald*), responded with a column entitled "Little David Swings His Sling." "With the persistency of a famous Biblical hero, David Clark has swung the pebbles of his particular type of rancid journalism at Goliath, the enemy, The University of North Carolina." Shoemaker challenged Clark's accusation that the UNC Press took state funds to publish books and journal articles "relative to socialism and communism," and expressed incredulity that Clark "tells the textile men of North Carolina that a small radical group of 'meddling professors' attempts to virtually dictate economic and governmental policies in the two Carolinas." The attack on the UNC Press, Shoemaker concluded, was "the proverbial last straw in Mr. Clark's bundle of militant chaff."[60]

In May 1935 Clark appeared on campus amid great fanfare, under the auspices of an organization called the American Liberty League, with the stated intention "to expose and make public all political propaganda taught in the classrooms of the University of North Carolina." Headlines blared: "Clark Will Defend Charges That University Is Radical Hotbed"; and Clark "Warns That University Will Fail Unless It Is Purged of Radical Influences Rampant among Faculty and Students." The day after Clark's appearance, a *Daily Tar Heel* reporter wrote that "hurling and ducking bombshell after bombshell into and from the amassed ranks of local undergraduates and faculty members, *Textile Bulletin* editor David Clark attempted to meet all questions last night as to his attacks on the University and the teaching of 'subversive doctrines of atheism, socialism, and communism.'" Clark's attacks on English professor E. E. Ericson (alleged to be a member of the Communist Party) and UNC Press director William Terry Couch were particularly vociferous, so much so that the two men were compelled to publicly refute his allegations.[61]

While speakers with controversial views on economics, politics, and social issues had appeared on the UNC campus for decades, the formation of the Carolina Political Union (CPU) in 1936 further aggravated an already tense situation. The purpose of the CPU was to invite and sponsor speakers at UNC from a variety of perspectives. During the 1930s, several members of the *Daily Tar Heel* staff were also members of the CPU, and the paper noted that it was the "only group of its kind in the US" and "embodies an attempt on the part of at least one segment of the nation's youth to study intelligently the processes of government—an element which is considered essential in any well-working democracy." Although the CPU was careful to balance the choice of speakers based on ideology—interestingly, the organization's first president was Frank McGlinn, who was active in Republican politics and from a wealthy Philadelphia family—not surprisingly it was the more radical invitees who attracted attention. The most notorious of these was the Russian Marxist revo-

Front page of the *Daily Tar Heel* announcing the barring of "Russian revolutionist" Leon Trotsky from speaking at UNC, September 1937.

WEATHER: *Clear and Continued Cool*

The Daily Tar Heel

THE ONLY COLLEGE DAILY IN THE SOUTH

VOLUME XLVI   EDITORIAL PHONE 4151   CHAPEL HILL, N. C., SUNDAY, SEPTEMBER 19, 1937   BUSINESS PHONE 4156   NUMBER 3

Trotsky Barred From Speaking Here

World News
By Ray Lowery

BOMBS FALL NEAR BRITISH DESTROYER IN SPAIN

London, Sept. 18.—Six heavy bombs fell close to the British destroyer Fearless today off Gijon, Spain according to a report to the London naval authorities.

Leading a belief in London that the plane might have been a Spanish government craft was the fact that after having completed the attack, the plane flew toward Gijon.

The Fearless carried the regular identification as a British warcraft. It has heavy anti-aircraft armament but it has not been disclosed whether it opened fire on its attacker.

The attack was another of the almost countless incidents that have occurred on the Bay of Biscay and the Mediterranean since the Spanish civil war broke out 14 months ago.

AMERICAN POSITIONS IMPERILLED AS JAPS ADVANCE AGAIN

Shanghai, Sept. 18.—More perils were brought to the American-defended sector of Shanghai's war-shocked international settlement today when Japanese artillery unleashed a new bombardment of the Markham road section.

Dodd Will Begin New C P U Year

German Ambassador Will Speak Here Sept. 11

Carolina Professor

William E. Dodd, United States ambassador to Germany, will inaugurate the year's program of the Carolina Political union when he speaks here September 27.

Dodd, who has been in this country several weeks on a vacation, will return to Germany early in October after his visit to Chapel Hill.

Governor Hoey has been invited by the Carolina Political union to introduce the ambassador, who is a native of this state, in Memorial hall at 8:30 p. m. October 27.

It is expected that over 40 state politicians will be seated on the stage at the 1937-38 inaugural program of the union.

Dodd, who was appointed German ambassador by Roosevelt in 1933, was a former member of the University's history department and a close friend of President Graham.

He received his Ph. D. degree from the University of Leipzig, having graduated from V. P. I.

Di To Elect

Star Concert To Be Heard In Fall Series

Gershwin, Beethoven Are On Program Tonight

Students who were not in school during the past summer session will have a chance to hear the open air concert, "Music Under the Stars," when it is resumed tonight at 8:30 in Kenan stadium.

The success of the program tonight depends entirely upon the attendance of the student body and townspeople, University Instructor Hal Gordon, who has charge of the recording concert, explained yesterday.

Each recording for tonight's concert has been carefully chosen by Gordon for campus appeal. The R. C. A. recordings of famous classics have included such popular artists as Lily Pons, Gladys Swarthout, Nelson Eddy, Grace Moore and Paul Whiteman.

Gershwin Recording

Included on the program tonight will be the Lawrence Tib-

Coed Invades Steele Dorm

Miss Amis Montgomery, junior coed from the state of Virginia, started to her first class on the University campus last Friday morning.

Her class was in Saunders hall, home of the decorous English department. She had been told that Saunders was the first building on the left as you enter the class room sector. Now Saunders is the first building on the left— if you eliminate Steele. But Miss Montgomery didn't eliminate Steele, so in she walked.

"It didn't look much like a class room," she said. There were several residents of Steele dormitory standing around, looking like residents of Steele usually look.

Miss Montgomery left much quicker than she had entered.

Noted Stars Will Appear In November

Entertainment Series To Feature Artists From Festival

Revolutionist Is Classed By Hull As Undesirable

Invited To Campus By Carolina Political Union; Earl Browder Will Replace Exile

International complications, arising through the Immigration Act of 1918 and 1920, have prevented Leon Trotsky, Russian revolutionist, from speaking on the campus under the auspices of the Carolina Political Union, it was announced yesterday by Alex Heard, chairman.

Plans Afoot For Set Of Coed Dances

Tea Will Be Given Friday Afternoon For Campus

President of the University Woman's association, Miss Nancy Nesbitt, yesterday made an announcement to the effect that plans were now being made to hold a tea and two dances for University coeds in the near future.

Place to be announced later, next Friday afternoon from 4 to 6 o'clock will be the date of the tea to be given in the interest of the new coeds.

After accepting the union's invitation to speak here, Trotsky was barred from entering the country by Secretary of State Cordell Hull, who stated in a letter to Heard that the Russian communist, now living in exile in Mexico, was classed as an undesirable because of his "known beliefs, activities, and advocations."

In accepting the union's invitation, Trotsky declined to lecture on a political subject because he "observes most strictly the principle of non-intervention into American politics."

(It was because Trotsky advocated the Third Internationale which seeks to spread communism over the world that he broke with Russian Dictator Stalin and fled to Mexico as an exile. Stalin wishes to develop communism in Russia only.)

Trotsky also observed in his acceptance note that perhaps "American Stalinists, and especially the direct agents of the G. P. U. in the United States, would attempt to disrupt the audience, *(Continued on page two)*

---

lutionary Leon Trotsky, who accepted an invitation to speak at UNC in the summer of 1937. Trotsky did not appear, however, as U.S. Secretary of State Cordell Hull intervened, and barred him from entering the country under the Immigration Acts of 1918 and 1920, calling him "undesirable." On the day the news broke about Trotsky in banner headlines in the *Daily Tar Heel,* J. McNeill Smith wrote a lead editorial entitled "Free Love and Communism," and he later poked fun at the idea that UNC students were so gullible as to

absorb everything a speaker might say to them. "The campus would hardly be afraid of Trotsky's ideas," Smith wrote. "Such a well-known international figure could incite little less than interest and enthusiasm. Maybe there's something to this idea of 'liberalism' after all." Smith's editorship during the Trotsky affair turned out to be prescient; nearly thirty years later he became the lawyer who sued on behalf of the *Daily Tar Heel* and other student organizations to overturn the infamous Speaker Ban Law, which sought to bar

speakers from UNC who were known communists (see chapter 4).[62]

After the Trotsky affair and further attacks on the CPU, the *Winston-Salem Journal* came to the aid of the organization, publishing a strong editorial about its importance and impartiality, which was reprinted in full in the *Daily Tar Heel*. Under the title "Potent Institution," the *Journal* columnist wrote that the CPU "has exhibited no partisanship in the selection of speakers. From its inception the union has sought to bring before Carolina students and others interested in political affairs the views of outstanding speakers representing every school of contemporary thought. The belief back of this is that only by full and free expression of opposing ideas is the modern mind enabled to strike a balance and find the true way of life." To this the *Daily Tar Heel* added that the CPU "has drawn for itself a nation-wide reputation for presenting on a non-partisan basis so many well-known speakers of nearly as many contrasting viewpoints."[63]

Contrasting viewpoints on race also continued to be exhibited at the university during the 1930s, with noted faculty and some students espousing utopian views about equality while practicing discrimination on campus. The discussion of race escalated from classroom discussions and UNC Press publications about the inequality of southern economic and societal structure, to polarizing speakers on campus, and finally to the ultimate question of whether the state-funded public university would admit African American students.

On November 11, 1931—Armistice Day, and the same day that Frank Porter Graham was inaugurated as president—the *Daily Tar Heel* ran a front-page story entitled "Negro Poet Will Deliver Talk on Race Problems." The fact that a black artist, educator, or even intellectual would speak at UNC was not a novelty. As early as the 1910s such speakers made presentations to all-white audiences on campus, and they would continue to do so throughout the 1930s. However this particular poet—Langston Hughes—was known as a radical leftist and activist. He had particularly offended some whites in the South through his writings, such as his poem "Christ in Alabama," which contains the lines "Christ is a Nigger, / Beaten and black—," calls Mary "Mammy of the South," and ends with "Nigger Christ / On the cross of the South." Hughes wrote the poem partly in response to the controversial arrest of nine young black men in Alabama for allegedly raping two white women earlier that year (the group of men later known as the "Scottsboro Boys" because they were jailed and initially tried in that Alabama town). Complicating matters for the university, Hughes's poem was reprinted in *Contempo*, an off-campus radical periodical published by two former UNC students, shortly before his visit in December. His appearance in Chapel Hill, however, was by all accounts not at all radical. The campus YMCA and Guy Johnson of the Sociology Department sponsored the talk, and the following day the *Daily Tar Heel* published a review saying that Hughes "gave a straightforward, humorous story of his life before a gathering of students and townspeople in Gerrard Hall."[64]

Predictably, David Clark spewed venom about the Hughes visit, and the *Daily Tar Heel* responded with a sharp and pithy column by Edward Kidder Graham Jr., who served on the paper's editorial board. Under the title "David and Goliath," Graham refuted Clark's statement that "Communism demands social equality with negroes and must have been taught at Chapel Hill," adding that it is "altogether terrifying to learn from a man who professes to know more about wholesome education than our own faculty that we are being subjected to so noxious an influence." "So Little David," Graham wrote, "picks up his trusty slingshot, lays in a goodly supply of spitballs, and sets out to destroy a mythical Goliath of Communism at Carolina." Graham pointed out that Clark's printed reference to *Contempo* as "a newspaper published by students of the University of North Carolina" was patently false, and that "the caliber of the man's character does not warrant his being taken so seriously."

Philip Hammer later remarked that bringing speakers like Langston Hughes to campus "was a good idea but it didn't do much to break down the racial barriers. You were bringing the blacks in to speak and others who would speak on the black issue, but the South was still segregated tight as a tick."[65]

The Langston Hughes affair, which certainly contributed to the Tatum petition that followed several months later, got the campus talking about race and the university's stand on the issue. The *Daily Tar Heel* decided to conduct a student poll on the question of admitting African Americans, and in March 1932, under the headline "Student Opinion Varies Regarding Negroes' Attendance at Carolina," it reported:

> That, on the whole, campus opinion here is hostile to the entrance of Negroes into the University of North Carolina, became apparent from the result of a symposium of student opinion recently conducted by the *Daily Tar Heel* feature staff member. Such hostility ran all the way from a mild distaste for such social and racial equality up to wild emotional talk of lynching, tarring and feathering, and the like. In between are those who feel that, if the colored applicant did gain admission to the college, life would be made so unpleasant for him by the student body that he would soon leave.

A few "Yankee" students gave an opposing opinion, noting that public schools in the North were already integrated and that it was just a matter of time before they would be in the South. "I think it would be a mighty fine thing for [UNC] to lead the way," one student replied, adding that "it was time for the school to put into practice the 'seat-of-liberalism-in-the-south' preaching that students have heard so much of. Admitting that he was in the minority, he nevertheless argued ardently for equality."[66]

Despite the university's reputation as an enlightened and liberal institution, the students, including the staff of the *Daily Tar Heel*, were at times surprisingly tone-deaf on matters of race. John Alexander, an associate editor during the early 1930s, is a case in point. In a column about the infamous Scottsboro Boys case, Alexander condemned the trial as unfair but wrote, "The negro race is at present an inferior one. The negro can not be permitted to infringe on white privilege or threaten in any way white supremacy." In February 1933 he wrote an editorial in support of the state's sterilization program, which involuntarily sterilized mentally ill and indigent women, a disproportionate number of whom were African American. The law, Alexander declared, "marked this state as progressive and a leader in sociological advancement." And in a column about sweatshops in the northern United States entitled "Slavery in 1933," he asserted that even in the antebellum South enslaved African Americans had been better treated.[67]

Paternalistic stories and romanticized representations of the Old South and African Americans appeared at UNC and in the *Daily Tar Heel* fairly regularly throughout the 1930s. For years white students celebrated Robert E. Lee's birthday, and the *DTH* reported that even the YMCA—the campus institution leading the way on racial equality—prominently displayed a donated painting of the Confederate general. In March 1933, during the darkest days of the De-pression, assistant editor Vermont Royster (later editor of the *Wall Street Journal*) encouraged students to give some of their meager resources to restore Stratford Hall, Lee's birthplace and ancestral home in Virginia. "Arlington, Lee's home which stands above the national capitol, has been seized by the enemy. Stratford is our last stronghold. We must not shirk our duty to our great [man]," Royster wrote. "All students of the University are urged to make contributions to the fund by purchasing medals of Lee, which will be placed on sale in Chapel Hill in a very short while." And the 1935 *Yackety Yack*—sister publication of the *Daily Tar Heel*—had a *Gone with the Wind* theme, including numerous color and black-and-white renderings of imagined scenes of the Old South and plantation life, specifically showing African Americans performing work as slaves. Inexplicably, UNC sociologist Howard Odum, leading proponent of racial understanding in the South, is credited as advising the *Yack* staff on the authenticity of the illustrations.[68]

The *Daily Tar Heel* could be sympathetic to the plight faced by blacks in the Jim Crow South, especially those who lived in Chapel Hill and Durham. In 1932 a story ran expressing concern that the "colored" employees of the university might lose their homes as a result of new tax assessments, and in 1936 the paper supported the efforts of a group boycotting Durham grocery stores that refused to hire African American workers. Despite a sensational headline—"Cab Calloway Refuses to Play When Gate Is Crashed by Mob"—the paper was somewhat sympathetic to the young black people who tried to gain admission to the whites-only concert by the popular African American jazz artist (which had been organized for UNC and Duke students). Over-

all, however, Philip Hammer remembered that during the 1930s the faculty and students "dealt more with ideas than actions. At that time nobody was really dealing with those issues at the action level. You were talking about them and you were thinking about long-term strategies for them, but actions were off in the future."[69]

The first actual test of racial segregation and African American enrollment at UNC came in March of 1933, when the paper ran a story entitled "Negro Will Sue for Admittance to Uni-versity?" The paper reported that Thomas R. Hocutt of Durham, a graduate of the North Carolina College for Negroes, had filed suit to enter UNC's School of Pharmacy, and that other African Americans were also considering applying (interestingly, the inclusion of Hocutt's name in the story deviated from the paper's policy in similar instances later in the 1930s). And though the article cited the unconstitutionality of not allowing admittance based solely on race, no editorials about this potential challenge appeared. The *Daily Tar Heel* followed the story as Hocutt's backers petitioned the legislature, reporting that the true intent was not to integrate Carolina, but rather to serve "as a test case by a younger group of negroes with the view of trying to get the state to provide facilities in pharmacy for the race." In fact the lawsuit was not supported by some of the state's African American leaders, including James E. Shepard, president of the North Carolina College for Negroes, who believed blacks benefited from institutions of their own. Shepard refused to release Hocutt's undergraduate transcript to UNC, and as a result there was no completed application to the School of Pharmacy, and on that technicality the case was dismissed. Despite the outcome, the case was the first filed in the United States to test racial segregation in higher education.[70]

In the midst of the increasingly public debate in the 1930s about racially integrating UNC, discrimination against Jewish students reared its ugly head, also calling into question the school's vaunted liberal reputation. The university's attitude toward Jewish students had always been one of measured tolerance. Jews attended UNC in the nineteenth century, though in limited numbers. Leslie Weil, class of 1895, was an active alumnus for many years and along with his brother established the Weil Lectures in 1915; and the first Jewish fraternity, Tau Epsilon Phi, was established in 1926. But thousands of years of prejudice did not die easily. In October 1932, an editorial appeared in the *Daily Tar Heel* criticizing "Semitic language" at a football game; two days later the paper in effect retracted the remark, claiming that no offense was intended. And unfortunately at the same moment that Hitler and Nazism were taking control of Germany, the university was embarrassed by the charge of anti-Semitism relating to its admissions policy.[71]

On September 30, 1933, the paper published a front-page story under the banner headline: "Dr. Isaac H. Manning Resigns." In fact, the story had been smoldering for months, and most of the drama occurred during the summer when school was not in session. Manning, who had been dean of the university's medical school for 28 years, had an unwritten policy of accepting four Jewish students a year, about 10 percent of the class. At the time the medical school was only a two-year classroom program, as the university did not have facilities for clinical training. After finishing the course of study at UNC, medical students were required to attend another school, usually in the Northeast, to complete their education. According to Dean Manning, it was difficult to place Jewish students in these schools, and so he restricted enrollment. When Morris Krasny, a Jewish student who had excelled as an undergraduate, was rejected for a second time in the spring of 1933 for enrollment in the UNC School of Medicine, he appealed the decision to President Graham. Graham's policy about admissions was that any qualified student should be

accepted, unless restricted by state law, and thus he overruled Manning and admitted Krasny. In protest, Manning resigned as chair, though he remained on the faculty.[72]

The story made national news, and President Graham was lauded for his action. The *Daily Tar Heel*, however, supported Manning. And though the story made front-page news when it broke, it just as quickly disappeared from the paper, without extended comment. The only editorial about the matter appeared under the banner headline on September 30, which was highly unusual. "In the present situation Dean Manning simply followed the policy he has adhered to unswervingly for the past 28 years," the editor wrote, adding that "racial discrimination and other charges will be hurled against Dr. Manning himself by those who are narrow-minded enough to over-

Pauli Murray, in a 1938 photograph just weeks before she became the first African American to formally apply for admission to UNC. (Schlesinger Library)

look the true and underlying facts of the case." It is notable that Morris Krasny's name never appeared in the *Daily Tar Heel* during the coverage of the controversy. The practice of not publishing the name of a student—potential, current, or even former—involved in a controversial situation began at the paper in the fall of 1933, and remained in effect during the cheating scandal of 1936 and during the most serious challenge to the university's "whites only" admission policy in late 1938 and early 1939.[73]

On December 12, 1938, the United States Supreme Court handed down a ruling in the case of Lloyd Gaines, an African American who, with the assistance of the National Association for the Advancement of Colored People (NAACP), sued the University of Missouri for admittance to its law school. In a landmark decision, the court ruled that no resident of a state could be barred admission from a state-funded school based on race if there was no other equivalent institution for the applicant to attend. Within days of the ruling in the Gaines case, Pauli Murray, an African American woman who had been raised in Durham, North Carolina, applied to enter graduate school at UNC. Later a noted author, activist, and the first black woman to be ordained as an Episcopal priest in the United States, Murray was living in New York City at the time. The story, which emerged soon after a well-publicized visit to campus by President Franklin Roosevelt, made headlines in the *Daily Tar Heel*. In an article titled "Officials Faced by Negro Entrance Application" and subtitled "New York Woman Seeks to Enter Grad School," the paper reported that "an application for admission to the University now lying on Dr. Frank Graham's desk may turn out to be an eight ball large enough

to hide all Carolina liberalism and the progressive philosophy of the University president, should a Negro woman now living in New York city be determined to push her demands to enter the graduate school." As with Morris Krasny, Murray's name was never published in the paper, and the fact that she grew up in Durham was also never mentioned. Instead, she was consistently referred to as a "New York woman," likely to make her seem even more of an outsider.[74]

The story about Pauli Murray broke the

same day that editor Allen Merrill wrote a column praising the organizational meeting of the Southern Conference for Human Welfare in Birmingham, Alabama, attended by Frank Graham. At the conference, when police chief Bull Connor—later infamous for turning dogs and hoses on nonviolent civil rights protesters in that city—forced blacks and whites to sit separately in the hall, First Lady Eleanor Roosevelt dramatically sat in the aisle between the segregated sections. After railing against threatened "lynching posses" on campus, and noting that the university had a history of seven decades of intolerance, Merrill called the conference a "bright spot." "Thousands of Southerners—business men, farmers, tenants, factory hands, white and colored—met together," Merrill wrote. "Free speech was a fact ... full and frank opinions on such pressing problems as tenancy, labor relations, housing, birth control, hours and wages, education, health, suffrage." Regarding the application of Pauli Murray, Merrill pointedly concluded in an editorial entitled "Equal Opportunity" that "our test case may not get to the courts, but if anybody finds that North Carolina hasn't been providing equal educational opportunity for both races we'll only be disappointed at the publication of our shame; we won't be surprised. What ostrich would be?" The paper's staff polled other college editors about the question, and the results were printed on the front page of the Daily Tar Heel the following week. Not surprisingly, most editors ducked the question or stated their institutions policies. Merrill stated his views on the matter forcefully and unequivocally: "Our actions in accepting [Negroes] will define our status as Americans. Our pilgrim, continental, Gettysburg tradition is freedom and

racial equality for all. It is our cue to pioneer the nation out of this last frontier of racial prejudice and superstition."[75]

The opinion of other UNC students, however, was harsh, even sarcastic. Under the heading "Ante-Bellum Air," the paper reported student reaction to the possibility of black students: "Campus opinion took on an antebellum note yesterday as one man declared 'I think the state would close the University before they'd let a Negro in. I've never committed murder yet but [would] if a black boy tried to come into my house saying he was a 'University student.'" Other students hearing of the movement "vowed that they would tar and feather any 'nigger' that tried to come in class with them." The Daily Tar Heel conducted a poll of grad students, and of 405 eligible students, 120 voted, 82 for admitting African American students, and 38 against. Some could not resist attempts at sarcasm. A front-page box under the headline announced that Carl S. Pugh, editor of the Buccaneer, would apply to North Carolina A&T (the state's college for African Americans): "I am applying as a protest to the gross injustice to which a Negro woman from New York was subjected when she applied for admission to the University."[76]

Murray's case could have been groundbreaking, but ultimately she didn't have the legal support needed to win and was refused admission based on her race. Though the NAACP was initially interested in providing Murray legal counsel, in the end they did not, out of concern that she was not a resident of North Carolina when she applied and because she had publicly released copies of letters she wrote to Frank Graham and Franklin Roosevelt seeking their support. It would be a decade before the next attempt to integrate Carolina, which ultimately proved successful, was undertaken.[77]

BREAKING A CHEATING SCANDAL

The *Daily Tar Heel* covered two scandals in the late 1930s that resulted in negative national press for the university, brought into question the school's vaunted honor code, and challenged the limits and authority of student government. The first, the exposure of an extensive cheating ring in 1936, was an early example of investigative reporting, and the stress of breaking the story almost broke Philip Hammer, the *Daily Tar Heel* editor at the time. The second, the banning and then burning by the Student Council of the November 1939 issue of the campus humor magazine, the *Buccaneer*, led to major opposition by the paper and cries of suppression of free speech.

The story of the cheating scandal was as much about Philip Hammer's editorship of the *Daily Tar Heel* as it was about the crime and its repercussions. Hammer joined the *DTH* staff as a freshman in the fall of 1932 because, as he later said, he wanted to do "something for the world." Though he did not major in journalism or harbor desires to become a journalist, he quickly realized that the *Daily Tar Heel* was the nerve center of the campus and its best public forum. Fortuitously his first assignment was the South Building beat, covering the university's administration. Like many other students, Hammer soon fell under the spell of UNC's charismatic president, Frank Porter Graham, though he was not afraid to take on the president when he disagreed with him. Along with Graham's influence, Hammer's worldview was also significantly shaped by courses he took in his major,

economics, and in sociology. Of his professors Hammer later noted that anthropologist Rupert Vance "was the greatest thinker, but [sociologist Howard] Odum was the most inspiring leader." Hammer served as a teaching assistant to Odum, and remembered him as being "delightful." Along with his academic pursuits and work for the *Daily Tar Heel*, Hammer helped found the Carolina Political Union to foster free speech on campus.[78]

After three years of working his way up the ranks, Hammer was elected editor of the *DTH* in the spring of 1935. Clearly the influence of mentors Graham, Odum, and Vance had an effect on his editorial perspective and his management of the paper. "The *Tar Heel* took on the configuration of the guy in charge of it," Hammer later recalled, and he described himself as an "activist." The school's yearbook, the *Yackety Yack*, gave a colorful account of Hammer's tenure as editor of the *Daily Tar Heel*, calling him an "energetic, fly-off-the-handle" guy who shouted "his bolts of sarcasm at everything he thought vulnerable ... [giving] South Building hell." Under Hammer, the *Yack* noted, "the *Tar Heel* was rambunctious and effervescent."[79]

One of Hammer's first acts as editor was to establish a front-page column that he penned daily, entitled "Campus Keyboard," which ran under a graphic of a set of typewriter keys. Rarely in the paper's history had an editor so consistently employed the front page to editorialize. Hammer used the column to take on all manner of issues, from the debate over turning university athletics into a semiprofessional operation to complaints about food service on campus. He wrote that the *Daily Tar Heel* was a "good, aggressive campus newspaper" that

carried on the tradition of being "representative [and] progressive." He further offered the opinion that "a campus newspaper is not just a news sheet. It has a large responsibility in its news coverage, yes; but it has an even larger one in its stand for improvements in student government, in living conditions, and in standards of education and athletics and campus activities.... Censorship of student expression," Hammer declared, "must not exist."[80]

In January 1936, soon after students returned from the Christmas break, senior Joe Barnett approached Hammer with explosive information. A wide-ranging cheating ring had been operating on campus for several years. He heard about the ring in the dorm in which he lived, and Barnett, as Hammer later recalled, was "a real idealist and got terribly exercised about it." Barnett had spent about a month putting facts together before approaching Hammer, and both agreed the *Daily Tar Heel* should break the story. Understanding the potential ramifications of the story, Hammer proceeded cautiously and asked Barnett to carefully check his sources. Once that was done, Hammer and Barnett went to President Graham with the full story. Graham, who understood that the student-administered honor code—fundamental to the academic reputation of the university—was in jeopardy, told them exposure of the cheating operation and subsequent disciplinary action "was a matter to be [handled] entirely by the students." Hammer and Barnett then went to the state attorney general and assistant attorney general, both of whom agreed that the students had the legal authority to conduct their own investigation. Having obtained approval to proceed from both the university administration and state leaders, Hammer

and Barnett then approached the student-body president, Jack Pool, and notified the Chapel Hill chief of police. On Saturday, January 25, the chief of police, Barnett and Pool surprised the main suspect in his rented room and, after conducting a search, began a five-hour interrogation. The dean of students also sat in for a portion of the interrogation, during which the suspect, Douglas Cartland, made a full confession.[81]

Hammer, who did not attend the interrogation because he didn't want to create the appearance of a conflict of interest for the *Daily Tar Heel*, felt it important that the paper break the story before it went to the Student Council, so that the details could be presented as "verified information." He sat on the story for six days and then, on February 1, splashed it across the front page in bold headlines, devoting most of the issue to various elements of the scandal and a detailed chronology of the investigation. In a prefacing statement Hammer announced that "a large ring of organized cheating" had been operating on campus for over three years, and that the story had been "purposefully withheld from publication until this morning so that all evidence which students uncovered could be presented to the Student Council." "It is urged that every student read the story completely," Hammer wrote, "in order to get the true facts instead of relying on the hundreds of false rumors and misrepresentations which are current on campus."[82]

The extent of the scandal was shocking, and the details seamy and salacious. Over a period of several years, Cartland developed an elaborate and extensive "gamut of services for students who would pay for them," ranging from providing exam answers to writing papers and theses. Hammer later recalled that "during tests and exams he would establish himself or his workers in the basement or in the men's room and say: 'You bring the question down. I'll give you the answers.'" Cartland "would either purloin or otherwise assemble previous exams on different subjects and have a stack of them so he could tell you what questions you were likely to face and he would give you the answer." Although Hammer made the decision to withhold the names of those accused of running the cheating ring—referring to the principal offenders

as "X" and "Y"—the *Yackety Yack* had no such qualms. The *Yack*'s breezy and colorful thumbnail version of the scandal summed things up succinctly:

Consternation covered the campus as rumors of a wholesale cheating ring excited the State. Douglas Cartland, former Phi Beta Kappa student of the University, had organized a business of illegally aiding students to pass their work. Aid was given on examinations, daily work and term papers. Whole correspondence courses were taken for substantial remuneration. Copies of examinations were stolen and stooges were planted in halls and toilets to aid customers. [After investigation by Joe Barnett,] Cartland was surprised in his room and without much trouble a complete confession was extracted. Bills and receipts incriminating scores of students were found in his room.[83]

According to the *Daily Tar Heel*, during the interrogation Cartland "wandered into a semi-hysterical worrying about what would happen to his mother, whose sole support he was," suggesting that he was driven to do what he did because of the effects of the Depression. But it was the school's honor code, not Cartland's motivation, that was the primary issue for the university. The honor code had not been much discussed on campus during the early 1930s, but the cheating scandal brought it front and center. In the same issue of the paper that first broke the story, Hammer wrote an editorial entitled "We Face a Crisis." "The honor system is in the balance, and with it our very student government," Hammer observed, and "if we fail to rally to answer

Front page of the *Daily Tar Heel*, February 1, 1936, with most of the issue
devoted to breaking the story of a major cheating scandal at UNC.

THE ONLY COLLEGE DAILY IN THE SOUTH

The Daily Tar Heel

"TO CREATE
A CAMPUS
PERSONALITY"

A JOURNAL OF
THE ACTIVITIES
OF CAROLINIANS

VOLUME XLIV   EDITORIAL PHONE 4351   CHAPEL HILL, N. C., SATURDAY, FEBRUARY 1, 1936   BUSINESS PHONE 4356   NUMBER 94

COMPLETE STORY OF CHEATING RING REVEALED

Foreword: The following story is the first official history of the successive student efforts to uncover a large ring of organized cheating which has been operating for over three years on the University campus.

It was purposely withheld from publication until this morning so that all evidence which students uncovered could be presented to the student council. This has been done.

It is urged that every student read the story completely in order to get the true facts instead of relying on the hundreds of false rumors and misrepresentations which are current on the campus.

The Boy heard about the cheating ring before we went home for the Christmas holidays. He told his father and his father made him promise to go back to Chapel Hill and assist in getting to the bottom of it and wiping it from the campus.

The Boy came back and told the Student, a friend of his. The student went to the room of A and told him what the Boy had said. A told the Student to ask the Boy to come over to see him and the Boy came.

By that time, rumors which had been unnoticed were picked up and they added weight to what the Boy had to tell. Pieced together, the story sounded like something.

Discussing the matter, the little group decided that the best thing to do would be to run the leader of the ring out of town. The leader was named X and the boy knew it and had told the Student and A.

Many Involved

Then it was found out, through rumors and other words, that X had a number of assistants who would possibly carry on the work if X had to leave. And there would still be the assistants to be attended to. Furthermore, there would be about 200 students (so they

Board of Trustees

The board of trustees, meeting yesterday in Raleigh, passed what might be regarded as a vote of confidence in President Graham by referring the consideration of athletic eligibility back to the president and faculty of the University and of State College.

The student council request, presented by Dr. Graham, which asked that the word "dismiss" in the trustee ruling on drinking, hazing and gambling be changed to "discipline," was granted.

The out-of-state tuition rate was raised by vote of the board.

Consolidation and its issues were deferred until the June meeting, at which time it will be made a special order.

The board ratified changes in student government and publications fee. More information on all these issues will appear in tomorrow's issue of this newspaper.

And, more important, Dr. Graham emphasized that it was a matter to be done entirely by the students. He said that the administration left the operation of the honor principle to them. It would like to be kept advised of all progress, but it would not interfere with student work in uncovering this breach of honor.

That night half of the later student group which uncovered the cheating ring was organized. First it was necessary to find out if they had a right to enter the premises of X and seize his papers to procure evidence of his dishonorable work. The State Attorney-General and Assistant-Attorney-General were contacted and, after a good deal of investigation, they advised

We Face A Crisis

The honor system is in the balance, and with it, our very student government.

Upon the student body rests their fate. If we fail to support our student council in its present deliberations, if we fail to rally to answer the challenge which this disgraceful episode has produced, then we have dug the grave of the honor system and we have built the coffin of the student government. For we will have been responsible, we, the student body.

If we hesitate, if we have not the courage to stand with our council at its most trying hour, we will cause this, the University's most precious treasure to be trampled in the dust and forgotten.

This cheating imbroglio has been uncovered by students. That is of utmost significance. And it is being removed, its cancerous self is being cut completely away, by the students. That is even more significant.

This proves that the honor system is working. But it does not prove that it has worked well or that it will continue to work.

THE RESPONSIBILITY IS THE STUDENT BODY'S. IF WE HAVE ALLOWED THIS NASTY SITUATION TO OCCUR, IF WE HAVE SLUMBERED WHILE OUR VERY FOUNDATION OF STUDENT LIFE HAS BEEN ATTACKED, WE ARE TO BLAME FOR THE UNFORTUNATE CONSEQUENCES OF OUR NEGLIGENCE.

AND IF THE HONOR SYSTEM IS TO BE MAINTAINED IN THE FUTURE ON THE HIGHEST LEVEL, THEN EVERY STUDENT MUST ANSWER THIS CHALLENGE WITH A VOW AND PLEDGE OF RESPONSIBILITY.

There must be a realization that we have failed and not the honor principle. And realizing this, we must swear by all things sacred, that it will not happen again, this failure. IT CAN'T HAPPEN.

Among us have been those hypocritical students who have preached the merits of the very principle which they seek to destroy. Many of them have gone or are leaving. But the rest cannot be allowed to stay, either. We must be for the honor principle to a man, or not at all. We have seen what happens when this is not the case.

This tremendous cheating activity has been broken up. The students themselves have done it. The administration has left it up to us and we have succeeded. But that is not all; we must continue to succeed.

That we have done what we have done, that we have asserted our faith and our devout belief in this principle of honor, that we have been able to place it before personal vanity and in spite of personal anguish—these are proof that we can and will maintain forever this heritage, which, through our unforgivable negligence, we have allowed to be besmirked by fellow students whom we trusted.

The student council is faced with a crisis and they are bearing up. The most difficult test that any student government has ever before met is theirs and they are succeeding by meet-

Student Council

The student council, hearing nine more cases, suspended seven students for violation of the honor principle in sessions running yesterday afternoon and last night.

Eight other cases which were considered involved students who are not in school and who consequently cannot testify in their own favor at present.

In the cases which did not merit suspension, one student was acquitted and the other's case was deferred.

Further hearings will continue today.

wandered into a semi-hysterical worrying about what would happen to his mother whose sole support he was. To quiet his fears about his mother and to bring his mind back to the business at hand he was told that he would be helped to rebuild his shattered career and that when he had made good, as many other boys have been helped provided his repentance and reformation were genuine and he were to frankly confess to any prospective employer this blot on his record.

He was not told that if he would give the names of those involved the student council would deal leniently with them. He asked several times what would happen to the students and was told that he would have to leave that matter to the council.

Urged to Confess

In all the discussion with him he was urged to give all the facts concerning his activities for the following reasons:

He owed it to the University to do everything in his power to clean up a terible situation that he had helped to create;

He owed it to the hundreds of

had. Y, on being quesioned, corroborated many of X's statements and added a number of his own. And at that time, as a result of that afternoon's conversation, A and the student body president found definitely that there had been a helper in the University mimeographing department who had turned over quizzes to X and Y, and that the pass key to Bingham hall was in their possession. Many other such disclosures were made in the hours of conversation.

Y, when asked for his papers, told the two students that he would get them and while A and the student body president questioned X, Y went away for 20 minutes, presumably to get the papers.

Gives Excuses

He returned, however, without them and the pass key, which had been demanded of him. He said, first of all, that he had moved the papers the night before to the room of a friend of his, although it later turned out to be the basement of a certain fraternity house. He said that he was unable to get the papers at that time as the friend was at the moving picture show.

Following further questioning (the whole conversation was again copied down completely by A on the typewriter), Y accompanied the two students to Y's room and made arrangements to meet the next day. At that moment A and the president realized that they must secure Y's papers that night, before Y had a chance to destroy them and their valuable evidence.

Although Y was unwilling at first to go immediately to get the papers, he finally consented and the three walked over to the fraternity house. The student body president, because of his position in student government,

95

the challenge which this disgraceful episode has produced, then we have dug the grave of the honor system and we have built the coffin of student government."[84]

The day the story broke, another bombshell exploded. Student-body president Jack Pool, who had participated in the interrogation of Cartland but had not been implicated, made a public confession that he had bought the answers to an exam when he was a freshman. Pool immediately resigned, but not before performing one last act as president: he asked the Student Council to suspend him for his participation, and then voted to approve the motion, thereby making it unanimous. Philip Hammer saw beyond Pool's freshman transgression and lionized his humbling public act extensively in the *Daily Tar Heel*: "What Jack Pool has done, in reporting his mistake of five years ago, in demanding his own suspension and in suffering like a man for his breach of the honor principle he loves so well, will live forever in the history of the University as an example of that honor and integrity which this University seeks to foster and maintain among its students.... In the glorious light of Jack Pool's magnificent stand, we press onward as he would have us do if he were still here to lead us."[85]

Eventually ninety-nine students were implicated for cheating, and twenty-four expelled by the Student Council. Under the "Campus Keyboard" column, Hammer wrote that "it is difficult to interpret the past week's happenings optimistically. But it is important that we do." Assistant editor Samuel R. Leaguer wrote a column putting the scandal into broader context: "The past week our campus has been so filled with nervous and emotional dynamite, of inter-

est to campuses throughout the country ... [UNC has demonstrated] that an unadulterated system of student government, combined with the honor principle, has teeth sufficiently strong to make it an effective and potent force in student life." Hammer later summed up the scandal in the 1936 *Yack* by stating that it "hurt in some quarters" but that it also worked for "the betterment of our University community as a whole."[86]

The effects of the cheating scandal were wide-ranging. *Time* magazine covered the story in a small article on February 10, 1936, entitled "Honor in North Carolina," stating that the university's honor system was "widely, shockingly violated." A committee was formed to investigate the honor code and to suggest changes, led by Philip Hammer and Fred Weaver (who would later serve as longtime dean of students at UNC). And in an effort to clean up all potentially damaging activity on campus, the Student Council, "in a spurt of activity following the cheating ring, abolished hell week," according to the *Yack*. Memory of the scandal and the *Daily Tar Heel*'s role in exposing it lingered at UNC for several years, and likely influenced all three of Hammer's immediate successors—Donald McKee, J. McNeill Smith, and Allen Merrill—who were on the staff of the paper in the winter of 1936.[87]

The effects of breaking the story were severe for Hammer. The *Yack* reported that "Phil Hammer left school because of an approaching nervous breakdown and he and the campus rested until he returned in the Spring Quarter." "It was such a shock to me that I left school for a couple of weeks after the scandal was over," Hammer later recalled. "I mean, we were up all night for a week writing this thing and another week to get it together for the Student Council. I was exhausted. I hadn't been to class for three weeks and I was fractured." As a result of the stress Hammer didn't take any of his written exams, but several of his professors, understanding the situation, gave him oral exams and passed him.[88]

THE BURNING OF THE *BUCCANEER*

The cheating scandal of 1936, which caused a crisis in student government and in which the *Daily Tar Heel* played a significant role, was followed in November 1939 by another scandal, almost as sensational, involving the humor magazine, the *Buccaneer*. This incident raised questions not only about the role of student government, but also about student autonomy and freedom of speech and the press. As such, it was of great significance to the *Daily Tar Heel*. In the era preceding World War II, the paper's relationship with the campus humor magazine—first the *Tar Baby*, then the *Boll Weevil* and finally the *Buccaneer* (briefly rebranded as the *Fin-Jan*)—was complex, incestuous, and often contentious. Frequently members of the newspaper's staff also worked for the humor publication, the most famous example being Thomas Wolfe. And after 1923, for better or worse, the *Tar Heel* was married to the humor magazine through shared oversight and funding by the Publications Union Board. For a time in the 1920s the two publications even occupied the same office. In 1925 the paper announced that the "*Buccaneer* boys have been granted permission to move in temporarily," and "should copy for the two publications get mixed up, the student body will please be tolerant."[89]

It was something of a shotgun wedding from the beginning, though in reality there was an unrecognized benefit for the *Tar Heel*. Because of the existence of the humor magazine, an official campus outlet was provided for the sophomoric antics of students who were so inclined, which allowed that element to be eliminated from the *Tar Heel* itself, and enabled the paper to rapidly professionalize during a critical era. This safety valve turned out to be invaluable to the paper, as the life of the humor publication would come to a blazing end, literally, in 1939.

During the 1920s and 1930s the humor magazine in its various incarnations sought to emulate sophisticated sister publications at Ivy League schools, as well as national periodicals such as *Esquire* aimed at urbane men, with the inclusion of bawdy and at times risqué articles and cartoons. As a result, the humor magazine and its editors often tested the limits of free speech—and the patience of the administration and alumni. In reality, the limits had more to do with decency than with free speech, as attempts at sophisticated adult humor blended with the expected locker-room hijinks of college-age men (despite the presence of female students on the magazine's staff). More than once the magazine ran afoul of the administration and was temporarily suspended, ordered to tone down, or reorganize. In February 1924, following a particularly objectionable issue of the *Boll Weevil*, the newly created Publications Union Board officially ended that periodical and announced the establishment of a new humor magazine, the *Buccaneer*.[90]

The name of the new publication was an obvious reference to North Carolina's colorful (if romanticized) early eighteenth-century swashbuckling pirate history, and small graphics of skulls and crossbones were used as borders and decoration on the magazine's pages. The *Buc-*

caneer soon followed in the footsteps of its predecessors and lived up to the salty reputation of its name, constantly testing the waters of good taste and propriety. In February 1926, the *Tar Heel* offered stern criticism of a recent issue of the magazine in a front-page article entitled "Reviewer Finds *Buccaneer* Crude." "Reviewing the *Buccaneer* is a waste of time. The magazine has to be reviewed because no one reads it, and some means must be made whereby the average student can talk about it intelligently." In November 1928 a sarcastic *Tar Heel* critic noted the "cleanest *Buccaneer* joke we have heard this year is that the esteemed editor of that publication called a staff meeting for Thursday night then forgot to attend."[91]

By January 1932 the faculty had had enough, and tried to establish a board to censor the magazine. Although clearly many on the *Daily Tar Heel* staff also disliked the magazine's content, the paper took the stand of fiercely defending its right to be published. In an editorial entitled "The Reactionaries at It Again," the paper strenuously objected to censorship of any kind, warning that such action would be "an indelible stain on the reputation of freedom in student publications that the University of North Carolina has long enjoyed. Once the germ of censorship receives the least bit of nourishment in any quarter of publications here, it will soon grow to such a size as to control completely every publication on campus ... [and will threaten the University's] nation-wide reputation of freedom of student expression." The *Buccaneer* survived the 1932 attempt at censorship and a further effort in 1933 to abolish it "because of mild attempts at pornography," as Philip Hammer later recalled. The magazine's name was subsequently changed to the *Fin-Jan* (an obscure Arabic phrase meaning "small coffee cup without a handle") in an effort to give the publication a fresh start. But phoenix-like, the *Buccaneer* reemerged a few years later.[92]

Skirmishes with the *Buccaneer* finally came to a head in November 1939, when the Student Council ordered that all copies of the new issue be burned before release, resulting in a heated debate about both freedom of speech on campus and student autonomy and self-government. On November 9, the day before advance copies appeared and apparently aware that something sinister was afoot, *DTH* editorial writer Don Bishop wrote a column arguing against abolition of the magazine, noting "like children after candy, Carolina students—male and female alike—clamor for their copies as soon as they come off the press." He added, however, that critics must be heard, as they "are the taxpayers who contribute a healthy chunk of cash every biennium to support of the University," and he warned that legislative funding could be affected. In fact, opposition to the magazine had been building for years outside of the university as well as within, and the staff brazenly decided to tempt fate that November by publishing what they called "The Sex Issue." Though the content was extremely tame by today's standards—slightly risqué cartoons and suggestive articles rife with double entendre, such as opinions gathered from students on the burning question "Is Sex Here to Stay?"—the cover art pushed the limits of propriety to the breaking point, especially for what was a student-funded publication at a state university. It featured a scantily clad woman seated on the sofa in apparently a cheap hotel, with a cigarette dangling from her lips, her legs spread apart and a white box covering her mid-section, with the bawdy caption inside: "We point with pride to the purity of our white space."[93]

The first hint of trouble came from Louis Graves, former professor of journalism and then publisher of the *Chapel Hill Weekly*, in whose shop the magazine was printed. Graves sent a letter to President Graham objecting to the issue, but saying he was being paid to print it and would do so unless told by the administration to stop. As soon as advance copies went out, a firestorm erupted and events unfolded swiftly. On November 10, *DTH* editor in chief Martin Harmon reviewed the issue. Overall his comments weren't very serious, but he remarked that, "even though this year's issues are mailable, I don't want Uncle Sam's post office department to catch me mailing a *Buccaneer*." Of the cover he wryly commented that though he didn't like the color combinations, "they are quite appropriate to the surroundings; at least that's what the boys who've registered in the fifty-cents-a-night hostelries tell me."[94]

The height of the controversy coincided with Armistice Day, celebrating America's World War I sacrifices for freedom, and on November 11, under the banner headline "Council Kills November Buc," the paper reported that all issues of the magazine were ordered destroyed before distribution. Jimmy Davis, president of the student body, was quoted explaining the drastic action: "It was taken with a realization that the *Buccaneer* is read throughout the state by persons from all walks of life, and it was judged that such an issue would seriously and permanently damage the reputation and lessen the prestige of the University in general." He added that it was not "a means of setting up a

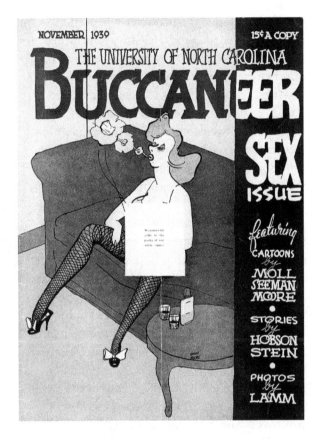

censorship of student publications or of student expression, but as a protective measure for the welfare of the student body."[95]

The following day's *Daily Tar Heel* headline read "Crisis in Student Government," and the editors announced, "We devote today's front page to the most important issue of student government to arise since the discovery of the illfamed cheating ring in the winter of 1936: student council suppression of the November issue of the Carolina *Buccaneer*." On the second page a large picture of a pirate surrounded by skulls, bones, and a large question mark was printed, with a caption that read, "We advocate immediate distribution of the present issue of the *Buccaneer* and recommend a 'clean-up' in future issues." Fred Weaver, involved as a student in efforts to revamp the honor code following the cheating scandal, and by 1939 assistant dean of students, supported destruction of the issue, arguing that "we do not have here or anywhere 100 per cent freedom. As a state institution we are subject to the representative judgment of the state. We maintain a continuous struggle for freedom.... Nothing more imperils student freedom than the continued publication of a magazine which is considered to be inimical to the objective ... of education ... [and we should] discriminate between rightful causes for freedom and specious causes of freedom." The paper also ran articles reporting that there was an unsuccessful attempt to break into the basement at the print shop where the 4,000 copies were being held, and pointing out that the entire incident happened while Bill Stauber, editor of the *Buccaneer*, was away from campus and unaware of the controversy or the Student Council's actions.[96]

On November 14, two front-page stories appeared: one reported that the Publications Union Board voted to approve funds for a replacement issue of the *Buccaneer*; and the other that the Student Legislature (a new and separate entity from the Student Council) voted not to destroy the existing issue (though it had no jurisdiction in the matter). In a column Don Bishop quipped: "the Student Council has decided it will not 'pass the Buc,' and has ordered that the November issue be run through a sifter ... the last time *The Buccaneer* was required to walk the plank, its name was changed to '*Fin-Jan.*'" Not everyone was pleased with the paper's coverage of the controversy, however. A letter to the editor appeared signed by eighteen students who supported destroying the offensive issue of the *Buccaneer*, and accusing the *Daily Tar Heel* of refusing to publish their previous letter, which they then printed themselves and distributed around campus.[97]

On November 15 the paper's headlines blared "4,000 'Over-Sexed' Bucs Meet Fiery End in Local Incinerator." The "issue which plunged the campus into its most controversial debate in several years and reverberated throughout the state—were unceremoniously dumped into the fiery depths of Chapel Hill's incinerator yesterday morning." The destruction occurred, the paper reported, "while students were attending classes, unaware that for the first time in history a student publication was being burned before distribution." Interestingly, even though this event occurred only two months after the start of World War II in Europe, no one at the time noted the obvious irony between the "fiery" end of the *Buccaneer* and the burning of books and periodicals deemed undesirable by the Nazis. As a final note, and probably as a means of thumbing a nose at the Student Council and the administration, two photos were published in the 1940 *Yackety Yack* showing the staff of the magazine working on the infamous issue, and the risqué banned cover is clearly visible. So in effect, the November 1939 "Sex Issue" of the *Buccaneer* was, in fact, distributed.[98]

Like the proverbial cat with nine lives, the UNC humor magazine cheated death several times. In October 1940, when *Buccaneer* editor Mark Hobson was imprisoned for the attempted murder of his girlfriend, the student legislature abolished the publication, with the support of the *Daily Tar Heel* management. It was reborn the following year as the *Tar 'n Feathers*, and an editorial in the paper noted that "the humor magazine has been discussed more than the so-called 'communist menace' in Chapel Hill. . . . It has not been abolished because, it has been held, its abolition would destroy freedom at the University." In its final incarnation, as *Tar'nation*, it was published periodically into the 1950s.[99]

PREWAR ISOLATIONISM AND THE STUDENT PACIFISM MOVEMENT

The 1939 controversy over destroying copies of a "dirty" humor magazine was a diversion at UNC as the war in Europe loomed increasingly larger. Much discussion and debate occurred on campus as guest speakers, faculty, administrators, and students offered predictions and opinions about when and under what circumstances the United States should get involved. The debate did not occur in a vacuum, and other factors colored various perspectives, notably the ongoing issues of "radical" teaching and promotion of communism and socialism at the university.

Reading of the *Daily Tar Heel* from the late 1920s and early 1930s reveals that the paper and the university community were keeping a close watch on the events in Europe (and later Asia). In January 1928 an article appeared entitled "The Blackness of Europe's Clouds," an interview with President Chase after his recent trip abroad, in which he expressed grave concerns about Italy and the rise of Benito Mussolini. In November 1932, Vermont Royster wrote a column about the political struggle in Germany between Baron von Hindenburg and Adolf Hitler—the first mention of the soon-to-be führer in the *Daily Tar Heel*. "Hitler has shown himself to be an embryonic Mussolini, a man of undeniable capabili-

ties," Royster wrote, suggesting, unfortunately, that a dictator in Germany could have a positive outcome.[100]

The effects of the First World War on UNC were not yet a distant memory in the 1930s. Though casualties in the Carolina family were relatively light, the conversion of the campus into a military base and the death of President Edward Kidder Graham left a lasting legacy. Armistice Day, November 11, was celebrated on campus throughout the 1920s and 1930s with almost as much pomp and ceremony as the annual University Day a month earlier. And as the possibility of another world war came into focus, Armistice Day became the logical opportunity to promote pacifism, a sentiment that was naturally strong on a college campus where so many of age could be called up to serve.

In addition to proclaiming America as a peace-loving nation every Armistice Day, the *Daily Tar Heel* published pacifist editorials as early as January of 1930, and by the middle of the decade an active antiwar movement existed on campus. The movement was tied to the larger American Student Union (ASU), which was organizing similar efforts at colleges around the country. The ASU had strong ties to the Communist Party, however, which compromised its effectiveness, and membership in the organization later came back to haunt some former students during the Cold War witch hunts of the late 1940s and early 1950s. In fact, the state representative to the national ASU was UNC student Junius Scales, who secretly joined the Communist Party in 1939, and who would appear a decade later as a "red" thorn in the university's public image.[101]

The ASU held war "strikes" at Carolina annually from 1934 to 1940, often pointing fingers at the greed of the munitions industry as driving the nation toward an unnecessary military conflict. Several faculty also became involved in the pacifist movement. Charles Phillips Russell, former editor of the *Tar Heel* and then a respected professor in the School of Journalism, was one of ten people representing American universities to attend a conference on the possible war in Brussels in 1935. All of this pacifist and anti-industry activity predictably incited the university's conservative critics, many of whom were more "hawkish" on the subject of war. As the *Yack* reported after the ASU event in 1936, "the ears of Mars burned April 22 when the annual anti-war strike condemned munitions and other systems that make for war. Speeches and banners marked an orderly demonstration, and except for a cry of 'communism' from Dave Clark everything went off quietly."[102]

As the war in Europe began, sentiment among hawks and doves on campus and throughout the state became more heated, and the line in the sand between the two sides became sharper. On September 22, 1939—exactly three weeks after the Nazi invasion of Poland—the paper carried a front-page story about opposition by a branch of the Winston-Salem American Legion to a proposed visit to campus by Fritz Kuhn, the American "Bund führer," or head of the American Nazi Party. The Legion threatened legal action if Kuhn spoke on campus, and, once again a debate ensued about free speech at UNC. *DTH* editor Martin Harmon wrote a column entitled "Hurricane," noting that the Raleigh *News and Observer* supported free speech on the campus, and added that Kuhn had actually not yet been invited. "We'd like to hear Mr. Kuhn in Memorial Hall,"

Harmon wrote, also noting that the Carolina Political Union board was sticking by its guns to invite whomever the members voted for (though in the end Kuhn did not appear).[103]

When it came to the issue of the United States' entry into the war, the question of free speech extended beyond the appropriateness of outside speakers to include student opinion, and culminated at a raucous Peace Rally on May 22, 1940. The *Daily Tar Heel*, under editor Don Bishop, was fully behind the antiwar movement, and announced the upcoming event in an unusual banner headline on the editorial page on May 17: "Keep America Out of Europe's War," running versions of it for the next five days. In an editorial the same day Bishop wrote: "The crisis is approaching for America, and it is time that we, who are the people—especially the youth of our colleges—rise up from the inertia and indifference which has been a plaque in our midst too long. . . . Now is the time for youth which has sipped its cokes too long, which has slumped in movie seats until its brain can do no active thinking—now is the time for this youth—to think about our position and to make a concerted stand to KEEP THE UNITED STATES OUT OF EUROPE'S WAR."[104]

The Peace Rally on May 22 did not go as the organizers planned. As students gave speeches and performed skits to a packed audience, rumblings were heard inside and outside of Memorial Hall. At one point eggs and other debris were thrown on the stage, and the event threatened to turn ugly. President Frank Graham got out of his seat and walked onto the stage, not speaking a word but simply looking out into the audience with a calming expression. Graham's commanding presence stopped the heckling temporarily,

and as the headline in the paper read the following day, "Mass Peace Meeting Subsides Into Forum after Approaching Near Riot." Newspapers across the state carried accounts of the incident and in a rare front-page editorial the *Daily Tar Heel* declared "Carolina Principles and Eggs Don't Mix."[105]

The May 1940 peace rally was effectively the end of the antiwar movement at UNC. In September, soon after students returned for fall classes, Graham made a speech clearly stating the university's position and intentions for the looming conflict, which was reprinted in the paper. "The United States of America cannot longer pretend to be isolated from movements and forces in either Europe or Asia and any other part of this interdependent dynamic world," Graham told the students. "The University of North Carolina, a child of the Revolution, and the first University of the people to open its doors ... offers its total resources to the nation for the defense of the freedom and democracy it

Orville Campbell, 1940–41 editor of the *Daily Tar Heel*. Campbell later published the *Chapel Hill Weekly*, where the *DTH* was printed for many years. (NCC/Hugh Morton Collection)

thinking people usually either agree with us or at least give us credit for thinking about the things that happen around us.

This "common sense liberalism" permits the *Tar Heel* to uphold the right of a free student press, yet oppose a dirty humor magazine [the *Buccaneer*]; to believe that America should not enter the war, yet allow the expression of opposing viewpoints in its public column ... to defend the right of alleged "super-liberal" faculty members to have their say, yet impress upon them the necessity of exercising a little common sense also.[107]

was founded to serve." Two weeks later the paper printed a draft registration form, announcing that students between the ages of twenty-one and thirty-five were required to register the following day; 966 complied, and the university was, for all intents and purposes, off to war.[106]

Bishop continued the futile cause a little longer, writing an editorial entitled "The Case for Pacifism" on November 2. In defending the paper's positions both on the war and more broadly on other issues, Bishop laid out the philosophy in a year-end summation:

"Common sense liberalism," the *Daily Tar Heel* terms its editorial policy. It is liberal within reason; thus, neither reactionaries nor radicals will countenance us. But honest, rational

In addition to the *Daily Tar Heel*'s role in the pacifist movement, the last student election for editorship of the paper before America's entry into World War II proved memorable. After a spirited and heated campaign in the spring of 1941, campus activist Lou Harris lost the election to managing editor Orville Campbell by twelve votes. Harris went on to become a pioneer in American presidential polling; his innovative polls were a key element of John F. Kennedy's winning campaign in 1960. Regarding his twelve-vote loss to Campbell, Harris quipped to *People* magazine in 1976, "the story is that I'm still trying to find those votes ... that's why I went into polling." Campbell later became longtime editor and publisher of the *Chapel Hill Weekly*, and something of an entertainment impresario, helping to propel UNC alums actor Andy Griffith and singer George Hamilton IV to national prominence.[108]

3

THE TRUTH IN EIGHT-POINT TYPE

1941–1959

THE *TAR HEEL* AT WAR

The American home front during World War II, including the UNC campus, is often remembered romantically as a place of abundant patriotism and a spirit of pulling together for the common national cause. While that was certainly true, it was also a period of great anxiety and uncertainty, and concern about the long-term effects the war would have on the university. It was a particularly difficult time for the student newspaper, which struggled with shortages of staff, money, and supplies. In addition, as the U.S. Navy moved onto campus, the *Daily Tar Heel* faced the real possibility of losing its established half-century history of autonomy and editorial freedom.

The war started for the *Daily Tar Heel* not with a bang, but with barely a whimper. In an unfortunate case of bad timing, the Japanese attack on Pearl Harbor on December 7, 1941, came too late to make the Sunday edition, and in that era the paper did not publish on Mondays. By the time the next edition appeared on Tuesday, the attack was old news. Even in the pre-digital information age, radio and big-city papers broke the story as soon as it happened. In a front-page story to mark the anniversary of Pearl Harbor in 1947, a *DTH* writer quipped that six years earlier the editors had been "caught with their columns down." To the paper's credit, however, the staff had been following events leading up to Pearl Harbor closely, and for two weeks preceding the attack articles and editorials appeared that made it abundantly clear that U.S. involvement in the war was imminent.[1]

The University of North Carolina was destined to play a significant role in the war effort, both by supplying so many of its young men to fight

Navy Pre-Flight training cadets in Lenoir Hall, 1942. (NCC)

and serve in the various European and Pacific theaters, and because of consolidated university president Frank Porter Graham's close relationship with the administration of President Franklin Roosevelt. Graham's ties to Washington led to two major war-related activities: his appointment to the National War Labor Board (NWLB), and the placement on campus of the Navy Pre-Flight Training School, one of only four in the nation.

In January 1942, the *Daily Tar Heel* reported that "University President Frank Porter Graham, already a key figure in the nation's war program and chieftain of the South's liberal educators, was named yesterday by President Roosevelt to a post on the all-powerful National War Labor Board (NWLB) as the public's representative." The board, first established during World War I and recommissioned by Roosevelt, consisted of twelve members representing labor and business who were charged with establishing policy and settling labor disputes so that work stoppages and strikes did not occur during the war. For the next three-and-a-half years, Graham commuted between Chapel Hill and Washington, dividing his time between the university and the NWLB. Some of the board's work became controversial, including ending distinctions between black and white workers in federal labor policy, an initiative championed by Graham.[2]

In the spring of 1944, the *Daily Tar Heel* became involved in a dispute between Graham and the UNC board of trustees over his service on the NWLB. On May 30 the paper ran an article under the headline "Trustees Demand That Dr. Graham Devote Full-Time To Post of University President." Accompanying the article was a three-column picture of Dr. Frank in shirt-sleeves pitching a horseshoe with a caption that read, "Today he is in there pitching for freedom, democracy, and progress." Editor Horace Carter—who would go on to serve in the navy and later win a Pulitzer Prize as publisher of the *Tabor City News* for a series of articles on the Ku Klux Klan—was highly suspicious of the motives of certain trustees, given that Graham had been successfully doing both jobs for two years. In an editorial, Carter charged that Graham was "being forced into the squeeze play" by "a small group of ultra-conservatives [who] want to discredit him in Washington." Carter also suggested there were other reasons for this "showdown," including the concern among "certain members of the board of trustees whose business interests may suffer as a result of Dr. Graham's continued service on the War Labor Board," as well as "a group right here in the University that would like to oust him and fill his President's chair with someone more conservative or to be more exact, more reactionary."[3]

Within hours of the editorial's appearance,

Carter later recalled, state senator John Umstead telephoned him and demanded that they meet at the Journalism Department right away. Before Umstead arrived, Oscar Coffin, former *Tar Heel* editor and then member of the journalism faculty, met with Carter and told him to stand his ground. "I don't give a damn what [Umstead says], but don't you back down one bit from what you wrote," Coffin instructed him. Carter credited Coffin not only with giving him the resolve to stand firm that day, but also with inspiring him "to be a newspaper crusader."[4]

At the same time the story broke, Carter and Sara Yokely, the *Daily Tar Heel*'s managing editor, sent a letter to President Roosevelt outlining their concerns about the motivations of some trustees. Roosevelt, to everyone's surprise, replied with a thoughtful letter that the paper speculated was "probably ... written from his personal typewriter." The letter—a photograph of which ran at the top of the paper's front page so large that it pushed the banner to the right-hand side—strongly supported Graham and praised him for his service. In the fatherly and somewhat patrician tone for which Roosevelt was famous, he wrote that he was "not surprised that they [the trustees] want his full energies and full time. But knowing North Carolinians, I am sure they rejoice in the knowledge that the University's sacrifice ... is an important part of the University's contribution to the successful conduct of the war." "I have known the University of North Carolina as one of our great institutions," Roosevelt continued, "which recognizes its responsibility for service not merely to its campus but to the commonweal." Roosevelt's carefully worded letter—dated June 16, 1944, just ten days after D-day—made it abundantly clear that he felt

June 16, 1944, letter from President Franklin D. Roosevelt to *Tar Heel* editor Horace Carter and managing editor Sara Yokely. This photograph of the letter, written just ten days after D-Day, ran twice in the paper (1944 and 1945).

THE WHITE HOUSE
WASHINGTON

June 16, 1944

Mr. W. Horace Carter, Editor
The Tar Heel
University of North Carolina
Chapel Hill, North Carolina

Dear Mr. Carter:

It was good of you and Miss Yokley to write me about the feeling expressed by some North Carolinians that Dr. Frank Graham should devote his full time to the presidency of the University of North Carolina. Knowing Frank Graham as I do, I am not surprised that they want his full energies and full time. But knowing North Carolinians, I am sure they rejoice in the knowledge that the University's sacrifice in sharing Dr. Graham's services with their country is an important part of the University's contribution to the successful conduct of the war. Other colleges, corporations and institutions are lending the nation their best officials and officers. The nation is grateful for their services, but I believe that in serving America, they also best serve the companies and colleges whose free future depends upon our full victory.

I have known the University of North Carolina as one of our great institutions which recognizes its responsibility for service not merely to its campus but to the commonweal. I know I can count on the University of North Carolina and the Old North State to continue to let the nation share Frank Graham's wisdom and energies in the cause to which the State and the University have sent so many of their daughters and sons.

Very sincerely yours,

Franklin D. Roosevelt

any effort to pressure Graham to give up either post was unpatriotic. The president's letter, subsequently published in newspapers across the state, effectively ended the matter.[5]

The presence of the Navy Pre-Flight Training School, along with the V-12 Navy College Training Program and an expanded Reserve Officer's Training Corps, transformed the UNC campus into a quasi-military base. The Pre-Flight Training School, the largest of the programs, brought approximately 18,700 men to the campus over three years for basic training and some college courses deemed useful to their military education. Among those who spent time at UNC during the war were future presidents Gerald R. Ford and George H. W. Bush, future baseball Hall of Famer Ted Williams, and future football coach Paul "Bear" Bryant. When the announcement about establishment of the school was made in February 1942, a lead article in the *DTH* excitedly reported that Carolina would become the "Annapolis of the air" and would host the "greatest aviation program in naval history." The navy men took over a dozen dormitories and the newly constructed Lenoir Dining Hall for their mess; other facilities, including Woollen Gymnasium and Horace Williams Airport, were expanded for training; and new buildings were constructed, including Nash, Miller, and what is today Jackson Hall. With wartime efficiency, the transformation was swift. In April 1942 the campus had its first blackout, and the annual spring carnival dance featured a naval motif.[6]

The official military presence on campus helped keep the university operating at full strength during what otherwise would have been a period of low enrollment, as the number of regular students fell dramatically. The staff of the *Daily Tar Heel*, while patriotic, nervously eyed the increasing military operation in the first eighteen months of the war, concerned that the paper would be taken away from the students and become either a mouthpiece for the university administration or an official organ of the war effort. In early 1942 editor Orville Campbell wrote:

There have been recent rumors to the effect that South building [UNC administration] determines the editorial policy of the *Daily Tar Heel*. Such rumors are totally unfounded. We want it understood that the editorial policy of this paper is determined by the editor and members of the editorial board. No one in South building has ever told us what to cuss or discuss.... When the time comes that college journalism is not free from censorship, the newspaper profession is in a pretty bad state. No, students, South building does not, and will not determine the editorial policy of the *Daily Tar Heel*.[7]

A little more than a year later, as the future of the paper was being discussed in relation to the war effort, editor Bucky Harward wrote several alarmist columns about freedom of the press, the importance of the *Daily Tar Heel*'s history, and rumors of suspending the paper for the duration of the war. "The future of a free press at Carolina is hazy," Harward warned, "and it is quite possible that there will be no free publication to bring to light errors that it believes may be rectified." Despite Harward's concerns, the paper reported that the Publications Union Board, after "consideration of the staff shortage, of printing difficulties, and waning finances [voted to] to shear the *DTH* down to a weekly paper. There have been a lot of Utopian schemes floating around which would supposedly enable the *DTH* to continue throughout the duration as a daily, but they all were blown up when rubbed with the question of a dwindling staff and advertising .... What the future of a weekly campus newspaper as regards to its freedom will be can be known only after it has been published a few times on the military campus."[8]

On May 20, 1943, the *Daily Tar Heel* went into limited wartime production, first as a weekly and later a semi-weekly, and the titled reverted to the *Tar Heel* until daily publication resumed again on February 5, 1946. The reduction occurred

IT'S THE OTHER WAY AROUND in classes. The girls outnumber the boys, but you can bet your bottom dollar that none of above male figures will regret such an overflow of feminine pulchritude.

just a week after the paper won its first award from the College Press Association. "Never before during its fifty-year history was the *Daily Tar Heel* more valuable to Carolina than in this war year," the *Yack* reported in 1943. "For, with the establishment of the Pre-Flight School and the consequential decentralization of the student body, its services were a necessary and invaluable asset." To emphasize the paper's new role on campus, beginning in September 1944 billowing American flags appeared on either side of the banner, and the masthead proclaimed: "Serving Military and Civilian Students at UNC."[9]

Despite concerns about press autonomy during the war, the paper's staff in fact worked fairly closely with the navy. The only time any serious friction occurred was in the summer of 1942, when the *Daily Tar Heel* became involved in a story the government considered potentially detrimental to national security. Under a cloak of secrecy, the government had procured a hosiery mill in nearby Carrboro, closed in 1938 during the Depression, and converted it into a facility that produced high-powered mortar shells. An enterprising young *DTH* reporter, Walter Klein, began hearing rumors about possible sabotage at the plant, and after some investigation he wrote an article entitled "Worker's Dismissal Starts Spy Scare," which ran on the front page of the paper on July 14. After determining that the story about employee Roderick McLean was an example of rumors gone wild, Klein wrote the article in a somewhat sarcastic tone. "Workers, whispering against signed statements of secrecy, are spreading the word today, 10 days after the episode, that a spy has been seized within the factory's machine shop where guards had broken into McLean's locker to find three thermite (incendiary) bombs, one time bomb and a pistol." Workers said McLean "didn't change his clothes regularly with the rest of the workers, and spoke with a foreign accent," which apparently aroused their suspicion. The actual cause for dismissal, Klein reported, was the discovery of five matches in McLean's locker—hardly the rumored "spy" arsenal but still a serious violation, as no incendiary devices of any type were allowed outside carefully controlled areas.[10]

The response from military authorities to the article was swift. Ensign K. W. Fairbrother, assigned to naval information on campus, called Roland Parker, dean of students, to express alarm about the story. "Don't your boys know we are fighting a war?" Fairbrother asked Parker. He went on to say that the "spy story" was "careless and unwise newspaper coverage" and that the reporter "flagrantly violated" a promise not to publish the story, which was "inaccurate and none of the *Tar Heel*'s business." In a rare instance of the university administration rebuking the paper, Parker wrote a long and pointed letter to summer editor Bob Hoke. "I believe that I am as anxious as you to preserve freedom of the press in our nation as a whole and Carolina in particular," Parker wrote, "but I realize very clearly that this freedom carries with it an arduous and grave responsibility, particularly in times of national and university emergency." In a final twist to the story, in August 1944 the cover of the plant was blown, literally. Apparently in an effort to save time, an employee who was not following safety precautions caused a violent explosion killing himself and extensively damaging the plant. The blast was heard as far away as Durham.[11]

The navy's appeals were heeded, and what were deemed important stories for the remainder of the war were cleared through the information office before being published. In an August 1945 special edition of the *Tar Heel* that gave an overview of the war and the paper's role in the effort, an article noted that "after an unfortunate incident early in 1942 relations with the Pre-Flight were amicable." The story on the munitions plant aside, the navy was pleased enough with the coverage and cooperation of the *Tar Heel* during the war that it awarded the paper a special commendation in 1947.[12]

Along with providing necessary war coverage, the paper took the opportunity on occasion to lighten the campus mood with humor. Student-drawn cartoons began to appear on a regular basis in the early 1940s, and one of the most talented and prolific cartoonists during the era was Al Kaufman, a naval ensign, whose subjects usually involved servicemen and attractive women. On April 1, 1942, the paper published its first April Fool's edition, aptly titled *The Daily Tar Heil*, a reference to the infamous "Heil Hitler" Nazi salute. Swastikas appeared on either side of the banner, and the masthead read "Official Newspaper of the Chapel Hill Gestapo," listing [Reich Minister of Propaganda] Joseph Goebbels as editor and Adolf Hitler as cartoonist. The issue was cleverly sarcastic, humorous but pointed about the dire consequences of a Nazi victory. One image showed Wilson Library, the university's elegant temple of knowledge and democracy, reduced to a bombed-out ruin and closed to students and faculty by order of the Gestapo.[13]

World War II caused predictable shortages on campus, not the least of which was a labor shortage as students enlisted and were drafted. The problem created an atmosphere of instability among the staff of the *Tar Heel*, with changes that were at times sudden and jarring: over a two-year period at the end of the war the paper was led by five different editors. From May 1943 until deployed by the navy in October, Walter Damtoft served in the position, a man the *Yack* described as a "staunch, conservative" editor who "steered the paper through safe, middle of the road channels." After Damtoft's departure a special fall election was held, and for the first time in the history of the paper a woman, Katherine "Kat" Hill, was elected editor in chief. Women had been part of the *Tar Heel* staff since the 1890s, but rarely in upper-level positions, and the transition shook up tradition. "The Editor's office changed from a pale white to a livid chartreuse," the *Yack* reported, and "headlines appeared on the editorial page." In addition to the unprecedented election of a female editor, "staff

changes were almost perpetual. Students came and left the University so suddenly that there was very little consistency in the names in the masthead." With Hill at the helm, "the *Tar Heel* began to lose its two-year policy of conservatism. It tended to become the more radical paper of two years back [when Don Bishop was editor]."[14]

Hill's successor, Horace Carter, was elected in the spring of 1944 but served only briefly before being called to active naval duty. The Publications Union Board decided to appoint a temporary replacement and to once again wait until the fall to hold an election for a new editor. Their choice for editor was another woman, Muriel Richter, who quickly became controversial because she made unconventional changes to the paper's operation. Managing editor John Thomas Kerr III, wrote a scathing, four-page letter to the Board in July 1944 outlining what he termed "blunders" and "aggressiveness of the editor," which he felt created a "precedent-shattering situation." According to Kerr, Richter went beyond the boundaries of the editor in chief and began trying to manage all aspects of the paper, for which she lacked adequate experience. Richter became "a complete dictator with the power of final judgment over everything that appears in the print of the *Tar Heel*," Kerr wrote. It is unclear how much of the complaining had to do with actual problems and lack of leadership by Richter, and how much was driven by male chauvinism, but her tenure was short, as Charles Wickenburg was elected to the position as soon as the fall semester began.[15]

In the spring of 1945, as the war wound down, the *Yack* noted that "the *Tar Heel* remained during this school year the only medium which bound together our perpetually emotional and

The Daily Tar Heil

—ALL GOOD GERMANS READ OUR GOOD NEWS—

VOLUME L | Business: 9887; Circulation: 9886 | CHAPEL HILL, N. C., WEDNESDAY, APRIL 1, 1942 | Editorial: 4356; News: 4351; Night: 6906 | NUMBER 131

Superior German Forces Crush Chapel Hill; Blitzkrieg Army Assumes Complete Control

Enemy Force Holds Out In Battle Park

Wisebram Named Enemy Leader By Louis Harris

The latest communique from the temporary Army headquarters at 101 [illegible] hall yesterday said that all but a small force of the enemy had been completely conquered by 10:30 last night. The remnants of the Carolina Volunteer Training Corps plus a few ill-equipped students continued to hold out in the forest about a half mile east of the campus.

Only sporadic firing was heard on this front, and it is computed that there can be no more than fifty or a hundred of the enemy still in action. Little has been seen of these remaining forces, and there can be no concentration of power, the communique stated.

Wisebram Leader

Reports gathered by our spies have been identified by Louis Harris, one of the few students to realize his obligation to society and cooperate with the German advance. Harris identified the leader of the marauding bands as Henry Wisebram, former CVTC tyrant, tool of the Jewish imperialists.

The ebb and flow of staccato gunfire on the fringe of the German entrenchments indicates guerilla warfare is the main plan of the small enemy action. Army officials hinted, however, that there may still be heavy resistance and warned that treachery should be expected.

German agents have intercepted a printed sheet by which the small unity of the enemy keep in contact, distribute orders, and encourage one another. Former Daily Tar Heel editor Orville Campbell is managing the journal. Agents reported that certain

See ENEMY FORCES, page 4

Superior Diet To Be Maintained For Duration

General Rudolf von Terpitz, supreme commander of the German food administration, prescribed the new diet that all residents will be forced to maintain for the duration of the National Socialist domination of the territory. Von Terpitz said that all violators would be dealt with severely with the maximum a complete denial of all food rationing cards, which is in effect complete starvation.

Sauerkraut and pig knuckles will replace the staple articles in the present diet and only ersatz pigs will be used to supply the meat for this, all other pigs remaining at the front with the German armies. Paperhanger

See SUPERIOR DIET, page 3

Plan to Continue Quad Renovations

Chief officer of the newly formed German Better Relations committee for Carolina students, Gofstunk von Heifnetz, announced today that Upper Quadrangle renovations would continue until the five buildings were "fit for use."

Following their completion they will be given back to the dispossessed students since the Naval Cadets would "not be coming this May."

Plumbing conditions will be improved as originally planned but students will have swastika wallpaper and ceilings in order to harmonize with the present German color scheme.

Heifnetz stated that "the High Command" would demand one favor from the students in return for use of their dormitory rooms. Students will be requested to sleep chained to their beds so that coeds will not be molested. Under the new ruling, coeds will be allowed out until 4 o'clock every morning and will not need chaperons if they desire to visit men's buildings.

Chief contractor, Herr Dedblatz, reported that the dorms will be ready sometime in April.

HIS MOST HIGH EXALTED, Majestic, Unconquerable, Unexcelled, Courageous, Knight of the Garter, Keeper of the Keys, Guardian of the Sanctuary of the Millenium, Reichfuehrer and General Manager ADOLF HITLER, who yesterday conquered the hinterland stronghold of democratic mania, Chapel Hill.

ADMINISTRATION CENTER of the former ruthless democratic regime, picturesquely named South Building, shown after being struck and destroyed by high-powered German demolition bombs. Squadron after squadron of the Luftwaffe raided Chapel Hill during the battle yesterday.

Masaryk Mortally Shot By Loyal German Guard

Hero Kills Traitor To Benefit Society

By Strudel Gofildofisch

Jan Masaryk, stinking Czech street cleaner and insane Dodger fan, was shot to death last night as he began his IRC address in Memorial hall.

Identity of the assassin was not immediately established, but many spectators reported that they saw a heroic disciple of the New Order, who had been placed on guard outside the hall, walk on the stage, pull his pistol from his holster, moisten the sight, stick it in Masaryk's right ear, and pull the trigger, apparently sending the bullet through Masaryk's head and allegedly killing him.

Shapiro the Hero

Entire situation was cleared last night when the glorious Nazi guard,

See MASARYK, page 4

Bands Parade in Reich After Von Schol Says Americans Sign Peace

BERLIN, March 31—Revelry spread through the Reich tonight with the speed of a Balkan blitzkrieg with the announcement from third minister Gurments Von Schol that the invasion of Chapel Hill was victoriously completed.

News of the peace pact signing was received by short wave radios in Berlin at 10:25 this afternoon and immediately announced to the thronging thousands who had been waiting for hours in the Wellemstrasse.

Bands struck up German victory marches while the joy intoxicated people danced and heiled until late in the

See BANDS PARADE, page 4

Courses Suspended at Once

The German High Command ordered today that all courses at the University be suspended immediately until new subjects have been substituted.

All degenerate language courses shall be abolished at once. Spanish, French, Latin, etc., are subjects fit only for people of low mentality and are not up to the high level of the Aryans that will attend the University. The teachers in these departments will be placed in protective custody.

The lying and exaggerating courses of History, Economics, and Political Science will be completely changed and the instructors also. History courses have been showing the growth of that decadent, race-destroying, corrupting thing called democracy. From now on, they wil concentrate upon such great periods as the Roman dictators, the period of reaction in Europe, and will center mainly upon the rise and growth of the greatest of world movements—National Socialism. Courses in the life of Der Fuehrer will also be given.

Both Political Science and Economics

See NEW COURSES, page 4

Kind Germany Aids Needy

Karl Suntheimer Recovers in Utah

Nazi Germany treats everybody, including the conquered millions in Europe and America, with great and extreme kindness by caring for the sick, the weak and the homeless. Even those who have spoken out against Germany are adequately cared for.

When Herr Karl Suntheimer muttered to a friend that Herr Reichfuehrer Adolph Hitler actually has wavy hair he was not seized and disposed of. Instead he was treated with the usual German kindness and tenderness.

Suntheimer Ill

Late last night it was discovered that Suntheimer was actually an extreme consumptive and that his exterior hides a very weak and fragile body. In trying to help him regain his health he has been sent to beautiful and restive recovery home for the ill in Utah. While there he will render his assistance in the salt mines.

Herr Ferebee Taylor, former Phi Beta Kappa student, was examined at 2 o'clock yesterday morning by Germany's very capable physician, Doktor Heinrick von Schnepps, and found to be mentally deficient. This mental collapse, suspected for some time by the German High Command, was revealed by Taylor when he expressed praise for democracy. He will be sent to our newly constructed air-conditioned, sun filtered home for the unbalanced shortly after the first shipment of super-strength barbed wire arrives from Germany.

The able head of the University

See KIND, page 4

Harris, Former Student, Joins Reich Management

The last stronghold of decadent America has fallen.

Early yesterday afternoon triumphant troops of the Third Reich followed their Glorious Fuehrer magnificently down the battered main street of this small village.

Thousands of splendid men of the New Order, fresh from victories over weak enemy resistance 12 miles to the north, stormed their way up this precipitous hill and poured in to take possession in the name of Germany and the Leader.

In Victory Exercises in the renamed Reichstag Stadium this morning, Der Fuehrer will officially designate Louis Harris as Commandant of this area.

Harris, who for the past four years has acted in the capacity of secret agent for the Gestapo and head organizer of internal dissension, has been termed the Quisling of Chapel Hill. Active duties for this personification of the New Youth and his assistant, Hunt Hobbs, begin tomorrow.

The Third Reich, according to its principles of freedom, will conduct a plebescite tomorrow morning between the hours of 6 o'clock and 6:01. Ballots will be printed in the classic tongue of German. Only pure Aryans will vote. A "yes" vote denotes the citizen's approval of rule by the conquerors. "YA" MEANS YES IN GERMAN.

Vastly superior German forces swung the tide of the battle. Thousands of weakling America troops were massacred in a fashion which they richly deserved. 6,939 enemy airplanes were destroyed before they left the ground. On different sectors of the Eastern Front the enemy broke after his unsuccessful attacks.

General Field Marshal Walther von Brauchitsch had yesterday completed the western engagements by capturing Winnemucca, Nevada, lead mine sector, after brief raids.

Our colleagues in the Far East, the Little Yuseful Braves, completed destruction of Bolshevist troops centered in the tropic hinterlands of Murmansk.

Most glorious announcement of the

See HARRIS, page 4

Americans Submit Women To Torture

Flabberlipz Tells Horrors To His Regiment

"Americans have committed more outrageous atrocities in this war than any other nation," charged Yard Marshal Herring von Flabberlipz in a victory address to the outstanding 72nd regiment after the successful conquest of the enemy stronghold, Chapel Hill, yesterday afternoon.

Speaking from a second story window of No. 1 Dormitory to the throngs of cheering soldiers in the quadrangle, Marshal von Flabberlipz easily demonstrated that the gallant German soldiers had successfully pursued their moral obligations to world society by cleaning out this last remaining, henious nest of democrats.

"The constant atrocities committed by these American dogs were a menace to the world," he said. "It is common knowledge that none of their womenkind could consider themselves safe before our merciful conquest. There, across the street, you see the grounds laid out for the scene of these atrocities by the authorities of the community," the Marshal further stated.

Mangled Feet

"Ample evidence has been found that the lower classes were forced to walk on dirt paths, filled with atrocious pebbles and other debris. Manuscripts reveal that at least one unfortunate individual was compelled to live in utter squalor, and that despite his constant complaint, the authorities refused to remove the pile of sand and debris outside his window," Marshal von Flabberlipz said.

The Marshal further demonstrated that the women of the community were forced into a veritable concentration camp each night and were kept under bolt and key despite their wailings and outcries to the contrary. Groans of agony resounded constantly from the Lower Quadrangle, and "we can not but believe that torture was the general practice in these buildings," the Marshal charged.

"Reports that we have found," said the Marshal, "definitely indicate that the ruling few removed the only joy that many of these individuals found by taking away the large dance orchestras to which these people are addicted. When the poor, downtrodden people tried to obtain justice by stuffing the ballot box, severe penalties were inflicted on the innocent victims," the Marshal pointed out.

"Who can doubt," Marshal von Flabberlipz concluded, "that we of the noble and exalted German race have preserved the dignity of mankind for our deeds of valor and brav-

See AMERICANS, page 4

Confederate Soldier Pays Fuehrer Homage

Symbolic of the mighty dignity and all-powerful masterfulness of our valorous Fuehrer, was the tribute paid him yesterday on his arrival on the Kapelle Huegel campus after a victorious entry into this, the latest conquest in the Fuehrer's march to dominance.

Leading his faithful troops after their valiant battle with the democrat dogs here on the outskirts of Chapel Hill, the Fuehrer rode from the main street into the campus proper.

As he passed before a bronze statue of a Confederate soldier, the statue expressed its thanks with a humble salute from its musket.

This seemingly supernatural feat gratified the Fuehrer immensely. He stopped for a moment before the statue and remarked that "even the inanimate recognizes the superior strength and virility of the German race."

Verboten

The following are VERBOTEN:

1. **To be in the Arboretum after 6 o'clock at night.**
2. **To drink anything in Harry's but Schnaps.**
3. **To leave the boundaries of Kapelle Huegel.**
4. **To read Hegel, Bosanquet, and Nie- propaganda speeches and German music.**
5. **To play or listen to "swing" music or to read any books against National Socialist doctrines.**

The following are COMPULSORY:

1. **To say "Heil Hitler" when greeting anyone.**
2. **To grow a small mustache.**
3. **To listen to Wagner, Brahms, and not Irving Berlin.**
4. **To read Heel, Bosanquet, and Nietzsche.**
5. **To click heels three times before getting up and going to bed, and before sitting or rising.**
6. **To look at Der Fuehrer's picture two hours before going to bed.**

By order of the German High Command,

(signed) Field Marshal von Uebelriechend.

April Fool's edition of the *Daily Tar Heel*, 1942, mocking the outcome of the war if the Germans won and took over UNC.

Katherine "Kat" Hill, first female editor of the *Daily Tar Heel*, 1943. *(Yack)*

changing campus. Three editors, one seaman, one female, and one marine [Carter, Richter, Wickenberg], guided the news sheet through regimes." Even with the changes in editor the paper won a first-class excellence award from the Collegiate Press Association, and it "began the new year with new blood and hope for an eventual return to a daily and just place in the student's appreciation and conception of U.N.C.'s liberalism for which [students and alumni] fought and frequently died."[16]

THE POSTWAR "HAUSER GENERATION"

The jubilation that accompanied the end of World War II was soon replaced at Carolina with the reality of postwar readjustment. The most pressing issue was the sudden and dramatic spike in enrollment of veterans, who had been given the opportunity to attend college by the federal GI Bill. Overall matriculation more than tripled in three years: it skyrocketed from 2,480 in 1945 (it had been as low as 1,788 in 1943) to 6,802 in 1946, and peaked at 7,603 in the fall of 1948. Older, tempered by war, and often married with young families, the veterans were generally more serious-minded than typical college students. They were also more physically separated from central campus than traditional students. Instead of living in dormitories, many of the former servicemen and their families moved into a group of prefabricated military apartments at the edge of campus, which was quickly dubbed "Victory Village."[17]

The *Daily Tar Heel* also went through an extended period of postwar readjustment. Converted to a semiweekly tabloid format in 1943, the paper again became a full-fledged daily in 1946, and reassumed its role on campus by boasting that it provided an "accurate, unbiased account of the Carolina passing parade. The *DTH* is the most cohesive unit on the campus, and plays a vital role in uniting the student body and cementing relations between the students and the University." There were also technical improvements as war production converted back to a civilian economy. The paper added United Press International wire service in 1946, and in 1947 former editors Orville Campbell and Horace Carter began printing the *Daily Tar Heel* at their new $30,000 Colonial Press plant—about three times the cost of an average new house at the time—which featured a duplex press capable of printing, folding, and counting an eight-page, eight-column newspaper at the rate of 3,500 copies per hour.[18]

As the university and the *Daily Tar Heel* struggled to regain normalcy amid the challenges of the postwar period, two factors emerged that were to affect the paper for much of the following decade. The first was the rise in importance of campus political parties. Though parties first appeared at UNC in the 1920s and 1930s, they weren't well organized or particularly influential in campus affairs. After the war, however, the Student and University parties quickly became players in student politics, including endorsements for campus elections—chiefly student-body president and editor in chief of the *Daily Tar Heel*. Soon an annual ritual developed where candidates for editorship of the paper appeared before each party's membership and made a plea for its support. To a fairly significant extent, the seeking of party endorsements changed the nature of the campaign for editor during the late 1940s, as it became as much a popularity contest as a considered election based on who was best qualified to run the paper. The staff of the *DTH*, alarmed by the new power of the parties to influence the process and concerned about poorly qualified candidates becoming editor, pushed in print for an end to student election for the position, favoring instead selection by the Publications Union Board. Managing editor Earl Heffner, just before leaving to begin a career with the *Charlotte Observer*, summed up the concerns: "So long as the *Daily Tar Heel* must remain the choicest morsel of the spoils system, the newspaper cannot be a free publication to inform and represent the student body." Despite attempts by *DTH* staff to change the process, the selection of editor by student body election continued for nearly half a century, though the influence of the campus parties waned by the mid-1960s.[19]

The second factor that would profoundly affect the *Daily Tar Heel* during the postwar decade was the appearance of Charles "Chuck" Hauser on campus in 1946. From a family with deep connections to the university (his middle name was McCorkle, as in McCorkle Place), Hauser went on to work for United Press International and *Newsday*, though he is best remembered as longtime executive editor of the *Greensboro Daily News*. In 1946 a freshman Hauser wandered into the *DTH* office, and quickly established himself as a first-rate newspaperman, serving in various capacities including news editor, managing editor, and for a brief period in the fall of 1951, as interim editor in chief. Because of his unusually long tenure at Carolina—a decade overall with interruption for service in the Korean War—he helped facilitate a period of unprecedented institutional continuity and exerted extraordinary influence over the daily operation and style of the paper.[20]

In a 1948 year-end summation of the *Daily Tar Heel*, the *Yack* declared, "Chuck Hauser reigned supreme in the news room." In fact he mentored or assisted almost all of the editors from the late 1940s into the late 1950s, from Barron Mills (1947–48) to Fred Powledge (1956–57), including a generation of men who went on to highly successful careers in journalism: Roy Parker, Barry Farber, Rolfe Neill, Charles Kuralt, Ed Yoder, and Louis Kraar. Interestingly, it was typical for members of this "Hauser generation" to major in fields other than journalism at UNC. In a sentiment expressed by Rolfe Neill, but doubtless shared by many others, "I learned all I needed to know about journalism at the *DTH*." Neill, who served as editor in 1953–54 and went on to a distinguished journalistic career most notably as chairman and publisher of the *Charlotte Observer*, described Hauser as "a superb newspaperman . . . a very good make-up editor [with] a strong sense of news judgment." Ed Yoder, co-editor in 1955–56 and later Pulitzer Prize winning columnist for the *Washington Post* as well as a noted author, remembered that even in college Hauser was "already a very proficient and professional newspaper person." Yoder recalled that it was Hauser's daily ritual to "dissect every issue of the *Daily Tar Heel* with his red crayon and put the result up on the bulletin board in the *Tar Heel* office every afternoon so people could benefit from the critique." Hauser was one of a long line of *DTH* staff more devoted to the paper than to his academic studies, which partly explains his extended tenure on campus. According to Neill, there were semesters Hauser worked on the paper but, undetected by the administra-

Chuck Hauser, who worked on the *Daily Tar Heel* in various capacities from 1946 to the mid-1950s. During his career he served as managing editor of the *Greensboro Daily News* and held executive positions at papers in Virginia and Rhode Island. (*Yack*)

tion, was not actually enrolled. After thirty-one months of service in Korea—during which time he contributed a periodic column entitled "*Tar Heel* at Large" and kept close tabs on both the paper and his protégés—he did finally graduate in 1954, though he enrolled intermittently as a special student through the fall of 1957.[21]

Hauser was a dedicated newspaperman; he was not an ideologue, and he served under both conservative and liberal editors, who set the tone for the paper. Perhaps the most conservative of the postwar editors was Richard "Dick" Jenrette (1949–50), who went on to be a partner in a highly successful New York brokerage firm and a UNC trustee. "With 'Old Reliable' Chuck Hauser still on the Managing Editor's desk," the *Yack* re-ported in 1950, "the paper continued to have the old zing in its make-up." As for the editorial content that year, the *Yack* article went on to state, "Published in the little village that has a reputation of being the liberal center of the South, the paper gave to its readers an unbiased view of the happenings." Unbiased was clearly a matter of interpretation. Dick Jenrette's views were often aligned with those of more conservative alumni and state leaders, and he instituted a policy of turning over the lead column on Sundays to students involved in campus religious activities. One of the most frequent Sunday contributors was Mike McDaniel, who, following graduation, became a prominent evangelical Lutheran minister. McDaniel's fundamentalist editorials—with titles such as "The New Radicalism" (on the failure of materialism and humanism in American society), "Giving Christ a Chance," and "Christ Has Risen!"—quoted liberally from the Bible and urged students to accept Jesus as their savior, something not seen before or since on the pages of the *Daily Tar Heel*.[22]

Not everyone in the student body was enamored of Chuck Hauser's power over the *Daily Tar Heel*. He ran for editor in the spring of 1950, only to be defeated by an outsider, Graham Jones. For unexplained reasons Jones did not return to campus in the fall, and Hauser, Roy Parker, and Rolfe Neill (who was then a sophomore and Hauser protégé) formed the editorial leadership of the paper until a special election gave the position to Parker. Jones's departure from the university and Parker's subsequent election as editor returned Hauser to his place at the *DTH* for another year. But Hauser's dominance continued to rankle some students, and his tenure was again threatened in the spring of 1951. In a

raucous campaign for editor in chief, four candidates ran for office—two endorsed by the campus parties, and two independents. One of the independents was Glenn Harden, a female junior transfer student who had worked sporadically as a reporter for the paper since coming to UNC. Harden embodied the dissatisfaction in some quarters with Hauser, specifically among those who felt he had established a fiefdom and was singlehandedly deciding who would work on the paper and who would not. At first the *Daily Tar Heel* staff didn't take Harden's campaign too seriously. But as the election drew closer and her support grew, a front-page article and ensuing editorials appeared calling into question her platform, the main planks of which were creating an "open shop" at the paper and, because of Korean War shortages, changing the format from a full-sized sheet to tabloid size in an effort to cut costs and maintain a six-day publication schedule. Hauser, Neill, and others ridiculed Harden's proposals, stating that it was the Publications Union Board, not the editor of the *DTH*, which made decisions about the size and frequency of the paper.[23]

Harden's campaign struck a chord, and from the crowded field of four candidates she emerged victorious, becoming the first female editor elected in a regular election for a full term in the history of the *DTH*. Stunned and licking their wounds, Hauser and Neill published articles predicting gloom and doom for the venerable *Daily Tar Heel*, though in a reference to the political parties Hauser did grudgingly admit that Harden "taught the professional campus politicians never to underestimate the power of a woman." Harden was in fact able to save daily publication by converting to a tabloid format as soon as she took

office in May 1951 (a format that continued until September 1952), and she also tried to end the factionalism caused by the election by retaining some Hauser loyalists, including Rolfe Neill. And though Hauser did leave campus and begin his military service soon after the election, Harden's triumph did not, in the end, mark his demise. Few things are as mercurial as the mood on a college campus, and the old guard would return to power in 1952 with the election of Barry Farber as editor (Farber would later come to prominence as a nationally syndicated talk radio host).[24]

Perhaps best known of the editors from the Hauser generation—and that is an accomplishment, considering the group as a whole—is Charles Kuralt, who went on to a celebrated

career as a broadcast journalist, winning the hearts of millions of Americans as well as a raft of awards, including Peabodys, Emmys, and Grammys. Kuralt was born into a North Carolina family. His father, Wallace, class of 1931, was prominent in the field of social work in the state, and his mother was a strong woman with progressive ideals. Both were staunch supporters of the New Deal. One family friend described the elder Kuralts as having "a deep social service streak," and together they provided their children with a home sympathetic to the likes of Franklin Roosevelt and Frank Porter Graham. Not surprisingly, Kuralt's worldview by the time he arrived at UNC was already several paces left of center, and his strong political perspec-

tive could often be found cloaked in the otherwise breezy and jaunty style of his *Daily Tar Heel* editorials.[25]

At UNC, Kuralt was a student in the Department of Radio, Television, and Motion Pictures; like most of the editors of his generation, he did not major in journalism, though his field was somewhat closer than history (Neill), English (Yoder), or business (Jenrette). His first wife, Sory Bowers, whom he dated during his time as *DTH* editor, remembered that Kuralt was "utterly in love with being editor of the *Tar Heel*" and "thought it was so romantic to 'put the paper to bed.'" Also, like many devoted to the *Daily Tar Heel*, he was an indifferent student and left Chapel Hill a few credits short of a degree. "Graduation proceeded without me," Kuralt later wrote. "I didn't care. I had found my career."[26]

Along with his service on the *Daily Tar Heel*, Kuralt broadcast on WUNC Radio and performed with the Carolina Playmakers, developing what would become his trademark vocal style. His hero was pioneering broadcaster and fellow North Carolina native Edward R. Murrow, and at UNC Kuralt had records of Murrow's *Hear It Now* radio program that he would listen to and study. His *DTH* colleague Rolfe Neill aptly characterized Kuralt as being "very good friends with the English language," in both spoken and written form. Certainly his editorials prove the latter to be amply true, and in reading them one can hear the marvelous cadence and mellifluous quality of his voice, which came to be a national treasure. For example, on his last day as editor in April 1955, he penned a love letter to Carolina:

From one building set in the Piedmont wilderness, the University has become North Carolina's most precious belonging—philosopher, teacher, doctor, sociologist, historian to the state. It has grown great in the sight of the world—and not alone by serving North Carolina, but by leading, with a stubborn liberal vision.

It is that liberalism which many thoughtful people feel to be dimming in the University today; and if it is so, it is a tragic truth, because the freedom from orthodox tenets and narrow, established forms is the spring, the very source of the University's stream of greatness.[27]

Kuralt's ode to the *Daily Tar Heel* was no less poetic:

Last door on your right at the end of the hall [in Graham Memorial] and you're in the newsroom with the white light and the old, green bulletin boards. This is not the *New York Times*. But the good, gray *Times* couldn't be as big in the minds of its reporters as the *Daily Tar Heel* is to those who give it their best hours and ideas.

You'll have to pardon [a student's pride] in the paper. It's the same pride E. W. Myers had in 1895 and Tom Wolfe had in 1920 and a thousand students have had after them. Years ago, in the masthead it said, "Oldest College Daily in the South," and that's still true; but this newspaper can claim a higher subtitle, freest college daily in the country, with a great liberal past and present. "The strongest force for progress on the campus," one teacher called it. "The most intelligent, responsible paper in the state, in many ways," a state newspaper's editorial writer remarked . . .

As long as the University itself is free, there will remain the seven-column streamer, the bold-face box, the truth in eight-point type.[28]

"THE DAILY WITCH HUNT": THE COLD WAR AND REDS ON CAMPUS

Kuralt's paean to academic freedom and the liberal exercise of ideas, both at the university and on the pages of the student newspaper, came at a time when these bedrock American principles were being seriously challenged in the post–World War II United States. On November 12, 1949, a former student penned a letter to the editor of the *Daily Tar Heel* that began, "I have returned to Chapel Hill this quarter after an absence of some years to find that the liberal traditions of freedom of thought and expression which have been the honor and fame of the University of North Carolina have, to all intents and purposes, been relegated to the junk heap." "Why?" the writer asked rhetorically, before coming to the conclusion that "the only answer I can find is that hysteria is ruling instead of reason and common sense—anti Communist hysteria."[29]

As the history of the *Daily Tar Heel* shows, UNC had been accused of both harboring Socialists and Communists and corrupting young minds since the 1920s. Attacks from the university's conservative critics continued through the 1930s and up until the outbreak of World War II; in May 1940, David Clark announced an investigation of the "Red Menace" in Chapel Hill, and the paper printed a large picture of him with an article on the front page. But as Americans were increasingly gripped by fear (real or imagined) as a result of the escalating Cold War, redbaiting reached new heights both nationally and on campus. At UNC the issue had always been something of a "red herring," to turn a phrase, as the number of actual card-carrying Communists at the university (students or faculty) was so small that they could comfortably hold meetings in a guest room at the Carolina Inn. President Graham estimated in 1941 that there might be six card-carrying students on campus, and the *Daily Tar Heel* speculated that there were perhaps twelve members among a student body of 7,500 in the late 1940s. More important, there was likely never any danger that even that handful of individuals had any real connections to Moscow or were plotting overthrow of the United States government. But the allegations proved an effective weapon for the university's critics, and specific accusations and incidents were treated seriously by the administration and trustees, resulting in actions that ranged from measured to near paranoid.[30]

The student newspaper played a significant role in the ongoing drama over potential subversives on campus from the fall of 1947, when the hysteria began in earnest at UNC, through the McCarthy era and up to 1959, when one of the onerous faculty loyalty oaths instituted a decade earlier by the administration was abolished. The *Daily Tar Heel* reported the relevant newsworthy stories, editorialized, provided a public forum on the subject for those on both sides of the issue in the university community, and even occasionally poked fun at it—something the paper's staff wouldn't do with the other major issue of the day, racial desegregation.

As the Cold War intensified in the late 1940s, the issue of communist infiltration at UNC coalesced around four people: a graduate student, a teaching assistant, an invited speaker, and even

a columnist on the *Daily Tar Heel*. The first was student Junius Scales, who enrolled at the university in 1936. Born into a wealthy and well-connected Greensboro family, his great-uncle had been governor of North Carolina and his father was a prominent judge. Scales, who rejected the traditional mainstream political values of his family, led the statewide antiwar efforts for the American Student Union (though he did serve in World War II), and secretly joined the Communist Party in 1939. After the war he returned to UNC as a graduate student in history, and on October 30, 1947, he issued a public statement not only proclaiming that he was a party member, but with the explosive news that in fact a campus branch of the Communist Party had existed at the University of North Carolina since the 1930s. In an exclusive interview with the *Daily Tar Heel* the day the statement was issued, Scales said he was coming forward publicly "in the hope that I may in a small way dispel some of the dangerous illusions and falsehoods about the Communists which are being used to distract us from the real problems which we must solve: a decent standard for all of the people, a peaceful world, a more democratic America without race discrimination." In a reference to the new atomic bomb, editor Barron Mills declared, "Junius Scales, by this formal announcement that he had a small band of Communists here on campus, delivered to the enemies of the University of North Carolina enough uranium to blast UNC for years to come." Only two hours after receiving Scales's statement, Mills noted, "newspapermen from all over the state had already swarmed Chapel Hill, including representatives from the wire bureaus." Editorial board member Roland Giduz tried to quiet the hysteria; in a column en-

Un-American Activities Committee. The *Daily Tar Heel* urged caution. Earl Heffner, a member of the news staff, wrote a column entitled "'Cold War' on Communists," agreeing with the first resolution but strongly opposing the second. Establishing an investigative committee, he wrote, "contains a dangerous potential," and he outlined a scenario that could easily develop:

> Immature, power-drunk, overly zealous students could grasp at isolated facets, could interpret falsely some liberal philosophies and attack the progressive thought on campus. Unskilled and unsympathetic with liberals, a conservative body could slash at the American heritage. The "send the nigger to the back door and keep the damn Yankees in the North" theorists on campus have proposed the creation of the anti-Communist committee ... [which potentially] would use the Red smear brush on others with a more liberal philosophy than their own.[32]

Ultimately the drama of Junius Scales—who was to have the dubious distinction of being the only American imprisoned under the 1940 Smith Act, which made it a criminal offense to advocate overthrow of the federal government—played out on the national stage over some fifteen years. Each time he resurfaced, the university's conservative critics pointed to him as a prime example of what could happen to the brightest of North Carolina's impressionable youth when they came to Chapel Hill and were exposed to the seditious environment festering at the university (though Scales's introduction to communist and socialist philosophy came as much, if not more, from the off-campus culture that centered around the

titled "Scales Does Not Bite," Giduz wrote: "Honest fellas, Junius Scales and his dozen-odd compatriots aren't worth all this fuss.... Nearly 7,528 of us are likely at complete political odds with him."[31]

The Student Legislature reacted immediately to the Scales bombshell by introducing two bills: the first, a resolution condemning Communism; and the second, legislation to create a committee to investigate potential subversion on campus, along the lines of the Congressional House

Intimate Bookshop). As sensational as the Scales story was, it was eclipsed a year and a half later by another that turned the national spotlight on UNC and further intensified the bonfire heating up university critics.[33]

In the fall of 1948, twenty-two-year-old Hans Freistadt entered the university as a graduate student, pursuing a PhD in physics. Small-framed and bespectacled, Freistadt had overcome great obstacles in his young life. Born in Austria in 1926, Freistadt was Jewish and the son of a liberal newspaperman. Prime targets of the Nazis by the mid-1930s, the family fled to France, where Freistadt's mother was killed in wartime bombing. His father took the teenage Hans and his sister to Mexico, and from there Hans entered the United States via an organization established to help European refugee children. Admitted to the University of Chicago, Freistadt excelled in physics, earned a bachelor's and master's degree, and became a naturalized citizen. He came to UNC financed by a $1,600 teaching fellowship—a large sum of money at the time—awarded by the National Research Council on behalf of the federal Atomic Energy Commission.[34]

At the University of Chicago, Freistadt had been involved with the campus Communist club. He continued his political activities at UNC, rooming at one point with Junius Scales. Freistadt's major activity was the writing of letters to the editor of the *Daily Tar Heel*, commenting on all manner of social and political issues, clearly espousing his leftist ideology—so much so that the paper's editor, Dick Jenrette, commented in the spring of 1949 that "readers of this page are thoroughly familiar with Freistadt's philosophy, for the [Austrian] native is the most prolific 'Let-

ters to the Editor' writer at Carolina." On May 10, 1949, conservative radio commentator Fulton Lewis Jr. whipped up hysteria by announcing on his national program that Freistadt, an avowed Communist and non-native citizen, was attending UNC on a large Atomic Energy Commission fellowship, implying that he might have access at some point to classified nuclear secrets that could be passed along to the Soviet Union.[35]

Although the possibility of Freistadt having access to sensitive atomic information as a graduate student was virtually nonexistent, the fact that he had received a previously unpublicized government scholarship while actively promoting his controversial political views was the Cold War equivalent of being marked with a scarlet "A." Following the Lewis broadcast, Jenrette banged out a furious lead editorial on his typewriter calling for the immediate rescinding of the fellowship. "The Commission certainly pulled a 'boner' in selecting Freistadt for the award," Jenrette wrote, lamenting the fact that so many worthy native young men were turned down for similar scholarships. "He has all the earmarks of a Communist.... [He] sits back in Chapel Hill, pen in hand, writing out his Communist beliefs for publication in the paper, utilizing to the fullest extent Carolina's liberalism." Jenrette continued:

> It is one thing for Mr. Freistadt to go to school and criticize our government while paying his own expenses. It is a horse of a different color for him to accept a scholarship from the U.S. and then turn on the hand that helps him. ... And the really great sufferer in the whole affair is the University of North Carolina. Through rumor and exaggeration the word

has gotten out that this institution is a hotbed of Communism. Nothing could be farther from the truth. Ninety-nine and a fraction per cent of the students have no interest in Communism whatsoever.... He should be deprived of his scholarship immediately, for the sake of the good name of the University of North Carolina, the taxpayer's money, and the welfare of the nation.[36]

The next day—Friday the 13th—the *Daily Tar Heel* ran the banner headline: "Freistadt Causes Furor in Washington." North Carolina senator and former governor Clyde Hoey condemned the scholarship, and other members of Congress issued similar statements. Freistadt, finding himself in the middle of a national firestorm, wrote a long letter to the editor pointing out errors and falsehoods in Jenrette's column. "By suggesting that academic awards be given on the basis of political orthodoxy rather than on the basis of scholarship, you are engaging precisely in the operation of mixing science with politics of which Communists have been accused," Freistadt wrote. "I submit that your vilifying and inflammatory editorial, filled with half-truths, exaggerations, and outright falsehoods, is a low of journalistic ethics." The following day Jenrette joked that Freistadt's "press clippings must already be the equal of those of [football star] Charlie Justice." He added: "The offices of the *Daily Tar Heel* have been besieged with visitors either demanding that Freistadt be deprived of his fellowship, defending him, or praising the paper's editorial stand on the issue." One letter compared the paper's editorial tone to that of the conservative Hearst newspaper syndicate, calling Jenrette "reactionary" and possessing "politi-

HANS FREISTADT, LOCAL GRADUATE STUDENT, is shown above sitting on the Old Well, familiar campus landmark, reading news reports concerning the awarding of an Atomic Energy Commission fellowship to him, a professed Communist Party member. Freistadt has claimed that despite his Communist affiliations, he is a loyal American and would "defend the United States against any aggressor."

cal immaturity," concluding that "we be more careful next year in our election of *Tar Heel* editors—let's have people who can give us more politically mature editorials."[37]

All through the last two weeks of May 1949, the Freistadt case captured national attention and filled the pages of the *Daily Tar Heel*. Freistadt was brought in front of a congressional hearing, the Atomic Energy Commission rescinded his fellowship, and he appeared on

Meet the Press, one of the first television inter-view news programs. But despite the scrutiny, Freistadt did not halt his political activities. In the fall of 1949, he and Junius Scales, unhappy with the way they were being portrayed in the *Daily Tar Heel*, founded an off-campus news-paper, the *Communist Student Bulletin*, in which they claimed thirty-eight UNC students were members of the Communist Party.[38]

The notoriety of the case exerted intense pres-sure on the university and led to a low point for academic freedom at UNC. Though the board of trustees courageously voted unanimously not to institute a "witch hunt" for potential subver-sives at state campuses in the spring of 1949, they passed the buck to the administration of each school to handle specific situations. UNC Chancellor Robert House did so by firing Frei-stadt as a teaching assistant, and, more signifi-cantly, instituting a policy that all faculty must sign two oaths, one proclaiming loyalty to the United States government and the other affirm-ing that he or she was not a member of the Com-munist Party. Only two faculty members dared to stand up in opposition to these proposed loy-alty oaths—one of whom was Charles Phillips Russell, a professor of journalism and former student editor of the *Daily Tar Heel*. In the fall of 1949, Russell also helped found the Committee on Freedom of Thought and Speech, with faculty from UNC, Duke, and Wake Forest, to address what was increasingly seen as a culture of fear and intimidation then descending on the state's college campuses. The threat was real; eventu-ally four faculty members lost their positions at UNC after refusing to sign one or the other of the oaths.[39]

In the pre-digital and largely pre-television world, print media was on the frontline of Cold War hysteria over Communist subversion in the United States. At UNC, between the Scales and Freistadt incidents, two controversies arose that raised broader questions about freedom of speech and the press, and both played out on the pages of the *Daily Tar Heel*. In January 1949, the Carolina Political Union invited John Gates, an American Communist Party leader and edi-tor of the party newspaper, the *Daily Worker*, to speak on campus. Hours before the speech was to be given, Chancellor House banned Gates from campus, citing both his federal indictment for violation of the 1940 Smith Act, and a North Carolina statute that barred anyone from using a public building who advocated overthrow of local, state, or federal government. The staff of the *Daily Tar Heel*, sensing a big story, took the opportunity to interview Gates in a room near the paper's offices in Graham Memorial, where he was sequestered after arriving on campus. Gates called the refusal to allow him to speak an "outrage," and editor Ed Joyner wrote a lead edi-torial criticizing the administration's handling of the situation. Calling the *Daily Worker* "an insig-nificant little propaganda sheet," Joyner noted that Gates had made a long trip to Chapel Hill in order to make a speech "in which he would have said precisely nothing that he and others who think as he does have not been saying for lo these many moons." Joyner predicted Gates would have drawn a large crowd, all of whom—except about a dozen of the party faithful—would have been hostile to his message. Joyner labeled the incident an embarrassment, as "all over the world people can be informed that in America, in the great democracy itself, in the bosom of a great center of learning, it was im-

John Gates, editor of the *Daily Worker*, the newspaper of the American Communist Party, addressing an estimated crowd of 1,000 on Franklin Street after being denied access to speak in Memorial Hall, January 1946.

JOHN GATES, EDITOR OF THE DAILY WORKER. Communist newspaper is shown at the extreme left as he addressed a crowd of approximately 1,000 students and townspeople on the Texaco service station corner of Franklin and Columbia streets Wednesday evening. Gates was forced to move his speaking rostrum to West Franklin street in front of the high school a few minutes after this picture was made by Staff Photographer Jim Mills. Gates was prohibited from speaking in Memorial hall, where his address had been scheduled, by Chancellor Robert B. House, acting on an interpretation of a state statute.

possible to assemble peaceably in a public hall to hear a statement of political creed."[40]

What resulted following the paper's interview of Gates was a highly charged scene remarkably similar to the better-known "stone wall" appearances of Frank Wilkinson and Herbert Aptheker seventeen years later at UNC, during the height of the struggle over the infamous Speaker Ban Law (see chapter 4). The next day, under a banner headline "John Gates Denied University Building," the paper reported that approximately fifteen minutes before the speech was scheduled to begin, several hundred students gathered outside the locked doors of Memorial Hall, where a policeman informed them that Gates would not appear. The crowd saw Gates a few hundred feet away and followed him to Franklin Street, where he attempted to speak at a gas station. When an attendant ran him off the property, the crowd followed him down West Franklin Street to a spot in front of Chapel Hill High School, where he gave his speech to the estimated audience of 1,000 that had gathered. "Our proud heritage of hearing all viewpoints and welcoming all ideas in the market place of free competition is badly shaken today," Joyner editorialized. "Our [public] appropriation may be more secure, but our freedom has need of buttressing."[41]

Unfortunately, Ed Joyner did not practice what he preached. In a stunning irony apparently lost on the paper's staff at the time, next to the January 13 front-page article on the John Gates incident was another noting that the Phi Assembly (one of the two campus debating societies) had voted to support Joyner's decision to dismiss columnist Bill Robertson, an avowed Communist, from the staff of the *Daily Tar Heel*. The Robertson story, which had played out over the

course of the previous fall, was perhaps more of a "low of journalistic ethics" than the handling of the Hans Freistadt controversy would be six months later. Joyner had hired Robertson to write a weekly column expressing his political perspective as a Communist, and Robertson did not disappoint. In the fall of 1948 he wrote a series of increasingly incendiary columns, including one entitled "Christ Was a Communist," and another, "Liberation of the Negro." Letters of complaint poured into the paper, but Joyner staunchly defended his decision to publish the columns: "as long as students write letters like this, he will be serving the purpose for which the *Daily Tar Heel* prints him. Robertson writing for Communism is the best argument we know for Democracy." At the end of November, however, Robertson went too far. It was not his blasphemous characterization of Christ, or his support of racial integration and civil rights that led to his

dismissal. The column that got him fired was entitled "Put Away Stars and Bars," calling for abolishment of the Confederate battle flag at UNC
football games, where thousands of small versions were waved by spectators in support of the
team. "The Confederate flag is the banner of a
government which defended the barbarous institution of slavery," Robertson wrote. "This government engaged in armed rebellion against the
fundamental principles of American democracy;
and for this reason, there is no difference between the Stars and Bars and the Nazi swastika."
Not surprisingly in the prosegregationist South
of the late 1940s, a furor ensued. Robertson was
called a "Kremlin stooge," and one student wrote,
"Mr. Editor, the Confederate flag symbolizes the
profundity and courageousness of conflicting
American thought in a turbulent era gone by. It's
a beautiful flag, an honorable one, and I'm proud
of it, suh!" In yet another irony of the story apparently lost at the time, on the day this letter
appeared, two articles ran in the paper about
African Americans who had refused to sit at the
back of segregated buses; one was about an incident in Chapel Hill, and another was about an
episode in Tennessee that ended in a shooting
wounding five people.[42]

Hans Freistadt rushed to Robertson's defense, which likely helped to seal his fate. "The
Civil War was not a football game, in which every
Southerner must cheer his team," Freistadt insisted, "it was a war fought over the issue of
slavery; in that war, there was a right side and
a wrong side." The debate over Robertson's dismissal was so intense that Joyner felt compelled
to write an editorial explaining the reasoning for
his action:

Seldom does the *Daily Tar Heel* consider it
necessary to explain the adding or dropping
of columnists from its pages, but to avoid any
misconception as to why Bill Robertson has
been discontinued we feel an explanation is
warranted. Columnists are free to write as
they please so long as their writings are not
libelous and are not offensive to good taste.
Robertson violated the journalistic precept
of good taste by using his column not for honest surveys into the merits of Communism
or "democratic socialism," ... but almost exclusively for the propounding of adjective-
colored Communistic propaganda.

Joyner continued with a curious statement with
which many former and future editors would
likely disagree: "As a newspaper, the *Daily Tar
Heel* is in an almost unique position. It does not
belong to its editor nor to the University. Because
of this, its editorial policy is to please as many
of the students as much of the time as possible."
He cited the "continuous barrage" of letters as
the reason for dismissal, and noted that Robertson was not being suppressed, as he could write
letters to the editor for publication whenever he
wished. Joyner's about-face on the matter, after
having defended Robertson so strongly in print
only a month earlier, may have been the result
of intense pressure from the administration and
alumni. An incredulous Robertson claimed that
it *was* his column on the Confederate flag that
caused his dismissal, but Joyner, perhaps half-
seriously, joked "it would be more accurate had
he blamed his dismissal upon the misspelling of
Charlie Justice's name in the same column."[43]

The anti-Communist hysteria of the post–

World War II era would acquire its well-known moniker—"McCarthyism"—from Wisconsin senator Joseph McCarthy, who came to attention in 1950 for his crusade to root out Communists in the government and wherever he could find them. Already seasoned by the unwanted attention and controversies surrounding Scales, Freistadt, Gates, and Robertson, the editors and staff of the *Daily Tar Heel* cast a wary eye on McCarthy's activities and accusations from the moment he stepped onto the national stage. On April 19, 1950, the paper ran an editorial that was highly critical of McCarthy and his methods, written by nationally syndicated columnist Drew Pearson. On May 13 what might be termed a late April Fool's issue was published, with the banner *The Daily Red Neck*, poking fun at both the current anti-communist mania and the university's location in the "country." Titled the "Pink Edition," the tabloid-sized special declared: "Our Policy: All the news that's left to print," a pun on the school's liberal reputation. A headline read "UNC Exposed: Carmichael Is a Red," taking a shot at then acting president William D. Carmichael (who, by UNC standards, was fairly conservative, and who was a vocal critic of Communism).[44]

Yet at the exact moment *The Daily Red Neck* issue appeared, the insidious effects of McCarthyism were seeping into North Carolina and onto the UNC campus, and it was no longer a laughing matter. That spring Frank Porter Graham, who had stepped down as president of the consolidated university in March 1949 following his appointment to the U.S. Senate (after the death of Senator J. Melville Broughton, who died only two months into his term), was embroiled in a heated primary campaign to retain his seat for the remainder of the unexpired term. Between 1900 and the late 1960s, North Carolina was a solidly Democratic state, and that party's primary was usually more significant than the general election, as Republicans rarely won statewide or congressional contests. Such was the case in 1950, and although Graham won a plurality in the special May election among a field of four candidates, he did not win a majority of the votes. As a result, another candidate, Raleigh attorney Willis Smith, challenged Graham to a runoff election scheduled four weeks later. What ensued is widely considered the dirtiest and most infamous political campaign in modern North Carolina history, as Smith's conservative supporters framed Graham as a Socialist (if not a Communist) and as being pro-integration and generally too friendly with the "Negroes." Vicious and incendiary posters and leaflets papered the state, in one of the last pre-television campaigns. One blared "White People Wake Up!," predicting the election of Graham would lead to blacks and whites sharing jobs, schools, even hospital beds and public toilets. Another showed a doctored photograph of Graham's wife dancing with an African American man, suggesting the ultimate act feared by die-hard white segregationists: miscegenation.[45]

The heavy mudslinging of this campaign not only covered Graham, but also splattered the university he had led for two decades. The *Daily Tar Heel*, as expected, fully supported Graham, but after a few editorials and articles accusing Smith's campaign of doing everything it could to defeat him, and calling the whole affair "dirty politics," the paper went oddly silent. The reason

WHITE PEOPLE
WAKE UP
BEFORE IT'S TOO LATE
YOU MAY NOT HAVE ANOTHER CHANCE
DO YOU WANT?

Negroes working beside you, your wife and daughters in your mills and factories?

Negroes eating beside you in all public eating places?

Negroes riding beside you, your wife and your daughters in buses, cabs and trains?

Negroes sleeping in the same hotels and rooming houses?

Negroes teaching and disciplining your children in school?

Negroes sitting with you and your family at all public meetings?

Negroes Going to white schools and white children going to Negro schools?

Negroes to occupy the same hospital rooms with you and your wife and daughters?

Negroes as your foremen and overseers in the mills?

Negroes using your toilet facilities?

> Northern political labor leaders have recently ordered that all doors be opened to Negroes on union property. This will lead to whites and Negroes working and living together in the South as they do in the North. Do you want that?

FRANK GRAHAM FAVORS MINGLING OF THE RACES

HE ADMITS THAT HE FAVORS MIXING NEGROES AND WHITES — HE SAYS SO IN THE REPORT HE SIGNED. (For Proof of This, Read Page 167, Civil Rights Report.)

DO YOU FAVOR THIS — WANT SOME MORE OF IT?
IF YOU DO, VOTE FOR FRANK GRAHAM

BUT IF YOU DON'T

VOTE FOR AND HELP ELECT

WILLIS SMITH for SENATOR
HE WILL UPHOLD THE TRADITIONS OF THE SOUTH

KNOW THE TRUTH COMMITTEE

for the silence was made clear by editor Graham Jones just days before the election—apparently there was concern that the paper's endorsement would hurt Graham. "Friends of Senator Frank Graham on campus have come to the office with suggestions that the *DTH* 'play-down' the present senatorial campaign," Jones wrote in a powerful editorial. "So for the past ten days the *DTH* has played-down the most news-worthy election to come out of North Carolina in fifty

years. The fact is that on Saturday the voters of this state will determine the wisdom of putting an honest man in the rather unsavory position of having to defend his innate Christianity against the vilest and most effective smear tactics ever used in North Carolina." Jones quoted a Republican as saying, "Frank Graham is the most Christlike man in the United States Senate," and fellow North Carolina senator Clyde Hoey stated flatly, "No more loyal American walks the face of the earth than Frank Graham." Jones outlined each of the charges against Graham: "They say he is a radical, a socialist, a communist ... They say [he] is too pro-labor ... They say Frank Graham is a 'nigger-lover,'" concluding in a mocking tone aimed at the accusers, "The Bible says that all men are brothers." Ultimately the attacks were effective; Graham lost the runoff election, though Willis Smith served only a short time, dying in office in 1953.[46]

Graham's appointment to the Senate in 1949 created a vacancy in the presidency of the consolidated UNC system, which then consisted of three campuses. Likely weary of the attacks on UNC's real or perceived liberalism over the preceding quarter century, and under the current cloud of McCarthyism, the board of trustees chose a new president who in many ways was the polar opposite of "Dr. Frank." Scion of a patrician Winston-Salem family—his father and brother were each in their day president of R.J. Reynolds Tobacco Company—Gordon Gray was a Carolina alumnus, class of 1930, and an attorney. Gray, it was felt, would communicate well with the state's more conservative leaders and business community. Unlike Graham, Gray was stiff and formal in public, and he was not a gifted speaker; Ed Yoder later recalled that in an attempt to break the

William D. "Billy" Carmichael Jr., vice president of the three-campus consolidated UNC system, 1940–1961 (left), and Gordon Gray, president of the consolidated system, 1950–1955 (right). (NCC)

ice at gatherings or when beginning speeches, Gray would often retell the same anecdote about former New York governor and 1928 presidential nominee, Al Smith. Yoder also recalled that when he and his coeditor, Louis Kraar, were summoned to Gray's office at the beginning of their tenure in 1955, the university president "spent most of his time [in a lawyerly fashion] trying to say what he was not saying, for fear of intimidating the editorial staff of the *Tar Heel*."[47]

One significant characteristic Gray did share with Graham, however, was his devotion to public service, particularly with regard to the federal government. Over the course of his long and distinguished career, Gray served every U.S. president from Franklin Roosevelt to Gerald Ford, working in a variety of positions, including at the Department of Defense. The *Daily Tar Heel* took great pains to welcome Gray in 1950, including publishing a special edition on the occasion of his inauguration. Despite his abilities in many public spheres, Gray was to prove an uncomfortable fit as president of the consolidated university during his relatively brief tenure. The paper's editorial staff quarreled with Gray on several important issues, notably regarding his role as chair of the three-person panel charged with evaluating the security clearance of the renowned nuclear physicist and so-called father of the atomic bomb, J. Robert Oppenheimer. In a case that once again linked UNC with the national debate about Communist infiltration, Oppenheimer was charged with befriending Communist Party members in the 1920s and 1930s (his wife had been a member), and his high-level security clearance allowing him access to classified United States nuclear secrets was challenged. Gray went to Washington to hold

the hearings in the spring of 1954, and the case captured national attention. *Daily Tar Heel* editor Rolfe Neill implored Gray in print to clear Oppenheimer, noting, "guilt by association ... is not yet the law of the land." In the end Gray did vote to rescind Oppenheimer's security clearance, an act Ed Yoder later characterized as both a "landmark event" that was "pivotal" in the national weariness over McCarthy-era witch hunts, and which contributed to the brevity of Gray's tenure as president of the consolidated university.[48]

The *Daily Tar Heel*'s stand on the Oppenheimer hearing was but one example of how the paper's editors, regardless of their personal political beliefs, kept up a steady drumbeat against McCarthyism during the first half of the 1950s. One of the earliest and most courageous stands was taken by the paper's only female editor in chief of the era, Glenn Harden. Alarmed by the chilling effect the dark mood, ongoing investigations, and in some instances administrative policies were having on intellectual freedom at the University, Harden penned a strong lead editorial in February 1952 entitled "Faculty for Freedom." In it she pointedly outlined the American Association of College Professors' stance on academics and political freedom. "The Association's ideal professor may or may not have political connections," Harden noted. "He may be a member of the Communist Party, the Republican Party, or a nudist camp. His sex life may be irregular. He may be of any color and any creed. These things are considered extraneous and unimportant to his ability as a teacher." At UNC this open policy was not followed, Harden charged, especially with regard to the "hidden loyalty oath." She continued:

> There have been other symptoms of fear. Professors who attempt to explain such educationally vital concepts as Communism, life and literature and history of countries politically or economically at variance with the United States, are actually afraid of their students. They apologize for the necessity of teaching the facts, and assure classes that they are not revolutionaries. Active political discussion is no longer encouraged in Political Science classes at UNC, and economics classes no longer hear students maintain that a particular system is the better. Unorthodox beliefs are actively discouraged by professors who

never know when some student may report that he is being tutored by a Communist. But unless individuals thrust away fear, express beliefs, and maintain stands on issues of freedom, that terror must consume us all. In our situation, the teacher must of necessity be the key individual in upholding freedom, though he shares the blame for the loss of freedom with students and administrators.[49]

Two days after her editorial appeared, Harden published a long and damning front-page expose about the damage the anti-Communist hysteria was causing to academic freedom at UNC, written by Richard "Dick" Murphy, a recent graduate who would go on to a distinguished career in the federal government, including serving as postmaster general under President John F. Kennedy. "Many of the events hashed over in the following letter have been hidden from the public eye," Harden wrote in an introduction, and "[for that reason] the ideas expressed are of such great significance to all agencies of the University and to the state, and indeed, to the nation, we are publishing this letter as a front page editorial, expressing the official policy of this newspaper." Murphy began with an eloquent statement about freedom and conformity:

> For the past few years I have viewed with the greatest alarm a creeping intellectual paralysis that has come to grip the American educational community. The paralysis finds its roots in fear and conformity generated by the nature of the cold war. In our efforts to combat the grave menace posed by the actions of Soviet Russia, we have allowed ourselves to become the prisoners of a doctrine of negativ-

ism, which has led us to repudiate the historic principles for which we claim to be fighting. Under the guise of anti-communism we have allowed professional patriots and opportunistic politicians to equate change with communism, and dissent with disloyalty. Paradoxically, this nation, which was once known because of its belief in freedom, as the country where a permanent peaceful revolution was continually taking place, to extend the benefits of the "good life" to more and more, has abandoned its historic role in favor of becoming a nation in which a premium is placed upon conformity and advocacy of the status quo.

With regard to academic freedom, Murphy wrote, "Our schools and colleges have manifested the most serious case of this illness—the very place where it can be least tolerated." Citing specific examples at UNC, Murphy listed the loyalty oaths that led to the firing of four members of the faculty, and the pressure exerted by a certain trustee on students who openly opposed segregation. Though this latter charge was serious and later to be proved true, UNC president Gordon Gray wryly noted that "the allegation that students are not allowed to speak on this campus is made by those who perhaps don't see the *Daily Tar Heel*."[50]

Harden's successor as editor, Barry Farber, whose political beliefs generally leaned more to the right, kept up the attacks on McCarthyism. In an editorial entitled "Stench, Smear, and McCarthy," Farber wrote, "the *Daily Tar Heel* feels that the actions of Sen. McCarthy present a clear and present threat to American democracy equal in potency to a Soviet invasion of Long Island." Farber charged that, not satisfied with simply exposing potentially political subversives, McCarthy had gone after "other citizens who may be sincerely desirous of improving unsavory conditions [but] are discouraged from expressing themselves for fear of being labeled a 'commie' ... [and being] indelibly stamped with the crimson curse for stating their unfeigned views." "All the perfumes of truth and sincerity," Farber concluded, "can never obliterate the stench of McCarthy smear." Along with publishing searing editorials, the paper supported and encouraged campus efforts to oppose McCarthyism. A "Joe Must Go" torch rally in May 1954, which followed a route from Fraternity Court to Emerson Field, was given extensive coverage. After the rally a front-page article reported that former president Frank Porter Graham had given a speech on campus declaring that McCarthy's power was on the wane and that "fear and hysteria are passing."[51]

On a less serious note, the paper hit a high watermark of parody and sarcasm when the 1954 April Fool's issue appeared, under the banner *The Daily Witch Hunt*. "McCarthy on Campus to Probe Subversives," the headline of the one-page sheet read, accompanied by a pair of large doctored photographs showing Senator McCarthy inspecting both ends of a horse with a magnifying glass—clearly implying that the crusading legislator was nothing more than a horse's ass. Killing two sacred cows with one editorial stone by also poking fun at recent controversy over big-time athletics at UNC, the subheadline read, "Big-Time Badminton Program Is Under Investigation." In addition, the farcical articles carried bylines of several of the noted editors and staff of the 1950s, all altering their last names with the addition of "Mc"—Rolfe McNeill, Louis McKraar,

1954 April Fool's edition of the *Daily Tar Heel*, poking fun at Sen. Joseph McCarthy's hunt for Communists and the campus debate over big-time athletics.

Fred McPowledge and Chuck McCorkle (Chuck Hauser's real middle name).[52]

In the extremely tense and brittle environment of the era not everyone was amused by the clever antics of the *Daily Tar Heel*. The day after its April Fool's issue appeared, an FBI agent assigned to monitor political subversion at UNC paid a visit to the paper's office. The purpose of his visit is unclear; Rolfe Neill, Ed Yoder, and Charles Kuralt all had somewhat different memories of the encounter. Neill, outgoing editor at the time, vaguely remembered nearly six decades later that the agent wanted to enlist the paper's staff to watch for subversive individuals or activities and report them to the FBI. Neill recalled that this was "an example of the times." After listening to what the agent had to say, he told him, "We don't really have any business," and asked him to leave. Ed Yoder remembered a more heated altercation. Noting that FBI director J. Edgar Hoover "had agents looking around college campuses, harassing college kids in that day and time," Yoder recalled that Neill had a "strenuous confrontation with one of those agents in the *Tar Heel* office one afternoon.... [He] roundly denounced him to his face for slipping around, snooping and bothering with college kids." Incoming editor Charles Kuralt's recollection was even more menacing. "There was an FBI agent who was ubiquitous on the campus, and he came by the *Tar Heel* office the next morning and said, 'Don't you kids know what you've done? You've ruined your lives ... your names are going to be in the files forever.'" The incident hardly seemed to warrant such a high level of surveillance of college students, though the FBI did in fact open a file on Kuralt several years later, after he went to work for CBS News.[53]

In November 1954 the ghosts of the late-1940s hysteria about Communism at UNC were resurrected, soon embroiling the *Daily Tar Heel* in another fight over editorial freedom. It began when Junius Scales was arrested and convicted under the 1940 Smith Act. Not only did the story make national news, but it involved several others with UNC connections: John Gates and Hans Freistadt came to Scales's aid, and his attorney was J. McNeill Smith, *Daily Tar Heel* editor in 1937 when Leon Trotsky was barred from speaking on campus. The paper's coverage of the Scales trial and similar examples of Red Scare hysteria continued to be critical and often razor sharp, especially when ink flowed from the pens of Charles Kuralt, Ed Yoder, and Louis Kraar. The editorial staff endlessly poked and prodded not only Senator McCarthy, but fellow Communist hunter Vice President Richard Nixon (referring to him on one occasion as President Dwight Eisenhower's "attack dog"). By March 1955, just before the spring elections for student-body president and editor of the *Daily Tar Heel*, certain members of the Student Legislature who disliked the paper's editorial tone sprang into action. Calling the paper *"The Second Daily Worker,"* a six-person committee was set up to investigate excessive leftist political bias and possible managerial incompetence. What ensued was just as Earl Heffner had predicted nearly eight years earlier if such a committee were to be established—an attempt by student government to control the editorial content and news coverage of the *Daily Tar Heel*. Kuralt, the paper's editor at the time, fought back by accusing certain student legislators of being "bogged down in preelection pyrotechnics like calling the *Daily Tar Heel* names, and worse," and labeled charges that he and other staff members were "Red" and "lazy" as "patently absurd." "It is a little saddening to find that the national mania for 'investigating' anything you don't agree with has descended upon the campus," Kuralt wrote. "The student legislature's watchbirds have the power of life and death over the *Daily Tar Heel*, not altogether a healthy situation. It could lead to a controlled press, except for a line in the student constitution 'Neither the Publications Board nor the Student Legislature shall exercise any control over the editor and chiefs of the various publications.'"[54]

Faculty and students rushed to the defense of the *Daily Tar Heel* and of freedom of speech on campus. Dean Norval N. Luxon of the School of Journalism told the legislative investigating committee, "You don't realize how lucky you are with this paper," adding that "Neill and Kuralt are two of the best student editors I've seen in my 34 years of experience." A transfer student, identifying himself as M. Wallace, wrote a letter to the editor summing up the situation: "As a transfer student, I have had an opportunity to see some other college newspapers and nowhere to my knowledge is there a college paper with so mature and readable an editorial page as yours. I do not know any of the Legislature members who brought the ridiculous charges against the newspaper, but I can only conclude that they are playing politics.... I think I speak for the overwhelming majority of students when I say that the forthcoming investigation can be summed up in one word—'childish.'" In the end the controversy died down, a result both of the unfounded nature of the charges against the paper and its staff, and of the weariness of the witch-hunt hysteria following public censure of Joseph

McCarthy by the U.S. Senate in December 1954. But charges of liberal bias at the *Daily Tar Heel* were now well established, and they would continue unabated for decades to come.[55]

The final act in the anti-Communist drama at UNC played out in late 1958 and early 1959. As Junius Scales petitioned the Supreme Court to overturn his conviction, pressure mounted on campus to abolish one of the two faculty loyalty oaths instituted in 1949. The *Daily Tar Heel*, in a campaign led by editor Curtis Gans, lobbied the administration to remove the oath requiring job applicants to declare if they were or had ever been members of the Communist Party. "It seems that the University of North Carolina does not take the words 'academic freedom' quite as seriously as it might," Gans wrote, arguing that the required oath was ineffective and only served to "tarnish" the school's reputation. By December the paper reported that consolidated university president William Friday approved UNC Chancellor William Aycock's request to remove the oath, and it subsequently disappeared from application forms in early 1959. The second oath required of all faculty and staff, however, declaring allegiance to the constitutions and governments of the United States and North Carolina, remained in effect until the early 1980s.[56]

"CODIFIED HYPOCRISY": BREAKING THE COLOR LINE

The timeline of the postwar Red Scare, both nationally and at UNC, ran concurrently with that of the fight to desegregate the campus. In fact, the two issues were bound together in the eyes of many conservatives, and because civil rights was in general a cause of the political Left, activists on the Right could effectively accuse supporters of racial equality as being subversive or "Red." This tactic was most evident in the 1950 senatorial primary runoff between Frank Graham and Willis Smith, which, in the minds of many North Carolinians, helped to link the university to the most radical elements of the civil rights movement. The reality was not so black and white; the UNC community remained predominately conservative well into the 1960s, and though in fact there were a few avowed Socialists and Communists involved the movement, their numbers and influence were limited. The question of subversive elements in the movement aside, the fight for civil rights in Chapel Hill was a three-stage process, extending over a period of about fifteen years. The first two stages involved the academic desegregation and social integration of the university, and the third stage (covered in the next chapter), dealt with equal access to businesses and public accommodations in the town. As the *Daily Tar Heel* took an active role in defending the university during the Red Scare, so too did it take an active—if not consistent—role in ending codified racial segregation at UNC and in Chapel Hill.

Following Pauli Murray's unsuccessful attempt to enter UNC in late 1938, and with the university soon focused on the war effort, the issue of desegregation was largely put aside during the first half of the 1940s. As the war drew to a close, however, the matter again began to regularly find its way into campus discussions and onto the pages of the *Daily Tar Heel*. In the spring of 1945, the campus YWCA conducted an opinion poll on the possibility of an integrated student body, the results of which were published in the paper. Although there were concerns, about two-thirds of those asked felt that

African Americans should be able to attend Carolina. Over the summer of 1945 two editorials appeared: one advocating an end to racial prejudice, and another calling for equal treatment of black veterans.[57]

By the fall of 1945—perhaps in the short-lived euphoric haze that offered a false hope of an utopian world rising from the rubble of the war—support not only for the end of segregation at UNC, but also for the end of Jim Crow throughout the South, became a cause officially championed by some campus organizations and by the editorial staff of the *Daily Tar Heel*. On November 3, 1945, a front-page story reported that the Dialectic (Di) Senate had voted "in favor of the abolishment of 'Jim Crow' laws in the South as well as the immediate entrance of colored students into the University of North Carolina." An important lead editorial also appeared that day praising the Di Senate's action:

This is not the first time that students of this University have shown their detest of racial discrimination. Perhaps Carolina is a bright spot from which this re-emphasis on human equality will spread ... the *Tar Heel* has gone on record against the senseless and unfair racial discrimination which is legalized by the laws of the Southern states, and we have not changed editors because of such. This clearly shows that the University of North Carolina is an oasis in a desert of prejudice. We must keep it that way and introduce at least conservatism in a reactionary South.[58]

The strong stand by the students in the Di Senate and by the *Daily Tar Heel* so early in the modern civil rights movement—nine years before the *Brown* Supreme Court decision and ten years before Rosa Parks refused to sit at the back of a bus in Montgomery, Alabama—was courageous. Not surprisingly, their actions provoked the university's most vocal right-wing critic, David Clark. He published a blistering editorial in his *Southern Textile Bulletin* accusing leftist faculty of brainwashing the students involved and laying blame on certain members of the Di Senate who "try to tell the people of North Carolina how to regulate themselves down to the level of East Side New York." Clark charged that these students were troublemaking Yankees who could not get into northern schools and ended up at UNC, and his mention of "East Side New York" was a blatant anti-Semitic slur, a reference to the Lower East Side of Manhattan, which had been heavily populated with Eastern European Jews since the late nineteenth century. Clark publicly challenged the *Daily Tar Heel* to publish the names and hometowns of all those members of the Di Senate who voted for the resolution. His aim was to embarrass "some very respectable North Carolina families [whose sons and daughters] were so weak-minded as to have yielded to the influence of professors and instructors who are members of the radical and communistic group at the University of North Carolina." The paper's editor, Robert Morrison, wrote an eloquent answer to Clark on December 1 that caused a firestorm of its own:

> Dave Clark, arch enemy of the University of North Carolina and bitter foe of Frank Porter Graham, recently threw out a challenge to the *Tar Heel* which we are prepared to accept.
> To those who are not acquainted with the notorious exploits of Clark, we give this brief

biographical data. Clark is editor of the *Southern Textile Bulletin*, member of the Board of Trustees of the University, and the degenerate offspring of a great liberal family of the state. For many years Clark has cluttered up his bulletin with false statements about Dr. Graham, and it must exceedingly exasperate Clark that Dr. Graham has stopped paying any attention to this petty trash. It was with considerable thought that we decided to answer his challenge here, but we think that the ravings of this warped reactionary are fit material to read during a boring lecture.[59]

Morrison went on to publish not only the names and hometowns of the entire membership of the Di Senate, but their religious affiliations as well. Twenty-four of the twenty-six students were native North Carolinians, and another was from Virginia. The only northerner on the list was Allard Lowenstein, later a well-known progressive activist and U.S. congressman, who was from upscale Scarsdale, New York, hardly the impoverished Lower East Side. Lowenstein and one other student were in fact Jewish, but the other twenty-four members—including the editor, associate editor, news editor, and business editor of the *Daily Tar Heel*, along with other student leaders—were Protestant.[60]

In the days following publication of Morrison's editorial, a significant amount of public and private pressure was put on the editorial staff to print a retraction for the reference to Clark as "degenerate," especially considering his status as a UNC trustee. Morrison stood his ground, acquiescing only to the point of publishing what he termed a "clarification," stating that his use of the word referred specifically to the regression

of Clark's politics in relation to those of his esteemed father, progressive judge Walter Clark, not to any personal characteristics. In a rare instance of the university administration feeling the necessity of publicly disagreeing with the paper, President Graham asked for his own statement on the matter to be printed, in which he expressed "deep regret" over the use of that particular word. "A man's character is his main possession and sometimes almost his whole possession," Graham wrote, and "I wish to state positively that [Clark's] personal life and morals are beyond question. Mr. Clark and I have differed on many issues but I have always found him to be exemplary in his personal life and habits."[61]

Douglass Hunt, then a member of the *Daily Tar Heel* editorial staff and later a lawyer who served the U.S. Secretary of the Treasury and as the university's vice chancellor of administration, wrote a powerful and eloquent lead editorial attempting to put the controversy into perspective. In praising Clark's progressive father, Hunt noted, "I, for one, sincerely regret that your father, champion as he was of human rights, is not alive today to be a candidate for public office and to speak out mightily against injustice and deceit wherever they may be found. It was his misfortune to be at least seventy years ahead of the nation and a hundred years ahead of his state. It seems to be his son's misfortune to be at least a hundred years behind both." "Negroes ... are men; they are human beings," Hunt asserted, noting in pointed comparison that Adolf Hitler disagreed with that statement. Hunt went on to suggest with remarkable prescience how the changes wrought by the war were profound, and that with the atomic bomb the "first fact of modern life" was that this now was "one world"

and that the "issue on which a new world war may well hinge is the issue of the maltreatment of the non-white races." In a further rebuke of Clark, Hunt noted about himself that he was in fact born and raised in North Carolina, and that regarding equality of the races, "my thinking on the subject was done for me at least two thousand years ago by one who recognized 'neither male nor female, bond nor free, Jew nor Gentile,' but saw them all as one in God's sight. . . . If you [wish to] look for the source for these seditious remarks, turn to that most revolutionary of documents, the New Testament."[62]

Desegregation at the university was again front-page news in the fall of 1949, as several African Americans began the legal process of trying to gain admittance to the UNC schools of dentistry and law, under the provision of the *Missouri ex rel. Gaines v. Canada* (1938) Supreme Court decision that blacks must be admitted to white schools in states where no "separate but equal" facilities existed. It was also part of a larger strategy (by the NAACP and other groups that would come together to form the core of the modern civil rights movement a few years later) to break the color line first in graduate schools, then at the undergraduate level, and finally in public elementary and high schools. *Daily Tar Heel* editor Dick Jenrette, concerned by these developments, challenged the paper's recent integrationist stance and wrote a column entitled "Should Segregation Go?" supporting the tradition and practice at UNC:

> It seems the "reformers" are on the warpath again.... Permitting a Negro to enter the University law school would not stop the persistent yelpings of the racial disturbers.... It all boils down to the fact that you cannot change Southern tradition overnight. There has been marked improvement in North Carolina's race relations and there is every indication that this improvement will be continued. However, admittance of Negroes to a University which has been open to whites only for 156 years would do nothing more than fan old flames of hatred and prejudice and encourage the return of organizations such as the Ku Klux Klan.

In taking what was known as a "gradualist" approach to integration, Jenrette sided with mainstream southern segregationists of the era. He also raised questions about social integration on campus—which would indeed prove problematic over the following five years—asking where African Americans would live, whether they would be allowed to use the locker rooms and the gymnasium pool, and "would the Negro students be seated in the student section at football games, meetings and class rooms?"[63]

Response to Jenrette's editorial was swift and strong. A few students wrote letters of support, but most of the responses were like that of John R. Harris. "Perhaps Mr. Jenrette has not heard that Negroes are North Carolinians, Southerners and, incidentally, people," Harris wrote, "some of whom want a good education just as we do. Yes, the reformers are 'on the warpath again'—AND NO BAD THING EITHER!" Jenrette, under pressure but holding firmly to his beliefs, wrote an editorial a week after the first, pointing out that he was offering an opinion of "realism vs. idealism" and was not suggesting that whites were superior to blacks. Although Jenrette noted that the paper had received a "deluge" of letters on the subject, only a handful were actually printed because he considered many too long or inappropriate.[64]

Considering Jenrette's views on racial integration, perhaps it is not surprising that the first actual challenge to Jim Crow on campus was virtually ignored by the paper. The March 1950 incident involved not a student or "radical" professor, but a nationally known African American singer, Hazel Scott, who had been invited to perform in Memorial Hall. Scott, the first African American woman to host her own national television show, was a staunch and early supporter of civil rights, and her standard contract included a clause stating she would not perform for segregated audiences. University policy, however, dic-

tated that whites could purchase tickets for the
main floor, but blacks were restricted to the bal-
cony. On seeing the racial separation of the audience, Scott refused to perform. Though the result was ironic—black patrons were escorted out,
and she performed for an all-white audience—
Scott's act was in fact the first civil rights protest
at UNC. No account of the incident appeared in
the paper, only an editorial and a column praising her performance. However a student, John L.
Poindexter Jr., wrote an angry letter to the editor that was published. Poindexter noted that he
and other (white) Carolina students who held
tickets shivered outside in line while the matter
was resolved, a situation he felt "'reeked' to high
heaven." "I am a native of this state and I did not
enter this tax supported institution to have tolerance shoved down my throat," Poindexter wrote,
suggesting that in the future, bookings should
be confined "to those individuals willing to perform before an exclusive audience of Carolina
students ... without any sort of concession whatsoever."[65]

Seven months later, and under a new editor, the issue of segregation in Memorial Hall
became front-page news in the *Daily Tar Heel*.
When the Ministerial Association of Chapel Hill
booked Dr. Toyohiko Kagawa, a Japanese evan-
gelist and Presbyterian minister for two lectures
in Memorial Hall, the university administration
informed the hosts that pursuant to "trustee-
passed policy," public seating would remain segregated. In protest, the lectures were moved to
local churches and the university was roundly
criticized. "Codified Hypocrisy," the title of editor Roy Parker's lead editorial announced, which
took the trustees to task for creating such a
policy. "For segregation on such a flimsy basis

as skin color to actually be put into law on a college campus is an absurdity," asserted Parker,
who believed that the policy insulted the university community and created "a blight on the good
sense of those in whose hands the power to rule
has been placed." Not satisfied with simply blasting the trustees, Parker encouraged students to
act. "Through their own open-minded, reasonable actions, students should assert the cause
of freedom to assimilate knowledge and understanding ... to battle with unreasonable prejudice
codified into hypocritical unbending policies

such as the one that has twice in [seven] months caused every fair-minded person to shake his head in understandable disgust."[66]

Parker's editorial was followed several days later by a carefully considered statement entitled "Policy over Conscience," by John L. Sanders, president of the student body, and Ed McLeod, president of the campus YMCA. In an unusual move, the paper covered the statement as a front-page story and then reprinted it in full on the editorial page. "The customs with which we have incrusted our relations with the Negro race are largely phenomena of fear and ignorance," Sanders and McLeod wrote, "so we cling to the tattered remnant of tradition, and say to our Negro fellow-citizens, 'We are sorry, but you must sit in the rear of the hall.'" They pointed out that integrated events had actually occurred on campus for years "without incident." Building the case for the end of segregation on campus, the

writers argued, "By its very nature, the University is and must continue to be free to go far beyond that which is accepted in society at large."[67]

As the legal challenges moved forward and as debate about integration at UNC raged during 1950 and 1951, the paper followed the developing story closely. A number of articles appeared about campuses throughout the South where, one by one, court-ordered desegregation was underway. Finally, in the spring of 1951, Carolina students learned from headlines in the *Daily Tar Heel* that the walls surrounding the 156-year-old practice of racial discrimination at Carolina had come down: a March 28 headline read, "Circuit Court Says Admit Negroes"; and another on April 5 announced, "Trustees Vote 61–15 for Negro Admissions." During the summer four African American men—including Floyd McKissick, who would later be a noted civil rights leader in the state—registered and took summer classes in the Law School. On July 20 the paper reported that the first black woman, Gwendolyn Harrison, had enrolled at UNC to pursue a PhD in Spanish. By the time the fall semester began, the presence of black students on campus was a reality, and rated only a page-five story in the paper's expanded first edition.[68]

Social integration of the university, however, proved a tougher nut to crack. Despite the fact that black graduate students were now on campus, a casual reader of the front page of the *Daily Tar Heel* on September 27, 1951, would likely draw the conclusion that the Old South was alive and well at Carolina. One article featured a photograph of young people in New York using the former Confederate battle flag as decoration on their cars, crediting the current fad to a 1949 football game between Carolina and Notre Dame, played at Yankee Stadium, where the Stars and Bars was much in evidence among UNC students, alumni, and supporters (the article did note that the practice generated "minor controversy"). And on the top right-hand side of the front page, a headline announced "Administration Has Qualified Negro Policy," breaking the story about African American law student James Walker, who refused his home-season football tickets because, he argued, they "were marked colored and entitled me to a seat in section 'K' which is reserved for colored persons" instead of regular student seating. "I feel that I am part of the student body and want to cheer and express school spirit as part of the student body," Walker stated, "not be set apart down behind the goal post in an undignified and humiliating manner as proposed by the administration."[69]

The story actually went somewhat deeper. Upon learning that the handful of black students had been issued a regular packet of season tickets for the student section of Kenan Stadium, Chancellor Robert House called them into his office and told them of the mistake. He asked for the tickets back, offering instead tickets for the section reserved for African Americans. House told the *Daily Tar Heel* that there was "a distinction between educational services and social recognition," noting that black students were now enrolled in graduate school, lived in dormitories on campus, and ate in Lenoir Dining Hall. But Kenan Stadium was run by the Athletic Association (the paper's former parent) and as such was a private facility, not an educational service. Student-body president Henry Bowers, appalled by House's actions, "challenged the right of the University Administration to place Negro students in the colored section of the stadium." The NAACP soon joined the protest, and filed suit in the matter.[70]

Editor Glenn Harden's response to the controversy was measured, as she took a middle-of-the-road stand that supported Chancellor House. While accepting that blacks are "here, now," Harden wrote that "we, like our good Chancellor, feeling somewhat 'conservative,' deplore the compulsory act" (of legal action that might force the issue), adding that it would be best if the students worked it out among themselves. The next day an editorial by Dick Murphy, entitled "A Student," was much more direct and defiant:

There should be no second-class student at the University of North Carolina. Any person who gains admission here is entitled to be a student first class. To admit students, and then to discriminate against them because of race, religion, creed, or economic circumstance, is thoroughly repugnant to the cardinal principle for which this venerable citadel of democracy and freedom has so long stood—equal treatment for all students, special privileges to none. To distinguish between Negroes sitting in Lenoir or Memorial Halls and Negroes sitting in Kenan Stadium is sheer delusion.... Our task is not to fight grudgingly the new social situation in which we find ourselves, but to make the transition as graciously and as smoothly as possible. It is about time we started getting to it. A student is a student is a student.[71]

The most spectacular verbal pyrotechnics over the issue of social integration were provided not from inside the university, however, but from outside it. The instigator was John Washington Clark, mill owner, a trustee of the consolidated university, and brother of David Clark. As David Clark was winding down his career and putting aside his poison pen after three decades of vituperative attacks on the university, his brother quickly picked it up. In February 1951, John Clark sent letters to the mayors of Four Oaks and Maxton, North Carolina, the hometowns of John Sanders and Ed McLeod, the two students who had written the editorial the previous October about ending segregation in Memorial Hall. Stating that these students and others were "insisting there be no segregation of races in meetings" at UNC, Clark asked for information about each student to determine if he came "from a family who advocates and practices this sort of thing or whether he has become imbued with these ideas since he became a student at Chapel Hill." Apparently the letters were not taken too seriously at first, and were not made public, but by

early 1952 Clark also began attacking the student newspapers at North Carolina State and the Woman's College (later UNC–Greensboro), accusing them of being "subversive" for supporting various causes, including full racial integration. In response, the staffs of the papers at these two schools banded together with staff of the *Daily Tar Heel* to protect free speech and freedom of the press.[72]

On February 14, exactly one year after Clark penned his letters to the two mayors, the *Daily Tar Heel* broke the story about his attempt to apply pressure to the UNC students as a part of a front-page editorial by Dick Murphy exposing the damage done at the university by anti-Communist hysteria. Murphy expressed concern about how academic freedom and freedom of speech at UNC were being challenged by certain trustees and outlined the inappropriate actions of the Clark brothers over the years. He used letters written by John Clark as a prime example, stating that he could not "recall or conceive of any other institution of higher learning which has permitted a man to sit on the Board of Trustees and at the same time to use the best methods of the Gestapo to intimidate students." Recriminations flew in all directions, with Carolina's resident Communist, Junius Scales, getting involved in the uproar by attacking Clark from the Far Left. After two of their letters appeared side by side in the Raleigh *News and Observer*, editorial board member Barry Farber wrote a column accusing both of having gone too far in either direction. Fed up with the situation, the university's board of trustees met on February 29 to resolve the matter (which the paper noted "might finish with fireworks"). Editor Glenn Harden predicted that "as to academic freedom, and the possible question of freedom of the student press, the *Daily Tar Heel* has no doubt as to the stand which will be taken by the administration of the Consolidated University.... With the backing of the administration, the three campus newspapers will, in all likelihood, be successful in fighting any encroachments on the part of the trustees."[73]

The meeting of the trustees was even more dramatic than expected. John Clark presented his charges concerning prointegration and subversive activities on the campuses, and a letter from John Sanders, Ed McLeod, and Dick Murphy was read answering the charges. As discussion ensued, Clark became increasingly agitated. Soon there was a showdown between the fiery and excitable Clark and the calm and patrician Gordon Gray, president of the consolidated university. When Clark charged that subversive Communist activities were as bad at UNC as those at the State Department (claims infamously made by Senator McCarthy), Gray, who had worked with the State Department and other branches of the federal government, uncharacteristically lost his cool and flatly refuted the wild allegations. Clark, flustered, began throwing out all sorts of other allegations, including accusations that black male students from North Carolina A&T in Greensboro were going over to the all-white Woman's College at night to use the library, "unsupervised," raising the age-old specter of black male sexual violence against virginal white womanhood.[74]

After this embarrassing public spectacle, most of the trustees had had enough. "UNC Trustees Rebuke Fellow-Member Clark," a *Daily Tar Heel* headline reported the next day. The formal censure of John Clark resembled that which would

befall Joe McCarthy in the U.S. Senate two years later. "The trustees at their meeting here accepted, by a 47–23 vote, a resolution branding the Greensboro industrialist's actions concerning segregation and racial affairs as the work of an individual and not representative of the board or its executive committee, of which Clark is a member." Governor Kerr Scott, ex-officio member of the board, quipped, "The cold war is over." The lead editorial in the *Daily Tar Heel* the following day praised Gray, while expressing disappointment that he was slow in doing what needed to be done. "President Gordon Gray stood before the trustees of the Consolidated University Friday, with his great dignity, and cleared the air of any doubts as to the administration's feeling on matters of freedom to teach and learn," Glenn Harden wrote, adding that "the sad—or if you choose, the tragi-comic—aspect of the affair is that the clearing of the air came so late."[75]

Undergraduate desegregation at UNC occurred following the ruling by the Supreme Court in the *Brown v. Board of Education* case, with enrollment in the fall of 1955 of LeRoy Frasier, Ralph Frasier, and John Brandon. All of the *Daily Tar Heel* editors from the spring of 1954 through the fall of 1955—Rolfe Neill, Charles Kuralt, Ed Yoder, and Louis Kraar—emphatically and unequivocally supported desegregation. The day following the *Brown* decision, Neill wrote, "It is time to stop postponing brotherhood ... Southern schools, the University among them, must now face the truth—that 'separate but equal' is a meaningless phrase, that places of learning, if separate, are inherently unequal." Apparently, the university administration continued to disagree. On October 5 the paper broke the embar-

Leroy Frasier, John Lewis Brandon, and Ralph Frasier (left to right), first African American undergraduate students to enroll at UNC, on the steps of South Building, September 15, 1955. (NCC)

rassing story on the front page that "while students in nine dormitories live three in a room, two students occupy private rooms in Steele dorm, and the two other rooms in that section remain empty. The two students are Negro graduate students." Accompanying the article were two photographs: one showing an empty room in Steele, despite the campus housing shortage; and another showing the two students, James Slade and Romallus Murphy, with a caption identifying them as "a future doctor and a future lawyer." In an editorial, Charles Kuralt wrote that "there is no excuse for the University's undergraduate facilities being limited to white students.... [How] much better it would be, how much more

in the progressive tradition of this University, if the authorities could be persuaded to let down the barriers of racial prejudice now."[76]

In November 1954, on the heels of the Steele dorm controversy, William C. George, professor of zoology at UNC for some four decades, began circulating a petition calling for continued racial segregation of facilities at the university. George made a statement in support of the petition, declaring that segregation was necessary to "protect both races from destruction," adding that "when you cross up different breeds of animals, including man, you soil the breed." The statements were shocking to Kuralt and many other liberal-minded people associated with UNC, especially coming from a member of the faculty who was respected in his field. Kuralt ridiculed George in several editorials, accusing him of taking up the "phonograph record" of racism from other white supremacists, particularly when the specter of miscegenation was raised. Not only was integration "not a matter of biology but a matter of legal justice," Kuralt pointed out, but "the ending of segregation in the schools does not involve 'cross-breeding,' the ancient and insistent claim of those who oppose desegregation." The mounting criticism of George failed to stop him, however, and he was to continue to espouse his racist philosophies well into the 1960s.[77]

Those on the board of trustees, on the faculty, and in the university administration who opposed integration did have allies among some students and alumni. William C. Grimes, class of 1954, fed up with the *Daily Tar Heel*'s proselytizing about race, wrote an emphatic letter to the editor in February 1955, printed under the title "You WILL Cease! That is A Fact":

Front page, October 5, 1954, breaking the story that two African
American graduate students were living in a segregated dorm.

Two UNC Negro Students Living In Segregated Steele Dorm Rooms

AN EMPTY ROOM IN STEELE DORMITORY

. . . and there are others, while men live three in a room

Search Can Find No Evidence Of Law Requiring Separation

By DICK CREED

While students in nine dormitories live three in a room, two students occupy private rooms in one section of Steele dorm, and the two other rooms in that section remain empty.

The two students are Negro graduate students.

President Gordon Gray, contacted yesterday after Chancellor Robert B. House refused to comment on the why' of the situation, said, "I just don't remember. I doubt that the Board of Trustees made the decision" to set aside space for Negro residents.

Continued Gray, "I'm sure that whatever happened came out of conferences with various University officials when the first Negro student entered the University two or three years ago." (The first Negro student was accepted into the Law School in June, 1951.)

House said yesterday that he could "not comment in advance of the State ruling" and that comments on the matter would have to come from the President's office or from the Board of Trustees.

"Don't involve me in the discussion," said House. He did not explain what he meant by "state's ruling."

Arch Allen, secretary of the Board of Trustees, said in Raleigh yesterday that he did not know of any state statue or ruling by the Board of Trustees requiring separate living quarters or toilet facilities for Negro and white students.

Similarly, Ed Rankin, secretary to Gov. William B. Umstead, said he knew of no such statutes.

Both said there were statutes requiring separate facilities in bus stations, airports, eating establishments and other public places. (Negro students here use the Lenoir Hall cafeteria.)

When the Board of Trustees acted on April 4, 1951, to allow Negro students to enter graduate and professional schools here, no action was taken on the question of where they may live on campus.

Housing Officer James E. Wadsworth said last week that the section in Steele was reserved for Negroes last fall even though there was a white waiting list and no applications for rooms had been received from Negro students.

Wadsworth would not say where his directions in reserving the rooms came from. About the Negro students he said, "They have gotten along very well with no problems. They seem to be happy, quiet members of the student body."

He said that during the past year "several students" had approached him for permission to move into the vacant rooms in the Negro section, but that he had directions to reserve the rooms for Negroes only.

Roy Holsten, of the office of the Dean of Student Affairs, said yesterday he thought Steele Dormitory was chosen to house Negroes because it was arranged in four-room blocks with a bathroom in each block, instead of open halls running the length of the building, as the dorms in the lower quad are arranged.

He said also that Steele's prox-

(See Two Negro, Page 2)

From A Woman's Viewpoint:

This Old House Houses Three Floors Of 'Unique Operations'

By BOBBIE ZWAHLEN

Have you ever wondered what it would be like to be the center of most of the extra curricular activities—to be visited by famous celebrities day in and day out? There is someone (or should I say something) on the campus that is.

For the time being let's refer to the brick, pillared Graham Memorial Building as a she (no disrespect to the masculine set.)

Miss GM houses all sorts of things. Within her walls, you'll find three floors of unique operations.

In her basement, you can find a wonderful place to dance, good music and the busy staff of the Yackety-Yack. Of course, if you like to shoot pool or need a coke, she can oblige that need, too. The ping pong tables are another popular place (now moved to the terrace during the heat wave).

If you have finally danced your date out, you might drag her up to the first floor and relax in one of those "sleep good" chairs in the main lounge; or, you can always strike up a bridge game by checking out a deck of cards from the information desk. Like a sandwich, a good hot cup of coffee and the world series, she can meet your needs there, too. I can see where this female is quite popular with the males.

Now this gal is usually very neat and well organized until you take your life in your hands and visit the third floor. Here is a mixture of everything from clicking of typewriters to strains of Chopin floating through the halls. The Daily Tar Heel occupies a good portion of these halls where its staff is always hard at work (naturally) and the GMAB which supervises the big job of keeping Miss GM trim.

I say again, is it any wonder that Miss GM gets my vote as the number one co-ed on the campus?

JAMES SLADE, LEFT, AND ROMALLUS MURPHY

. . . a future doctor and a future lawyer . . .

[You] are rapidly becoming a ball and chain around the University neck. You, with your nigger-loving socialism, are turning the people of this state against their leading educational institution. Because of your putrid liberalism you are causing them to regard the entire University with suspicion. [You] even dare to write cheap editorials berating such state leaders as John W. Clark ... you are spouting [an] incessant stream of liberalism. You are getting much too loud ... You WILL cease! That is a fact. Those who put the future of the University ahead of the propagation of socialism and the destruction of the Germanic races in the South are going to cut you off. John Clark is the voice of this group. You had better listen to Clark, because if he takes too long to eradicate your school of thought, you may go the unfortunate way of all niggers and Reds who have stepped out of line in the South. Go north, young man.[78]

In support of Grimes, Milton McGowan wrote: "You flaming Yankee liberals come to a Southern, state-supported university and by dent of your brash egotism gain control of the Student Legislature and newspaper, and then you proceed to publicize unpopular beliefs and doctrines in such a way as to the delude the people of the state into thinking that your wild ideas on racial questions are held by the general student body." A wry editorial note accompanying this letter pointed out that editor Charles Kuralt was from Charlotte and everyone else in positions of authority at the *Daily Tar Heel* were native North Carolinians, except the one "Yankee"—the sports editor, who was from Virginia.[79]

Stunned by the vitriol, a number of students voiced support of the paper's staff and other campus leaders who held progressive views on the race issue. Paul D. Mason and Fred W. Dieffenbach wrote a letter stating that they were "disgusted" with Grimes and "ashamed and embarrassed" that he was a graduate of the university. "We pity you, Mr. Grimes, if you are unable to express yourself without using the word 'nigger.' In your mind, does a person automatically become Red if he expresses liberal views? What courses did you take while you were attending the University? Narrow Mindedness 22 and White Supremacy 53?" "More power to Kuralt, Kraar [and others] for their 'liberal views,'" the letter continued, "What this University needs is more people like them and fewer like you." Another letter, from a multiracial woman named Mary Lynn, read in mock sarcasm: "Shame, Mr. Editor, that you should permit an ill logic, such as advocating a love between individuals regardless of racial characteristics or any other differentiating factors, that you should let your paper stand for open-mindedness and brotherly love and racial equality."[80]

The paper continued to be the one official university entity calling for an unqualified end to racial discrimination. In the spring of 1955, as the exact date for enrollment of the first black undergraduate students was being debated, Kuralt wrote:

The *Daily Tar Heel*'s oft repeated contention this year has been that students should not passively wait for the year or two that remain before Negroes may attend Carolina by Supreme Court direction; they should say—and say now and say loud enough so the state might hear—to Negro high school graduates:

We welcome you here. For this is your University as much as it is ours.

We believe that it is so: we can find no reason in the human law or in the human heart that says it is not so.

A welcome by Carolina's students to Negroes would be heard around the world.... "Proceed calmly" we are told. What calmer or greater procedure is there than this: to tear down barriers built on the flimsy foundation of bigotry, to do it voluntarily, to do it now?

As it turned out, 1955 marked the end of a dark era for UNC. The university was officially opened to African American students at all academic levels that September with the matriculation of three black undergraduates. And in 1955 David Clark, prosegregationist and university antagonist for three decades, ceased publication of the *Southern Textile Bulletin*.[81]

Despite the end to codified segregation, racial divisions and discrimination persisted at UNC in various forms for decades, and the school's progressive reputation on this issue was often at variance with tradition and practice. The *Daily Tar Heel* continued to expose examples of this dichotomy on a regular basis, and needled institutional discrimination throughout the late 1950s. In November 1956, Fred Powledge wrote an editorial about the lack of true integration on campus, pointing out that trustees were slower to effect change than faculty or students: "This is bad, we feel, because integration would help the University, the state, and the South." And a front-page story in October 1958 entitled "Discrimination Still Practiced at UNC" criticized campus fraternities and sororities, which remained officially closed to African Americans (a situa-

tion that persisted well into the 1960s). During the period the *Daily Tar Heel* also closely followed local and national events in the civil rights movement, particularly with regard to desegregation of public education at all levels, from elementary schools through college. For example, the paper reported favorably on a vote by Chapel Hill residents in late 1956 against the Pearsall Plan, a program created by state government to circumvent the Supreme Court's 1954 ruling on public school desegregation. The paper's opinion was negative, however, in its extensive coverage of the 1957 fight between Arkansas governor Orval Faubus and President Dwight Eisenhower over school desegregation in Little Rock. *Daily Tar Heel* editor Neil Bass called the recalcitrant, prosegregationist governor a "hillbilly" and a "hog-caller," christening him "Ozark Orval: The Pied Piper of Violence."[82]

FOOTBALL'S UPS AND DOWNS: THE *DAILY TAR HEEL* CAMPAIGN AGAINST BIG-TIME ATHLETICS

As if the bitter fight over integration that reached into the hallowed ground of Kenan Stadium weren't enough to upset the university's more traditionally minded students and alumni, in 1953 the *Daily Tar Heel* initiated a war over the role of what was called "big-time" athletics at UNC, which periodically flared up for nearly a decade. More personal an issue to many in the university community than the presence of Communists or African Americans on campus, this battle ultimately threatened the paper's carefully protected six-decade history of freedom of the press and resulted in recall elections of the editors in chief in 1956 and again in 1957. To understand the context of the issues involved, it is

Cartoon by Al Kaufman that appeared on the front page of the paper, November 11, 1946, showing football star Charlie "Choo-Choo" Justice as engineer of a train with the UNC team chasing the "Dook" devil down the tracks.

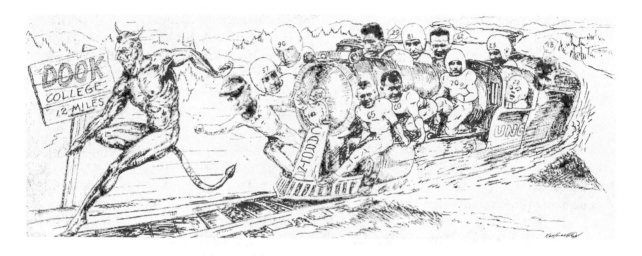

useful to track the development of the UNC football program during the decade following World War II.

In November 1945 the paper ran an editorial entitled "Big-Time Sports," the first time that phrase was used to describe Carolina football. The editorial, positive in tone, came at the same time as the return of Carl Snavely as head coach of the Tar Heels (he had coached the team for one year in the mid-1930s). During his seven-year career at Carolina, the football team achieved the highest rankings in the school's history, due in part to the efforts of a tailback from Asheville, North Carolina, named Charlie "Choo-Choo" Justice. Twice nominated for the Heisman Trophy, Justice led Carolina to two conference championships and a number-one ranking during his career, 1946–50.[83]

The football program and its public image in the years following World War II were, to a significant degree, controlled by the father-and-son team of William "Billy" Carmichael Jr. and his namesake, Billy Carmichael III. The senior Carmichael, class of 1921, was a member of the

basketball team as a student. After graduation he went to New York to seek his fortune, which he found both as an investment banker on Wall Street and as an advertising executive on Madison Avenue. In 1940, Frank Graham visited Carmichael and asked him to come back to the university as controller (the title was later changed to vice president). Despite his reputation as a gifted leader of the consolidated university system, Graham knew he had a public-relations problem because of the real and perceived liberalism at the flagship campus where he was based. Carmichael, with his connections to the business and banking communities in North Carolina, could help calm the concerns of more conservative alumni, legislators, and donors to the university.[84]

Carmichael's contribution to the development of UNC over the ensuing two decades was pivotal, though often behind the scenes. As part of a shrewd marketing and public relations campaign, he rebuilt, remodeled, and reinvented various campus facilities, most notably the Carolina Inn, to create a more traditional "Old

South" public facade for the university. He took on projects intended to build school pride, including reconstruction of the historic Old Well in 1954. He also orchestrated the first strategically planned capital campaign to solicit large donations from alumni, which he began in spectacular fashion by cultivating the 1947 gift of a state-of-the art planetarium from John Motley Morehead III, class of 1891 and one of the founders of Union Carbide Corporation. Overall, Carmichael's presence on campus and the myriad projects he initiated were critical to maintaining good relations with powerful and generally conservative alumni and state leaders during the turbulent Red-scare era of the late 1940s and early 1950s (especially as the university felt the residual effects of the 1950 campaign against former president Frank Graham). Twice during this period, after Graham left for Washington in 1949 and again after Gordon Gray resigned in 1955, Carmichael served as interim president of the consolidated university.[85]

Billy Carmichael loved Carolina sports. He also understood that it was one of the best means of cementing relations between alumni and the university. As a result, he became the biggest booster of intercollegiate athletics on campus, which would prove a double-edged sword. On the one hand, his efforts opened the spigot of donations to UNC on an unprecedented scale, but on the other, it also fed the growing appetite for big-time athletics, and the inevitable problems that followed. To assist his promotion of the school's athletic program during the height of the post war boom, Carmichael had a direct line to the *Daily Tar Heel* in the form of his son, Billy Carmichael III, who entered Carolina in 1946 and graduated in 1951. The younger Carmichael, sports editor of

the *DTH* for several years and a member of the Publications Union Board (where he served for a time as chair), exerted much the same influence over athletic reporting as his friend Chuck Hauser did over the newsroom. As a result, the paper during the late 1940s and early 1950s was—as originally intended when established a half century earlier—the number one booster of intercollegiate athletics, especially football.[86]

The *Daily Tar Heel* had good material with which to work during a period that is often referred to as the golden age of Carolina football, with Carl Snavely coaching the team and star Charlie Justice on the field. The high-water mark of the era occurred on November 12, 1949, when 2,000 students and some 30,000 alumni flooded into New York City to attend the game between Carolina and Notre Dame, which was to be played in Yankee Stadium. For several weeks in advance the paper was filled with stories of preparations for the big day—and speculation about whether the injured "Choo-Choo" would play. In a jubilant mass exodus from campus, students arrived in New York by plane, train, and automobile. The *Daily Tar Heel*, under the banner "NYC Bureau: Statler Hotel," put out two special "Air Mail" editions that were flown from Manhattan to Chapel Hill. The whole event had the exuberant atmosphere of an MGM musical starring Mickey Rooney and Judy Garland, replete with students cramming into hotel rooms and causing a ruckus by building a bonfire in the middle of Times Square and staging a pre-game pep-rally parade, which shut down traffic. With some 32,000 true blue Carolina fans in the city, the paper reported that "hotel space is more scarce than tickets to *South Pacific*," a reference to the new hit musical on Broadway.[87]

UNC students, alumni, and fans cheering on the football team in front of the Hotel Astor in New York City, ahead of the game with Notre Dame, November 1949. The confederate battle flag was a staple at UNC games in the 1940s and 1950s. (*Yack*)

Despite the pregame enthusiasm, the event had a dark side that went beyond the mood following the team's loss to Notre Dame (the result, in part, of the absence of Justice, who was in fact sidelined because of his injury). Even the extensive hype about the game couldn't displace the ongoing tension about race and political subversives. On the day of the game, editor Dick Jenrette chose to run an editorial entitled "Difficult to Explain" about riots that were occurring in Harlem, the city's center of African American life and culture. The editorial pointedly noted that there was no segregation in Harlem for residents to protest, and he blamed the agitation on "Negro" Communists. Two days later the paper reported that New Yorkers were "impressed by the Rebels": Carolina students driving through the streets of Manhattan waving handheld ver-

sions of the Confederate Stars and Bars in support of the team (exactly one year after Bill Robertson's column condemning the flags got him fired from the *DTH*).[88]

Boosterism of big-time athletics at UNC, both by the *Daily Tar Heel* and various university entities, continued into the early 1950s. But that would change in the fall of 1953, when editor Rolfe Neill traveled with the football team to Athens, Georgia, and attended a much-hyped game with the University of Georgia. That experience, Neill recalled, "opened my eyes" to the fact that the athletic program had "grown too big, and was torturing the basic academic purposes of the institution." Alarmed by what he witnessed up close, and by information he learned on the trip, Neill came back to Chapel Hill and wrote a landmark column, "Big-Time College Sports—

The Educational Cancer." At issue was special treatment given football players, the unseemly role of certain alumni, and most notably the revelation that one-quarter of the profits of the student stores was being turned over to the athletes via the euphemistically titled "Educational Foundation" for what amounted to improper scholarships. In Neill's view:

> Big-Time college sports are a cancer at the heart of education. Long suspected as a serious disease, the ravages of intercollegiate athletics becomes a certainty when state funds are tabbed for specific uses as grants-in-aid to athletes.
>
> What really hurts is that it has happened to us. One-fourth of the profits from campus stores has been given to the Educational Foundation. The University officially has joined the alumni and "friends" who provide the cash to buy better teams.

Neill continued by declaring that the term "grant-in-aid" instead of scholarship was an admission that the funds were given for athletic, not academic, ability, and "thus the dollar premium on athletic prowess is in the open at last." "We'll miss the student with the curious mind and puny fame who otherwise might have received the benefit of these state funds," he opined. "It is not just education's loss, but North Carolina's." Noting that the players were victims of a situation that had gotten out of hand and that the administration and alumni were to blame, Neill wrote, "We would rather have fewer students come here because of our reputation for learning, rather than the many who come to cavort in a playboy's paradise." Seeing no other option, Neill concluded with a bombshell: "We believe Carolina should withdraw from the big-dollar arena."[89]

Reaction to the editorial was swift, by both students and the administration. The following day, Charles Kuralt wrote the front-page story "Gray Defends Sports Aid," informing readers how the consolidated university president tried to walk a tightrope and mitigate the damage caused by the embarrassing revelation. Gray announced that the university's board of trustees had approved the use of student-store profits for athletic grants as a onetime allocation, because a similar situation existed at N.C. State and the trustees wanted, in a manner of speaking, to have a level playing field between the two schools. Neill was incredulous. Writing a lead

Ed Yoder, 1955–56 coeditor of the *Daily Tar Heel*. Yoder was later a Rhodes Scholar and Pulitzer Prize–winning columnist. During his career he wrote for the *Greensboro Daily News*, the *Washington Star*, and the *Washington Post*. (*Yack*)

editorial entitled "An Unwanted 'Fairness,'" he declared that this equated "one bad with [another] bad" and that the board's action did nothing but "smudge Carolina's hands." Newspapers across the state applauded the stand of the university's student newspaper and its editor. The *Asheville Times* reported that the *Daily Tar Heel* "fired its heaviest editorial artillery" at the problem, and it called the paper "courageous," adding that "we hope [this is] much more than a small voice in the wilderness of confusion and manufactured excitement" surrounding big-time intercollegiate athletics. "If the conclusion of that student newspaper represents the majority sentiment of the student body," the *Asheville Times* declared, "then those who feel that education should be the most important function of a great university can take fresh hope."[90]

Rolfe Neill reignited a debate about the role of big-time athletics at UNC that had lain mostly dormant since controversy over the Graham Plan in the mid-1930s. In the process he inextricably linked the *Daily Tar Heel* with the debate, and the paper became the crucible for heated discussion about the issue for much of the remainder of the 1950s. The paper quickly became so synonymous with anti-big-time athletic sentiment that in the campaign to succeed Neill as editor in the spring of 1954, candidate Charles Kuralt secured the endorsement of the University Party (the more conservative of the two political parties on campus) only after publicly pledging that he would not continue the assault on intercollegiate sports. Kuralt largely stuck to his pledge, which was likely made easier by more pressing issues demanding attention during his year as editor, including McCarthyism and racial desegregation.[91]

But the relative quiet on the subject during Kuralt's tenure as editor proved to be the proverbial calm before the storm. He was succeeded in the spring of 1955 by a first for the *Daily Tar Heel*—coeditors. Ed Yoder and Louis Kraar both joined the paper as freshmen in the fall of 1952 and wrote periodic columns. Hugh Stevens, himself coeditor in 1964–65, later described Yoder as "a genuine intellectual ... a character trait which marks him still as one of the rarest of birds ever to inhabit the *Tar Heel* office." Kraar, in Stevens's estimation, was "a newspaperman of the old school—tenacious, crusading, and endowed with a typewriter from which he squeezed both genuine humor and undisguised vitriol, as the occasion demanded." Their columns became regular features on the editorial page during their junior year, with Kraar generally focusing on campus politics and Yoder, an English major, focusing most often on literary subjects. The craftsmanship of both men, according to Yoder, benefited greatly from the writing course they took with former *Tar Heel* editor Phillips Russell (it is also interesting to note that another former editor, Walter Spearman, served as faculty adviser to the paper at the time).[92]

Understanding that editorship of the paper was something approaching a full-time job, and not wishing to split votes in the annual election, the two men decided to run as a team. During their tenure, the lead editorials were usually written by one of the two coeditors with agreement from the other regarding theme and content (these editorials remained unsigned, the tradition at the *Daily Tar Heel*). In the fall of 1955, following a series of distasteful incidents, Yoder and Kraar began focusing on the football program. When a dispute arose over the price of nonstudent tickets, the pair suggested that students should be given control of the school's athletic program. When the commissioner of the Atlantic Coast Conference, Jim Weaver, stated that "you have to have a good conference to compete for the entertainment dollar in this day and time," Yoder and Kraar responded that college athletics ought to be exclusively "for training students and giving them recreation and providing the campus with a pillar for school spirit." After a 25–0 routing by Wake Forest, the editors got wind that head coach George Barclay's days at Carolina were numbered, and they took the opportunity to issue a stinging indictment of the role zealous alumni played in the football program:

Talk today will center around who will replace the present coach (not whether he should be replaced), and alumni will have their heads together conjuring up new gridiron talent for next season.

Frankly we'd rather see alumni put their

heads together over the amount of foundation money, or the quality of teaching, or the state of dorms at the University.

But some men can't grow up and always must play the game of college boys, paining bitterly when they lose a football game. Perhaps some of this talk to college students about growing up, about maturity, should be administered in stiff doses to footballing elders.[93]

Matters grew more tense when it was announced that Jim Tatum was to be the new head football coach. Tatum—known as "Big Jim" and "Sunny Jim"—was a 1935 graduate of UNC and had played under former coach Carl Snavely. He returned to Carolina in 1939, serving as assistant coach until 1941, and as head coach during the 1942 season. After leaving Carolina he coached football at the University of Oklahoma, and later at the University of Maryland, where he led the team to a national championship in 1953. But he was also strongly criticized in some quarters at Maryland, including on the pages of the student newspaper, the *Diamondback*, for bringing big-time sports to the school in the form of vast sums of money spent on a massive stadium and large athletic scholarships for players. He was well known as a coach who would do anything to win: he famously stated that "Winning isn't the most important thing—it is the only thing." What was not as well-known at the time was that Tatum and consolidated university vice president Billy Carmichael were cousins, and Carmichael and president Gordon Gray argued strenuously over the coach's hire. Likely it should have been a sign of trouble when the *Diamondback* breathed a heavy sigh of relief upon word of Tatum's de-

'Any Good Quotes Today, Coach?'

parture for Chapel Hill, expressing the hope that Maryland might now return to "more of the academic fundamentals for which the University exists."[94]

Many at UNC, including *Daily Tar Heel* editors Yoder and Kraar, were stunned and appalled that the university would hire someone so closely associated with the pitfalls, if not outright evils, of big-time athletics. In response, Yoder penned a column that remains one of the most (in)famous in the history of the *Daily Tar Heel*. Entitled "From University to Cuckoo-Land," he blasted the hiring of Tatum:

> Amateur football has suffered acute asthma at this school for two decades. With the arrival of Jim Tatum as head football coach, it will draw its last painful gasps and suffocate.

Now that we have this parasitic monster of open professionalism in our midst, let's not hold onto any delusions about it. Let's not think, naively ... that it will fail to take its toll on the academic health of the school.... The University of Maryland has adopted big-time sports so ravenously, and raised its idolatry so high, that its academic reputation, however much it had, is withering.

The *Daily Tar Heel* believes as strongly in winning sports as anyone else. But we do not believe in subsidies for athletic prowess alone. We do not believe that a football coach should receive more money than the President of the University. And we would sooner see intercollegiate sports stopped than the University made over into an athletic Cuckoo-Land.[95]

This editorial, and coverage of the Tatum hire in general, brought anger over the paper's opinions to the boiling point. After a few upset members of student government discovered a provision in the campus constitution that allowed for elected officials to be recalled for incompetence or malfeasance, a petition calling for the removal of Yoder and Kraar was circulated. The requisite signatures were gathered, and a campaign to replace them was mounted in early 1956. Many rushed to support the coeditors, including Chuck Hauser, who was back on campus as a special student. In a letter to the paper, Hauser wrote that, though he was in "violent disagreement" with Yoder and Kraar's position on Tatum, he would vote to retain them because "they have been guilty of nothing more than stating their honest convictions.... If they did otherwise, they would be compromising their own integrity and that of this newspaper, which has always stood

Front page announcement of 1956 recall election of
DTH coeditors Ed Yoder and Louis Kraar.

Editors Of The Daily Tar Heel To Face Recall Election This Month; New Group For Better Student Government Is Born

Nance & Reid Not Debating

E. L. (Junior) Nance, who began the circulation of the petition to recall the editors of The Daily Tar Heel, and Atty. Gen. Dave Reid have refused to participate in a debate with Daily Tar Heel Editors Louis Kraar and Ed Yoder on the editorial policies of The Daily Tar Heel.

Nance and Reid were invited to participate in a panel discussion by the newly-organized Council for Better Student Government on the question of whether or not the editorials of the student newspaper should reflect majority student opinion.

Kraar and Yoder told Council Chairman Richard Fowler they would participate in the discussion. Reid later told Fowler he would participate if Nance wanted him to.

Chairman Fowler then received a letter from Nance refusing to participate. Nance said his petition had nothing to do with student politics and he did not want his petition to have any connections with any person associated with student politics.

Nance said the suggested topic for discussion did not relate to the principal purpose of his petition. He said his contention was that the editors of The Daily Tar Heel had exceeded the limits of expression that he felt they possess in their present position. He said he believed there have been instances when a little "common sense" would have told the editors they were grossly misrepresenting the overall views of the student body.

(See REFUSE, page 8.)

PETITIONER E. L. NANCE (LEFT) AND DAILY TAR HEEL EDITORS ED YODER AND LOUIS KRAAR
... recall election for editors is scheduled in next two weeks

Candidate Seen For Paper Job

Apparently one candidate has been ruled out and one candidate has announced definite intention of running in the spring election for editorship of The Daily Tar Heel.

Deconsolidation Under Inspection

CHARLOTTE, Feb. 1—A statement by the chairman of the newly-created State Board of Higher Education started a new round of speculation today that the Consolidated University of North Carolina might be broken down into three separate institutions, each with its own president, by the 1957 General Assembly.

D. Hiden Ramsey, chairman of the board which recently named

Ramsey commented that individuals and some newspapers in the state have called for an end to consolidation because many of the duties of the Consolidated University office have been taken over by the Board of Higher Education, which was created by the 1955 Legislature.

It would be wise to make a decision on deconsolidation, according to Ramsey, while the post of

Art Forum Scheduled For WC

GREENSBORO, Feb. 1—The annual Woman's College Arts Forum — one of the highlights of the year—begins this weekend with lectures and demonstrations on choreography. Special guests will be Joe Limon and his dance group, Mrs. Susanne Langer and representatives from 20 colleges and universities.

Editorial Policies Are Cited

The student body will vote "within two weeks" on whether to recall Editors Louis Kraar and Ed Yoder of The Daily Tar Heel.

President Don Fowler said the election, brought about by a petition circulated during examination period, will be held "within two weeks after return for second semester." Fowler's statement came in a letter to Yoder and Kraar, advising them of the coming election.

More reports on the recall situation appear on Page 6.

The petition, allegedly started by E. L. (Junior) Nance, senior from Charlotte, merely calls for the editors' recall. It does not give reasons.

COUNCIL

Meanwhile, a newly-organized Council for Better Student Government will meet tonight in an effort to organize and make plans for the immediate future, according to Chairman Richard Fowler.

The meeting will be held at 9:30 p. m. in the Roland Parker Lounges of Graham Memorial for representatives of campus organizations interested in the preservation of a free campus newspaper and in the deterioration of student government. Fowler said,

After the petition was circulated, it was presented to President Fowler. Fowler said he checked the 700 names on the petition and found everything in order. He then checked the validity of the petition with the Student Council, he

---

proudly for editorial freedom." The dean of the School of Journalism, Norval N. Luxon, went on record stating that removal of Yoder and Kraar for expressing their opinion, no matter how unpopular, would be "a crime."[96]

Despite anger against the editors in some corners of the university community, the election itself proved to be anticlimactic. Yoder and

Kraar remained officially silent in print, reporting only on the preparations for the special election and allowing the letters to the editor to provide most of the opinions on both sides. In the end the opposition had a difficult time fielding a viable candidate (the first one dropped out), and Yoder and Kraar won the election handily. But the incident was a pivotal moment in the history of the paper. Though debates about how editorial opinion on the *Daily Tar Heel* is determined had occurred for decades, this was the first time since 1908 that freedom of the press was actively challenged through an attempt to forcibly remove the editors. Hugh Stevens, in a lengthy feature story on the 1956 recall election that appeared in the seventy-fifth anniversary edition of paper in 1968, declared that the episode "came closer to destroying the *Daily Tar Heel* as a free, unfettered newspaper than any issue before or since."[97]

A NEW UNC SYSTEM PRESIDENT, THE ASCENDANCY OF BASKETBALL, AND ANOTHER RECALL ELECTION

The furor over the hiring of Jim Tatum in 1956 proved to be a prelude to a five-year string of scandals and embarrassing revelations about intercollegiate athletics at UNC and State College (now North Carolina State University) in Raleigh, all of which were laid in the lap of the new consolidated university system president, William Clyde Friday. In fact, the battle to keep college athletics clean and nonprofessional was to be one of the major issues of Friday's thirty-year tenure, and he continued to crusade against big-time sports throughout his long life. Raised in Dallas, North Carolina, Friday graduated with a degree in textile management from State College, where he served as student-body president and was sports editor of the campus newspaper, the *Technician*. As a result Friday gained a working knowledge of both campus politics and the student press, which would serve him well in UNC administration. Following service in World War II, Friday entered the University of North Carolina as a law student, where he became an

acolyte and protégé of Frank Porter Graham. After graduating with a law degree, Friday began a legendary career in higher education, serving briefly at State College before becoming dean of men at UNC in 1948. Along with Graham, Friday worked closely with Billy Carmichael, a man he came to greatly admire (despite his wariness about big-time athletics). In many ways, Friday absorbed the best qualities of the two men, which allowed him to become perhaps the most effective and influential president in the history of the UNC system.[98]

The *Daily Tar Heel* greeted the appointment of William Friday, along with that of the new chancellor, William Aycock, with enthusiasm. Both men were comparatively young, and following the administrations of the older and more conservative Gordon Gray and Robert House, the paper declared a "new Progressive Era" at UNC. Part of that progressivism was a skillful and usually behind-the-scenes relationship with the press, including the *DTH*. During his five-decade career, Friday cultivated strong relationships with literally dozens of editors at the paper, working quietly with them on causes he considered important to the campus, the larger system, and the state. He called the *Daily Tar Heel* "the university's gyroscope" and said it played a key role by "shining a light in the dark corners of the university." That light, in his estimation, included keeping a close eye on intercollegiate athletics to ensure that they remained clean, in proper perspective, and above all, an amateur enterprise.[99]

Within months of the unsuccessful recall election of editors Ed Yoder and Louis Kraar, Friday faced his first public challenge over big-time sports. And as athletic scandals began to erupt at both UNC and State College, Yoder's warning

against the "parasitic monster of open professionalism" now seemed prescient. Like the leaves falling from the trees that autumn, colorful revelations fell to the ground almost daily. The problems began in November 1956, when the National Collegiate Athletic Association (NCAA) put the State College basketball team on probation for four years (thus making the team ineligible for postseason play) as the result of "improper recruiting of basketball talent." At the time, it was the stiffest penalty ever imposed by the NCAA. In seamy and sensational hearings over the following month—covered as front-page news in the *Daily Tar Heel*—it was revealed that Jackie Moreland, a top basketball prospect from Louisiana, had taken illegal cash payments provided by alumni (and delivered by assistant coaches) to attend State after signing a letter of intent to Texas A&M and accepting a grant-in-aid from the University of Kentucky. In addition, his girlfriend had been promised a seven-year scholarship to pay her way through medical school. The *DTH* reported that William Friday, trying to get to the bottom of the allegations, was stymied by State College head coach Everett Case, who refused to provide the system president with evidence in the case. It was a seminal moment in the history of ACC college athletics; never again would William Friday allow himself to be pushed around by a coach or anyone else attempting to cover up an athletic scandal or impede an investigation. In a final irony to the story, Moreland never played in a single game at State, being barred for one year by the NCAA and subsequently transferring to another school after one semester.[100]

While Carolina students clucked their tongues disapprovingly at improprieties at State College,

the UNC athletic program was facing troubles of its own. In early November the paper ran an editorial about the preferential treatment given football players on campus, including access to academic tutors free of charge and reserved seating in a cordoned-off section of Lenoir Dining Hall. While that information was embarrassing to the university, what followed was far worse. On December 8, the *Daily Tar Heel* broke the story that freshman backfielder Don Coker had accepted a country club membership paid for by UNC "alumni and friends." A scant ten days later, the university was forced to forfeit nine football games from the 1956 season because it was revealed that head coach Jim Tatum had allowed a former player for Temple, Vince Olenick, to join the team under an assumed name (Olen), apparently to extend his eligibility.[101]

As these sports scandals were playing out in public, a story of ultimately greater interest to the UNC community was developing behind closed doors: a power struggle between Frank McGuire, hired as head coach in 1952 to build the Carolina basketball program, and the new head football coach, Jim Tatum. Though no one knew it at the time, basketball was on the road to becoming Carolina's premier intercollegiate sport. That transition involved growing pains in the Athletic Department that became evident in the fall of 1956, in part through reporting by the *Daily Tar Heel*. The story first broke on December 14, in a column on the editorial page entitled "Lifting the Sweatshirt Curtain," by news writer Neil Bass. "Tatumian tactics are overpowering the entire athletic set-up, and students actually know nothing about it," Bass wrote, citing refusal by the athletic director to allocate funds for several requests by McGuire, including allowing him to hold weekly press conferences during the basketball season as was done for the football program. This refusal, along with others, was seen as an attempt by Tatum to ensure that no other sport outshone football. "Will athletics ever be the same as they were in the B.T. Era (Before Tatum)?" Bass queried, noting that McGuire "may be in for his greatest season here, and possibly one of the greatest seasons we have ever had." Realizing the impact of the story, Bass wrote that "it might be argued by sources from which this reporter got information that revelation of the turbulent athletic situation is not proper or appropriate at this time," though elements had appeared a week earlier in the *Durham Sun*.[102]

On December 18, the same day both the news of Moreland's girlfriend's tuition deal and of Ole-

nick's ineligibility broke in front-page headlines, a rare above-the-banner headline in bold type proclaimed "McGuire and Tatum Deny Split Rumors." On the sports page an editorial appeared entitled "Clash in Woollen Gym," by sports editor Larry Cheek, outlining the power struggle under way between the football and basketball coaches and attempts to rectify the situation by athletic director Chuck Erickson and the sports publicity director, Jake Wade (who had been editor of the *Tar Heel* in 1922–23). "Reportedly both of these two kings of the athletic world are now somewhat mollified," Cheek wrote. "Apparently the skillful diplomatic maneuvering of Erickson and Wade paid off.... We hope these waters remain calm."[103]

The sum total of what transpired during the fall of 1956—the exposing of athletic improprieties at both UNC and State College, along with revelation of the tension and power-struggle between Jim Tatum and Frank McGuire—prompted *DTH* editor in chief Fred Powledge to launch a blistering three-part editorial in January 1957, the first installment of which was entitled "Modern College Athletics: An Unheeded, Rotten Mess." In the strongest language yet printed in the *Daily Tar Heel*—no mean feat considering editorials stretching back to the 1890s, and the recent anti-big-time-athletics campaign of Neill, Yoder, and Kraar—Powledge went in with guns blazing:

Football and basketball, the two biggest money sports for most colleges and universities, bring in millions of dollars from thousands of fans. And along with the people and money, football and basketball bring in corruption, dishonesty and the worst of all: A forgetting of the purpose of an educational institution.

[The average student] is just a paying customer.... The team that plays on Saturdays is not his team. It is the donors' team, the coaches' team, the sportswriters' team, the team that belongs to the 'friends of the team.'

Students who play on the team are athletes first, and students second.

[The student athlete] is given special handling.... He often has special living quarters, tutors, special eating arrangements, many benefits that the average student only hears about. His grant-in-aid takes care of most of the financial worries of his college career. All he has to do is play football or basketball and stay in school.[104]

Powledge followed this shot across the bow with a second attack that hit below the waterline. In the second part of his editorial, entitled "Educational Cowards' Fault," he took direct aim at the faculty and administration. "The cowards in top educational offices are weaklings who will do what any alumnus with a fistful of dollars asks them to do" Powledge wrote. "They are only too happy to bow to whatever the public, press, coaches, and athletes demand." He noted that though some faculty and administrators were "courageous or semi-courageous" and stood up to the pressure, it was not enough. "So the academic community tumbles along, fighting over petty things, ignoring one of the situations that threatens its whole definition—modern athletics."[105]

Powledge continued his barrage against the football program in February, charging Tatum with turning athletes into "machines" and accusing Chancellor Robert House of not doing enough to fix the problem, as well as asking House in print to "raise his standards" for the university. Apparently Powledge felt he might have gone too far in his attack on the chancellor, and in an unusual move for a *Daily Tar Heel* editor, he sent House a congenial and contrite letter (though not an apology), to which House responded graciously. What caused Powledge to write such a letter is unclear, but perhaps he thought better of antagonizing the administration too severely. As expected, the latest iteration of the *Daily Tar Heel* campaign against big-time athletics brought criticism as well as support. One unsigned letter to the editor commended Powledge, and issued a grave warning: "You are following a trend not only set by previous editors but one which all thinking people who are concerned with this university follow.... Sooner or later this university will be brought to its senses, and perhaps its knees. We can do it the easy way by abolishing big-time athletics, or the hard way by waiting till the bottom drops out of everything."[106]

In the midst of the pummeling of big-time sports, the paper was caught in the unusual position of following what was to become the university's legendary first NCAA basketball championship team. Coverage of the team's success was supportive but relatively sparse through late 1956 and early 1957, especially when compared to that given championship teams in later decades. But the sport was still emerging from the shadow of the football program; for example, when the football team won a game against archrival Duke in the fall of 1957, the paper ran the five-inch-high headline "WE WON! above the banner, far larger than for any of the basketball team's wins. And though expectations for the 1956–57 basketball season were relatively high, the paper reported in early February that three players were lost from the team, two for academic reasons and one for ineligibility. By mid-February the paper began excitedly tallying the winning games in what would be a 32–0 season, and running a "human interest" story that followed the number of days that player Pete Brennan left his old car parked in the same spot on campus, superstitious about moving it lest the team lose (ultimately it remained there for some eleven months, during which time it was spattered with red paint). When the team won the title game in late March—in triple overtime against a University of Kansas team that included future NBA superstar Wilt Chamberlain—Powledge praised the young men in a column entitled "Champions and Gentlemen: An Excellent Combination."[107]

Fred Powledge's successor as editor in the spring of 1957 was Neil Bass, whose investigative reporting had helped break the story about the friction between coaches Jim Tatum and Frank McGuire the previous December. Bass had won election over veteran staffer Charlie Sloan, whose campaign was run by Wallace Kuralt, the younger brother of former editor Charles Kuralt. The campaign had been hard fought, and the divisions it created did not soon heal. When classes resumed in the fall, Bass took on a number of issues in a crusading and freewheeling style that quickly made him enemies across campus and in some instances veered dangerously close to libel. He covered an Asian flu outbreak with sensationalized headlines and editorials that questioned the competence of the doctor in charge of UNC's infirmary, causing alarm among students. He charged the School of Journalism and its respected dean, Norval N. Luxon, with

plotting to take over the newspaper in order to add the annual $23,000 student fee stipend to the school's coffers. Even when Bass's editorial opinion was on point, his cavalier language crossed the boundary of propriety and civil discourse. In editorials he called Jim Tatum a "ruthless monster," and labeled UNC's athletic program "scholastic prostitution," resulting in a firestorm of negative reaction.[108]

Aside from publishing potentially libelous stories and using questionable language, issues of the paper that fall exhibited sloppy editing and poor layout, and apparently some number of letters to the editor critical of Bass went unpublished, a move that was at variance with established policy at the *Daily Tar Heel*. In print Bass was called "incompetent, irresponsible, and incapable of functioning any longer in his present capacity," and in private he was described as a "loose cannon" and "somewhat unbalanced." Complaints about the new editor were swift and loud from many corners of the university, as Bass's political enemies were joined by those unhappy with the paper's editorial tone and lack of professionalism. In late October a bill was introduced into the Student Legislature to study how other college papers and their editorial policies functioned, and Wallace Kuralt, with the backing of leaders in student government, began a campus-wide petition to have Bass recalled. The petition quickly garnered the necessary 1,050 signatures, and a recall election was scheduled for late November. In a stunning reversal of sentiment, many of the same people who had come to the defense of Ed Yoder and Louis Kraar in the March 1956 recall election supported the removal of Neil Bass in November 1957. The issue in this instance was not freedom of the press, accord-

Front page, March 24, 1957, following the national championship win by the UNC men's basketball team.

WEATHER

The Daily Tar Heel

REVIEW

VOL. LVII NO. 128   CHAPEL HILL, NORTH CAROLINA, SUNDAY, MARCH 24, 1957   Offices in Graham Memorial   FOUR PAGES THIS ISSUE

Win In Three Overtimes, 54-53

TAR HEELS ARE NATIONAL CHAMPIONS

Pressure Mounted Then Broke Loose

Legs Crushed

N. C. State Legislature Attacks News Reports

Dr. Demerath Here On Visit

HOUSE

Candidates Must Attend Meet Tomorrow

1957 National Basketball Champions

The happy group pictured above is the UNC basketball team which Saturday night defeated the University of Kansas Jayhawks, 54-53 in three overtimes. Joe Quigg sank two foul shots in the fading seconds to bring the Tar Heels from behind to take the win. Kneeling, left to right, are Roy Searcy, Gehrmann Holland, Danny Lotz, Ken Rosemond, Bob Cunningham and Tommy Kearns. Standing, left to right, are Coach Frank McGuire, team manager Joel Fleishman, Bob Young, Lennie Rosenbluth, Joe Quigg, Pete Brennan and Assistant Coach Buck Freeman. Not pictured is John Lotz, trainer.

Quigg Sinks Free Shots For Victory

By LARRY CHEEK
Special To The Daily Tar Heel

THE BOX

TO WORK IN PHYSICAL THERAPY

Riebel Resigns Y Position

By NANCY HILL

DUTIES

Goide Students Gives Program Tonight At 8

TO STUDENTS

Evans Vows To Bring Administration 'Closer'

EXPEDIENCY

EXAMPLES

Ragsdale To Be Chairman Of Council For Next Year

DATE TICKET

After The Game Celebration On Franklin St.

Five made victory in Kansas City and while they sat extinguished two thousand students celebrated their victory. The student pictured at left climbed atop the post office corner tonight to lead the cheering crowd which, right, formed on the photographer.

Franklin St. was blocked for 30 minutes. Students would not let the cars backing up for two blocks inch way pass. They sat on the cars and threw toilet paper rolls on top of them.

Photo by Norman Kantor

ing to individuals involved with the paper at the time, but rather maintaining the high journalistic standards of the *DTH*.[109]

The bitter fight over the recall of Neil Bass consumed the campus in November 1957, and dramatically illustrated the *Daily Tar Heel*'s importance to the university and the depth of sentiment about the paper in the broader community. Bass used every available resource at his disposal—some of which were quite considerable—to beat back the attacks and hold on to his job. In editorials, he accused Wallace Kuralt of engaging in a "bitter and personal attack" and called the recall petition a "dangerous scheme" that threatened both freedom of speech and freedom of the press at UNC. "Were such an action to be successful," Bass wrote, it "would so severely limit freedom of expression that ensuing editors would be afraid to breathe, without restraint, on the necks of the student body." He defiantly added: "I shall not be intimidated." In a low point of the campaign, Bass sought to embarrass Norval Luxon, who had come out publicly in favor of removing the editor. In a front-page article run under the banner along with a photograph of the dean, Bass quoted extensively from Luxon's strong and eloquent objections in 1956 to the earlier recall election, when he had expressed his grave concerns about freedom of speech and the press on campus.[110]

Many came to Bass's defense, even those who disagreed with him, arguing that the far more important issues of editorial freedom and the integrity of the *Daily Tar Heel* were at stake. Among Bass's defenders were two staff members and future editors, Davis Young and Curtis Gans. Young penned a letter, signed by seventeen other staffers, in support of Bass's right to control the editorial page as he saw fit. Gans wrote a long op-ed piece admitting that he hadn't voted for Bass, didn't agree with him most of the time, and rated him at or near the bottom of the four editors under which he had served—yet he was voting to retain him, as the broader issues were far more significant than the foibles of an individual. Both city and college newspapers also rushed to defend the embattled editor. The Raleigh *News and Observer*, then under the editorship of Jonathan Daniels, himself editor of the *Tar Heel* in 1921–22, labeled the recall election "self-kicking" and declared that if Bass was removed, it would be tantamount to the student body "admitting both the failure of their own democracy and the unwillingness to tolerate opinions with which they disagree." The Raleigh paper also noted, pointedly, that the subjects of the 1956 recall had gone on in less than two years to great success: Yoder was a Rhodes Scholar, and Kraar a "brilliant" reporter for the *Wall Street Journal*. The editor of the University of Florida *Alligator* also wrote in support of Bass. "The *Tar Heel*'s factual and interesting news stories and its well written and pointed editorial page are among the most outstanding in the country," he observed, adding that "the eyes of college newspapers all over the South will be on UNC student body this week to determine what happens." Even the rival N.C. State student paper, the *Technician*, warned that setting the precedent of removing the editor could result in a "college newspaper which never mentions controversial issues—this could be the future facing the University of North Carolina's *Daily Tar Heel*."[111]

The campaign itself was dramatic, garnering more interest than usual for a campus election. Three hundred students attended a debate between Bass and his two opponents a week before the election. But when neither of the student political parties chose to endorse any of the three candidates, a surprise nominee was drafted—Doug Eisele, who was then managing editor of the paper. Bass cried foul in print, and stories appeared that all manner of political collusion and intrigue were involved in the Eisele nomination. Eisele denied any such machinations, but he did mount a surprisingly organized campaign at the very last minute, which included a slick one-page leaflet and a large rally the day before the election. The leaflet, entitled the "Recall Fact Sheet" and laid out like a small newspaper, included an editorial by Louis Kraar that enumerated his reasons for supporting the recall of Bass. "I have never known the *Tar Heel* to be as poor journalistically," Kraar wrote of Bass's tenure, and "I have been embarrassed and distressed by its editorial tone, and its general technical performance." Noting that "competency and fairness, not the viewpoint of the editor, is in question," Kraar expressed the concerns of many in the university community by pointing out that the "past reputation for accuracy, literacy and responsible independence that the *Tar Heel* has built over many years—a reputation that stretches throughout the campuses of the nation and among the people of North Carolina"—was at stake.[112]

Despite the warnings against setting a dangerous precedent, the forces that opposed Bass proved stronger than his supporters, and Eisele won. The election was held the Tuesday before the Thanksgiving break, and when the next issue of the paper appeared the following week, there was no mention of the results on the front page, perhaps to ensure as smooth a transition as possible. Eisele did write two short editorials outlining his plans for revamping the *Daily Tar Heel* and asking for student support as new policies and procedures took effect.[113]

The recall election of Neil Bass in November 1957 was only the third such event in the long history of the student newspaper, and the outcome marked the only time the editor was removed from office. It is worth noting that throughout the post–World War II era, the three organized attempts to remove *Daily Tar Heel* staff—Bill Robertson in 1948, Ed Yoder and Louis Kraar in 1956, and Neil Bass in 1957—centered not around the highly controversial issues of political subversion or racial integration, but at least in part around the paper's criticism of big-time UNC football. As a footnote, coach Jim Tatum survived the various bombardments of the *Daily Tar Heel*, but not for long; he died suddenly of a virus in July 1959. His early death, however, did not bury the problems associated with big-time athletics at UNC, as the most notorious sports scandal in Carolina history—involving basketball, not football—loomed over the horizon.

4

PRINT NEWS AND RAISE HELL

1959–1971

A NEW FRONTIER AND THE END OF THE DIXIE CLASSIC

As the *Daily Tar Heel* approached its seventy-fifth anniversary, it had become a sophisticated newspaper with makeup and layout on the order of the best big-city dailies of the era and an informed and generally progressive editorial page read across the state and beyond. Generations of editors and staff had worked to build such a paper, first in the 1920s and 1930s, and then again after the disruption of World War II. The student caretakers of the 1960s understood the established legacy of professional journalistic standards and freedom of speech that formed the core of the *Daily Tar Heel,* and they carefully protected those attributes through a decade that would witness some of the most tumultuous social, political, and cultural change in American history and on the campus of the University of North Carolina at Chapel Hill.

One of the hallmarks of the paper in the mid-twentieth century was its broader worldview, presented both in national and international news coverage and in editorials. Wire-service stories, nationally syndicated columns, and political cartoons like those of the *Washington Post*'s Herblock were regular features. As the 1960 presidential campaign began to take shape in the fall of 1959, the *DTH* covered it in far more detail than had been done in previous election cycles. In-depth articles and editorials ran about the potential candidates, and after the nominating conventions a daily front-page feature entitled "What They're Saying" appeared that included pictures of Democrat John F. Kennedy and Republican Richard Nixon alongside the latest campaign news. The paper had often been critical of Richard Nixon during his two terms as

vice president, and as the campaign began also took a dim view of his Democratic challenger, Kennedy. In September of 1959, managing editor Jonathan Yardley, who would go on to a highly distinguished career as a Pulitzer Prize–winning columnist for the *Washington Post* and the *Washington Star*, wrote: "Senator John F. Kennedy, the current Democratic front-runner, is severely hampered by his Catholicism and by the impression of a basic sneakiness which he leaves behind him. His youthful effervescence, his charm, his good looks, and his attractive young wife are political assets which any candidate would love to possess, but whether he can overcome his liabilities with these is open to a good deal of doubt." When Kennedy delivered a seminal speech the following April in West Virginia about his Catholicism, which was very much an issue in 1960 America, Yardley, by then editor of the *DTH*, was highly critical of the tone. "It is obvious that Kennedy did not really think that he could go through the entire campaign without meeting some mud head-on," he wrote. "It is terribly disappointing and rather indicative that he chooses to face it with such a self-righteous attitude. The United States does not want such a quality in its next president."[1]

But buzz and excitement for the dashing young candidate was evident on the UNC campus, as it was at many colleges across the country. Students opened a Kennedy campaign office, and the candidate's mother, Rose Kennedy, visited Chapel Hill and spent the night at the Carolina Inn. Even the doubtful Yardley came around. In September, Kennedy and his entourage hop-scotched across the state in his private plane, the *Caroline*, and Yardley was invited to join other newspaper editors and political re-

porters in a follow-up press plane—an indication of the respect the professional journalism community in North Carolina held for the *Daily Tar Heel*. The skeptical Yardley was smitten, both by Kennedy's star power and by the depth and import of a speech he gave in Greensboro. He later likened the reaction of screaming young girls reaching out to touch Kennedy to the adulation given rock star Elvis Presley. Soon after the press trip, Yardley was ready to endorse Kennedy, while taking the opportunity to have one more swipe at Nixon. "In the past we have written many harsh words about Kennedy," Yardley admitted, "attacking what seems to be opportunism and a willingness to take advantage of the expedient." While noting that these concerns remained valid, the editor called Kennedy "a mild offender when compared with Vice President Richard Milhous Nixon," and he added, presciently, that "the latter's history will bear this out." "The Kennedy program is one of progress," he continued, "and it also seems to be one of honesty, of realization of the problems of America.... We support John Kennedy, then, with great enthusiasm. He is the best of these two men." The election was so close that the paper had to be put to bed before the results were finalized, and the headline the next day read, "Kennedy Apparent Victor." When Kennedy's election was secure, Yardley wrote an editorial in support of the new president, again making a statement that would prove sadly prescient: "John Kennedy faces a task so strenuous as to be killing."[2]

Kennedy's razor-thin victory was due in part to the early support of the 1960 Democratic candidate for governor of North Carolina, Terry Sanford, a Carolina alumnus and close friend of consolidated university president William Friday. Sanford was the only southern gubernatorial candidate to publicly support the Catholic Kennedy and seconded his nomination at the national convention in Los Angeles. The *Daily Tar Heel* was unsure of the young Sanford (who, at forty-four, was the same age as Kennedy), and in the primary only reluctantly endorsed him over opponent archconservative I. Beverly Lake, declaring the choice between the "two rather disappointing men . . . a largely negative decision." "We

endorse Sanford because there is a glimmer of hope that he may continue the admirable course set by Luther Hodges," editor Yardley wrote. (As it turned out, Sanford was to be one of the most progressive and effective North Carolina governors of the twentieth century, and as he did with Kennedy, the young editor came to change his opinion of him.) In an expression of gratitude to Governor Sanford for his support, which helped Kennedy carry North Carolina, the president agreed to speak in Chapel Hill on University Day, October 12, 1961. In the crisp autumn sunshine he rode triumphantly into Kenan Stadium—in the custom-built, open-top Lincoln limousine in which he would be assassinated two years later—to a cheering, capacity crowd of some 38,000. The paper had speculated in the weeks leading up to the visit that Kennedy would use the occasion to give a major speech on foreign policy, perhaps related to the then-tense situation in Berlin. Instead he delivered a rather standard fifteen-minute talk, received an honorary degree from UNC, and at some point in the proceedings pocketed a favorite pen of William Friday's, a story the university president would tell with delight for the rest of his life. Though expressing disappointment regarding the speech, the *Daily Tar Heel* covered Kennedy's visit extensively, and staff photographer Jim Wallace snapped pictures that would become iconic in university history.[3]

Coverage of the presidential visit was almost overshadowed on the front page during early October by the cyanide deaths of two UNC roommates (apparent suicides or murder/suicide), but neither story was the biggest of 1961; that distinction belonged to the scandals and repercussions surrounding college basketball, which would collectively come to be identified with the

Top of the front page, October 13, 1961, with photographs
of President John F. Kennedy speaking in Kenan Stadium
on University Day by Jim Wallace.

Kennedy Stresses Vitality In UNC Education; Pledges 'We Shall Be Neither Red Nor Dead'

We Are All Destined . . . To Live Most Of Our Lives . . . In Uncertainty And Challenge . . . And In Peril

The Daily Tar Heel

A Difficult Course
See Edits, Page Two

FRIDAY OCTOBER 13, 1961

ABOVE PHOTOS BY
JIM WALLACE

Complete UPI Wire Service

Dixie Classic, a wildly popular tournament of the era. Since the *Daily Tar Heel* began focusing a spotlight on the problems of big-time athletics in 1953, each new story about irregularities and violations in the football and basketball programs at UNC and State College seemed to get more sordid. But all the previous incidents proved to be only a prelude to the Dixie Classic scandal, which William Friday later called "an unspeakably harsh experience for all of us." The resulting fallout vindicated the paper's courageous but often unpopular editorial position, which had remained consistent since 1953, and reverberated through intercollegiate sports at UNC for decades to follow.[4]

The Dixie Classic was a basketball tournament played a few days after Christmas every year from 1949 to 1960 at Reynolds Coliseum on the campus of North Carolina State College in Raleigh. Created by legendary State head basketball coach Everett Case, the invitational tournament pitted the four leading North Carolina college teams—UNC, State, Wake Forest, and Duke—against four of the best teams from other conferences around the country. In the era before the NCAA Final Four, the Dixie Classic quickly became one of the biggest college tournaments nationally, bringing in tens of thousands of dollars (large amounts in those days), mainly to State's athletic fund. It also quickly became a source of pride for alumni of the host schools, particularly N.C. State. But the tournament had surprising detractors as well. In a 1957 interview with the *DTH*, UNC head coach

12th Annual

DIXIE
CLASSIC

N. C. State   North Carolina

Villanova   Maryland

Wake Forest   Duke

Marquette   RALEIGH, N.C.   Wyoming

Reynolds Coliseum, N. C. State College

December 29, 30, 31, 1960

Frank McGuire went on record advocating the end of the Classic, referring to it as "a $60,000 slot machine," and suggesting instead a round-robin-style tournament restricted to Atlantic Coast Conference teams. As events unfolded, McGuire's allusion to gambling proved to be right on the money.[5]

What came to be called the Dixie Classic scandal was actually the culmination of a series of events that began in September of 1960, though the incidents did not become public until the first half of 1961. In early January the *Daily Tar Heel* reported that an NCAA investigation into basketball recruiting irregularities at UNC had resulted in a one-year probation, which the paper supported. In February, two UNC basketball players were suspended by the ACC for fighting with Duke team members during a game. But the real trouble began in March, when details emerged about players on the Seton Hall team taking bribes to throw games. That led to a wider NCAA investigation, and the UNC community was shocked to learn in late April that a former reserve player, Lou Brown, was indicted on charges of trying to bribe current team members, bringing the burgeoning national scandal onto the Carolina campus. Apparently the previous fall Brown had approached star UNC forward Doug Moe about a scheme to "point shave," which involved purposefully missing shots and allowing the opposing team to score, thus throwing the game or reducing the point spread. Funded by professional gamblers often attached to the criminal underworld, point shaving was a means of controlling the outcome and increasing bookie winnings on illegally placed bets. Moe accepted a "softening-up" gift of $75 to fly to New York to meet professional gambler Aaron Wagman, then thought better of it. As the scandal unfolded, it was reported that certain players on other teams had accepted up to $2,500 to throw a particular game, including two N.C. State players who threw a game with UNC in March 1961. The revelation of the involvement of professional gamblers linked to the criminal underworld marked a new low in the long history of pitfalls related to big-time intercollegiate athletics. Recently elected *DTH* editor Wayne King followed in the footsteps of his predecessors by condemning the evils and corruption that came with semiprofessional sports. He did not mince words about the whole rotten mess and who was to blame—not only Aaron Wagman, then widely identified by the investigation as the mastermind of the scheme, but alumni:

Some of the [players] who took bribes emerged from dirt-poor homes and rode to the crest of fame through their athletic prowess-to-be shoved back into that selfsame dirt ... But perhaps the greatest contributors to the scandal will go unpunished. They will be the most shocked of all at the filthy affair, shaking their heads at the whole matter and dismissing it with a pious air of aloofness. Yet they have created the atmosphere on which the Wagmans capitalize ... [An alumnus] who slips an athlete a sum of money to get him to attend a certain school—thus treating him like an animal that can be bought and sold—is as reprehensible as Wagman. Corrupting athletes was business with Wagman.... With the alumni it is a hobby—a hobby that is no less dangerous because it stems from school spirit.[6]

At first the administration allowed the Men's Honor Council, part of the school's vaunted self-policing honor code system, to determine Doug Moe's fate. After the council decided not to discipline Moe (as he ultimately rejected the large bribes to throw games), Chancellor William Aycock suspended him, citing information that had not been made public. In what was the first student demonstration of the 1960s at UNC, 300 students marched across campus in protest of the suspension. Aycock invited the angry students to talk with him in a hastily arranged forum in Gerrard Hall, which led to a raucous session that lasted until 2:30 in the morning, but ended with Aycock convincing most of the protesters of his

position and receiving an ovation. Wayne King jumped into the fracas, first writing an editorial praising the administration for allowing the students to handle the matter, and then blasting the situation as mishandled: "It has become readily evident ... that student government is trusted only to the extent that the administration deems sufficient." He concluded, however, that the Moe case might have certain "good effects," as "never, that we can remember, have students been as interested in the intricacies and problems of the Honor System."[7]

In early May, Lou Brown and another former basketball player, Jim Donohue, stole a penny chewing-gum machine from a hospital in Wilmington. It was unrelated to the point-shaving scandal, but now UNC varsity athletes were branded as common criminals. King responded with a powerful editorial entitled "Athletics: The Fly in the Academic Ointment." "Everyone seems to be unwilling to admit that the whole tenor of big-time athletics is little better than rotten," King wrote. "Athletes who are average scholastically and morally are pointed to as proof that big-time college athletics are great. But these examples are only pointed out because they are rare." "Why," King asked, "are coaches supposed to be good coaches only because they win, and not because they put out teams that are above reproach as men? Why does this University pour fantastic sums of money into an athletic program that is geared only to winning?" Summing up the situation, the editor concluded: "All the storm of controversy, all the slaps that this university has received because of it, will come to nothing if they do not serve to make athletics subordinate to academics and popular opinion subordinate to honest evaluation."[8]

Front-page story of April 1961 about Lou Brown, part of
the investigation that led to the cancellation of the
popular Dixie Classic basketball tournament.

Lou Brown Named In Basketball Bribe

FOR BOOKS

Students Asked For Permission To Search Homes

Students in an 11 a.m. mathematics class yesterday were asked to sign statements permitting University and police officials to search their homes for missing library books.

The request was made by Kenan Professor A. T. Brauer.

The class, consisting of advanced undergraduates and graduates, included students on scholarships from the Academic Year Institution. Visiting Professor Merrill E. Shanks was conducting the class, but stepped aside for Brauer's request.

Several members of the class have reported that Brauer told them any student refusing to sign such a statement would not receive a favorable job recommendation or recommendation for admission to another school from him.

Missing Books Cause

The increasing number of books missing without leave from the Math Library opens

Lou Brown
... Former Carolina Cage Star

Former Cage Star 'Co-Conspirator'

By Steve Vaughn

Lou Brown, former Carolina student and basketball player, was named yesterday as a co-conspirator in attempts to bribe college basketball players, in an investigation by New York authorities.

Brown is said to have contacted and was "most successful at St. Joseph's and LaSalle in setting up players" for Aaron Wagman, the prime mover in the latest eruption of the fix scandal.

Wagman was recently indicted by a grand jury on 37 counts of bribery and corruption of college basketball players.

According to different sources, nine to ten athletes from five to six colleges were up before the jury. All, however, were granted immunity and will serve as witnesses for the state in the case against Wagman.

Five other men, including Brown, were cited as go-betweens for Wagman to contact players. Brown has not been granted immunity and is liable to prosecution.

Under Surveillance

Brown had been under surveillance for some time, and was taken to New York on March 22 by members of the

Hill March 29 and withdrew from the University.

He was under no pressure from the university, according to Chancellor William B. Aycock. However, he may not re-enter UNC without permission of the chancellor. Brown was a sophomore.

No UNC Players

No Carolina players have been named as having taken bribes. Carolina was named as having had members of its squad contacted by Jerry Vogel, a graduate of the University of Alabama, but nothing involving Carolina players as having accepted them was unearthed.

"The administration has co-operated fully with the New York police," Chancellor Aycock stated. "We are open at

---

As sordid as details of bribery and point shaving were—three N.C. State players were indicted for these violations in early May—the next revelation of the scandal horrified even the most ardent supporters of big-time athletics. On May 13, commencement day at UNC, President William Friday was informed that after one of the Dixie Classic games the previous December,

purported mobsters appeared in the locker room and shoved guns into the stomachs of certain players who had not performed as they had been paid to do. In the wake of this stunning news, Wayne King's words became even stronger: "It is this glorification of athletics beyond reason that is at the root of the current basketball scandals which have been so disastrously linked with the greater University.... The time has come for the Greater University to pull athletics down from its ill-ascended pedestal and replace it with scholarship." Reform of the athletic program, King argued, would "require administrative courage."[9]

Threats against the lives of players and the involvement of the criminal underworld marked the breaking point for President Friday, who had learned invaluable lessons from the previous athletic scandals that accompanied his first year in office, and his inability to control the situation. He appeared before the consolidated university's board and announced new procedures and imposed strict penalties—including indefinite suspension of the Dixie Classic tournament. Fallout was intense; N.C. State and UNC alumni screamed and threatened to remove the president, who successfully fought back detractors. Coaches Everett Case and Frank McGuire, however, both left their respective schools shortly after the scandal.[10]

Friday's rulings came a few days after the end of the spring semester and were not covered in the *Daily Tar Heel*; however, editorials in support of the president's actions appeared over the ensuing two years as various efforts were made by alumni to resurrect the Dixie Classic. Certainly the policies and self-policing that Friday instituted in 1961 helped keep the worst of the athletic abuses under control at UNC for half a century. The *Daily Tar Heel*'s crusade against the evils of big-time sports at UNC joined a list of important causes the paper championed over the decades, from the elimination of hazing in the first decade of the twentieth century through various battles over freedom of speech at the university, to the fight for desegregation and civil rights for African Americans in the post–World War II era.[11]

THE FIGHT FOR CIVIL RIGHTS AND THE RISE OF ACTIVISM AT THE *DAILY TAR HEEL*

On February 1, 1960, four black students from North Carolina A&T, one of the state's public universities for African Americans, sat down at the lunch counter in the downtown Greensboro Woolworth's (a popular discount chain store) and politely refused to leave until they were served. This act of civil disobedience captured the attention of the nation and began the nonviolent protest phase of the modern civil rights movement. In May, students and civil rights leaders from across the country gathered at Shaw University in Raleigh and formed the Student Nonviolent Coordinating Committee (SNCC) to expand civil disobedience throughout the racially segregated South.

The University of North Carolina at Chapel Hill, the state's flagship public school and one of the great public universities in the United States, was caught, geographically and philosophically, between the events in Greensboro and Raleigh. Sit-ins and other nonviolent protests would eventually force both the university and the town to face the painful problem of racial discrimination openly and forthrightly. Though UNC was officially desegregated by 1960, fewer than a dozen black students were enrolled, and virtually all of the town businesses that catered to students were segregated, many refusing to serve African Americans entirely. Despite the university's vaunted reputation as the liberal mecca of the New South, the Carolina community and the town of Chapel Hill would struggle with the reality of equal access and civil treatment throughout the tumultuous decade of the 1960s.[12]

Fairly early in the civil rights movement, the

Daily Tar Heel became an important advocate for change, which ultimately had a profound effect on the paper and the university. The *DTH* not only became a champion for civil rights on a moral and intellectual level, it also transformed into an activist publication. Because of the nature of the editorial management of the paper, which changed hands annually, this transformation was not always consistent or progressively linear. Of the fifteen editors who served during the 1960s, however, fully two-thirds called for activism directly through editorializing or indirectly through news coverage. And though the history of the paper over the previous seven decades included examples of strong support for progressive causes, for the first time during the civil rights era the *DTH* became itself actively engaged in efforts to support legal and social change. This development was largely the result of being where the action was; a new sensibility that resulted from editors and reporters leaving their offices on campus and being present as actual events unfolded, fostering a less detached and clinical assessment of the news. The transition began with reporters and staff photographers on the scene at protests in and around Chapel Hill in the spring of 1960, and soon expanded to coverage of many of the crucial events of the civil rights struggle throughout the South. Remarkably—and certainly unique among college newspapers nationally—the *DTH* had staff on the ground in Oxford, Mississippi, in September 1962 as Governor Ross Barnett attempted to bar James Meredith from enrolling at the University of Mississippi and for the riots that followed; in Birmingham, Alabama, in May 1963 to hear Dr. Martin Luther King Jr. speak in a barricaded church just before he was jailed for lead-

ing protests; and in Selma, Alabama, in March 1965 as King led voting rights activists across the Edmund Pettus Bridge, where protesters had been recently beaten by police.

Daily Tar Heel coverage of civil rights demonstrations began a week after the first Greensboro sit-in, as the story gained national attention. "Three Cheers," wrote editor Davis Young, who declared that the students were "displaying courage" and comparing the sit-in to the successful protest that followed Rosa Park's refusal to sit at the back of a Montgomery, Alabama, bus in 1955. Amid calls for the students to back down and negotiate in private, Young characterized their actions as the "good fight," urged them to "stick to their guns," and proclaimed, "We hope they win BIG and we hope they win SOON." However, Jonathan Yardley, in his regular column "Perspectives" on the editorial page, was conflicted. On the one hand, "the intent of the action is excellent," Yardley wrote, noting that it was "ridiculous that a city as vital as Greensboro should allow nineteenth century practices to remain in a highly accelerated twentieth century community." And he was brutal in his description of the "militant white element," the teenagers who, "taking the fellows in Little Rock as their examples, have decided that they are the ones responsible for maintaining the myth of white supremacy." He graphically painted a picture of how they sought to intimidate the protesters: "They cling to the outskirts of the Negro group, hands in their pockets, cigarettes dangling insultingly from their lips, tight Levi's suspended from somewhere south of their navels, leather jackets dangling from seemingly impotent shoulders." But Yardley went on to question the method employed by the students; while agreeing that African Americans "have every right to expect this privilege," he added that "they should petition to do so in a less conspicuous manner." Concerned about the potential for violence in such a highly charged situation, Yardley concluded, "We admire the intent of such actions, but cannot condone the manner in which they are being carried out."[13]

By early March the protests reached Durham and Chapel Hill. Black and white students from five colleges, including UNC, staged a sit-in at the Howard Johnson's restaurant located on the Durham-Chapel Hill Boulevard. The *Daily Tar Heel* sent photographer Charlie Blumenthal to the scene, and his powerful pictures were published across the front page above the banner. Three days later another photograph appeared on the front page of the paper that would have been unthinkable scarcely a decade before: the photo showed an African American UNC student, David Dansby, carrying a placard and marching in front of a segregated dairy store on West Franklin Street in Chapel Hill. In the face of these protests, now at the university's door, Jonathan Yardley urged gradualism. "We are wholly in sympathy with the oft-repeated and rarely heeded cries of the Southern moderates who realize the psychological necessity of making the process a slow, careful one," he wrote. "A hundred years' tradition cannot be changed in a fortnight. But the fates, as they were, have determined that the change is to be made and resistance seems ineffectual and, in a way, tyrannical." As the protests continued throughout the spring of 1960, Young and Yardley (who became editor in April) continued to offer differing perspectives on the effectiveness of the protests, though both were concerned about potential vio-

lence. After Governor Luther Hodges stepped in to try to stop the protests, Young wrote, "as long as the demonstrations remain peaceful, I consider them an effective means of communicating certain inequalities which exist in this state." He added, however, that "there is a fine line between a peaceful demonstration and violence."[14]

Beginning in April, and continuing through the end of 1961, the integration efforts in Chapel Hill coalesced around movie theaters, a popular source of entertainment in an era when few students owned televisions. For the first time, a substantial number of white students took a stand by passing out pledge cards stating that they would only patronize integrated theaters. Concurrently, students supporting civil rights began wearing small metal buttons featuring a drawing of a black hand and a white hand clasped in friendship (the newly adopted SNCC logo). In an editorial entitled "Buttons and Cards," Yardley wrote that while he was sympathetic to the cause, these efforts were silly and did nothing but cause friction. In his opinion, the buttons were "obnoxious" and "a kind of indecency" that fostered "an implicit effort, it seems, to divide the campus." "Because these thoughts will probably be misconstrued by most of our readers," Yardley added, "we feel it only fair to state that *Daily Tar Heel* policy supports to the hilt the concept that all men are created equal, with equal opportunity. We do not, however, support any moves which serve to arouse antagonism or lead to violence." He concluded by decrying the "hand of the North reaching into the South," referring to rumors of activists from the Northeast aiding in the cause, and raising the specter of a second Yankee invasion on the eve of the centennial anniversary of the bloody Civil War (against the highly symbolic backdrop of which the civil rights movement played out).[15]

Yardley's language was similar in tone to that of editor Dick Jenrette on integration exactly a decade earlier, and like Jenrette, Yardley received a number of letters criticizing his calls for moderation. However there is an important distinction between the two editors. Just as his views on Kennedy evolved, Yardley was to become an ardent supporter of civil rights. In hindsight it may appear that support for immediate action would have been the right course, but on a daily basis, as events occurred, the right course was not always immediately evident. Nonviolent protest was new and untested, and no one wanted to see violence erupt on the campus or the streets of Chapel Hill. There was also a difference between armchair intellectual liberalism and activism, especially for the generally privileged young white students at UNC who were not living the daily oppression of racial discrimination. Yardley was the last *Daily Tar Heel* editor to advocate moderation and gradualism with regard to racial equality, and his personal evolution on the subject reflected a similar transformation among thousands of UNC students of the era.

The evolution of white students on the matter of civil rights moved dramatically forward in May 1960 following the campus visit of Martin Luther King Jr., head at the time of the Southern Christian Leadership Conference. The event was almost overshadowed, however, by what at first appeared to be a prank in poor taste, or possibly a racist act, three days before King's scheduled speech. On May 6, someone removed the American flag in front of South Building and replaced it with a homemade white flag featuring a red swastika along with a white dove, the Ger-

Flag had serious purpose, raisers said

man words "Christliche Raus" (meaning "Christians get out"), and, most shockingly, what the paper described as "a dark-skinned child being crushed by a spike-impaled foot." The perpetrators greased the flagpole and tangled the ropes for good measure, making it necessary to use a ladder to remove the offending flag. The *Daily Tar Heel* ran a large picture of the flag on the top of the front page, together with an accompanying interview of the four students responsible by reporter Wayne King (who had been covering the civil rights demonstrations in and around Chapel Hill). The article began with a statement by Jonathan Yardley in boldface type, calling the interview a *DTH* exclusive and stating that the paper would keep the students' names anonymous; he also requested that readers not call the office asking for their identities. "We put the flag up as a symbol," one of the unnamed students told the paper, "in the hope that it will shock someone out of his middle class complacency." The Nazi swastika—a powerful symbol only fifteen years after the end of World War II—was "meant as a representation of the American attitude toward minorities—religious, racial, and ethnic. The same person who becomes outraged at the swastika as a symbol of racial intolerance is precisely the same individual who would become outraged if a non-white or non-Christian family moved into their neighborhood. This is a prime example of village idiot mentality." "The child," another of the students explained, "represents a race, not necessarily the Negro race, but any race that is being ground under the heel of the so-called Christian, who preaches brotherhood but does little to encourage it." Asked by the reporter if the staging of this event was timed with the appearance of Martin Luther King, they replied it was not, stating it was "just a general buildup of dissatisfaction with American society in their hypocritical piety and complacency." Despite that statement, it seems clear that the timing was indeed intended to stir up controversy just prior to King's visit. The students, who were subsequently identified in the paper when they voluntarily came forward, were brought up on charges of violating the campus honor code.[16]

The *Daily Tar Heel* covered King's visit to UNC on May 9, 1960, in detail, including his speech in Hill Hall to an overflow audience that was three-quarters white. The paper extensively quoted King's eloquent language, his own words making the best argument for the cause of civil rights. "It is non-violence or non-existence," King proclaimed, and "we must all live together as brothers or perish together as fools." "The

Negro," King argued, must "remain passive physically but active mentally and spiritually in his struggle for equality." In the lead editorial two days after the speech, Jonathan Yardley wrote of King's power and poise:

> Rev. King speaks with great fervor and great emotional appeal. The audience, encouragingly integrated and encouragingly contentedly so, responded to Dr. King's talk with a reaction approaching awe. . . . The white audience responded with deep admiration and respect; it was recognized by all that this man is a leader of men's bodies and minds and that he is a figure of great power. A figure of great intelligence, strength and knowledge . . . a man to be reckoned with: a person of extraordinary ability and insight regardless of the color of his skin.

Declaring that there was "no psychological, scientific, or archaeological validation of white supremacy in any way," Yardley wrote that African Americans had a long way to go to achieve equality, but he added that "the white man has a long, long, long way to go as well . . . in terms of understanding, self-effacement, and willingness to accept a fellow human being for his total, real worth rather than his partial, imagined value." At the end of the editorial, Yardley once again proved prescient: "Martin Luther King may well go down in history, when they write the books a hundred years from now, as one of the great men of our time. If he does, it will be because he has the courage and the foresight to realize the prejudices of mankind and to battle them, and the patience and understanding of a love which obscures and conquers hate."[17]

King's powerful appearance at UNC only strengthened the resolve of those attempting to integrate Chapel Hill's theaters, a struggle that continued into early 1961. A protest that January in front of the Carolina Theatre during showings of *Porgy and Bess*—a George Gershwin "folk opera" with an African American cast—graphically illustrated the irony and absurdity of the situation. The *Daily Tar Heel* headline quoted a protest placard that said it all: "All Negro Cast, but in Chapel Hill All White Audience." Jonathan Yardley, by this point an ardent supporter of the civil rights movement and a skillful critic of segregation, urged a boycott of the theaters and an end to the discrimination. The actions of the theater owners, Yardley wrote, amounted to "rank unadulterated prejudice, untouched by human sympathy or pride. It is the doctrine of white supremacy, a doctrine as archaic as the slave system that fostered it." Urging Chapel Hill to "wake up," he accused "this comfortable, complacent little center of liberal thought" of being "in reality, as steeped in prejudice as any southern hamlet." "Our town is being disgraced," Yardley concluded, "and only we can erase that disgrace. Do we have the courage to do so?"[18]

The *Daily Tar Heel*'s next editor, Wayne King, had a significant effect on the paper's activism throughout the first half of the 1960s. Seasoned as a reporter during the early civil rights demonstrations, King challenged the forces of hate and discrimination head-on and helped propel the paper into the role of participant in the struggle. His language was often vibrantly colorful and bitingly sarcastic, and he rarely pulled his punches. In May 1961, soon after taking the helm, King skewered a ball being held in Raleigh to kick off the centennial of the Civil War. In an editorial entitled "A Cotton-Pickin' Ball in Raleigh: The South Reconstructs Its Image," he wrote:

> The smell of magnolias will hang sick-sweet in the Raleigh air this week as the North Carolina Confederate Centennial Commission sponsors a black tie formal to commemorate the glorious days of the ante-bellum South. For the nominal fee of only $15 per couple, all good southern belles and beaus will be able to cavort to the honeyed strains of old Southern favorites as they reminisce about honeysuckles, mint juleps, whupping slaves and picking cotton in the sun-drenched South. Unfortunately, the law forbids lynchings, so this traditional southern pastime will be absent from the festivities, as will a re-enactment of the Mack Parker and Emmitt Till death scenes, much to the disappointment of the crowds of Confederates. In view of this lack of traditional southern entertainment, perhaps it would be better to forget the whole thing, and raise money for selling slaves.

"It's amazing how many people want to go there," King concluded, "on a segregated bus, of course."[19]

But the editor wasn't the only member of the *Daily Tar Heel* staff to use razor-sharp language to express incredulity at the actions of arch-segregationists. Following the bloody beating of the Freedom Riders in Montgomery, Alabama, Jim Clotfelter penned a column entitled "Montgomery vs. Paul Revere," sarcastically comparing the white supremacist thugs who beat up the nonviolent protesters to the British, and the Freedom Riders to American Revolutionary War heroes. "A group of self-appointed Paul Reveres were routed yesterday by some modern-day Tories," Clotfelter wrote, continuing:

> In one of the most glorious exhibitions of white supremacy ever seen in this country, a mob of enraged Montgomery whites attacked the bi-racial "Freedom Riders" as they got off their bus in the city's terminal. Two white "nigger lovers" were beaten to the ground before the eyes of four white Montgomery policemen, who did nothing to stop the mob. Newsmen attempting to report the story were chased down and beaten ... It is truly disgraceful, the lust for blood which these "Riders" so openly show. The manner in which these evil people travel from city to city beating up innocent mobs of distinguished white citizens is too terrible for belief.[20]

To dramatize the civil rights struggle locally, Wayne King assigned sophomore Jim Wallace,

MARGARET ANN RHYMES, Managing Editor; WAYNE KING, Associate Editor; MARY STEWART BAKER, Associate Editor; BOB HASKELL.

the principal *DTH* photographer, to capture the protests on film. Wallace, later longtime curator of photography at the Smithsonian, remembered: "Editor Wayne King gave me my first civil rights assignment and led the paper's continuing coverage of the movement, as did the series of coeditors who were elected annually by the University of North Carolina student body and who followed him." In addition, Wallace recalled, "It would have been impossible for me to take many of the photographs without the help of Chapel Hill Police Chief William Blake and Detective Lindy Pendergrass. While they were working to maintain calm in Chapel Hill, they gave me unprecedented access to the events." Wallace's photos, which continued to appear in the paper through the summer of 1964, provided dramatic testimony to the protests and served to bolster the both the paper's news coverage and its editorial policy.[21]

By the fall of 1961, the campus debate about the town's segregated theaters intensified. King, in an uncharacteristically cautious editorial that may have been intended to appear moderate, urged support for integration of the theaters but added, "We are not suggesting the committee expand its operations to other areas." In November, twenty-eight white students from Avery Residence Hall signed a pledge to boycott the Varsity Theatre until it was integrated, which was published in the paper along with their names. When the Student Legislature condemned local theater segregation by a vote of 23–10, King criticized the students who voted against the bill, expressing concern that they were influenced by claims of connections between the protesters and the Congress for Racial Equality (CORE) and the NAACP, which leading conservatives considered radical and subversive organizations. All of the months of pressure proved successful; by early December the paper reported that the Varsity Theatre was integrated.[22]

In March 1962, following the orderly integration of Chapel Hill's movie theaters (and despite his contrary position five months earlier), Wayne King wrote a powerful editorial in support of complete integration of public accommodations entitled "The Social Barrier: It Must Fall." King pointed out that the "relative lack of reaction to the integration of the theaters is significant," and a "first step" toward racial equality, which would be achieved through "social interchange." He further explained what he believed lay at the root of the issue:

> The great barrier that stifles total acceptance of the Negro is the social taboo that permeates the South. The image of the Negro at the bedroom door that is impressed on most white Southerners from birth usually manages to work itself into any segregationist's argument sooner or later. Let a young Negro in a South-

ern town so much as smile at a white woman and the racists conjure up the most inspired of charges. Let him enter a restaurant and white womanhood has been insulted. Let him try to vote and a Negro plot is being hatched to take over the government and allow mongrelization of the races. Let him sit at the front of a bus and your sister is in danger. Let him educate himself and he becomes a threat.[23]

From the spring of 1962 through the spring of 1965, three sets of coeditors followed Wayne King, all of whom continued the *Daily Tar Heel*'s strong support of the civil rights movement. The first was the team of Chuck Wrye and Jim Clotfelter, whom King had supported in the election. Clotfelter was already an established supporter of the civil rights movement, but Wrye, a student athlete and member of a fraternity, did not fit the stereotypical image of a college-newspaper radical. The new coeditors, along with King (who was still a student and remained on the *DTH* staff), were soon on the front lines of the biggest civil rights story that year, the attempt by Mississippi governor Ross Barnett to keep an African American student, James Meredith, from enrolling at "Ole Miss," the state's all-white public university. The paper covered the unfolding drama closely, both on the front page and in editorials, and the editors excoriated Barnett to an extent not seen since Neil Bass attacked Arkansas governor Orval Faubus during the Little Rock desegregation crisis five years earlier. As he had done with the white mobs that attacked the Freedom Riders the previous spring, Clotfelter employed scathing sarcasm to ridicule the situation. Following Barnett's declaration that integration meant "genocide" for whites, Clotfelter wrote a parody of the governor in a lead editorial entitled "No Genocide for Ross Barnett": "Get out there and keep those niggers from going to school, getting an education, voting, eating at our lunch counters, sitting in the front of our buses, praying in public and anything else that might lead to the extermination of the white race. Beat them up. Put them in jail. (Use trumped-up charges if you have to). Shoot at them. Scare their children. Burn their churches and houses. Hang some of them occasionally."[24]

A week later Chuck Wrye added his voice, penning an editorial entitled "Ignorance," in which he expressed shock and exasperation at the reaction of the white Ole Miss students and rhetorically inquired about the apparent absence of the faculty in the situation. "To read of the students attending university-level courses who line up and jeer, 'nigger, nigger, nigger,' is disconcerting to say the least," Wrye wrote. "We wonder just what they teach down at that university. What do the professors tell those children?" "We wonder," he further pondered, "how it happens that students can stand in a mob and jeer ridiculous phrases about the color of someone's skin, and then stroll, comic books in arm no doubt, into a university course in sociology or ethics or religion. Surely someone at the university must feel that they are wrong. Surely some professor or instructor, some radical grad student must be an 'integrationist,' whatever that term means."[25]

By the end of September the editors decided not to ponder the matter from afar any longer. The *Daily Tar Heel* did something it had never done in the seven decades of its existence—staff members Mike Putzel and Ford Rowan, along with former editor Wayne King, were dispatched to Oxford, Mississippi, to report from the scene of the unfolding drama. The national press was barred from campus, but the enterprising *DTH* reporters got in by posing as Ole Miss students. Putzel and Rowan conducted interviews with students and campus leaders, sending back exclusive stories, and King photographed events, including riots that ensued following Meredith's enrollment under the protection of federal troops sent in by President Kennedy. "At about 4:00 or 5:00 in the morning, I was crouching facedown in a ditch trying to breathe through the weeds to filter the tear-gas filled air while I took notes and strained to open my eyes," Putzel remembered. "I realized I had found my future." At UNC, Wrye organized a campus rally in support of Meredith, running the announcement for it, "A Minute For Meredith," in giant red type above the paper's banner. Two hundred students attended the rally on the steps of South Building in what was the first demonstration of the civil rights movement on university soil. The line had been crossed: the *Daily Tar Heel* was not only reporting the news and offering editorial opinion, it was now playing an active role in the civil rights struggle, and urging UNC students to act as well.[26]

The decision by Wrye and Clotfelter to send student reporters to Mississippi was controversial on campus and led to weeks of discussion and debate about the role of the *Daily Tar Heel*, and journalism in general, in the civil rights movement. The writer of one letter to the editors asked: "What overpowering reasons led to the departure of 4 'accredited reporters' of the *Tar Heel* staff to Mississippi? What justifications can cover up the obvious nature of their trip, 'Fire-engine chasing?'" Another letter from three students criticized the "new policy" of sending reporters to the scene of events outside the university and darkly suggested the next location be war-torn Laos (implying that they might not return, thus bringing an end to off-campus reporting on controversial topics). Other students chimed in with similar opinions, suggesting that the *DTH* should stick to stories about UNC and not get involved in politics and social causes. In defense of extensive *DTH* civil rights coverage, a front-page story appeared about editors at other colleges and how they were handling the situation. And in an editorial entitled "Rough Editorial Road: Sanity and Responsibility," Clotfelter and Wrye wrote, "The lot of college editors is not an easy one.... In the South their problems are greater than anywhere else—particularly when they buck the staunch segregationist feelings of their neighbors and friends."[27]

The question of whether to cover civil rights off campus was further complicated in the chill of the Cold War by the persistent charges from opponents that Communists had infiltrated the movement. The *Daily Tar Heel* did little to quell those charges by running a major story about Ole Miss from the *Village Voice*, an alternative, leftist newspaper published in New York City, and a letter about the incident from the International Union of Students, a Communist-controlled organization in Prague. Regarding the letter, however, an editor's note commented that the statement was "typical of the line taken by the Communist propaganda toward the Meredith incident, especially that it plays down the role of the Federal troops." Segregationists and arch-conservatives were apoplectic in late November 1962 when the paper announced, and supported, a campus concert by folk singer and activist Pete Seeger, with proceeds going to SNCC (Seeger had once been a member of the Ameri-

can Communist Party and had run afoul of the House Un-American Activities Committee in the 1950s). Turning the line of one of Seeger's best-known songs into a pun, an editorial entitled "The 'Hammer of Justice': Seeger and His Critics" added fuel to the fire by noting that during her appearance at UNC a year earlier, fellow radical singer Joan Baez had complimented Seeger as a man who stood by his beliefs. More than a thousand people attended Seeger's concert in Memorial Hall, and the following day a photograph by Jim Wallace on the front page showed a right-wing twist on the protests—a man carrying a sign, showing a hammer and sickle (symbol of the Soviet Union) dripping with blood, and the slogan "Save Your Dollars for Democracy."[28]

The pressure and criticism Clotfelter and Wrye faced turned out to be mild in comparison to that of their successors, Gary Blanchard and David Ethridge, who happened to sit in the editorial hot seat when the fight for racial equality in Chapel Hill turned dangerously confrontational and at times violent. Continuing the activist stance recently established by the paper, Blanchard and Ethridge took on the issue of segregated restaurants and lunch counters in Chapel Hill, urging protests and boycotts. In an April 1963 editorial, "Segregated Breakfast," the editors issued a strong statement on the issue: "We are a student body almost 10,000 strong and should be willing to defend any member of our group. We are not blacks and whites, we're a family of students, and the abrogation of the rights of one of us is an attack on all of us. We can afford no more Little Rocks, Oxfords, Albanys, Montgomerys or Birminghams. They are too costly to our vitality and dignity as a nation. Neither can we hide our heads and hope that the problem will go away. It won't."[29]

Dave Ethridge (left) and Gary Blanchard (right), 1963–64 coeditors of the *Daily Tar Heel*. *(Yack)*

Two days later, an incident in Raleigh involving a UNC alumnus inflamed already heightened tensions over restaurant desegregation. In an event staged to bring attention to the absurdity of segregation, the United Nations ambassador from Liberia, Angie Brooks, in town for a lecture, was turned away from a downtown cafeteria in the state's capital city and also from the dining room of the Sir Walter Hotel, the favorite home-away-from-home for state legislators. Protests outside the cafeteria and hotel followed—in full view of state legislators—organized in part by UNC alumnus Allard Lowenstein, then an assistant professor of political science at N.C. State.

Along with reporting on the high-profile Raleigh demonstrations, on May 2 the editors decided to publish a list of fourteen dining establishments in Chapel Hill that remained segregated, urging action and sharply adding that the University community needed to be "busy at the task in our own backyard."[30]

Less than a week later Blanchard and Ethridge sent two *Daily Tar Heel* staffers, Mike Putzel and Joel Bulkley, to Birmingham, Alabama, to cover the demonstrations that were being staged by protesters attempting to integrate businesses in one of the most racially divided cities in the country. Martin Luther King was also in Birmingham to assist in the efforts, and the subsequent televised events riveted the nation—most notably the actions of police chief Bull Connor, who unleashed dogs and high-pressure water hoses on the nonviolent protesters, including large numbers of children. The sight of peaceful American men, women, and children being subjected to such violent tactics, graphically broadcast on national television, was a turning point in the civil rights movement. King was jailed in the midst of the protests, and many were fearful for his life. Placed in solitary confinement, King was only able to speak to his wife by phone after President Kennedy intervened. It was while in jail that King composed his impassioned plea for equality, "Letter from Birmingham Jail," written in pencil on the margins of newspaper pages.[31]

Once again, the *Daily Tar Heel* had reporters on the scene filing exclusive front-page stories and photographs during one of the key moments of the civil rights struggle. Putzel and Bulkley were two of only four reporters from across the country to get into the barricaded Baptist

Exclusive photographs and coverage of Dr. King and civil rights protests in Birmingham, Alabama, April 1963, by *DTH* reporter Mike Putzel.

Rev. Martin Luther King, Jr. (left) tells over 1000 students assembled in the 16th Street Baptist Church that "a new sense of dignity and destiny shall be derived here from this movement." Before the volunteer picketers were sent out on the street, they were given instructions on the use of non-violent tactics and "brotherhood."

Upon leaving the church, the students singing "We Shall Overcome" (above), encountered fire trucks and police pointing to paddy wagons and school buses a half-block away, where they were arrested and taken to jail.

Spectators (right) stand behind police lines and watch the demonstrators march from the church. Some sang along. Many just watched.

These pictures are exclusive shots taken from inside the church ruled "off-limits to all whites" by Police Commissioner "Bull" Connor.

—Photos by Mike Putzel

church where King delivered a powerful speech while heavily armed police encircled the building, waiting to arrest the protesters. After the siege, Bulkley was able to interview movement leader Dick Gregory, imprisoned along with King, who told the *Daily Tar Heel* reporter that he had been beaten in jail by law enforcement officials. Also arrested and jailed during the Birmingham protests was John Dunne, a white student attending UNC on a prestigious Morehead Scholarship (and later chair of the Chapel Hill chapter of CORE). Dunne's presence heightened interest in the story by the university community and throughout North Carolina and intensified debate about the role of college students in the movement. Not surprisingly, the *DTH* praised Dunne's actions, but there were calls from people who opposed integration—some of whom were quite influential—to strip him of his scholarship. "We cannot help believing that any action taken against Dunne by the Morehead Foundation for his actions in Birmingham would make a hollow mockery of all in which the Foundation professes to believe," Blanchard and Ethridge wrote. The editors also took the opportunity to make an important statement about activism, which clearly represented their own philosophy: "The leaders of our generation of 'war babies' have new areas and methods of leadership. Instead of debating an issue in the Di-Phi, they act publicly on personal conviction. They believe this is the only kind of leadership which is significant today." As happened the previous fall, the *DTH* received criticism on campus for its decision to send staff out of town to cover a civil rights story. This time senior class president Richard Vinroot (later mayor of Charlotte and Republican gubernatorial candidate) chastised the paper for its attention to Birmingham at the expense of campus news, and a public squabble ensued between the student leader and the editors of the *Daily Tar Heel*.[32]

In addition to calling for the boycott of segregated restaurants in Chapel Hill and sending reporters to Birmingham, Blanchard and Ethridge gave African American students a voice in the paper. In April 1963 an article appeared entitled "The Negro at Carolina: How Integrated Are We?" by Kellis Parker—the first byline of an African American student in *Daily Tar Heel* history. Parker noted that progress had been made at Carolina, but with only thirteen black students, no black athletes, and racial discrimination at UNC's Memorial Hospital, much more progress was needed. Several months later a front-page story ran about George Miller, an eighteen-year-old graduate student in political science whom the paper described as a "prodigy." Miller, who happened to be African American, offered his opinion about racial issues: "The South can truly rise again if it realizes its resources and if the white and Negro youths combine. But the South cannot rise again as a racist South. . . . The New South must be an era of partnership between the races. When the Negro is given what is duly his and when everyone works together through peaceful co-operation, then both races will then indeed be free."[33]

Following his return from Birmingham, Mike Putzel was named editor of the *Tar Heel*, a weekly published during the summer sessions. In previous years the summer editions had been more of a campus calendar and rarely covered major news or took strong editorial stands. But events in 1963 changed the pattern not only that year, but for the remainder of the turbulent 1960s. Putzel, now a veteran civil rights reporter,

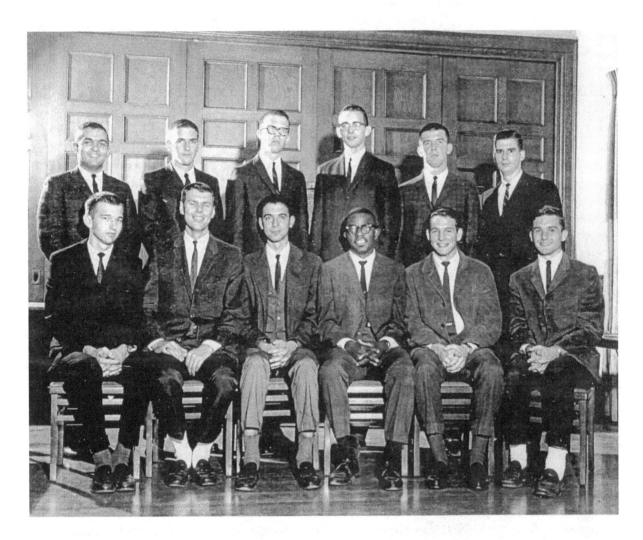

kept up coverage of the increasingly contentious protests targeted at integrating Chapel Hill's dining establishments, including the first to occur on UNC property, when fifty-one black and sixteen white students marching between South Building and the Old Well demanded the university administration take action. Accompanying these stories were Jim Wallace's powerful photographs, which often illustrated the absurdity of the situation. One front-page picture showed two "anti-picketers" carrying signs outside the Colonial Drug Store on Franklin Street who turned out to be sons of the owner. The caption noted that a black protester had pointed out to the boys that they had misspelled a word on one of their placards, which read, "We Won't Intergrate."[34]

Turning a Shakespearean phrase, Putzel termed those months in 1963 the "Summer of Our Discontent," and he kept up pressure on the remaining recalcitrant restaurant owners with strongly worded editorials. On the nation's birthday, July 4, Putzel quoted from another famous document, the Declaration of Independence, in an editorial entitled "Free, White & 187," in which he reiterated the words that "all men are created equal," and "are endowed by their Creator with certain unalienable Rights," adding that "187 years ago, these truths were espoused and these rights declared, but they were not granted then, and upon millions of Americans they have not yet been bestowed." Two weeks later, amid failed "half-hearted" efforts by the mayor and a citizens' committee to stop the demonstrations and negotiate desegregation of Chapel Hill businesses, Putzel decided to print Martin Luther King's letter from the Birmingham jail in its entirety, in which King voiced disappointment at moderate whites for not becoming more actively involved in ending racial injustice. Putzel prefaced the letter with the simple statement, "We feel that the views expressed here may have particular pertinence to the present unrest in Chapel Hill."[35]

Despite the soaring rhetoric, and the paper's now well-established position on civil rights, a sharp letter to the editor a week after King's letter was published revealed a certain level of hypocrisy at the *Daily Tar Heel*. "If the editors of the *Daily Tar Heel* and (summer) *Tar Heel* are genuine in their advocacy of desegregated public facilities in Chapel Hill, to the extent that they urge their readers to avoid business contact with discriminating merchants of the town," the writer asked, "why do they not adopt the policy consistently for themselves by rejecting advertising from such merchants?" Noting that other southern college newspapers had begun to refuse such advertisements, the writer inquired, "Does the

Tar Heel yield in its liberalism to comparatively 'benighted' institutions further south?" Putzel replied with a terse statement that this matter had been previously addressed, but in fact no satisfactory answer was given.[36]

It was also surprising that Putzel, who had witnessed firsthand the demonstrations in Oxford and Birmingham, did not foresee the importance of the March on Washington that August, when Martin Luther King would deliver his seminal "I Have a Dream" speech on the steps of the Lincoln Memorial to a crowd of over 250,000. In one of his last lead editorials, entitled "Cut Off One's Nose," Putzel noted that about fifty students and Chapel Hill residents were planning to attend the march, which was to call for equal economic rights and a higher minimum wage. Though he praised the cause as "noble and certainly worth fighting for," he questioned its effectiveness, comparing it to "charging at a windmill." "We do not object to the march," Putzel wrote, "though we fear that violence may be difficult to avoid and poses a terrible threat to the march and to the movement itself."[37]

While the March on Washington proved peaceful, the fall of 1963 and the winter of 1964 brought horrific acts of violence many Americans thought impossible in a modern democratic society. On Sunday September 15, four young African American girls were killed in the bombing of the Sixteenth Street Baptist Church in Birmingham. The *Daily Tar Heel*, whose reporters had been in the city only five months earlier, covered the story extensively through United Press International team reports. On November 22, President Kennedy was shot while riding through the streets of Dallas in his open-top limousine. Kennedy was declared dead at 2 P.M.

Daily Tar Heel staff photographer Jim Wallace was on hand for many of the key civil rights demonstrations in and around Chapel Hill in the early 1960s. This January 1964 photograph shows some of the violence against the nonviolent protestors in front of Watts Restaurant (where one angry waitress urinated on a prone protestor). Wallace later served as director and curator of photographic services for the Smithsonian Institution. (Jim Wallace)

(Eastern Standard Time), sending the staff of the paper rushing about to write and layout a new edition. The decision was made to run nothing on the front page except the banner and a picture of the slain president, with the dates, "1917–1963." The picture chosen—taken by Jim Wallace, showing Kennedy flashing his famous smile in Chapel Hill on University Day, 1961— was too large to be made into a halftone plate at the *Chapel Hill Weekly* (where the *DTH* was then printed), and had to be taken to the *Durham Morning Herald* for engraving. The assassination, funeral, and capture and killing of the suspected assassin pushed virtually everything else off the pages of the *Daily Tar Heel* for the next five days leading up to the Thanksgiving holiday, as it did in newspapers across the grieving nation.[38]

The weeks following the Kennedy assassination, with the country in a dark mood, marked the ugliest period of the civil rights protests in Chapel Hill. In December, two UNC students were arrested and jailed as sit-ins continued. One of those students, Karen Parker, a journalism major and the first African American woman to enroll as an undergraduate at Carolina, emulated Martin Luther King by writing a letter while incarcerated, "The Chapel Hill Jail: Gloom," which was later published in the *Daily Tar Heel*. In early January the paper reported five separate incidents of attacks on protesters, as frustrated and angry white segregationists began employing increasingly violent tactics against the peaceful demonstrators, including dousing them with ammonia. The most shocking incident occurred in front of Watts Restaurant, located between Pittsboro and Chapel Hill. As protesters lay silently on the sidewalk in front of the building, one of the waitresses came out, hiked up

her skirt, and urinated on one of the men. "We could hardly believe it," read an editorial in the *DTH*, calling the behavior "depraved" and an "animal act." "It just does not seem possible that any woman could be so debased as to straddle the head of a prone demonstrator and urinate on him."[39]

The *Daily Tar Heel* editors and staff poked and prodded everyone with any power to effect change—the student body, student government, the administration, business owners, and town officials. News articles and photos about the pro-

tests and violence ran above the banner, and editorials appeared such as one entitled "Chapel Hill—North Carolina or Alabama?" Following the ammonia and urination incidents, the paper conducted a poll that found 25 percent of the town's businesses practiced discrimination, and it published the names of those establishments. In February, under intense pressure, student-body president Mike Lawler introduced a controversial resolution calling for a student boycott of segregated businesses that split campus government, resulting in the resignation of the student attorney general. Paying Lawler's action a backhanded compliment, the *Daily Tar Heel* editors wrote that "the fact that he has waited until now to [call for the boycott] does not detract from the meaningfulness of his words." Amid the turmoil, Kellis Parker and Karen Parker—whose bylines had appeared in the *DTH*—submitted a letter to the editor explaining that while they might not agree with the most controversial tactics employed by more radical elements of the civil rights movement, they did agree with their ideals and would boycott segregated businesses. Eight days later a full-page ad ran with the names of some 1,000 students, faculty, and townspeople who had signed a petition based on the letter from the two black students, along with a banner in bold type at the bottom that read, "Won't You Join Us?—Boycott Places Where ALL Cannot Go."[40]

In March 1964, the persistence of the *Daily Tar Heel* reporting and editorializing about civil rights activities in and around Chapel Hill resulted in another first in the paper's history: editors Gary Blanchard and David Ethridge were called to testify in the case of William Wynn, an associate professor of philosophy who had been

arrested in the demonstrations outside the Watts Restaurant. Blanchard and Ethridge had been on the scene as reporters and were called by the defense to support Wynn's assertion that he had broken no laws during the demonstration. Prior to their testimony, however, an editorial appeared in the paper calling the strict courtroom rules of the presiding judge, Raymond Mallard, "nonsense." The county prosecutor, seeing a possible opportunity to discredit the young editors' testimony, questioned Blanchard directly on the stand about his opinion of how the judge was handling the case. Knowing that Mallard was not on the side of Wynn or the demonstrators, Blanchard found himself caught between perjury and contempt; either he could disavow what he had written in the editorial, or he could repeat it, risking the ire of the already unsympathetic judge. Blanchard chose to carefully confirm what he had written, and the judge ordered him to reappear on contempt charges. The case drew attention across the state and was covered in virtually every newspaper, as it was seen as a challenge to freedom of speech and the press and as rough handling of the editors by county officials who were irritated in general by the *Daily Tar Heel*'s position on civil rights. Perhaps because of the attention, and the realization that he had put himself in a potentially embarrassing situation, Judge Mallard chose to dismiss the charge at the hearing, but not until he had admonished Blanchard, calling his words "immature."[41]

On July 2, 1964, President Lyndon Johnson signed the Civil Rights Act, effectively ending racial segregation in restaurants, businesses, and public accommodations across the United States. The legislation did not, however, address nearly a century of political disfranchisement in the South. Leaders of the civil rights movement now turned their attention to passage of a voting rights act to rectify the situation. Once again, the *Daily Tar Heel* followed the developing story closely and had a reporter on the scene in Selma, Alabama, for another of the pivotal events in the struggle for equal rights. In March 1965, two days after peaceful protesters were beaten by Alabama state policemen while marching across the Edmund Pettus Bridge from Selma to the state capitol in Montgomery—an incident known as Bloody Sunday—a second march was organized, and *DTH* managing editor Mike Yopp flew to

Selma to cover it. Yopp's intention was to interview Freedom Ride organizer and CORE cofounder James Farmer, which he did. He also managed to hear and briefly interview Martin Luther King.[42]

On March 10 the paper ran "A *DTH* Exclusive," by Yopp, with the headline "THE SITUATION: Tense Peace in Selma." "There was no violence here yesterday," Yopp reported, "Dr. Martin Luther King led about 700 marchers across the Edmund Pettus Bridge toward Montgomery about 2:30 PM in defiance of an order from Federal Judge Frank Johnson. After a tense, but peaceful confrontation with state troopers, King ordered the marchers back to Brown Chapel A.M.E. Church, the start of the march." The paper's staff, understanding the importance of King's words, took the unusual step of printing them in boldfaced type on the front page: "I cannot stand in the midst of all of these glaring evils and not take a stand against it. I have no alternative but to lead the march from this spot in an attempt to convey our grievances to the seat of government in Montgomery. I have made my choice this afternoon. I've got to march. I had rather die on the highways of Alabama than make a butchery of my conscience."[43]

The Voting Rights Act of 1965, signed into law in August, struck down barriers many southern states had put in place to restrict African American political participation. Despite the two pieces of landmark civil rights legislation passed in 1964 and 1965, however, problems of equal access to quality public education and economic opportunity persisted. By the late 1960s, the nonviolent phase of the civil rights movement gave way to new and more confrontational efforts to create equal opportunity and a stronger public

Exclusive coverage of the march from Selma to Birmingham, Alabama, over the Edmund Pettus Bridge, March 1965, by *DTH* staff reporter Mike Yopp.

THE SITUATION: Tense Peace In Selma

The Daily Tar Heel

CHAPEL HILL, NORTH CAROLINA, WEDNESDAY, MARCH 10, 1965

Volume 72 — Number 109

THE MARCHERS: Before The Journey—Excitement

Selma, Alabama
A DTH Exclusive

EDITORS' NOTE: With racial tensions mounting in Selma, Ala., DTH managing editor Mike Yopp flew to the scene Monday afternoon. He will return to Chapel Hill late this evening. Yopp's coverage of the last two day's events, including an exclusive interview with James Farmer, appear here.

THE LEADER: Farmer Looks To The Day Ahead

By MIKE YOPP
DTH Managing Editor

Dr. Martin Luther King

BULLETIN

Johnson Hits Selma Police For Brutality

MIKE YOPP

A junior from St. Petersburg, Fla., Mike Yopp has served as Managing Editor of the Daily Tar Heel this year. He is a journalism major, entering UNC last fall after spending two years at St. Petersburg Junior College.

Marines Join Viet Rangers For 1st Time

DA NANG, Viet Nam

---

identity for black Americans, which would lead to controversies at UNC for decades to follow, especially as those efforts occurred at the same time as the rise of the New Right.

THE RISE OF THE NEW RIGHT, CONSERVATIVE VOICES AT UNC, AND THE SPEAKER BAN LAW
The drama of the civil rights movement played out against the backdrop of broader social change and political realignment in the United States during the 1960s. The national Democratic Party, moving steadily to the left from the days of Franklin Roosevelt, was increasingly at odds with staunch segregationists in the South. The Republicans, once the party of Abraham Lincoln and supported by politically active African Americans in the late nineteenth and early twentieth centuries, were going through a long and arduous process of redefinition. The GOP evolved during the decade into a coalition of economic conservatives who championed business interests and small government (usually from the northeastern and western United States, these members were often libertarian on social

issues and hawkish on foreign policy) with more socially conservative white southerners who opposed racial integration. This coalition became known as the New Right, and was led in the early days by Senator Barry Goldwater of Arizona, California Governor (and later president) Ronald Reagan, and North Carolina's Jesse Helms, media commentator and later U.S. senator.

Realignment of the national political parties also grew out of the Red Scare that followed World War II, as debate shifted from ideologies and individuals being labeled "Communist" versus "American," to being "liberal" versus "conservative." In North Carolina, a series of comparatively progressive governors after World War II gave the state the national reputation of being a leader in the so-called New South; however, most politicians walked a fine line on the volatile matter of race. Though in many ways the university, alumni, and even to a significant degree the student body remained conservative, Chapel Hill was the epicenter of a small but vocal liberal (or New Left) movement in the state. From the first days of the decade, the *Daily Tar Heel* carried numerous stories and regularly ran editorials about this political polarization nationally and statewide, revealing that the staff of the paper, if not the entire student body, was keenly interested in these topics. A sampling of coverage includes editorials such as "Rise of Conservatism?" following a vote by the controversial National Student Association; "Liberal-Conservative: What's the Difference?" which noted that *DTH* editor Jim Clotfelter "considers himself a radical moderate"; and the news story "Editorialist Predicts GOP Growth," an interview with William Snider, who had been associate editor of the paper in 1941 and was then associate editor for

the *Greensboro Daily News*. Coverage of related campus activities was also extensive, including stories about the formation and activities of various clubs and organizations: on the left the Progressive Labor Club ("espousing a Marxist-Leninist point of view"), the New Left Club, and Students for a Democratic Society; on the right, the Young Republicans, the Conservative Club, the John Birch Society, and Young Americans for Freedom.[44]

By late 1962 and early 1963, in the wake of the Cuban Missile Crisis, escalating political debate at UNC reached new levels of rhetoric. In early October a story ran noting that staff members of *UNC News* (the title of the weekly summer edition of the *Daily Tar Heel* at that time), had reserved Gerrard Hall on campus for a speaker sponsored by the recently formed Progressive Labor Club. Once again cries of subversive activities at Carolina—this time directly involving the student paper—arose from the leadership of the state's American Legion, as had happened during the McCarthy era. A week later the paper published a well-researched multipart series by reporter Virginia Carnes on the history of Communism at UNC, in an apparent effort to respond factually to conservative critics. Liberal-leaning *DTH* editors, however, more often resorted to brittle sarcasm that bordered on name-calling; when 500 students marched down Franklin Street in opposition to Cuban president Fidel Castro, burning him in effigy, editor Jim Clotfelter wrote a sharp editorial entitled "Conservative Lizards." Some months later, as the sparring with the American Legion continued, summer editor Mike Putzel referred to the group in a headline as the "American Lesion" and wrote that "by proposing a witch-hunt on this campus, [the organization] has once again shown how un-American it is possible to be under the guise of Patriotism and Freedom."[45]

Student groups across the political spectrum—left, right, and center—regularly invited speakers to campus during this period. The New Left Club invited Norman Thomas, perennial Socialist candidate for president who was no stranger to UNC, and the Young Americans for Freedom hosted Fulton Lewis Jr., the conservative radio commentator who had brought Hans Freistadt's federal government fellowship to national attention in 1949. The officially nonpartisan Carolina Forum sponsored both a spokesman from TASS, the Russian news agency, and William F. Buckley Jr., editor of the *National Review*. Buckley—whom the *DTH* characterized as "the nation's most articulate conservative spokesman"—was the topic of much campus conversation surrounding his appearance in December 1962. "We would suggest that every member of the student body attend the lecture," the editors wrote, "though we may not agree entirely with what he says, we do anticipate being entertained by the way in which he will say it." Praising Buckley as an intellectual, the editors added: "We would stress a difference which should be apparent between the 'conservatism' of an extremely wealthy (aren't they all?) and educated editor of the *National Review* and the conservatism of 'negation' which is too often in evidence on the campuses of southern universities." Despite the paper's welcome of Buckley, his talk in Memorial Hall was roundly criticized, not for what he said, but because he read aloud a piece he had recently written for *Playboy* magazine (and because he apparently absentmindedly scratched himself inappropriately at sev-

eral points during the appearance). At first the Carolina Forum, which sponsored the talk using student fees, refused to pay Buckley for simply reading a published article, but after several months of wrangling and finger-pointing, closely followed by the *Daily Tar Heel*, his fee was paid.[46]

If the editors and staff of the student newspaper were generally seen as left-leaning partisans during the 1960s, there were also strong conservative voices pushing back at UNC and statewide. Retired faculty member William C. George, whose arguments regarding the biological superiority of whites first made news in 1954, continued to espouse his ideology throughout much of the decade. The *Daily Tar Heel* published a column by George during the 1960 gubernatorial campaign, entitled "Why I'll Vote for Dr. [I. Beverly] Lake," expressing his support for the avowed pro-segregationist candidate. The paper covered George's activities extensively, including his 1962 study on race, commissioned by the state of Mississippi during the height of efforts to desegregate Ole Miss, and his public comments that college professors, particularly at schools like UNC, "indoctrinate integration." One *DTH* editorial noted sarcastically that George was "anxious to help our Negro people develop the talents they possess but is unwilling to sacrifice our white children needlessly and foolishly, in the process."[47]

In the early 1960s, residents of the Triangle area could turn on their black-and-white television sets every weeknight to watch conservative commentator Jesse Helms, who appeared at the end of the local evening news on WRAL-TV, broadcast from Raleigh. Helms's career included work on the Willis Smith campaign during the 1950 Senate race that unseated Frank

Porter Graham and a stint as a sportswriter
for the *Raleigh Times*, the capital city's evening
newspaper, which was generally more conservative than its morning counterpart, The *News
and Observer*. In 1960, WRAL station owner A. J.
Fletcher hired Helms to serve as executive vice
president of the company and to provide on-air
commentary. In his daily "Viewpoint" editorials, Helms promoted all manner of conservative
causes, including racial segregation, and sharply
and often cleverly jabbed liberal perspectives
and institutions. Chief among the latter were
UNC–Chapel Hill and its student-run newspaper. Soon the university and the editors of the
Daily Tar Heel found themselves with another
David Clark on their hands, but this time the pulpit was not a trade publication but the powerful
new medium of television. The opening salvo in

what would become an eight-year running battle
of words and wit between the conservative commentator and the paper came in December 1962.
Helms charged that "not only does the *Daily Tar
Heel* slant news, it prints Communist advertisements as well," a reference to book titles offered
in an ad for the Intimate Bookshop, the site of
early Communist Party meetings in the 1930s
and a notorious target of conservatives. Helms
apparently failed to notice the equally large ads
some months later that were placed by the Colonial Drug Store (one of the town businesses
most reluctant to desegregate) offering a book by
Sarah Watson Emery entitled *Blood on the Old
Well*, a salacious tale branding UNC as a nest of
Communist vipers and degenerate homosexuals.
Once Helms found a target that resonated with
his audience, he would pummel it mercilessly.[48]

But the *Daily Tar Heel* also had its own conservative voices from within. The most notable was the columnist Armistead Maupin. From the fall of 1962 to the spring of 1966, Maupin, who hailed from a prominent southern family, served on the *DTH* staff, and his regular column, "A View from the Hill," offered thoughtful and at times biting counterpoint to the liberal perspective. In one of his first columns he declared that "the conservative has never had an easy time of it at Carolina," and indeed during his four years on the paper he found himself no stranger to controversy. Maupin routinely criticized what would later be called political correctness: he poked fun at black leaders who objected to racial stereotypes in American popular culture such as Aunt Jemima and ridiculed those who sought to ban the Confederate song "Dixie" at N.C. State events. He called the Student Nonviolent Coordinating Committee (SNCC) "The Student Non-Coordinated Committee," and when Students for a Democratic Society formed a chapter at UNC, he said in a column titled "The Leftovers" that it was established for no other reason than "to provide a meeting place for liberals and radicals."[49]

Maupin reserved his harshest criticism for those involved with the civil rights movement, providing opinions consistently at variance with both the paper's editorial perspective and its news coverage. He took the African American community to task, pointing to low literacy rates, voter apathy, and black males' desertion of their families. Maupin was particularly critical of black leaders such as Dick Gregory, whose speech at one rally he characterized as proclaiming "dependence on relief checks is an honest living and that, until the white man has assuaged the Negro's economic pains, the Negro should

continue to draw government welfare." Maupin argued that "instead of stressing the civic and moral consciousness that comprise 'first-class citizenship,' these clever professionals aimed, rather, to stimulate only bitterness and a sort of righteous irresponsibility. Glossing over their own shortcomings and those of their race, they labeled all critics as 'prejudiced.'" To provide evidence to support his assertions, Maupin listed Washington, Chicago, and Philadelphia as northern cities "where years of integrated schools, restaurants, and recreational facilities have failed to alleviate a problem that most Negro leaders blame on 'discrimination' or 'white oppression.'" When the field secretary for CORE, Rev. B. Elton Cox of High Point, threatened to burn himself on Easter Sunday to protest segregated restaurants, Maupin darkly quipped: "If you feel so inclined, go ahead and light the match, Reverend Cox. But frankly, it won't make me feel any more inclined to eat lunch with you."[50]

Like Jesse Helms, for whom he worked at one point, Maupin stood firm in the face of his critics. Liberals on campus constantly registered their objections to both the columnist and his opinions, but Maupin remained steadfast, and he continued to be prominently featured on the editorial page. As one letter to the editor put it, "Mr. Maupin has in effect become the campus mouthpiece of Jesse Helms, thereby allowing the Raleigh broadcaster to get his foot further into the door of this campus to subvert the University of North Carolina." Alden Lind, a faculty member in the Political Science Department, could not restrain his disgust and chastised the editors of the paper for allowing Maupin and other conservatives to have a bully pulpit. "This august newspaper has made many intellectual and artistic

Armistead Maupin, conservative columnist for the *Daily Tar Heel*, 1962–1966, and later celebrated novelist whose works include *Tales of the City*. (*Yack*)

contributions to the campus of the University," Lind wrote, but with "increasing frequency it has graced the campus with its devotion to the darker of the achromatic colors." Lind accused the paper of "misreporting activities, attitudes, and motivations of those with whom it does not agree, by printing 'clever' editorials and 'clever' cartoons," adding that some in the university community "grow a little nervous when the *DTH* becomes the judge of what is or is not patriotic." The criticism also came from within—staff cartoonists lampooned Maupin, and the grudgingly backhanded compliment of another columnist, Chuck Neely, expressed what many thought: "Although we are in almost total disagreement with Mr. Maupin's rather unenlightened racial views ... [he has at times] put forth a lucid, logical argument against the irresponsibility of certain segments of the Negro leadership." Despite Maupin's strident conservative views, his life after UNC went in a completely different direction. Following graduation he served in Vietnam and then did an about-face in the 1970s; he came out as a gay man, wrote a celebrated series of novels about gay life in San Francisco, and became more politically liberal.[51]

The tension that had been festering for decades in North Carolina between competing political ideologies, exacerbated by the explosive issue of race, reached a breaking point in the early 1960s. The most significant result of this fissure for UNC was passage of "An Act To Regulate Visiting Speakers at State Supported Colleges and Universities"—otherwise known as the Gag or Speaker Ban Law—by the state legislature on June 25, 1963. One of the most infamous pieces of legislation in North Carolina history, the law was the greatest threat to free speech and academic

freedom ever faced at the state's public universities. Its three main provisions barred from speaking on publicly funded campuses anyone who was "a known member of the Communist Party," was "known to advocate the overthrow of the constitution of the United States or the state of North Carolina," or had "pleaded the Fifth Amendment of the Constitution of the United States in refusing to answer any question, with respect to communist or subversive connections, or activities." Responsibility for policing the campuses on this matter was given to the consolidated university board of trustees, whose membership largely opposed it. President William

Friday, reflecting years later on the Speaker Ban Law, summed up the situation: "I always felt that freedom is the basic lesson you have to teach every student. . . . No self-respecting university can call itself a first rate educational institution without the right of free expression."[52]

The Speaker Ban Law and the efforts to repeal it have been much discussed and examined over the decades, ever since a federal court struck the law down as unconstitutional on February 19, 1968, nearly five years after it was enacted. However, reading about events as they happened, through coverage and editorials in the *Daily Tar Heel*, adds to the understanding of the story and reveals previously overlooked elements. In addition, a study of the history of the *DTH* makes clear that the roots of the issue were complex and some four decades in the making. A direct line can be drawn from the political controversies involving the university from the mid-1920s to the enactment of the Speaker Ban Law in 1963. These controversies began with the fight over the teaching of evolution in public schools and support by university faculty for workers' rights at the state's mills and factories in the mid- and late 1920s, continued through the flirtations with Communism by a few students and the presence of far-leftist speakers on campus in the 1930s and 1940s, through the Red Scare and McCarthyism in the late 1940s and early 1950s, and to racial integration and civil rights activities in the 1950s and early 1960s. Even cancellation of the Dixie Classic in 1961 by UNC President William Friday was likely a contributing factor to creation of the law, as a number of the state's conservative leaders were furious with him for ending the popular tournament. Specific incidents foreshadowing the law include the banning of Leon

Trotsky from UNC in 1937 by U.S. Secretary of State Cordell Hull, and the barring of John Gates from speaking on campus in 1949 by UNC Chancellor Robert House, which led to the dramatic spectacle of Gates speaking extemporaneously to some 1,000 students in front of Chapel Hill High School. In 1952, a front-page *Daily Tar Heel* editorial on academic freedom noted the effect of such precedents: "Since the unfortunate experience of the John Gates affair, few organizations have dared to bring controversial speakers to the campus. . . . The tendency now (which is due in large part to the Administration's past attitude) is toward 'safe speakers'—namely, local Democratic politicians, military men in abundance, or safe conservatives."[53]

As with the issue of civil rights, the editors and staff of the *Daily Tar Heel* sought to cover the Speaker Ban Law as news, to offer editorial commentary, and to serve as a public forum on the matter. Eventually it would also assume an activist role in advocating for abolishment of the law. The paper decried the Speaker Ban Law from the start, and it never waivered from that position; however, as with racial segregation, there was not always agreement about how best to overturn it. The story first broke in late June 1963, when the state legislature hurriedly passed the bill in the final days of the session, apparently to get it on the books before major opposition could be organized. But if the state politicians thought they would also catch the universities unaware between semesters, they sorely misjudged the attentiveness of some students—particularly those responsible for the summer edition of UNC's student newspaper. Editor Mike Putzel sprang into action by covering the rushed legislation in banner front-page headlines, and ferociously attacking the law in lead editorials. In a front-page boxed editorial entitled "Burden of Shame," which ran in the *Tar Heel* two days after the bill passed, Putzel wrote:

The American university, by tradition and definition, has been and should continue to be a place of inquiry—an institution where students and scholars are free to explore, to question and to doubt ideas of their own and of their predecessors ...

We do not believe that destruction of North Carolina's higher education system is the goal of the state legislature, nor is it their intention, but such will be the result of their speaker ban law ...

The reputation of this University is a great one, and we can all afford to be proud of its history. But when academic freedom is lost, the heart and the reputation of the University are lost with it.

This burden, no institution can be expected to bear.[54]

Reaction to the bill was swift, and university officials unanimously opposed it. President Friday tried unsuccessfully to have the bill repealed, and he and Chancellor William Aycock were among the first to publicly condemn the law. Former UNC president Frank Porter Graham, himself no stranger to attempts to muzzle freedom of speech at the state's public universities, put the situation into broader context in a speech he gave in August 1963, which was quoted extensively in the *Tar Heel*. "North Carolina, the historic home of complete freedom of political and ideological discussion," Graham declared, "has suddenly shown a lack of faith in

the robustness of our free American democratic institutions by restricting the complete freedom of political and ideological discussion in our state colleges." Despite unified opposition to the Speaker Ban Law in the university community, it was unclear how to rescind it, and the administration urged students to proceed with great caution. Apparently this included asking the newspaper to comply, as two weeks after the law was passed, Putzel wrote a lead editorial, somewhat grudgingly, entitled "We Must Be Gagged." "The Trustees have placed upon the students the responsibility for enforcing the gag law," Putzel wrote, "and to be sure, we do not relish the job, nor see it as an easy task. But nonetheless, for the immediate present it is imperative that the law be upheld." Urging a measured response, Putzel added, "there are many of the law's opponents, this newspaper and the Trustees included, who are anxious to see it erased from the books, but the means used in any attempt to do so could be important."[55]

Some observers blamed the *Daily Tar Heel* for the Speaker Ban Law. One letter to the editor in July 1963 cited the paper's "bad diplomacy and poor public relations which, in a sense, may have particularly necessitated—and even fostered—the enactment of the controversial law." Specifically the writer pointed to the paper's ridiculing of the state and local chapters of the American Legion, including having "branded" their actions with regard to leftist groups at UNC as a "witch hunt." Passage of the law, in fact, emboldened the membership of the American Legion, which stepped up attacks on what it saw as subversive elements on campus. Days after the law went on the books the statewide organization passed a resolution decrying the UNC Progressive Labor

Club as a "red nest" and calling it "atheistic and hate-embittered." In August, Legion officials charged UNC with flagrantly violating the ban by inviting Communist Party leader Milton Rosen to speak. Apparently in an attempt to show that the university welcomed all sides of the debate, the state head of the American Legion, L. J. Phipps, was invited to be the featured speaker at University Day in October.[56]

Early debate over the Speaker Ban led to a running battle of words between the *Daily Tar Heel* and Jesse Helms. In the fall of 1963, Helms allegedly made a comment on a radio program that he would welcome a face-to-face debate with the coeditors of the *DTH* about the controversial law. In a lead column entitled "An Editorialist's Dilemma," Gary Blanchard and David Ethridge cleverly and somewhat sarcastically pondered the question of whether to reply. A week later the paper officially issued Helms and other state conservatives an open invitation to come to UNC and publicly debate the matter. Helms issued a dismissive reply, labeling the invitation "distasteful and vague." He stated that he was on television every day and that his views were well known, and he denied having issued the debate challenge in the first place. He suggested the editors invite former U.S. president Herbert Hoover, who had come out in support of the ban. Calling Helms a "hypocrite," Blanchard and Ethridge pushed back, convinced they had caught the conservative commentator in a contradiction, claiming that he had offered to "cancel prime time" to confront them about the Speaker Ban. The spitting match dragged on into early 1964, when the owner of the radio station was asked to review the tape of the broadcast to determine exactly what Helms had said. The matter was never fully settled however, as—in shades of the Watergate scandal a decade later—the vital part of the tape was mysteriously missing.[57]

Throughout the summer and fall of 1963, the *Daily Tar Heel* kept the university community informed of developments regarding the Speaker Ban Law and continued to call for its repeal. It also pointed to obvious hypocrisies: when the North Carolina Council on Women invited a female representative from the Russian embassy to speak in the new State Legislative Building, the paper noted the irony that the same talk could not be legally held on public university property. An in-depth series on the Speaker Ban, beginning with a piece entitled "A Shot in the Stomach," appeared on the front page over three days in early October, written by Hugh Stevens, who would be elected coeditor of the paper the following spring. Fred Seely, who would become the other half of the editor in chief team in 1964, and who described himself as politically moderate, urged students to act. "The Gag Law controversy is more than just a liberal-conservative argument," Seely wrote. "It affects you and I as surely as any University decree, and you and I are the people who must lead the fight against it." Each time an institution, prominent individual, or other entity came out publicly against the law, the paper reported it as news. These included the UNC Student Legislature; the Wake Forest student paper, the *Gold and Black*, and the conservative-leaning *Wall Street Journal*, whose editor, Vermont Royster, was a UNC alumnus who served on the editorial staff of the *Daily Tar Heel* in the 1930s. In late October, after the UNC board of trustees and the Faculty Council passed resolutions condemning the Speaker Ban, the editors wrote, "We no longer feel like orphans. … We are a good deal more confident about the future of the University."[58]

Clearly, the increasingly strident protests and demonstrations by civil rights activists were a leading cause of enactment of the law, though at first legislators and conservatives denied it. The *Daily Tar Heel* saw through the facade, as summer editor Mike Putzel wrote in August 1963:

In the short period of only three months there have been events in Chapel Hill and in the state which have been cause for revolutionary change in the minds of men.

The State Legislature has instituted legal boundaries on academic freedom in what appears to be an attempt to protect the citizens of the state from totalitarianism.

Negroes in Chapel Hill and throughout North Carolina have risen up to claim their rights as full and first-class citizens, and they have taken a stand from which it would be almost impossible to back down.

And behind both these issues lies a fundamental concept of freedom, something to which we as human beings, as Americans and certainly as students should give sober thought.

In November the paper ran an editorial entitled "The Stench of Truth Is Gagging," breaking the story that North Carolina secretary of state Thad Eure, in an unguarded moment, admitted that the Speaker Ban bill was introduced because he and other officials were infuriated by civil rights protests orchestrated to cause disruption in and around the Sir Walter Hotel in downtown Raleigh, where many of the North Carolina General Assembly members stayed during the legislative session. Participants in these protests included students from various public universities, at least one UNC professor, and Allard Lowenstein, well-known UNC alumnus and then an assistant professor of political science at N.C. State. Eure's accidental admission confirmed what had been widely suspected, and exposed state officials as being not only pro-segregationist, but also in a vindictive mood against UNC.[59]

In spite of Eure's statement, and except for the ongoing squabble between the *Daily Tar Heel* and Jesse Helms, the debate over the Speaker Ban was relatively quiet following the Kennedy assassination in late November 1963. After nearly a week of national mourning, public attention and news coverage focused once again on civil rights, as the next several months turned out to be the most intense period of protests in Chapel Hill. In addition, there was apparently a decision by William Friday and other UNC administrators to largely forgo public opposition to the law until after the election of a new governor, who would take office in January 1965. The results of that election did not bode well for speedy repeal of the Speaker Ban, however; the new governor, Dan K. Moore, was considerably more conservative than his predecessor, Terry Sanford.[60]

While Friday and other officials within the university system pondered a new approach to removing the onerous law, student opposition began to ferment in various quarters. A series of events from February 1965 through March 1966 brought the issue back onto the front pages of the state's newspapers and led to the lawsuit that would eventually bring the ban to an end. The first sign of renewed opposition came from conservative college students, interestingly, who were torn between a libertarian belief in free speech and a strident distaste for Communists. The *Daily Tar Heel* reported in early February 1965 that when the state Young Republicans passed a resolution at their annual conference supporting the law, the UNC chapter voted to oppose that action. Seeing the split between the campus chapter and the state organization, a *Daily Tar Heel* editorial cleverly announced: "The YRC [Young Republicans Conference] Bites Its Own Tongue."[61]

The spark that lit the fuse of active student opposition to the Speaker Ban Law came as the result of a rally held in February 1965 in the Y Court (a brick area in front of the YMCA building, which served such purposes in the days before the "Pit" was constructed in 1968). The rally was organized because a white student, James W. Gardner, alleged that as he walked in front of the Sigma Alpha Epsilon fraternity house with a Liberian student who was visiting UNC for a model United Nations Assembly, racial epithets were hurled at the two of them. "Insult May Spark Legal Action" and "Demonstrations Threatened," declared *Daily Tar Heel* front-page headlines in the following days. The paper also ran a sharp editorial rebuking Gardner, declaring the incident minor and not worth stirring up controversy that might harm efforts to end the Speaker Ban. In fact, it is likely that CORE, the NAACP, and campus organizations including the Free Speech Movement and the Student Peace Union (of which Gardner was a member, and which opposed the Vietnam War), whipped up furor about the incident as a pretext to publicly challenge student complacency over the Speaker Ban Law. Though the paper reported the insult was settled a few days later, the rally went ahead

on February 19. The keynote speaker was Floyd McKissick, who had a long history of civil rights activism at UNC. He was one of the four African American men to successfully desegregate the Carolina law school in 1951, and later became a leading figure in CORE and the NAACP in North Carolina.[62]

At the rally, McKissick appealed to students to uphold UNC's liberal reputation, get involved, and actively oppose the Speaker Ban. The *Daily Tar Heel* quoted his speech extensively on the front page the following day: "The liberal attitude at the University of North Carolina has changed.

People can't express themselves anymore. It's a far cry from the day when Frank Porter Graham was here.... There has been no positive objection to the Speaker Ban Law from the students. In other parts of the world where there is concern for freedom and dignity of man, the movements have started on the campuses." In a rare instance of disjunction between page one news coverage and page two opinion, the paper offered conflicting accounts of the rally. In the editorial, "Much Ado about Nothing," the editors expressed relief that the protest caused no great disturbance, entirely missing (or ignoring) the importance of McKissick's statements. Following the rally, the editors did allow James Gardner and a compatriot, Timothy Ray, to write a series of columns on free speech, civil rights, and the Speaker Ban, which elicited much commentary from the university community.[63]

McKissick's call for "positive objection" resonated with at least one student: Paul Dickson. An Air Force veteran who had served in Vietnam, Dickson was several years older than most students, and his experiences gave him a broad perspective. In February 1964, as chair of the campus Student Party, Dickson called for that organization to take a firm stand on civil rights, and he moderated a panel calling for the hiring of black professors and recruitment of black athletes, "provided they are academically qualified." Within days of McKissick's speech at the rally in February 1965, Dickson declared his candidacy for student-body president on a platform of actively working to repeal the Speaker Ban Law, and subsequently won the election. In his inaugural address, Dickson called the law "un-American" and issued an ultimatum: "If the General Assembly does not take action against the

law in the current session, let no man say that we are not willing to ripple the waters." In an orientation speech in front of 2,000 freshmen and transfer students in September 1965, he spoke with equal conviction, receiving a standing ovation. "I want it known, as long as I am student-body president," Dickson declared, "Student Government will not fear to risk its very being in fighting for repeal of the Speaker Ban law."[64]

Once again, the Speaker Ban Law was in the news and garnering national attention. The stakes for North Carolina's public universities were raised in May 1965, when it was announced that the Southern Association of Colleges and Schools was considering revoking accreditation of the state schools as a result of the Speaker Ban. "So What Else IS New?" a *Daily Tar Heel* editorial asked. Also that May, Carl Braden, of the Southern Conference Educational Fund, was denied permission to speak at UNC because of a conviction in 1959 on a charge of contempt of Congress for refusing to answer questions during a House Un-American Activities Committee hearing. The NAACP picketed the decision in front of South Building, and after Braden did appear at a local church, the paper summed up his speech in a headline: "Braden Denounces Speaker Ban, HUAC, KKK and [UNC] Administration." As a follow-up, the *Daily Tar Heel* made a strong point of noting the absurdity of the Speaker Ban Law by carrying a story a few months later about a Ku Klux Klan member who might be barred from keeping his scheduled speaking engagement at N.C. State University because he too had refused to answer questions during a congressional hearing.[65]

The *Daily Tar Heel* continued to keep up pressure against the Speaker Ban by publish-

ing interviews on the subject with national figures. Humorist Art Buchwald, in North Carolina to speak at N.C. State, told a reporter from
the paper in his trademark droll manner, "In my
opinion it doesn't matter if UNC loses its graduate students and accreditation, just so the remaining students are 100 percent American." The
1964 Republican presidential candidate, Senator Barry Goldwater of Arizona, caused a stir
when he told the *Daily Tar Heel*, "I don't believe
anybody—including Communists—should be
prevented from speaking on a state-supported
campus," though he added that he thought anti-
Communist speakers should be allowed to provide rebuttal. An editorial crowed: "It's one thing
when some idealistic academician or hopelessly
liberal newspaper condemns the speaker ban
law, but it's a pretty low blow to a '100 per cent
American's' pride when Mr. Conservative himself cuts loose on the law." One letter to the editor
called Goldwater's statement "a bombshell."[66]

Despite the *Daily Tar Heel*'s active opposition
to the Speaker Ban, the dramatic events leading to its repeal almost did not occur, as student-
body president Paul Dickson became embroiled
in a personal scandal in the fall of 1965 and soon
found himself at odds with both the university administration and the editor of the paper,
Ernest McCrary. During the summer of 1965,
Dickson was caught after sneaking a female student into his room at the Chi Psi fraternity house
overnight, and the matter was referred to the
university's Men's and Women's Honor Coun-
cils. Dickson's action was considered a serious
offense in the mid-1960s, a violation of both accepted social norms and the UNC campus code
of behavior. The female student received suspension by the women's council, but Dickson only

received what amounted to a slap on the wrist
by the men's council. The matter would likely
have ended there, but Chancellor Paul Sharp
and other administration officials decided Dickson should step down as student-body president,
and they tried to force the issue by threatening
to publicly reopen the case once the fall semester
began unless he resigned. Dickson, a Vietnam
War combat veteran, was not easily intimidated,
and he refused. The paper reported that Sharp
and dean of students C. O. Cathey declared Dickson "unsuited" for office, and they did not extend
to him the traditional invitation to participate in
University Day ceremonies. Jesse Helms jumped

into the fray, suggesting in his WRAL-TV editorial that Dickson's parents should give the twenty-four-year-old veteran "a spanking" and that the administration should have removed him so he could no longer "inflict upon us his asinine declarations of philosophy."[67]

Eight student leaders, including *Daily Tar Heel* editor McCrary, also felt Dickson should resign. McCrary chided the student-body president in print for "setting a poor example" and referred to the incident as carrying "implications of moral laxity." However, he was equally appalled at the actions of the university administration, whom he charged with attempting to "blackmail" Dickson, stating that their tactics only "inflames the situation." The triangular struggle between the administration, the student-body president, and the *Daily Tar Heel* roiled the campus. One student wrote to the paper, shocked by the actions of both the leaders and the paper: "If eight students and a newspaper can controvert the electoral decision of thousands of students, student government is meaningless." "Do the eight 'student leaders' and the *DTH* have some special powers in this case?" he asked. "Are these eight students and the *DTH* duly constituted to remove the president of the student body?" Dickson stood his ground, even in the face of a student petition for a recall election (which narrowly failed to get the requisite signatures). Ultimately he remained in office because students' distaste with the meddling of the administration was greater than any qualms they may have with his moral conduct.[68]

Just days after the UNC student court declared the petition to recall Paul Dickson invalid, the Speaker Ban was once again front-page news. "Out of the Ban and into the Fire," the lead editorial announced, referring to the recommendations of the so-called Britt Commission, a body appointed by Governor Moore and headed by state representative David Britt, to try to broker some sort of compromise regarding the controversial law. After months of hearings and testimony, the commission recommended that the law be amended to give the authority to approve speakers at a public college or university to that school's board of trustees and administrators. Supported by UNC President William Friday and the *Daily Tar Heel*, the compromise was approved by the board of the consolidated university and the state legislature, which was tiring of the matter. The compromise was not acceptable to everyone, however, and soon more radical groups decided to challenge it, which caused the editor of the paper, Ernest McCrary, to reassess the situation.[69]

In early February 1966, one of the most radical groups on campus, Students for a Democratic Society (SDS), decided to openly challenge the newly amended Speaker Ban Law by inviting two avowed Communists, historian Herbert Aptheker and activist Frank Wilkinson, to appear on campus. Aptheker had spoken at Carolina previously, and the *Daily Tar Heel* noted that his books were available in Wilson Library. When both men were approved to speak at Duke, the paper charged that their banishment from UNC gave the school "a black eye." Governor Moore came out publicly against Aptheker, and the paper, referring to the Britt Commission that Moore had established, charged that the governor "openly washed his hands of the problem, and the dirty water dripped on the University." At this point McCrary decided that the principles of free speech and academic freedom were too important to ignore and, despite any personal disagreements he had with Paul Dickson, concluded that the *Daily Tar Heel* must not only speak out on the matter, but become actively involved. In conjunction with student government and the Carolina Forum, the paper officially issued its own invitation to Aptheker to speak, as McCrary explained in a statement to the press, published as an editorial:

> We feel that the basic question of whether or not Aptheker should be allowed to speak has been confused and clouded by the association of the invitation with a group identified, justifiably or not, as leftist radicals.
>
> Because of the controversial nature of SDS we feel the trustees have been placed in the position of judging both the group and the man invited.
>
> We have extended the invitation to Aptheker to remove this complicating factor from the decision facing the executive committee of the board of trustees because we wish the decision to be made solely on the grounds of academic freedom, not emotional opposition to the inviting organization. The *Daily Tar Heel* and Student Government do not represent any elements deserving of this emotional opposition.[70]

Daily Tar Heel alumni, opposed to the attack on freedom of speech at their alma mater, also sprang into action after the Britt Commission compromise was adopted. Vermont Royster wrote a column in the conservative-leaning *Wall Street Journal* (his second on the subject) calling the Speaker Ban a bad law, and outlining lessons that should be learned from it. Several other alumni of the paper worked behind the scenes to repeal the law. J. McNeill Smith, editor of the paper in 1937 when Leon Trotsky was denied a visa to speak at UNC, and now a Greensboro attorney, privately counseled Paul Dickson. Ed Yoder, then associate editor for the *Greensboro Daily News*, revealed in an interview decades later a fascinating story involving himself and his colleague Chuck Hauser, at the time executive editor of the same newspaper. Alumnus George Watts Hill, a member of the executive committee of the consolidated university's board of trustees, would leave closed meetings held in the office of Governor Moore (an ex officio member of the committee), hasten to the nearest telephone, and relay the proceedings of the meeting on background to Yoder. In turn, Yoder would relay the information to Chuck Hauser, who immediately wrote a story for release in the *Greensboro Daily News*. As a result of this direct pipeline—which Yoder later called his "Deep Throat," a reference to the Watergate informant for the *Washington Post*—the Greensboro paper had for a period the best-informed articles on attempts made to deal with the Speaker Ban Law.[71]

As predicted, the UNC–Chapel Hill trustees instructed the university's new chancellor, Carlyle Sitterson, to refuse the request to allow Aptheker and Wilkinson to speak. In a dramatic public spectacle, the men appeared, Wilkinson on March 2 and Aptheker on March 9. They each stood on the sidewalk on Franklin Street, inches from a low stone wall that marked the boundary of the campus, and spoke to thousands of UNC students assembled on the other side. *Daily Tar Heel* photographer Jock Lauterer climbed a nearby tree to capture iconic images of the March 2 event, which were picked up by the

The Daily Tar Heel

The South's Largest College Newspaper—All-American Award Winner

CHAPEL HILL, NORTH CAROLINA, THURSDAY, MARCH 10, 1966

Founded February 23 1893

Ban Showdown:

Students Shout 'Louder, Herbie!'

Aptheker Tests Ban Law; 3,000 Listen Across Wall

Speech Attempted Under Silent Sam

IN THE CONFUSION at the foot of Silent Sam Herbert Aptheker (right) is led by Campus Security Chief Arthur Beaumont by arm and made to speak on the campus.

— DTH Photo by Jock Lauterer

Ban Law Deciding Factor In Resignation Of Arndt

Mathis Before Showtime:

A Down To Earth Singer

You Would Think Aptheker Was The 'Pied Piper' Of Chapel Hill

— DTH Photos by Jock Lauterer

Red Scholar Accepts Bid

Front page of the *Daily Tar Heel*, March 10, 1966, with photographs by *DTH* staff photographer Jock Lauterer.

wire services and sent to newspapers around the country. NBC News arrived for the Aptheker appearance, and broadcast footage on national television. The spot where the two men spoke was in view, symbolically, of the Confederate Soldiers' Monument colloquially known as "Silent Sam." Adding further irony to the situation, few students could actually hear either speaker, as the town of Chapel Hill had rejected an application by the student organizers to use a public address system.[72]

The Aptheker and Wilkinson appearances were carefully orchestrated by Paul Dickson and McNeill Smith to provide a solid basis for a lawsuit to challenge the law. On April 1, 1966, in one of his last acts as editor, Ernest McCrary, along with Dickson and ten other student leaders, signed the complaint filing suit against the university. Because the *Daily Tar Heel* was an official university publication, it could not bring suit against the school, but using his title as editor, McCrary signed as a private individual. The case wound its way through the federal courts for nearly two years, with the paper following its progress. Finally, on February 19, 1968—three years to the day of Floyd McKissick's call for action on campus—the law was struck down. A front-page article the next day announced, "State Speaker Ban Ruled Unconstitutional," and the lead editorial, "Score One for UNC," summed up the sentiments of many in the university community: "This law was evil, in the most Machiavellian tradition, and it would not be tolerated— even in its diluted form. It was one of the clearest breeches of the right of free speech, one of the most flagrant attempts of red neck politicians to curtail academic freedom, to which this University had ever been a victim." "The good guys," the editorial concluded, "won again."[73]

THE 1960S: A DECADE OF CULTURAL AND INSTITUTIONAL CHANGE AT UNC

All through the fall of 1970, in what was referred to as a case of "hair-rassment," the *Daily Tar Heel* followed the trials of UNC male cheerleader, Bernie Oakley. After the first home football game in September, a small group of alumni complained about Oakley's long hair and beard, both of which were on prominent display as he cheered the team on the sidelines. What at first seemed a humorous situation soon became the talk of campus, and an excellent example of the so-called generation gap wrought by cultural changes of the 1960s. When pressure from alumni resulted in Oakley's removal from the squad in early October for his refusal to cut his hair, the paper rushed to his defense. A lead editorial cried foul. "The complaints of alumni, all 13 of them," the paper declared, should not "decide that the image of the University should be the image of what the University was like ten years ago." Cheerleaders should reflect "an accurate portrayal of the student body ... and that reflection includes long hair." Apparently student opposition worked: on October 9, the *Daily Tar Heel* ran a headline above the banner reading, "Oakley Reinstated to Cheering Squad." This was not, however, the end of the story. In mid-December, in a letter printed on the paper's editorial page, Oakley announced his resignation as a UNC cheerleader. Soured both by the furor over his hair and by what he had witnessed of the football program up close, he wrote, "I feel we have lost all perspective as far as sports are

Front page photo of cheerleader Bernie Oakley, fired from the squad because of his long hair, October 1970.

Longhair Cheerleader Removed From Squad

Bernie Oakley

by Karen Jurgensen
Staff Writer

Long-haired, bearded cheerleader Bernie Oakley has been removed from the UNC cheering squad for refusing to cut his hair.

Squad coaches Barbara Yarborough Fred Sanders issued a cut or quit ultimatum to Oakley Monday. Head Cheerleader Gunnar Froman relayed the ultimatum to Oakely.

Oakely said he woudn't cut his hair and refused to quit. Froman said he then ordered Oakley to turn in his equipment.

Pressure from alumni was the reason for the ultimatum, according to Miss Yarborough.

After first reports of alumni unhappiness with Oakley's hair and beard two weeks ago, the squad adopted a policy which said long hair was all right as long as it was neat, clean and didn't hamper the cheerleader.

However, Miss Yarborough said the squad's vote conflicted with an Athletic Association rule that "any athlete on a team must keep his hair above his collar and ears."

Athletic Director Homer Rice said Wednesday night that there "is no standing rule concerning hair length."

"All we do is leave it up to each individual coach," Rice said.

The cheerleading squad is working this year under the jurisdiction of the Athletic Association. In previous years the squad was a part of student government but made the change last spring because of financial troubles.

Miss Yarborough added, "Under the Athletic Association we feel we have to abide by their rules. If we don't, it's going to hurt us financially...The alumni will withhold money, so I have to take the stand I do. This position is most advantageous for the group."

Asked for his reaction, Oakley said, "The whole situation is so illogical. We were told we'd have to have a rule. I said I'd abide by what the cheerleaders decided. We got a good rule, and the advisors didn't like it. So I guess what we say doesn't really matter.

"The only reason anyone has given me is the money from the alumni," he said. "They say some alumni would actually withhold money if I don't cut my hair or get off the squad."

Miss Yarborough said Athletic Director Homer Rice got 13 complaints about Oakley from alumni after the N.C. State game Sept. 19.

After the squad voted, head cheerleader Froman was told by Rice that Miss Yarborough and Sanders were coaches for the squad instead of advisors.

Froman said of the coahces, "It's their decision and we have to do it. There's an image we have to try to uphold although the students and I might not agree with it. That's the image of the cheerleader.

concerned," and he cited money and winning as "ruining" collegiate athletics. Echoing concerns voiced by *Daily Tar Heel* staff since 1953, Oakley further lamented, "All the emphasis on sports has been shifted from participation to economics. Those involved in sports now are little more than mercenaries, and any compromise in standards for admittance only worsens the situation."[74]

Long hair was not the only change concerning UNC alumni and the greater university community during the era. As the state's population rapidly expanded and demand for an educated workforce grew with development of new economic drivers such as the Research Triangle Park, pressure was put on the increasingly outmoded consolidated UNC system. Twice during the period, in 1963 and again in 1971, the organizational model created in 1931 was restructured and schools were added to what ultimately became the new sixteen-campus University of North Carolina System. The 1971 changes were the most sweeping, scrapping the old consolidated UNC framework and creating a new, streamlined board of governors. William Friday transitioned from being president of the old system to being appointed president of the new one, though not without some difficulty and controversy.[75]

The *Daily Tar Heel* followed these changes with varying levels of interest. The 1963 changes, which included admitting women as freshmen to UNC and men as freshmen to the former Woman's College (now renamed UNC–Greensboro), were not of particular concern to the staff of the paper, who were focused on civil rights and the Speaker Ban Law. The events leading up to the 1971 restructuring, however, garnered significant attention in the paper's news coverage and editorials. Of particular concern were attempts by the chancellor and alumni of East Carolina College (ECC, later East Carolina University) to build that school into a rival of UNC–Chapel Hill. The most visible example of this effort was the drive to create a full school of medicine on the Greenville campus, which was publicly opposed by William Friday. "So East Carolina 'University' President Leo Jenkins has asked Consolidated University President William C. Friday for help in obtaining funds for ECC's ailing medical school program," one editorial noted derisively. "That's a lot like President Nixon asking Sen. McGovern to endorse Vietnamization."[76]

The paper expressed grave reservations about the conflict between the two schools, concerned that UNC would become a "political football" in the process, especially as Governor Bob Scott was siding with the ECC proponents. The sports analogies continued when staff writer

Lou Bonds suggested in print that Scott's support for the ECC plan was payback for Jenkins's support in the 1968 gubernatorial election, and a lead editorial accused the governor of "playing educational politics in [the] wrong ballpark." The *Daily Tar Heel* called the plan to scrap the original consolidated system "a smokescreen," declaring that "building overlapping facilities across the state is a foolish waste of tax resources." Rumors abounded that President Friday could lose his job in the struggle, though these proved not to be true. As the battle over a new system reached the end, a lead editorial put the issue into perspective:

> A plan that would expand the Consolidated University rather than destroy it is a political compromise, and many (including the *Daily Tar Heel*) have voiced concern over political maneuvering placing higher education in a worse condition than at present. But something must be done to improve the state's universities. If changes are to be made, they should be made around a system that has proven itself as the Consolidated University has done for almost half a century, a system that now includes schools with some of the most progressive programs in the southeast.[77]

Changes in the UNC system coincided with changes in the landscape on the Chapel Hill campus. The "Collegiate Colonial" style, adopted as the official architectural design in the master plan developed after World War I, reigned supreme for nearly half a century. But by the early 1960s, driven in part by the influence of faculty at the renowned School of Design at N.C. State, modernism began to take root in North

Carolina. Even the conservative state legislature moved into a radically modern building in Raleigh designed by Edward Durell Stone—passing one of its first bills, the Speaker Ban Law, in the new edifice. At UNC, growth in enrollment and a $20 million state appropriation brought the first major building campaign since the Public Works Administration projects in the 1930s, which also broke aesthetically with the traditional neoclassical design. The architecture of what became South Campus reflected the new modernism, with high-rise dorms and Chase Dining Hall. The centerpiece, however, was development of the area east of Wilson Library. Three new dramatic, white two-story concrete and stone buildings—a student union, a student store, and an undergraduate library—rose around a paved sunken courtyard in what had at one time been Emerson Athletic Field. The common area was quickly dubbed "the Pit," and it became the campus town center, hosting all manner of events, protests, and student activities.[78]

The stark white, stone-and-concrete modernist buildings, which contrasted with most of the existing warm redbrick architecture, were not without controversy. "Student Union Plans Raise Roof," the Daily Tar Heel announced in November 1964, when drawings and models of the new complex were unveiled. Debate raged for several months, but one recent graduate, Arthur Ringwalt Jr. (who had transferred from N.C. State), wrote a thoughtful and lengthy letter to the editor putting the new designs into context. "Let us be consistent concerning the architecture of our campus," he wrote. "Four-story buildings are erected on the campus, laboratories and other modern facilities are placed in them and they are then called 'colonial.' Isn't having an eighteenth

century campus as silly as having eighteenth century learning? If we are really on the new frontiers of learning, why don't we apply them to all the disciplines including architecture?" Ringwalt pointed out to critics of the new designs that while the older structures were attractive, they were often not practical: "Human beings have to adjust to these buildings ….[They] were built partially for their 'colonial' exterior appearance. If you do not believe me, observe the main entrance to Dey Hall between classes; try to find the stairs in Phillips Hall; or try to find the men's rest room in Saunders Hall."[79]

The new architecture was not simply an academic matter for the staff of the Daily Tar Heel. When construction on the new student union (named for former UNC president Frank Porter Graham) was completed in 1968, the paper moved in, leaving its home of thirty-seven years, Graham Memorial. Despite the excitement and modernity of the fresh new building, Wayne Hurder, who was the editor at the time, remembered feeling sorry to leave the old redbrick structure behind. The student union was to be the Daily Tar Heel's last home on the UNC campus, and its longest in one location; offices remained there until 2010, when the paper moved into a building on Rosemary Street.[80]

The coming of modern architecture to campus coincided with the cultural revolution of the era, which widened the generation gap between students and most adults in the university community (faculty, administrators, and alumni), and provided convenient fodder for UNC's critics. Along with hairstyles and dress, cultural changes were particularly evident in popular music, the developing use of recreational drugs, and, most notably, attitudes and practices re-

For the paper's seventy-fourth anniversary in February 1967, staff photographer Jock Lauterer assembled a number of the senior staff in a corner of the *DTH* offices in Graham Memorial and mimicked the 1893 photograph of the first staff (page 12). Among those shown here are 1966–67 editor Scott Goodfellow (seated center, holding pen); 1968–69 editor Wayne Hurder (seated far left); cartoonists Jeff MacNelly (standing far left) and Bruce Strauch (standing far right); Sandy Treadwell, later a writer for *Sports Illustrated* and active in national Republican Party politics, serving at one time as New York's secretary of state (seated third from right); and Don Campbell, who went on to be a longtime columnist for *USA Today* (seated far right). (Jock Lauterer)

garding sex and traditional gender roles. As it did with the major social and political issues of the day, the *Daily Tar Heel* both covered these changes as news, and commented extensively on them in editorials. The paper also supported specific causes, such as lowering the voting age to eighteen (a position it noted was a rare instance of agreement with the Republican Party); and in January 1964 running a large front-page story when the U.S. surgeon general issued his seminal report linking cancer to smoking, a habit widely practiced on the campus of the largest public university in the state that produced the most cigarettes in the country.[81]

The biggest cultural issues of the 1960s and early 1970s on the UNC campus, and in the pages of the *Daily Tar Heel*, involved the related subjects of premarital sex, how the University should regulate interaction between men and women, the role of women in society, and women's social and reproductive rights. *Daily Tar Heel* coverage of sex had been virtually nonexistent into the early 1960s, aside from reporting about sex-related lectures and discussions in an academic context (usually regarding when one should marry and have children). There was the occasional sly reference or double entendre, but the bawdy banter often found in college papers was usually relegated to the various humor publications at UNC and kept off the pages of the *DTH*. The subject was simply not considered appropriate for public discourse. A 1950 column on the editorial page said it all: the heading, "Sex on Campus," was followed by blank space where text would normally appear.[82]

The so-called sexual revolution of the 1960s was soon evident, however, both at the university and in the student paper. In March 1963, a front-page story and photo ran under the headline "Playmate Bunny Likes UNC Males," about the visit to campus of a "bunny" who had appeared in the men's magazine *Playboy*. The magazine's founder, Hugh Hefner, appeared at UNC in May 1965 in Memorial Hall, "puffing on his ubiquitous pipe," as the paper reported, telling a packed audience of students that "sex and life are wonderful, enjoy them." Hefner's message went beyond the titillating and spoke to the changing role of women in the sexual revolution. "Women can begin to play a fuller role in American society," Hefner said, adding, "I don't think they've learned that yet."[83]

Only a few months after Hefner's appearance, the story of Paul Dickson's indiscretion with a female student was splashed across the pages of the *Daily Tar Heel*, and hotly debated through most of the fall of 1965. The story had a number of significant implications beyond the honor of the two students involved; the incident occurred on the cusp of changing attitudes both about premarital sex and the place of women in society at large, and the inequity of the punishment meted out to the two students shone a bright light on the double standard of the day. As other newspapers around the state noted, the young woman was judged to be immoral, yet Dickson's indiscretion was dismissed with the notion that "boys will be boys." The situation provided Jesse Helms with an opportunity to editorialize, charging UNC with applying "curious standards of morality." The affair also began a campus conversation about who should regulate morality in a democratic, secular society. A column in the *Daily Tar Heel* labeled the petition to recall Dickson "deplorable," arguing that it was "a symbol of public face versus private morals."[84]

The Dickson episode also occurred during a period when there was much discussion at Carolina about "in loco parentis"—a Latin term used to refer to the role of the university acting as parent in absentia for students—and the related arguments over "visitation," involving whether members of the opposite sex should be allowed in dorm rooms (and even apartments off campus), and the ending of curfews for women, as none existed for men. Both issues appeared in articles and editorials in the paper from 1963 until the last of the regulations was dropped in the fall of 1970. There was also serious conversation that year about the creation of non-gender-specific dorms, with the *Daily Tar Heel* arguing that such dorms would actually "dissuade campus sex." The paper noted that national poll-

ing showed sexual activity on college campuses was the same in the 1960s as it had been in the 1940s—25 percent of women reported being sexually active, and 50 percent of men.[85]

The state's conservative leaders were alarmed by the erosion of traditional values and permissiveness wrought by the sexual revolution and the movement toward a broader role for women in society. In May 1971, as a result of the relaxation of policies at UNC, state senator Jyles Coggins introduced a bill in the legislature to stop visitation of members of the opposite sex in dormitories at state-supported schools. That measure failed, but it was not the first attempt to regulate morality on public campuses. An earlier episode in the fall of 1966 had been of greater concern to the university community as it brought UNC's leading conservative critic, Jesse Helms, into a debate about what was taught in classrooms, and had drawn a great deal of unwanted national attention to the university.[86]

The incident began innocently enough. Michael Paull, a graduate student who was teaching an introductory course in English literature, assigned his students to read "To His Coy Mistress," a seventeenth-century poem by Andrew Marvell, and asked them to write a twentieth-century version of it along the same lines. The subject of the poem was man's mortality, using the literary device of a man describing how he would approach a woman if time were endless. Apparently several young male students in the class misunderstood either the assignment or the poem—or were simply attempting humor—and wrote rather risqué papers. When one or two of these papers were read aloud in class, in front of several female students, it was clear the contents were inappropriate and Paull asked the students responsible to redo the assignment. The incident came to the attention of Helms, who by coincidence was planning an editorial about a racy love story recently published in the *Carolina Quarterly*, the campus literary magazine, which Paull was editing at the time. During one of his televised editorials, Helms called Paull "sexually preoccupied" and described the piece in the *Quarterly* as "a bit of fiction which spells out details of a sordid bit of fornication on a 100-pound block of ice." Regarding the "To His Coy Mistress" affair, Helms whipped up his viewership with an embellished and inaccurate account of events, declaring that there was "no doubt, the boys enjoyed the vicarious frolic of talking about erotic matters in the presence of girl students."[87]

Two days after the Helms editorial aired, all hell broke loose. Following a quick inquiry into the matter, UNC Chancellor Carlyle Sitterson relieved Paull of his teaching duties, citing "words that were inserted merely for shock value" in one or more papers read aloud, despite the fact that the investigation also showed that "apparently Mr. Paull's class misinterpreted the assignment." Fred Thomas, editor of the *Daily Tar Heel*, was stunned. In an editorial, "Who's Afraid of Jesse Helms? The University—That's Who" (a pun on the title of a recent popular film starring Richard Burton and Elizabeth Taylor, about a college English professor and his wife), Thomas wrote a scathing condemnation of the situation, and of the attack on the university's academic freedom:

The relegation of graduate instructor Michael Paull to 'duties other than teaching' is a monumental tribute to WRAL-TV's manager Jesse Helms and his never-ending campaign to mis-construe the image of and cast public disfavor upon the University. It is also sad commentary on the ability of public opinion—or better stated, public misunderstanding—to alter the course of academic freedom. Helms, who would make a good running mate for Lester Maddox, has long been noted for his reactionary approach to everything that happens in Chapel Hill.

We were not at all surprised to find Helms in the center of such a contorted picture. We've more or less resigned ourselves to accepting him as one of the unavoidable evils of our society. But we were quite distressed that his rasping tongue should be so powerful as to cut through the respected walls that protect academic freedom from an often misunderstanding citizenry and influence our administrative leaders to remove this instructor from his classroom.

Thomas's powerful editorial went on to win a prestigious Hearst Journalism Award, but he was not the only voice at the *Daily Tar Heel* to speak out. Associate editor John Greenbacker wrote that Sitterson took the action because he was "hounded by the vicious ignorance of Jesse Helms, the unofficial leader of those elements of the state who would tear the University of Chapel Hill apart in a frenzy of rabid hatred." Greenbacker also noted that the chancellor "had his mind tormented by the reactive criticism of the faculty, which has misconstrued his decision as being based upon the dictates of the University's enemies."[88]

For three weeks the story dominated not only the *Daily Tar Heel* and many state newspapers—in his column in the *Greensboro Daily*

News, former *DTH* editor Ed Yoder called Helms a "bully television pundit" and referred to WRAL as running "poisonous innuendos against the university"—but also national media, appearing in the *New York Times*, *Life* magazine, and on the CBS Evening News. Students marched in protest in front of South Building, because, as one student told a *Daily Tar Heel* reporter, "people in similar positions are open to the same kind of statewide WRAL pressure." When a group of English professors threatened to walk out over Paull's suspension, a panel of five faculty members was created to investigate the matter. The panel quickly exonerated Paull, and in early November, chancellor Sitterson reinstated him to the classroom.[89]

The situation, as serious as it was, also had its humorous side. The inevitable poetic parodies appeared in the *Daily Tar Heel*, as did searing cartoons by Bruce Strauch. A photograph ran showing a protestor carrying a sign that read, "Helms for chancellor; eliminate the middle man." But the "Coy Mistress Caper"—as *Life* named it—marked a significant moment in the developing "culture wars" of the era, both because it represented the morality-based nature of the New Right then consolidating in the South and because it was an attempt by conservatives to reach into the public university classroom and reshape the parameters of academic freedom. This was not a new battle for UNC, but it was an assault being fired from a new weapon: television.[90]

Jesse Helms never admitted that he had blown the situation out of proportion, but he did take a final potshot at the *Daily Tar Heel*. In a front-page interview, noted as a "Special to the *DTH*," Helms stated that his television editorial had "no effect in putting pressure on Chancellor Sitter-

son." Asked why he thought it important to comment at all on a classroom incident, he replied, "Happenings on the UNC campus are political situations because the University is a part of government and subject to criticism from the state." "How much enlightenment can be gained from bawdy themes?" Helms asked rhetorically. "Shakespeare did not dip into the sewer for the main subject of his themes. Do students mean by academic freedom the right to do anything they want, anytime they want?" In reply to a question about how he felt regarding the way he was covered in the student newspaper, Helms became coy himself. Saying he was not "well acquainted with the *Daily Tar Heel*, and couldn't comment on it"—despite several public battles he'd had with the paper since 1962, and the fact that his wife, Dot, was on the *DTH* staff as a student in the 1940s—he added dismissively, "I assume that its workers are young people learning to become professional newspapermen."[91]

But not even the increasing cultural muscle of Jesse Helms and the conservative Right could stop the coming of the sexual revolution and the women's movement that followed. In February 1967 a story appeared on the front page entitled "Should University Health Service Provide THE Pill?" While the paper supported availability of the pill, Dr. Edward Hedgpeth, who was head of the Student Health Service, went on record in the article saying that unmarried women would not receive the pill "under any circumstances" and that, "for medical and moral reasons," any such woman requesting it would be confronted with staff who would try to "straighten her out in other ways." The Student Health Service, Hedgpeth declared, would not "sanction indiscriminate promiscuity."[92]

The title graphic used for the "Elephants and Butterflies" column in the *Daily Tar Heel*, which began running in December 1970.

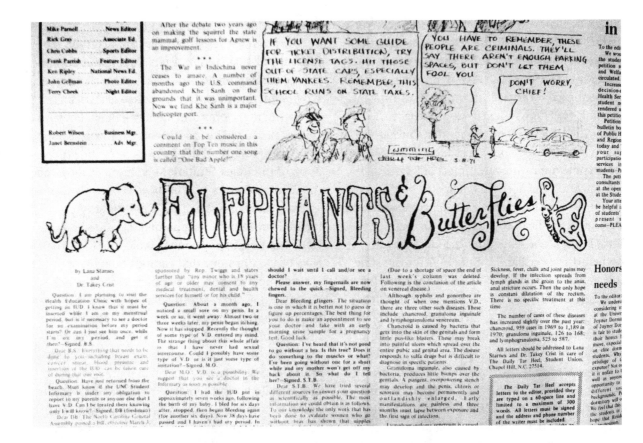

Unable to move administrators like Hedgpeth, students took matters into their own hands. In the fall of 1970, a pamphlet entitled *Elephants and Butterflies*, created by students under the supervision of faculty in the school of medicine, was introduced on campus. "Dedicated to the prevention of the tragedy of unwanted pregnancy and venereal disease," the pamphlet addressed a wide range of issues related to human sexuality in a straightforward manner and was soon was reprinted in multiple editions. The staff of the *Daily Tar Heel* took notice of the impact of the pamphlet and asked Lana Starnes, a graduate student involved with its creation, and Dr.

Takey Crist, an assistant professor of obstetrics and gynecology in the UNC School of Medicine, to write a weekly column under the same title for the paper's editorial page (which migrated at about this time from page two to the back page of each issue). The "Elephants and Butterflies" column appeared first in December 1970 and subsequently ran for several years. The first column, "Cunnilingus Can Spread VD," foreshadowed what was to come, with future topics including female orgasm and detailed descriptions of various types of contraceptive devices.[93]

Frank discussion of sexuality coincided with the fight over women's reproductive rights, which by 1970 was a subject of national conversation. As the *Roe v. Wade* test case on abortion worked its way toward the Supreme Court, debate raged in North Carolina when a bill to legalize the procedure was introduced in the state legislature. There was little doubt where the *Daily Tar Heel* stood on the matter. Calling the bill "a chance for women," associate editor Rick Gray came out in strong support of its passage. "To question the necessity of such a bill," Gray wrote, "is to question the right of women to exist outside of the lie of the stations wagons, split-level homes, housekeeping, 2.4 kids, the garden club and husband's dinner." After the state legislature failed to pass the bill, an angry Lana Starnes commented on the darker side of defeat, writing that "college coeds can continue to travel to New York for legal abortions or more likely continue to seek quick, inexpensive, yet illegal abortions." And in an attempt to drive home the human cost of not legalizing abortion, Starnes and Crist published an "Elephants and Butterflies" column that consisted of a black-bordered box, mostly empty, with a brief statement in the middle: "We leave our column blank today in memory of an 18-year-old coed who died from an illegal abortion. Would proper birth control and counseling have avoided this tragedy? What good did our so-called liberal abortion law do for her? We mourn in silence."[94]

THE BLACK STUDENT MOVEMENT, THE FOOD WORKERS' STRIKE, AND THE VIETNAM WAR

Despite protests over civil rights and the Speaker Ban, and despite the university's long-standing liberal reputation, the student body at UNC was not as radicalized during much of the 1960s as were students on other high-profile college campuses. In addition, the African American presence on campus remained very small and made little imprint on student life. But a major shift occurred as the nonviolent phase of the civil rights movement ended and a new sense of African American autonomy and agency—Black Power—rose nationally. The most significant expressions of this shift on the UNC campus were the creation of the Black Student Movement in 1967 and the food worker's strike of 1969.[95]

Even after passage of the Civil Rights Act, racial discrimination remained ingrained on the UNC campus. In September 1964, the *Daily Tar Heel* broke the story that campus housing was still segregated, publicly embarrassing the administration and resulting in a speedy end to the policy. A 1965 editorial, entitled "Holding Back Liberalism," noted that there were only eighty-four black students at the university—a decade after the first African American undergraduates enrolled—and remarked that at UNC "there are thousands of 'Carolina Gentlemen' who still carry the prejudices of their hometowns, even though they have lived three or more years in this 'liberal' community." The statement was a thinly veiled reference to fraternities, and it exemplified the level of tension that had developed between the *Daily Tar Heel* and the campus Greeks during the 1960s. As early as 1962 the paper exposed racial discrimination clauses in the constitutions of UNC fraternities, and editors pushed and prodded the matter for years. There was particular resistance from the Kappa Alpha house: in March 1965 a front-page photo ran of members growing beards in honor of Robert E. Lee (the fraternity patron), and standing in front of the general's portrait holding a Confederate flag. In the fall of 1966, the paper chided KA members for a "Beat Dook" float that included six small African American boys trailing behind it waving little Confederate flags and wearing placards decorated with painted watermelon slices that read, "KA Sez Spook Duke." "Way to go KA," the *Daily Tar Heel* declared sarcastically. "Keep the Nigra in his place.... Sure, you had to get the discrimination clause out of your bylaws [but] you show 'em." In September 1967 the lead editorial, "Fraternities and Negroes: The Twain Should Meet," indicated that not much progress had been made in racially integrating campus fraternities. Basketball star Charlie Scott was admitted into St. Anthony's Hall around 1968, but the absence of African Americans in UNC fraternities was still discussed in the paper into the early 1970s.[96]

The fraternity system may have been a convenient target, but it was not the most serious offender at UNC. African Americans were also few and far between on the faculty and in administrative positions well into the 1960s. In September 1967, a front-page story announced "Discrimination Complaint Filed Against University," as Dr. B. T. Elliot Jr., a black pediatrician at North Carolina Memorial Hospital, filed a complaint with the U.S. Department of Labor, citing "persistent, overt discrimination" in the hiring of not only hospital employees, but of workers in skilled and unskilled positions across campus. The lead editorial that day took the allegations seriously: "The University—which owns just about everything in this town from N.C. Memorial Hospital to the telephone system—has been accused of racial discrimination in its hiring policy. This is a very serious charge to level at anyone, and especially for an institution whose sole reason for existing is supposed to be as a

center of enlightenment." The paper followed the story closely for five months as the administration attempted to resolve the problem and to minimize the public-relations fallout. In the end the Department of Labor issued something of a "nondenial denial," clearing the university of outright discrimination but making detailed suggestions for changes in hiring practices.[97]

Two events in 1967 brought Black Power to the university. In an effort to diversify the almost all-white faculty, Howard Fuller was hired as an instructor in the sociology department in September. Fuller was a civil rights activist from Durham, and his nontenure appointment brought loud protests from Jesse Helms and Governor Dan Moore, who called the hiring "a serious mistake." The *Daily Tar Heel* was accustomed to attempts by Helms to discredit faculty he thought too liberal or radical, but the editorial staff was appalled by the governor's public stance and accused him of embarking "upon his own little binge of McCarthyism against this University and one of its instructors." The paper also tried, without much success, to quell the debate by defining Fuller's activism and the true mission of Black Power, noting that Fuller's efforts carried "a mood of militancy, not violence." University President William Friday once again found himself defending academic freedom at UNC, and attempted to silence the matter by stating that the hiring of Fuller was "a routine appointment of a fully qualified professional." Ultimately, Fuller remained on the UNC faculty only five months, but he played a significant role in campus protests that were to follow, and his hiring cast a long shadow across conservative perceptions of the university harboring radicals in the classroom.[98]

The second event that brought Black Power to campus was the formal dissolution of the UNC chapter of the NAACP in November 1967, and creation in its place of the Black Student Movement (BSM). Despite the NAACP's highly visible efforts to end discrimination on campus during the 1960s, a group of black students felt progress was not being made swiftly enough and that a new approach was needed. The group was headed by Preston Dobbins and Reggie Hawkins, who modeled themselves in both style and message on leaders of organizations such as the Black Panthers. "We're going to be more of an action group than the NAACP ever was," Dobbins told the *Daily Tar Heel*. The paper's reaction was positive but cautious. Bill Amlong, who was the editor at the time, remembered being friendly with Dobbins and sympathetic to the issues. An editorial published the week the group was founded, "The Black Student Goal: Harnessing the Panther" called the establishment of the Black Student Movement "a good thing," especially if middle-class blacks banded together to help less fortunate members of their race—otherwise they would be "guilty of even more than indifferent white[s]." "For the Black Panther is indeed a powerful creature," the editorial declared. "And if it can be harnessed, self-identity can do much to bolster this nation's efforts to cope with the racial problems of this turbulent age."[99]

In the wake of violence following the assassination of Martin Luther King Jr. in April 1968, the BSM stepped up its efforts to increase both the presence of and opportunities for African Americans on campus, and to assist the broader black community in attaining social and economic equality. The new editor in chief of the

Daily Tar Heel, Wayne Hurder, was perhaps even more supportive of the group's efforts than Amlong. Hurder's perspective was formed as a result of witnessing first-hand the evils of extreme prejudice and discrimination in the summer of 1966 when he served as a reporter and bureau chief for the *Southern Courier*, a newspaper founded by a group of Harvard students to cover African American issues in Alabama, Mississippi, and southern Georgia. A self-described radical, Hurder applauded planned campus appearances by black activists Eldridge Cleaver and Stokely Carmichael. When Cleaver was unable to speak as scheduled because of legal troubles in California, Hurder lamented that stu-

February 1969 cartoon by Bruce Strauch showing BSM president Preston Dobbins, which *DTH* editor Wayne Hurder decided was potentially too controversial to run. It was published in an issue of the *Carolina Alumni Review*, with the caption "Rejected by the *Daily Tar Heel*."

Rejected by The Daily Tar Heel

dents were "missing out on a great opportunity" to learn about "characteristics of the New Left and the militant Blacks." In a remarkable statement by the white editor of a southern college newspaper, Hurder wrote: "For the blacks, who have been frightened into submission for the past 350 years by public officials and police, the contempt that Cleaver shows is psychologically boosting. It helps give them the courage to drive for the changes they seek from the system."[100]

In the fall of 1968, the BSM issued a series of demands to Chancellor Sitterson and clearly implied that if those demands were not met, trouble would follow. At the same time, campus food workers, who were predominately African American, were organizing to protest low pay, lack of compensation for overtime, lack of job security, and disrespectful treatment by white university management. Twice during 1968 the BSM and the *Daily Tar Heel* supported brief protest actions by the food workers. By early 1969 the BSM had taken up the food workers' cause and tension mounted on campus. In the midst of this volatile situation, both the university admin-

istration and the paper attempted to avoid the real threat of violence; although the *DTH* staff were certainly sympathetic to the BSM and the plight of the food workers, the paper found itself walking a razor-thin line between supporting these groups' agendas and not lighting a match in the highly flammable environment.[101]

In February, Bruce Strauch, who had been editorial cartoonist for the *Daily Tar Heel* for three years, drew a cartoon of BSM leader Preston Dobbins as a wind-up doll with a key in his back, and a caption that read: "The BSM Doll—Wind it up and it threatens to burn down the university." Hurder, concerned about the delicate situation, rejected the cartoon. Strauch redrew the cartoon, toning down certain elements, but Hurder again rejected it, stating that it had "no social value" and, more importantly, because the editor "wanted to prevent violence on campus." Strauch was incensed, quit the paper in protest, and publicly charged that his freedom of speech was being denied. The situation made for strange bedfellows as more conservative media outlets cried foul. The *Carolina Alumni Review* picked up the story and ran the cartoon, and Jesse Helms used the incident on his television editorial as an example of preferential treatment for radical groups at UNC by the student newspaper.[102]

As discomforting as the situation was for the *Daily Tar Heel*, it turned out to be fortuitous. Suddenly without an editorial cartoonist, Hurder approached Jeff MacNelly, who had worked as a sports cartoonist for several years and was then drawing for the *Chapel Hill Weekly*. MacNelly, who went on to be one of the most celebrated American political cartoonists of the twentieth century—winning three Pulitzer Prizes, among

other awards, and creating the comic strip *Shoe*—had by early 1969 developed his signature style. His contributions during the height of what became known as the food workers' strike are likely the best and most sophisticated student-drawn cartoons in the history of the *Daily Tar Heel*.[103]

Debate about freedom of speech aside, Hurder's concern about the volatile atmosphere at UNC was soon confirmed. Members of the BSM staged a protest in Lenoir Dining Hall turning over tables and shouting with raised fists in support of the food workers' request for changes. When the food workers walked out, sympathetic students helped set up an alternative "soul eatery" in the recently vacated Manning Hall. Newly elected governor Bob Scott was eager to flex his muscle and show that the state of North

Carolina would not be intimidated by such actions. To the horror of William Friday and most of the university community, Scott sent state troopers to occupy campus and ensure that order was maintained. The concept of protecting "law and order" had been a rallying cry for the campaign of Richard Nixon, and as Hurder noted in the title of an editorial: "'Law and Order' Means Keep Niggers Down." Interestingly, radical black leaders also publicly employed the racial epithet that in later generations would be taboo. When Howard Fuller appeared before protesters at a large rally at the height of the food workers' strike, the *Daily Tar Heel* ran his words as a front-page headline: "Students Are 'Real Niggers' Fuller Informs Lenoir Rally." Fuller's point was that all students, regardless of race, had little voice on campus and should embrace the food workers' cause as their own and support it. After tense negotiations, grievances with the food workers were settled, but in what was seen as an act of bad faith, the university turned around and contracted dining services to a private company, which led to a second round of protests in the fall of 1969.[104]

Reading issues of the *Daily Tar Heel* from the late 1960s does reveal some progress on racial matters. Aside from the gains made during the food workers' strike, the BSM was able to increase its appropriation from the Student Legislature to help recruit African Americans to UNC and to work with organizations in surrounding communities on poverty and other social issues. The first African American Morehead Scholar was named in 1968, an action praised by the paper. In addition, there was more general acceptance of black students into campus culture, which was helped along by the on-court skills of

The Scene Inside Lenoir Cafeteria Tuesday Night
Before The Police Came To Restore Order

Staff Photo by Tom Schnabel

Charlie Scott, the first full-time African American player on the Carolina basketball team (and first black scholarship athlete at UNC). Scott was part of the U.S. Olympic team that brought home a gold medal in the summer of 1968, and in the spring of 1969 he led the Tar Heels to an ACC championship and a run all the way to the NCAA Final Four. For those in the UNC community uncomfortable with the militancy of Black Power and the BSM, Scott offered something of an antidote, presenting a more clean-cut appearance and participating in traditional campus life (although he did attend at least one rally supporting the campus food workers). Also in 1969, Chapel Hill elected its first black mayor, Howard Lee, who was strongly endorsed by the *DTH*. Lee, who earned a master's degree in social work at UNC, was one of the first African American mayors in the South.[105]

The coming of black activism to UNC in the late 1960s occurred against the backdrop of student activism on college campuses across the country, particularly with regard to rising resistance to the Vietnam War. The various conflicts in southeast Asia—Vietnam, Laos, and Cambodia—were covered in news stories and editorials by the *Daily Tar Heel* over the span of a decade, though in limited numbers before 1970. In May 1963, staff photographer Jim Wallace took a photograph of a small group of protesters marching in front of the Chapel Hill post office with signs featuring the "peace" symbol. These early antiwar demonstrations were organized by two campus groups, first the Student Peace Union (SPU), and later Students for a Democratic Society (SDS). The subject of the escalating war, however, was barely on the radar screens for most UNC students in the early years, as focus during the period was on civil rights and the Speaker Ban Law—and because college deferment for eligible males was in effect until 1969. In addition, unlike the positions espoused by the *Daily Tar Heel* on civil rights and the Speaker Ban Law, the paper's stance on the war was neither well defined nor consistent. For example, in September 1963 a letter from a young Vietnamese ran under the headline "From Vietnam, a Plea for Aid," yet less than three weeks later a sharp editorial appeared criticizing the SPU for protesting American involvement in the war.[106]

As the SPU became better organized and more visible by 1965, small-scale protests were organized on campus and various locations around the state. The group participated in a closed-circuit nationwide television "teach-in" on the war in May 1965, and twenty members protested at Fort Bragg in Fayetteville that October.

Though the *Daily Tar Heel* reported the teach-in as a news story, columns on the editorial page vilified the Fort Bragg protesters. Staff member Fred Harwell wrote a column entitled "UNC and SPU Are Now Bound Together In Carolinian Minds," citing a placard carried by a demonstrator reading: "We're from the University of North Carolina." Harwell argued the protesters broke the law by demonstrating on federal property, and "made a scene in front of four and one-half million North Carolinians—and the rest of the world, too." The antiwar group Students for a Democratic Society was also a favorite target of conservatives, who accused the organization of being infiltrated by radicals and Communists. In the midst of the battle over the Speaker Ban Law Harwell declared that the actions of the SDS "damaged this University." Apparently a number of students agreed with Harwell, as the paper reported over 1,200 people participated in a Veterans Day rally that November in support of U.S. policy in Vietnam—more than ever attended a civil rights protest on campus.[107]

Throughout the late 1960s, the nation, the university community, and the *Daily Tar Heel* increasingly grappled with the growing morass that was the Vietnam conflict. In September 1967, the front page of the paper carried two articles expressing opposing viewpoints on the war: one was entitled "Peace Group Plans Action in Washington, Durham"; and the other, "Viet Nam Creates One Million Jobs." In October a black-bordered box appeared on the editorial page, mostly blank white space, with a short statement in small type in the center: "(UPI) The toll of American dead, missing and wounded in the Vietnam war has soared to over 101,000." Editor Bill Amlong and associate editor Don Campbell

wrote columns condemning the war, but they also condemned the way national protest groups were opposing it. Campbell called their actions "the wrong way to oppose the war," and Amlong, who went to Washington in September 1967 to cover the large protest for the paper, wrote a lead editorial entitled "The Peace Mobilization: Wolf in Dove's Clothing."

Most of the leaders are of the very radical left, a great many of whom have arrived at the point of the political continuum that they now practice the politics of Despair.... And today their bitterness is threatening to erupt and spill like lava over those persons who are opposing the Vietnam war by more legitimate means ... a great portion of those who staunchly oppose the Vietnam war—us included—cannot throw in its lot with those involved in the national Mobilization to End the Vietnam War. For even those we see the Vietnam war as an unjust assault on another people, and as a festering cancer on the American body politic, this nation and what it stands for must be preserved—reformed perhaps through evolution, but protected always from revolution.[108]

After returning from Washington, Amlong continued to criticize student protests of the war. When seventy students from different North Carolina colleges and universities picketed the draft center in Raleigh, the editor wrote: "Plainly and simply sidewalk protests of the draft and of the war [do] no good whatsoever. Should you need proof of this, just flip on any newscast and listen to reports of how the war is being escalated day by day." However, Amlong endorsed antiwar presidential candidate Senator Eugene McCarthy in December 1967, nearly a year before the next election, calling him the "responsible candidate." Coverage of the election of 1968, in which the war was the central issue, was unusual for the *Daily Tar Heel* in several ways. For the first time paid advertising for candidates appeared in the paper in the spring ahead of the Democratic primary, and the day before the general election the lead editorial read: "the *Daily Tar Heel* does not endorse anyone for president this year. For us to do so we feel would be to mislead you, for we can find no candidate running for office that can provide this country with the leadership it needs or has a platform that is substantially in agreement with our own editorial policy." The opinion, written by Wayne Hurder, expressed the disillusionment many college students across the country felt after McCarthy was defeated for the Democratic nomination by Vice President Hubert Humphrey. "We came closest to endorsing but had to reject him," Hurder wrote, primarily because he looked upon Vietnam as "an unfortunate mistake" and not what it truly was, "in the broadest sense of the word, a racist foreign policy."[109]

Though UNC did not witness large-scale antiwar protests as occurred on some other university campuses in the late 1960s, two Carolina student leaders did garner national attention by making official trips to Washington to oppose the war. In January 1967, student-body president Bob Powell joined ninety-nine other college presidents in writing a letter to President Lyndon Johnson in opposition to the war, and Powell and the student president of Harvard were chosen to speak for the group, publicly and in a private meeting with Secretary of State Dean Rusk. Fred Thomas, editor of the *Daily Tar Heel* at the time, supported Powell's stand. But in an example of how the paper's opinions on the war vacillated, when Thomas left school abruptly and was replaced by Scott Goodfellow, the new editor expressed concerns over Powell's action. "The Vietnam War is of prime concern to all of us. When our student-body president speaks, we would like to know how we are represented." The paper's reservations about Powell's action led to a campus-wide referendum on the war that spring, which showed that students supported Powell's activism. And in April 1969, following the lifting of college deferments, Wayne Hurder, who had just stepped down as editor of the *DTH*, went to Washington and spoke for a group of students from schools across the country who pledged to defy the draft. During the course of the visit he and members of the group's steering committee met in the Situation Room in the West Wing of the White House with Nixon advisors Henry Kissinger and John Ehrlichman.[110]

Despite these high-profile protests by individual student leaders, demonstrations on the UNC campus remained limited until President Richard Nixon ordered the bombing of Cambodia in the spring of 1970. The *Daily Tar Heel* reported that an antiwar festival in April, a few weeks after the bombing began, was attended by 3,000 students, far fewer than the 10,000 expected. But on May 1, the Student Legislature urged a boycott of classes to protest the action in Cambodia, and editor Tom Gooding wrote, "U.S. aggression in Cambodia must be stopped.... We agree with the resolution and hope all students will join the protest." An antiwar "Jubilee Weekend" held in early May drew 25,000 to Kenan Stadium, but the paper reported that amid the

The Daily Tar Heel

Weather

On The Inside

Volume 79 Number 43

78 Years Of Editorial Freedom

CHAPEL HILL, NORTH CAROLINA, THURSDAY, MAY 7, 1970

Founded February 23, 1893

Thousands Rally, March To Protest Kent State Deaths, Indochina War

'On Strike, Shut It Down' Cry Of Marching Students

By Rick Gray
Associate Editor

Tommy Bello leads march down Columbia Street

Professors Grant Amnesty

Number May Reach Hundreds

3000 March By Night To Sitterson's, Friday's

By Mike Parnell
Staff Writer

Pat Wood pours "blood"

Bello: 'Today We Begin To Live The Dream'

224

music and fun, "Cambodia was soon forgotten." The mood changed radically the following day, however, following news that National Guardsmen on the campus of Kent State University in Ohio had opened fire and killed four students and wounded others, including bystanders. Tension at Carolina reached its highest point during the Vietnam era in the wake of the Kent State shootings, with 11,000 students demonstrating and someone setting fire to the Air Force ROTC building. The paper came out in complete support of a proposed student strike at UNC "as a two-fold protest against the U.S. invasion of Cambodia and the murder of four students at Kent State University." Likely remembering the presence of state troopers at UNC during the food workers' strike a year earlier, the editorial declared that the murders "could have just as easily happened on this campus." The student strike lasted several weeks and along with boycotting classes resulted in several large-scale marches on campus, as well as one at the State Capitol in Raleigh, that counted 1,500 UNC students among the crowd of 6,000. After the marches, Gooding noted that the tide of widespread student activism against the war had happened suddenly, calling it "hectic and tiring," but that it had brought "a political awareness to the students of this campus that only once existed in dreams."[111]

THE *DAILY TAR HEEL* UNDER FIRE

In the span of a decade, the civil rights movement, the Speaker Ban Law, the sexual revolution, the rise of Black Power, the food workers' strike, and the war in Vietnam all served to liberalize and radicalize significant numbers of UNC students, mirroring a similar transforma-

tion on college campuses across America. The *Daily Tar Heel* also became increasingly radicalized during the era, though most editors strove to provide a forum for all points of view. Quoting a nineteenth-century Chicago newspaper editor (and often repeated by former *Tar Heel* editor Walter Spearman, then teaching in the UNC School of Journalism), the masthead of the 1966 summer edition of the paper announced: "The job of a newspaper is to print news and raise hell."[112]

By the late 1960s, however, a conservative political movement represented by a new coalition within the Republican Party began to rise in prominence and push back against the liberal agenda. Following national violence triggered by racial unrest and antiwar demonstrations, Richard Nixon was elected president in 1968—only the second Republican to occupy the office since 1933. His campaign used slogans such as restoring "law and order" to what many conservatives saw as a society that had lost its moral bearings, and Nixon called his constituency America's "silent majority." In the South, where conservative white Democrats who felt betrayed by the pro–civil rights agenda of the national party were rapidly switching political affiliation, another group joined the fold: Christian fundamentalists. Soon to be labeled the Religious Right, these new Republicans focused on social and moral issues such as school prayer and abortion.[113]

Despite UNC's reputation as a bastion of liberalism, much of the student body and larger university community remained moderate to conservative throughout the 1960s. By the end of the decade, the political Right was well organized and energized by what was happening in the

South and across the nation, and it actively opposed radical groups and initiatives on campus. The *Daily Tar Heel*, seen as a principal offender, was soon the target of this new conservative movement. Morality became the new Communism, as the battleground on which the Religious Right chose to attack liberalism became cultural as much as political. With witch hunts for closeted Reds passé, and attempts to maintain racial segregation a lost cause, the Right turned to stamping out what it defined as social permissiveness, including the breakdown of "traditional" values and the moral laxity brought about by the sexual revolution. Significantly, this marked the beginning of a difficult period for the *Daily Tar Heel*: a quarter-century of outside pressure and internal analysis that would eventually become a contributing cause of the paper's separation from the university in 1993. In the 1950s, students and others angry over the paper's editorial policies attempted to correct the situation by cutting off its proverbial head through special campus recall elections of the editor. By the late 1960s, many conservatives saw the paper as unfixable, rotten to the core, and beginning in 1969 a variety of attempts were made to greatly weaken its influence, if not shut it down entirely.

On February 5, 1969, barely two weeks after Richard Nixon's inauguration and amid rising tension over the situation with university food workers, a group of students founded the Hayakawa Society at UNC, whose mission was to combat radicalism on campus and promote a conservative agenda. The society was named for San Francisco State College President S. I. Hayakawa, who was something of a right-wing hero after he personally tore out the wires of a sound system during a campus protest led by the Third

World Liberation Front, the Black Panthers, and Students for a Democratic Society in December 1968. "This organization," one member stated, "constitutes a new coalition of the center." "Ordinary students here are upset by the trend of militancy by a small minority. The organizations that are heard of most often ... give the impression that they dominate campus, yet they do not represent a majority of students and have little influence with what is known as the Silent Majority." Jesse Helms, during one of his nightly television editorials, praised creation of the society, which he declared "speaks well for the student body" at Carolina.[114]

The Hayakawa Society members were relentless in their attacks on the *Daily Tar Heel*. Grainger Barrett, president of the society, accused the paper of "slanted, extremely selective news coverage focusing almost exclusively" on radical groups such as SDS, the Southern Student Organizing Committee, and the Black Student Movement. "The *Daily Tar Heel* flouts the canons of journalism," Barrett charged, and "dealing in questionable journalism, the editors have by-passed truth, condoned distortions in news, and have failed to cover the campus while ignoring or down-playing legitimate news of happenings of interest to the great majority of students." One of the main activities of the society was creation of the *Carolina Chronicle*, the first of a series of campus publications established to provide a counterpoint to what was seen as the liberal perspective of the *Daily Tar Heel*. Though the *Chronicle* only survived for three issues in the spring of 1969, it laid the foundation for similar conservative publications that followed at Carolina.[115]

The short-lived Hayakawa Society was more

influential than it probably would have been because of the strong support of Pete Ivey, who was director of the UNC News Bureau at the time. In the first week of the society's life, Ivey wrote or authorized no fewer than seven press releases that clearly promoted the organization. Such highly visible involvement in student politics was unusual for an administrator and added to an already contentious relationship with the staff of the *Daily Tar Heel*. The trouble apparently began in early 1967, when Ivey issued a press release listing the ten most significant events on campus during the previous year. Ivey, who was on record opposing any radical activities he felt reflected badly on UNC, left the biggest story of 1966 off the list—the "stone wall" speeches of Herbert Aptheker and Frank Wilkinson, in defiance of the Speaker Ban Law. A lead editorial in the *DTH* noted the obvious omission, and although it did not mention Ivey by name, relations between the News Bureau and the paper subsequently soured. In March 1969, following publication of a stinging attack on Ivey and the News Bureau by Lawrence Kessler, a faculty member in the history department, Ivey publicly and privately excoriated editor Wayne Hurder for not publishing his reply on the same day. Hurder's explanation that Ivey's letter had not arrived in time to be published that particular day, and the fact that the paper did subsequently publish it, did not mollify the News Bureau director.[116]

Hurder's successor as editor, Todd Cohen, inherited the disdain for the *Daily Tar Heel* in conservative circles, along with the ire of Pete Ivey. Soon Jesse Helms came after Cohen as well. As he had done with the incident involving Michael Paull several years earlier, Helms took words

used by Cohen in one of his first editorials out of context and used them to bash the editor, the *Daily Tar Heel*, the University of North Carolina at Chapel Hill, liberals generally, and "radical" students across the United States. Helms also set off a chain of events that ultimately threatened to destroy the *DTH*. On May 9, 1969, Cohen wrote a column, entitled "Poppycock," about amendments to a bill then in the state legislature regarding the appearance of student representatives at board of governors meetings for the proposed new UNC system. The amendments would require students to be neatly dressed, to be clean-shaven, and to have "a normal businessman's haircut." Cohen objected, saying appearance alone should not determine "the measure of a man." On May 14 the paper ran a letter to the editor from a student who disagreed with Cohen, calling his opinion, in essence, "bullshit." Cohen wrote an angry response entitled "Go To Hell," in which he reiterated the word "bullshit."[117]

Helms, ignoring the fact that the editorial was in response to a student letter published on the same page, took the opportunity to rail against the *Daily Tar Heel* in a series of his WRAL "Viewpoint" segments. Accusing Cohen of having a "fetish for barnyard language," Helms declared "it used to be that ill-bred children scribbled their uncouth obscenities mostly on sidewalks and the walls of the school restrooms.... [Now] it is fashionable for such immature mentalities to be elected to edit college and university newspapers." Chiding William Friday for not doing anything about the situation—and noting (incorrectly) that Frank Graham had ordered the racy "sex issue" of the *Buccaneer* burned three decades earlier—Helms suggested the trustees "remove the requirement that all students subsidize the circulation of trashy attempts at journalism." Making a rhetorical leap and connecting unrelated issues, Helms also proclaimed that "taxpayers should not be asked to foot the bill" for such "filth." In fact, the fees used to subsidize the paper came directly from students and did not come from state appropriations made to the public universities.[118]

Stirred up by Helms's opinion about the *Daily Tar Heel*, nine conservative students from the Young Republicans Club formed an organization called the Committee for a Free Press over the summer of 1969. As soon as the fall semester began, they called for an investigation into the editorial policies of the *DTH*, which they felt were heavily biased to the left, and demanded that student funding of the paper cease. Helms applauded their actions: "The campus newspaper at Chapel Hill can scarcely be regarded as a great source of pride for the University. During the past several years it has become increasingly irresponsible to the point that it is now widely regarded as a sort of juvenile amplifier for far-left and militant causes." The charges made by the nine students were taken seriously, and two committees were formed: one by the Student Legislature, and another by the Faculty Council. To the surprise of many, Todd Cohen came out in support of ending student funding, stating, "It appears quite clear to us that the way the *Daily Tar Heel* is funded, namely by student fees, is both unfair and in conflict with the nature of a free press." In hearings held by the Student Legislature, Cohen declared, "The paper should be independent of the University and students should not be required to pay for it." Instead he proposed "a corporation to run a daily paper, serving not only the University but the community of Chapel Hill." Cohen's proposal would come to pass, but not for another 23 years.[119]

At the time, the fee of about $2 per student provided $35,750 of the *Daily Tar Heel*'s $110,500 annual budget, slightly less than one-third. The student legislative committee studying the matter issued a report in February 1970, finding that "there exists on our campus a basic need for a student-oriented newspaper existing completely free of any administrative control." The committee further found that although a plan could be put into place to cease the student fee portion over time, in the immediate future "the *DTH* could not exist without the funds." Opponents of the paper understood this and pushed for a referendum on the matter, which was approved for the spring ballot (when student leaders and the editor of the paper were elected). The *Daily Tar Heel* now found itself in a battle for survival. One of the paper's columnists charged the Committee for a Free Press with seeking not only simply to eliminate student funding, but "to end the *DTH* because it disagrees politically." Cohen and other members of the editorial board argued vigorously in print for defeat of the measure: "A yes vote Tuesday," one column read, "means there will be NO newspaper in the fall."[120]

Cohen had to keep not only Jesse Helms and the Committee for a Free Press at bay, but also the UNC News Bureau. As debate churned on campus about the fate of the paper in the spring of 1970, bureau director Pete Ivey issued press releases that clearly showed his bias in the matter. Soon a public war of words broke out between the editor and the director. In a lead editorial, Cohen described Ivey's press releases as "a classic style based on ambiguities, obscenities, and half-truths." Pointing out that "Ivey's releases were the official sources of information for the public about the University," Cohen charged that they "carry with them the unique character of being the distortions of the facts as created by Ivey." Despite the added handicap of fighting the head of the campus news bureau, the campaign to keep the paper alive was a success, with the measure failing by a margin of nearly five to one.[121]

When the referendum failed to bring down the *Daily Tar Heel*, conservative students turned to the state legislature, and a new approach—the issue of sexual mores. On April 23, 1971, a full-page "Insight" feature story about being gay in Chapel Hill appeared on page three of the paper. Though titled "Homosexuality ... has its problems," the article was a remarkably frank and nonjudgmental piece for its time. In bold type, it stated: "The picture of the homosexual of five or ten years ago is changing. Today, homosexuals want to be accepted as people." Accompanying the story was a large photograph of two bare-chested young men, their heads not visible, in a clearly romantic and sexually suggestive embrace. This was the proverbial last straw for several students, who clipped the article and sent it to state senator Julian Allsbrook of Halifax County. The article, and particularly the photograph, deeply disturbed Allsbrook, who carried the clipping around the State Legislative Building in his wallet, showing it to any other member of the legislature he could collar. Soon Allsbrook introduced a bill into the Senate to prohibit student fees from being used to fund student news-

papers on public university campuses. As he explained to the press: "I have been considering the bill since about two years ago when some students came to me and complained about articles in the *Daily Tar Heel*. Finally when the picture and story appeared, something had to be done about it. I thought it was as rank pornography as the public should be subject to. It is not the type of material that should appear in a paper, and I don't think the students should be subjected to it. Students who do not wish this smut in their mailboxes should not be required to pay fees for these newspapers."[122]

Sensing another Speaker Ban in the works, UNC system president William Friday, UNC student-body president Joe Stallings, and *Daily Tar Heel* editor Harry Bryan mobilized to defeat the bill. Appearing before the Senate Higher Education Committee, Friday argued that it was best to "leave this kind of issue in the hands of the boards of trustees rather than subject it to statutory action." Senator O'Neill Jones of Anson County called the legislation a "subterfuge to get the *Daily Tar Heel* and other college newspapers." "These papers depend on the money from students to survive," Jones said, adding, "They serve a good, useful purpose ... I know a witch hunt when I see one, and this is a witch hunt." Cooler heads prevailed, and the measure went down in defeat, 21–15. After the vote, Harry Bryan reflected on the situation:

If it had passed, it would have meant the downfall of the *Daily Tar Heel*. The *Daily Tar Heel* has produced some of the best journalists in the country in its 79-year history, and I would hate to see that stopped. ... I believe

Homosexuality...

Story and Photo
by Harry Smith
COPYRIGHT (C) 1971

The Daily Tar Heel Insight

> Most homosexuals "... think they have made a normal adjustment to life and they happen to be different from other people. They're not as guilt ridden as they once were."

... has its problems

> Some homosexuals are disturbed by the notion that all homosexuals are promiscuous. "There ... are some homosexuals who rarely go to bed; others are what we call real whores."

Gay bar: a social place

> "Over 80 per cent of our customers would never be recognized as gay."

Sen. Allsbrook would not have introduced this bill if he was in agreement with the *DTH* political philosophy. Because he is a conservative, and the *DTH* and most college newspapers are not, he tried to silence the papers that disagreed with him.

Over the years the paper has built up a reputation as a crusader in issues affecting the student body and, at times, society as a whole. ... Attacks on the paper will continue, just as they will continue with every newspaper that stands up for what it believes is right. But as long as the *DTH* continues to speak out for the majority of the UNC student body, those who challenge it will not stand a chance of success.[123]

5

A FREE PRESS MUST PREVAIL

1971–1993

Despite the defeat of the 1970 campus-wide referendum and the 1971 bill in the state legislature, both designed to end the use of student fees to partially underwrite the *Daily Tar Heel*, the battle over defunding became even more intense during the years that followed, consuming large amounts of the paper's resources and staff time. Although the wheels that Jesse Helms and conservative students set in motion in 1969 would, in fact, eventually lead to the paper's separation from university funding and oversight, the process would take a quarter century. Equally significant, the battle would also create an effective model for conservative students on campus to use against organizations and social movements with which they disagreed.

In August 1972, four students filed a lawsuit in federal district court on behalf of the UNC student body, arguing that the *Daily Tar Heel* did not represent the views of all students and thus no portion of their mandatory annual activity fees should be used to support the paper. Such use, the plaintiffs argued, was a violation of their constitutional rights of free speech under the First Amendment, and their civil rights under the Fourteenth Amendment. The suit, which bore the names of plaintiff Robert Lane Arrington and principal defendant Chancellor N. Ferebee Taylor, wound its way through the court system for a total of five years, including appeals. Among the other defendants named were UNC system president William Friday, the newly formed UNC Board of Governors and UNC–Chapel Hill Board of Trustees, and *DTH* editor Evans Witt (who petitioned the court to be added). Several lawyers with ties to the paper supported the legal

To offset the costs associated with the *Arrington v. Taylor* lawsuit, the *Daily Tar Heel* established a legal defense fund. This 1972 photo shows donations being collected outside the Frank Porter Graham Student Union, which housed the *DTH* offices. (*Yack*)

team of Jordan, Morris & Hoke in representing the defendants. Hugh Stevens, editor in 1964–65, and Robert W. Spearman, son of Walter Spearman (editor in 1928–29, and long-time professor in the School of Journalism), served as counsel for editor Susan Miller, when she succeeded Witt as editor in 1973. John Sanders, an attorney and the former student-body president who had run afoul of conservative critics when he coauthored a landmark column against campus segregation published in the *DTH* in 1950, took depositions and offered legal advice.[1]

The student plaintiffs in *Arrington v. Taylor* claimed that "the mere existence of the system of financial support for the *Daily Tar Heel* now in effect chills the free expression of ideas so as to violate the First Amendment," noting that it served to "drown out" their opinions and could lead to "diminished economic capacity" to express their own views. To dramatize the latter claim, one of the plaintiffs, William Robert Grady, refused to pay the $4 portion of his student fees for the fall semester of 1972 that would support the *DTH*, and was assessed a late fee of $5 by the university. The lawsuit listed several editors since 1969 with whom the plaintiffs disagreed politically, and enumerated a host of issues on which the editorial positions of the paper differed from those of the plaintiffs, including: "the adoption of a Chapel Hill and Carrboro Bus System, the use of busing to integrate public schools, James C. Gardner, Spiro T. Agnew, the United States intervention in Cambodia, the impeachment and removal of Richard M. Nixon, the appointment of William H. Rehnquist, the death penalty, the Equal Rights Amendment, student strikes, Food Worker's strikes, protests against the war in Southeast Asia, and abortion." The

plaintiffs also disagreed with the paper "reportorially," objecting to its news coverage on such wide-ranging topics as Vietnam, Cambodia, the Equal Rights Amendment (ERA), student political polls, the Black Student Movement, and civil liberties in Pitt County. As an example of censorship—and violation of Fourteenth Amendment civil rights—the lawsuit noted an incident in September 1969, when editor Todd Cohen refused to print a column by conservative activist and occasional *DTH* contributor Louise Trent Oliver in which she advocated cessation of student fees to support the paper.[2]

Extensive news stories and editorials about the case ran in the paper. Calling the lawsuit "crucial for all students," and noting that it could shut down publication, editor Witt insisted that "students' rights and the continued survival of the *Daily Tar Heel* are at stake in the current lawsuit to cut off student fees for this newspaper. If the suit is not won, the immediate result would be the death of the *DTH* as it now serves the campus. It would end a 79-year old tradition of freedom and irreverent dissent that has contributed to what UNC is today." A legal defense fund was established, and students and alumni rushed to contribute. The residents of Morrison Residence Hall contributed $25, and former editor Charles Kuralt sent $100. In a letter accompanying the contribution, Kuralt wrote: "The *Daily Tar Heel* has not always been sensible, but it has always been free." Calling the lawsuit "nothing less than an attempt to shut down the paper by extremely conservative forces at Chapel Hill," Kuralt added that if such forces "had the imagination to try to take the paper over, and the energy to succeed, then the attempt would be perfectly honorable. But the extremist imagination is always limited where free, clear speech is concerned—they always try to strangle it because they can't stand it."[3]

The case was not adjudicated for two years, delayed in part by a preliminary ruling on whether the complaint constituted a class-action suit, and further by the desire of the federal district court to await the decision in a related case. Both matters were settled by September 1973, with the court first ruling that the four students who filed the suit could not do so on behalf of the entire student body. The related case, *Joyner v. Whiting*, involved the *Campus Echo*, the student newspaper of North Carolina Central University (NCCU), one of the UNC system's historically African American schools. In the wake of the Black Power movement, the editor of the *Echo*, Johnnie Edward Joyner, announced that the paper would only employ African American staff and would accept advertising exclusively from black-owned businesses. The president of

NCCU, Albert Whiting, withdrew student funding from the paper and ordered it shut down. Whiting was concerned that the paper's actions promoted racism (in this case, against whites), and insofar as UNC system schools were officially integrated, that Joyner's new policy violated the Fourteenth Amendment to the Constitution and could jeopardize federal funding. Joyner in turn filed suit, arguing that the withholding of funding constituted violation of the paper's freedom of the press rights under the First Amendment. NCCU won an initial decision, but an appeals court overturned the ruling, declaring that the university administration "shall take no action to control the contents of the *Echo* unless he or they can reasonably forecast substantial disruption of material interference with school activities on account of the distribution of such printed material." The lawsuit, which was followed closely by the *Daily Tar Heel*, determined that a newspaper at a public university was a "manifestation of state action" and, as such, was protected against abridgment of freedom of the press under the First and Fourteenth Amendments. In the lawsuit against the *Daily Tar Heel*, the judges subsequently ruled that "the test for determining what campus related activities at state universities constitute state action for the purpose of civil rights actions was set forth in *Joyner vs. Whiting*."[4]

The *Arrington v. Taylor* lawsuit occurred within the context of a national debate about freedom of the press, the result of the 1971 Supreme Court ruling in favor of the *New York Times* and the *Washington Post* regarding publication of the so-called Pentagon Papers, detailing America's involvement in Vietnam, as well as the *Post*'s subsequent relentless coverage of the Watergate scandal. A number of the judicial statements made in the *Arrington v. Taylor* ruling—which was handed down only two weeks after President Nixon resigned in August 1974—not only addressed the *Daily Tar Heel*'s constitutional protections, but also settled the legality of mandatory student funding and went a step further by strongly supporting the paper's role on campus. "Plaintiffs' economic capacity to advocate their views has been only incidentally lessened," the court ruled in reference to the small mandatory annual fee, "and this slight infringement is not of such proportions as to render the procedure unconstitutional." The court found that partial subsidization of the newspaper with student fees did not establish an institutional "orthodoxy." The ruling cited as an example that the "occasional reference to subjects of a religious nature in the *Daily Tar Heel* does not constitute establishment of a religion, and is therefore not in violation" of the constitutional rights of students who hold differing views. Further:

The *Daily Tar Heel*'s position on a given subject is no more attributable to (and therefore imposed upon) plaintiffs than is the position of the Federal Government on South Vietnam attributable to each of the citizens who annually pay their federal taxes.

... The University subsidizes the *Daily Tar Heel* for several purposes, none of which involves the desire to propagate a particular position or point of view. The publication is a useful device to inform the student body of noteworthy campus activities. It also prints pertinent local, national, and international news. Perhaps its most important function is to complement classroom education by ex-

posing the student body to various points of view on significant issues.... Far from being a "predictable conduit" upon which the state can depend to express its views, the *Daily Tar Heel* has published diverse views on a variety of issues, often conflicting with and criticizing governmental policies. There is simply no factual basis for concluding that the University's motives in maintaining financial support for the *Daily Tar Heel* are other than laudable.

The justices also related the issue of the freedom of a subsidized college newspaper to that of academic freedom: "Teachers, with salaries paid in part from tuition, present differing views on pertinent subjects in an educational setting. That a teacher may present one viewpoint as more meritorious than another surely does not deny to students in that classroom their constitutional rights."[5]

Within days of the decision in *Arrington v. Taylor* the plaintiffs announced they would appeal, and the suit wound its way through the appeals court until 1977, when the initial ruling was upheld. Ultimately the proceedings cost the *Daily Tar Heel* approximately $10,000 in legal fees, a considerable sum in the mid-1970s. Hugh Stevens remarked that the opinion showed the role of the student newspaper at UNC to be "proper and legal," adding that in reference to constitutional protections, "I have always felt that although it does have some quirks in the way it is circulated and financed, the *Daily Tar Heel* is really just another newspaper."[6]

As they pursued their case in court, conservative campus critics of the *Daily Tar Heel* applied pressure in other ways, including an attempt to institute control over the paper's editorial autonomy during the 1972 national presidential election cycle. David Boone, a plaintiff in the lawsuit and a member of the Student Legislature, proposed an amendment to a bill on campus election spending, unrelated to the lawsuit, that would, in the words of editor Evans Witt, "prohibit editorial endorsements [for national or state offices] by the editor or by columnists ... limit campaign coverage, dictate the form of paid political advertisements, and mandate equal space to be given to all candidates." Witt defiantly fired back at Boone and his attempt to silence the paper. "The *Daily Tar Heel* will comment on and make endorsements in this year's political races in which we think such action is justified," the editor wrote, adding, "even some of the more ignorant members of the student legislature would not have attempted this attack on the First Amendment." Referencing the recently filed lawsuit, Witt declared that regarding the amendment, "we'll ignore this one too." When the tactic failed, Boone, a second-year law student, decided to run for student-body president in January 1973. "For the last several years, student government has been run by a clique of students ... and the *Daily Tar Heel* office," Boone declared when announcing his candidacy. "Evans Witt runs the *DTH* with other people's money like he was God. I think the phrase yellow journalism must have been coined with Evans in mind. Thousands of dollars of student money have been thrown away on luxurious offices, secretaries, and junkets for the clique." With the lawsuit pending and existing bad blood between the editor and the student legislator, Witt declined to endorse any student candidate, though Robert Putnam III, the paper's resident conservative voice at the time, backed Boone in a column. Out

of a crowded field of ten candidates, Boone received only 2.3 percent of the vote, and the *DTH* avoided the adversarial relationship that would have almost certainly resulted from his tenure in office.[7]

The fight over use of student fees to support the *Daily Tar Heel* occurred during a period of sustained growth for both the university and the paper. As the size of the student body hovered near 20,000 in the early 1970s—double what it had been a decade earlier—daily circulation of the *DTH* grew to an average of 17,500, requiring an increasingly complex distribution system. A full-time professional business manager and secretary were added to the payroll (the first nonstudent employees in the paper's history), and the annual budget rose to $250,000. This growth made the *DTH* the largest capitalized student organization on campus and a formidable small business in its own right. But with growth came problems, especially with regard to student government's increasing control and regulation of the paper's financial matters. Chief among the issues was the inability of the paper's staff to control cash flow, as by the early 1970s all funds went in and out of the Student Activities Fund Office (SAFO), under the management of the student treasurer.[8]

The lack of fiscal control complicated efforts by the *Daily Tar Heel*'s staff to wean the paper off student fees, a goal supported by virtually everyone in the university community, whether for business or ideological reasons. The paper had received funding from student fees since it became an official university publication in 1923, and student government had exercised some control over distribution of those funds since 1946. In 1958, student fees constituted 50 per-

cent of the *DTH*'s annual budget, but that proportion was reduced to 13 percent by 1975. The reduction was the result of voluntary decreases that began in 1972, following filing of the *Arrington v. Taylor* lawsuit, and in the wake of the failed campus referendum and bill in the state senate to end student funding. The voluntary reduction was, in the words of student-body treasurer Mike O'Neal, "in keeping with a shared philosophy of an eventually independent *DTH*." Cole Campbell, the paper's editor in chief in 1975–76, wrote that "in the long run, the University administration, Student Government, the Media Board and the *Daily Tar Heel* must work for the independence of the *DTH* from Student Government. Only in

this way can a free and responsible press stay clear of the political process and dedicate itself to the service of the readers."[9]

While there was consensus that a financially independent *Daily Tar Heel* was preferable and necessary to assure editorial freedom, a viable business plan to achieve that goal was not developed in the early 1970s. As a result, financial cracks soon appeared, and in September 1972 the paper stopped publishing Saturday editions, except on football weekends, to save money. By the spring of 1975 it was starved for cash and required a $10,000 emergency loan from student government. As the new academic year got underway, the *DTH* found itself in an untenable financial position. Cole Campbell decided to run an unusually large orientation issue that August, followed by two more expanded editions. By early September the number of printed pages already totaled eighty, at a time when the standard was eight pages per issue. Although a proportionate amount of ad space had been sold, many advertisers had not yet paid their invoices and cash was in short supply. The *DTH* staff was not overly concerned about the matter, as the paper had operated for several years under the practice of drawing down a large percentage of the student fees appropriation in advance, until the flow of advertising revenue became large enough to sustain the paper.[10]

This time, however, that practice led to the most serious financial crisis in the paper's eighty-two-year history and resulted in an ugly public showdown with student government. In early September the staff requested the remaining semester's worth of student funds from the Media Board, which was approved. But the student body treasurer, Mike O'Neal, refused to comply, blaming the capital shortage on "failings of the [Media Board] to monitor *DTH* finances," and "errors by the *DTH* business staff." Calling the paper's staff "uncooperative," O'Neal asserted that withholding funds was "the only sensible, businesslike way to handle the problem." Warning that the paper would have to stop production, the *DTH* staff made an unsuccessful appeal to the Campus Governing Council's Finance Committee to release the funds. "There has been much hysteria and unfortunately a shortage of concern and understanding in dealing presently with the finances of the *Daily Tar Heel*," O'Neal stated in a column on the editorial page. He noted that the paper had operated with a deficit since November 1974, even with payment in January 1975 of a "surplus" of over $23,500 not taken between 1972 and 1974, and the $10,000 loan four months later. O'Neal charged that the situation was not as dire as predicted, as the staff could go out and collect revenue due on advertising.[11]

The story largely played out behind the scenes until September 5, when it took over most of the front page in an abbreviated issue of the paper. Calling the situation "complex," a lead article reported that "the *Daily Tar Heel*'s funding troubles reached critical proportions Thursday as a lack of funds forced the newspaper to print a four-page issue today and endangered next week's publications." "It is extremely difficult to cover news when the news reporters are the news makers," a rare front-page editorial declared. "But when an organization has a budget of $250,000 and provides a daily service to the entire university community, threat (internal or external) to that organization unavoidably makes the news."[12]

No paper appeared on Saturday, September 6, and on Monday, September 8, UNC students awoke to find copies of N.C. State's *Technician* at *Daily Tar Heel* distribution sites on campus. In sympathy for the plight of the *DTH*, the editor and staff of the *Technician* took the unprecedented step of coming to the aid of the rival school's newspaper, running 20,000 extra copies for UNC students. The extra cost was borne by the *Technician* and Hinton Printing Company in Mebane, which normally printed the *DTH*. A front-page story described the situation and included an interview with editor Cole Campbell, who blamed UNC's student government for the crisis. *Technician* editor Kevin Fisher explained his rationale for assisting: "What is happening to the *Tar Heel* constitutes an abridgment of freedom of speech through financial means. I detest government intervention in newspapers in the so-called real world, as well as the University structure."[13]

As accusations flew back and forth, students and others in the university community took sides, supporting the *Daily Tar Heel* staff and putting intense pressure on student government to release the paper's funds. The owners of Hector's and Zeus, popular eateries for *DTH* staffers, gave anyone who worked on the paper free meals for several days during the crisis. Frustrated and unable to resolve the matter, student-body president Bill Bates signed a petition for his own recall. Finally treasurer Mike O'Neal relented, and a check for $7,379.47—the remaining semester funds—was delivered to Campbell. The paper resumed publication on September 9, and took stock of what had happened. "In an unprecedented show of support yesterday, North Carolina State University's stu-

In a rare show of solidarity, the *Technician*, the student newspaper of North Carolina State University, printed 20,000 additional copies in support of the temporarily suspended *Daily Tar Heel* and delivered these copies to *DTH* distribution sites on the UNC campus on September 8, 1975. (NCSU)

Technician

North Carolina State University's Student Newspaper Since 1920

Volume LVI, Number 6   Monday, September 8, 1975

Daily Tar Heel at temporary standstill

by Howard Barnett
Assistant Editor

The University of North Carolina at Chapel Hill's student newspaper, the *Daily Tar Heel*, is not publishing this morning due to lack of funds. Cutting out this week's Monday issue follows a reduction in size last week because of the money crunch.

The financial dilemma came after UNC's Student Body Treasurer, Mike O'Neal, refused to release the newspaper's student fees for the semester, around $13,000, in a lump sum. O'Neal instead decided to release he funds in seven monthly installments.

O'Neal said he was concerned that the amount under "accounts receivable" (payments which have yet to be collected from advertisers) was too much, and therefore decided to portion out the newspaper's student fees to force them to collect more of

the debts faster.

THE AMOUNT O'Neal agreed to give the paper was insufficient, according to *DTH* Business Manager Reynolds Bailey, because the paper was unusually large for the first three issues, and needed the capital for those issues.

Carolina regulations require all organizations receiving any funds from Student Government, such as the newspaper, to requisition funds against a cash balance before doing business.

Since O'Neal released only $3,900 of the nearly $13,000 allocated to the paper, the advertising staff was forced to collect part of the remaining accounts receivable in order to have enough of a cash balance to pay for printing costs. Last week, the *DTH* was no longer able to do so.

"We collected around $4,000 last Friday," *DTH* Editor Cole Campbell told the *Technician* yesterday, "and that should be enough for us to publish

Tuesday, and hopefully the rest of the week, but we will not be able to publish Monday."

Campbell said that the money the advertising staff has been collecting concerns mainly debts from last year and the sum· erl Advertisers owed the paper in the neighborhood of $24,000, or about 13 percent of its total budget for the 1975-76 year.

"THE AD STAFF has been going around to friendly merchants and asking them if they can pay us sooner than they planned. We have been getting some money, but the ad staff hasn't been able to sell any new ads," Campbell explained.

O'Neal felt that the 13 percent figure for accounts receivable for the newspaper was excessive, but Dick Pope, a graduate business student and member of the Campus Governing Council (CGC) who mediated between the two sides, said, "I think it's a perfectly acceptable business practice. Mike is doing an acre· table job of monitoring the treasury, but this is one area where he didn't have the

expertise to immediately see what the accounts receivable meant."

O'Neal said that arrangements should have been made to get more of the $24,000 in accounts receivable, and that the merchants had no reason to not to go ahead and give the paper the money.

Campbell, however, pointed out that the fall is a time when merchants normally have cash reserves tied up in larger-than-normal inventories to accommodate the back-to-school rush.

IN AN EDITORIAL printed in the *Tar Heel* Friday, Campbell said, "Ads have been turned away because there is not enough cash on hand to pay for papers large enough to include all the ads...Current advertisers have been alienated because we have not been able to extend them credit regardless of their prestige and credit rating within the business community."

O'Neal agreed to release an additional $2500 from the September allotment of student fees, but the *DTH* staff is trying to get the entire amount for the semester released. it would reportedly take at

two-thirds majority of the CGC to bring such a measure before the body, since the finance committee has not introduced one.

The reason for the crackdown, according to Campbell, was a drop in cash reserves last year which forced the paper to borrow funds.

The CGC set up a system by which the paper could borrow the cash from the university," *DTH* News Editor Jim Roberts explained, "and there was some question abou' it, since the money was suddenly there and we used it. Also, it took longer to pay back than we thought it would."

"THERE HAS BEEN a long political battle between student government and the *Daily Tar Heel*," said Campbell. "Student Government is composed mainly of conservatives. During the summer student government put out its own weekly newspaper almost in direct response to an editorial in the *DTH*."

O'Neal, however, blamed the newspaper's problems on financial instability and inefficiency within the business staff.

DTH Editor Cole Campbell

"Internal business practices of the *Tar Heel* are not in order," O'Neal said in a *Chapel Hill Newspaper* interview.

"The *Tar Heel* is on the right track now. The problems will correct themselves. Outside professional help is what the *Tar Heel* needs."

Campbell said that the newspaper would seek to obtain half of the money remaining allocated money.

See "Tar Heel," page 3

Anticipation...

staff photo by Kearns

State mascots Jim Hefner and Jan Seymour watch with anticipation during the Wolfpack's season opener against East Carolina Saturday night in Carter Stadium. These two State student cheerleaders are only two of the 47,000 fans that looked on as State defended the Pirates, 26-3.

Technician editor blasts Carolina Student Government's DTH policy

The University of North Carolina student newspaper, *The Daily Tarheel*, was forced to cut back on the size of the paper last week due to a financial crunch. *Technician* editor Kevin Fisher was asked how the events and subsequent developments might affect the operation of the newspaper on the State campus.

"From the information available to me thus far, it seems apparent that the *Tarheel* is castrated by the student

government of the University of North Carolina at Chapel Hill," said Fisher. "What it comes down to as far as I can see is a case of the student government there being unable to come up with creative projects of its own, so instead they've decided to play 'hot shot' and exercise their financial control over the *Daily Tarheel*."

Fisher added that the system of publication at State was such that student government had no control over the operation of the newspaper.

"THIS SITUATION points out how much better it is to have the kind of publications structure where student

Fisher added that the *Technician* was making a "substantial profit" so far in the semester, but that he didn't know if the paper would be under a system such as Carolina's.

"In the 'real world,' the thought of government regulation of newspapers is met with disgust," Fisher said. "It should also be that way with university newspapers and university student governments."

"IF STUDENT governments that have some sort of financial control over their university's newspapers can't come up with anything better to do than hassle the newspapers, then the value of having

---

dent newspaper, the *Technician*, was distributed to UNC's student body in the absence of the financially plagued *Daily Tar Heel*," the paper reported. "The *Tar Heel* was forced to cancel its planned Saturday and Monday issues because of a lack of cash on hand." An unrepentant Mike O'Neal called the *Technician* incident "ridiculous" and implied non-publication was an orchestrated stunt. "The students are being sold a bill of goods," O'Neal declared. "The facts are that the

Daily Tar Heel didn't print because it didn't want to." Campbell fired back, denying O'Neal's accusation, and expressing offense that the treasurer was, in effect, calling him a liar.[14]

The showdown between the *Daily Tar Heel* and student government in September 1975 had both short- and long-term repercussions. Though Bill Bates kept his position as student-body president, O'Neal was forced out of office after weeks of refusing to resign. Student gov-

February 1976 cartoon by John Branch, commenting on the shrinking size of the *Daily Tar Heel* during one of its regular funding shortages of the era. (*Yack*)

ernment commissioned a study of the Media Board and *DTH* operations, and Cole Campbell cofounded a committee with the stated goal to "preserve the *Tar Heel* as a daily publication with sufficient copy space to permit complete treatment of campus and community news, according to the policies set by each editor." The result of these efforts was a proposal to amend the student constitution to create a new board to oversee *DTH* business operations, and to set the annual student fee appropriation given the paper at 16 percent (then amounting to $51,000) of the total SAFO budget. The new board would operate under the auspices of the existing Media Board and consist of six members: four students, one each appointed by the student-body president, the *DTH* editor, the Media Board, and one at large; and two faculty members, one from the School of Journalism, and the other from the Business School. "The *DTH* separation was necessary," as one Media Board member explained, "because the newspaper monopolized the board's

time.... It was a case of the *DTH* being too large for the board to handle." A campus-wide referendum creating the new board and setting the 16 percent student fee appropriation passed by a wide margin in February 1977, and this structure remained in place until the early 1990s.[15]

OTHER VOICES: THE WOMEN'S MOVEMENT AND THE DAWNING OF LGBTQ ACTIVISM
The civil rights movement of the 1960s brought the struggle for racial equality into national consciousness and opened the door for other groups traditionally marginalized in American society. The most prominent of these groups to form in the early 1970s to fight for social, legal, and political rights were women and the same-sex community. The women's movement, and especially what was first known as the gay rights movement (later LGBTQ), were controversial and complicated, involving diverse populations and questions of societal structure and views of morality that were often not as clear-cut as racial dis-

crimination. The University of North Carolina, with its tradition of liberalism and dedication to a fully inclusive democratic society, provided an environment for some of the earliest activities of both movements in North Carolina. As had been the case with civil rights, however, those associated with these movements also faced harsh criticism and discrimination even in Chapel Hill. And as it did throughout the long struggle for racial equality, the *Daily Tar Heel* took a leading role in fighting for the expansion of rights and acceptance of all, regardless of gender or sexual identity—though not without some controversy and occasional equivocation.

Though women had been students at Carolina—and had served on the staff of the paper—since the 1890s, the population and culture of the campus remained male dominated into the early 1960s. After women were fully admitted as first-year students in 1963, however, the balance quickly began to shift. In March 1964, the *DTH* reported on two events focused around women's issues: one was a lecture on the position of women at UNC by Gladys Coates of the School of Government, and the other was a campus meeting of the North Carolina Council on World Affairs, with a theme of equal opportunity for women. That month the paper also carried a large ad by the New York firm of J. Walter Thompson announcing, "A career where it is an asset to be a woman: Advertising." And as the history of the *DTH* reveals, women increasingly fought for social and reproductive rights on campus throughout the mid- and late 1960s. By the early 1970s, in tune with the national movement, "women's liberation" was in full flower at UNC. The paper reported that Female Liberation, No. 27, a radical feminist group, was established, with a mission

of "working in various aspects of women's lives." Numerous conferences and festivals themed around women's issues were held, at times in conjunction with national organizations such as the National Organization for Women (NOW), and a host of prominent feminist speakers appeared at UNC, including Gloria Steinem, Jane Fonda, Betty Friedan, Shelia Tobias, and Angela Davis.[16]

The Association of Women Students (AWS) also emerged on campus during this era, with a moderate agenda that appealed to a wide base and ultimately outlived the first blush of more radical feminism at UNC. In 1973 the AWS started a female-oriented program on the UNC radio station called Calliope's Corner and began publication of *SHE*, a newspaper organizers were quick to point out was "not a women's lib publication." With an initial circulation of 3,000, and supported in part by student fees, *SHE* was one of a small group of periodicals that appeared at Carolina in the late 1960s and into the mid-1970s, focused on a specific audience. These publications usually stuck to narrowly defined missions and tended to represent one end or the other of the political spectrum, and as such were at times at odds with the *Daily Tar Heel*, which generally remained only a few steps to the left of center in terms of news coverage and editorial opinion.[17]

The women's movement differed from other causes, notably civil rights, in that equal access at UNC proved a somewhat less difficult path for women, the result of the dramatic shift in balance of the student population: by 1975 there were more women than men in the first-year class, and by the early 1980s women outnumbered men in the entire student body. Barriers soon fell across campus, and female students assumed positions of authority. In the fall of 1973,

the student-body vice president, the editor of the Black Student Movement (BSM) publication, *Black Ink*, and the director of the Carolina Forum were all women—and the *Daily Tar Heel*, for the first time since 1951, had a female editor in chief.[18]

Elected the previous spring, Susan Miller had run on a platform that included a proposal to have the UNC School of Business conduct a study to develop a plan to end the paper's reliance on student fees. Under Miller's leadership, the *DTH* focused primarily on campus news and took on a more informal layout style that suited the era and offered respite from both the so-

cial turmoil of the late 1960s and the recent bitter fighting over the paper's political opinions. Miller did take on a few select issues, however. In October 1973, she wrote an editorial calling for the "unreasonable" President Richard Nixon to be impeached, three days after special Watergate prosecutor Archibald Cox was fired on Nixon's orders for issuing a subpoena for secret White House tapes (and after the resignations of the attorney general and assistant attorney general for refusing to fire Cox, the so-called Saturday Night Massacre). As twentieth-century investigative journalism reached an apex in the United States during the Watergate scandal, the public lost faith in government and authoritative bodies. In this atmosphere of distrust, Miller called for transparency and press access to meetings of the university's Affirmative Action Advisory Committee, which were held behind closed doors. "The committee should quit fooling around with semantics and pseudo logic and get on with the people's business—eliminating discrimination in the University—in open meetings," Miller wrote.[19]

The most significant issue Miller tackled as editor of the *Daily Tar Heel* was a crusade to open the prestigious Morehead Scholarship program to women. Established in 1951 by university alumnus and benefactor John Motley Morehead III, the program offered full four-year scholarships and other benefits to an elite group of students who excelled academically and showed promise of becoming citizens who would provide "the state and the country with a true caliber of leadership." Though the Morehead Scholarships were opened to African American men in 1968, five years later women were still barred from applying, and Miller and the *DTH* staff decided it was time for the gender wall in this high-profile program to fall. In late October 1973, a front-page article appeared above the banner with the boldface headline "Was Morehead a male chauvinist?" The story, covered exclusively by female staff, charged the head of the Morehead board of trustees, Hugh G. Chatham, with being tone-deaf to the political sensibilities of the era. When asked why women were not allowed to apply, Chatham replied: "Well madam, any young lady who achieves the notoriety I wish for my scholars would obviously be immoral." Despite the uproar this article created, Chatham continued to defend his antiquated views. Managing to offend both women and Native Americans, the board chair told a reporter several days after the story broke that "if I could get an honest-Injun pledge written in blood that a girl would not get married and have children, but be a politician or a leader, then we'll have women in our program."[20]

Comments like these enraged supporters of women's rights on campus—and on the staff of the *Daily Tar Heel.* "So Morehead was a male chauvinist," Dawn Marie Clayton wrote in a column on the editorial page. "Hot damn. He was probably racist too, but that didn't deter the trustees of the scholarship from naming several black Morehead scholars in 1973. It is the fuddy duddies who run the program now who should be branded and roasted as male chauvinist pigs due to their senile thinking and male superiority complexes." Miller was more tempered in her language, though no less firm in her resolve: "There may be a good reason not to give the Morehead scholarship awards to women, but we sure haven't heard it." Noting the current leadership roles held by women on campus, Miller wrote: "Women, too, can achieve success in a career and as a wife and mother, just as men can

achieve success as a husband and father ... we would like to bring the Morehead trustees back from the fifties' vision of women's roles in society." The paper's attention to this issue, and the unfortunate words of the Morehead board chair, brought swift results. Three weeks after the initial article appeared, the Faculty Council passed a resolution supporting the inclusion of women in the Morehead program, and by the fall of 1974, the paper reported, approximately one-third of the applicants were female. The first women Morehead Scholars arrived in 1975, and the same year a women's studies curriculum was established at UNC.[21]

Throughout the 1970s and early 1980s, the *Daily Tar Heel* went on record in support of the three major national issues involving women: legalization of abortion, passage of the Equal Rights Amendment (ERA), and implementation of Title IX of the Educational Amendment of 1972, requiring equal opportunity for women in federally funded institutions. The *DTH* had consistently supported women's reproductive rights since the sexual revolution of the 1960s, including advocating for student access to the pill once it became available and for the legalization of abortion. The Supreme Court decision in *Roe v. Wade* was handed down in January 1973, shortly before Susan Miller became editor of the *DTH,* and the paper's position on reproductive rights became even more evident. Later that year, ads appeared for "Pre-Fil" contraceptive foam, and in early 1974, when Senator Jesse Helms attempted to weaken *Roe* by introducing an amendment to a bill in Congress that would define life as starting at the moment of conception, Miller blasted the move in an editorial entitled "Unborn Rights Unfair to the Living."[22]

The disproportionately low number of women on the faculty at UNC also fueled campus support for the ERA. As with ongoing criticism that the university was not promoting opportunities for African Americans, the progressive reputation of UNC was challenged by a similar problem regarding women. A 1973 report on the situation found clear gender bias and, as the *Daily Tar Heel* reported, "discrepancies between men and women in the areas of hiring, promotion, and salary." Following release of the report, NOW issued a scathing statement about the situation at UNC, but the problem persisted for years. When religion professor Mary Carroll Smith filed a gender discrimination suit in 1976, the North Carolina Equal Employment Opportunity Commission investigated and found bias in both faculty and non-faculty hiring at UNC. Another suit followed in 1980, filed by four current and former female faculty members, and yet another in 1989, all covered by the *DTH*. In the midst of these discrimination suits, bills to ratify the ERA were introduced in the North Carolina state legislature no less than five times between 1973 and 1981, failing to pass each time. In 1973, on the first attempt at passage, a lead editorial noted that it took North Carolina an embarrassing fifty-two years to ratify the Nineteenth Amendment (giving women the right to vote), and wondered if passage of the ERA would have to wait until 2025. "Equality before the law, one of the cornerstone traditions in our American heritage," the editorial declared, "will remain a hollow gesture until it is guaranteed for all citizens regardless of sex." When the bill was introduced for the fifth time in 1981, the Carolina Union sponsored a public debate between nationally known conservative leader and ERA opponent Phyllis Schlafly and NOW founder Betty Friedan, which was covered extensively in the *DTH*. All of the *DTH* editors of the time supported passage of the ERA, regardless of whether their personal politics were to the left or right on the political spectrum. Editor George Shadroui, whose political perspective was right of center, called for passage even though he wrote that he knew it was a lost cause, calling the struggle for ratification in North Carolina nothing more than "political games."[23]

Of the three national issues involving women's rights in the 1970s and early 1980s, none was to have a more significant effect on the university than Title IX. Passed by Congress in 1972, the law prohibited discrimination based on gender in any aspect of an institution that accepted federal funds. Though the mandate was intended to cover all aspects of a given institution, in the case of universities the impact was most significant in athletic programs. Specific provisions of the law went into effect in June 1975, and institutions were given three years to comply. Many in the university community and the UNC Athletic Department grumbled, but major changes were made to accommodate women and meet the new requirements. The news and sports staff of the *Daily Tar Heel* worked during the period to cover developments and to provide context and background. In November 1974, reporter Jane Albright wrote that "the '74–'75 academic year will go down in history as the year women moved from the physical education department to the administration of the Athletic Department." Carolina's answer to the threat of Title IX, Albright wrote, was to make women part of the Athletic Department, give them their own athletic director, and award them with academic scholarships. She also noted that efforts were hampered by questions of funding, as the rising cost of athletics was already putting pressure on the university: due to inflation and other causes, the men's athletic programs budget had grown more than 400 percent in six years, from $800,000 to $3.5 million.[24]

The university administration established a committee to implement Title IX at Carolina, which was charged with overseeing various changes and meeting federal requirements as monitored by the Department of Health, Education and Welfare (HEW). This was a daunting proposition, as the UNC system was by the mid-1970s already enmeshed in a protracted and very public battle with HEW over racial discrimination on its campuses. The *Daily Tar Heel* reported that the Title IX Committee took up a variety of issues aside from athletics between 1975 and 1979, including ensuring equality with respect to the number and condition of university dormitories, and the opening up of formerly male-only service fraternities on campus (which resulted in the admission of women to Alpha Phi Omega, and the merger of the honorary male-only Order of the Grail with the female-only Valkyries). The paper took on one Title IX issue itself: the number of lockers for women in Woollen Gymnasium. In a front-page story in November 1977, the paper reported that while nearly half of the student population on campus was female, only 15 percent of the gym lockers (and attendant changing facilities) were available to women. Running a large photograph of the cramped women's locker room, and citing Title IX, the paper called for change. Two weeks later, women students were given access to 450 additional lockers formerly used by male faculty.[25]

Ultimately, Title IX transformed the athletic programs at UNC. More than a dozen women's sports teams were created, and full-time female coaching staff was hired. Ironically using a line from a popular cigarette ad of the era aimed at women—"You've come a long way baby"—the *Daily Tar Heel* reported in August 1980 that over the previous decade the number of female athletic scholarships had accelerated from zero to 103 at Carolina, and that the thirteen women's varsity sports had an annual budget of $700,000. Title IX led to the creation of the storied women's soccer program at UNC, and the team won the first NCAA championship in 1982, beginning an unprecedented series of title wins. Getting students to the games proved difficult, however, even though the *DTH* began in the early 1980s to promote women's sports in front-page photographs and articles. When women's soccer coach Anson Dorrance lamented to one of the paper's reporters in October 1984 that only forty or fifty students attended games, despite three national titles and a 40–1 winning streak, the *DTH* ran an article entitled "A Sad Song for UNC's Women Athletes," encouraging students to show support.[26]

Though the *Daily Tar Heel*'s editorial policies on major women's rights issues of the 1970s and 1980s were consistently progressive, the staff found itself in a difficult position with regard to one issue that challenged the boundaries of free speech: pornography. As the national conversation about women's rights expanded to include combating sexual violence, pornography was increasingly cited as contributing to the problem. Mainstream pornographic publications came under severe criticism, and on several occasions the *DTH* was caught in the debate

over objectification of women versus freedom of the press. The first incident occurred in September 1976, when a large, sexually suggestive ad for one such publication, *Oui*, appeared in the paper. A withering letter to the editor a few days later rebuked the *DTH* for making the decision "to join the flesh trade." The writer also referenced the paper's recent funding crisis, and equated the ad to racism: "In its financial situation, the *DTH* no doubt found it a lucrative proposition to pander to puerile taste. Would they also, I wonder, have run an ad depicting blacks as shuffling Step N' Fetchits, just for the money it would bring?" Though the letter was printed, it did not deter the editors from running an ad for *Playboy* a week later. And in 1978, when *Playboy* decided to feature college women in its jubilee issue, the *DTH* carried front-page stories about the magazine's photographer who visited campus to shoot prospective student models (noting in one article that a small group of protesters had picketed a

similar shoot at the University of Southern California). Revealing his own insensitivity, the photographer told a *DTH* reporter that he was often "disappointed" when some women disrobed. "It's a shame that so many beautiful girls from college have figures that aren't what they should be.... It's shameful." He did quickly add: "I can appreciate what they are going through, though, having grown up in husky pants with love handles on each side."[27]

The issue involving *Playboy* advertising and the *Daily Tar Heel* heated up again in 1983. A quarter-page ad appeared in early February, seeking young women from UNC to appear in an upcoming "Girls of the Atlantic Coast Conference" issue. Apparently there was some debate about running the ad, but editor John Drescher (who would later become executive editor of the Raleigh *News and Observer*) remembered that most of the editorial staff, including the three women members, had no objections. The day after the ad ran he wrote a somewhat tongue-in-cheek editorial, noting that it had provoked "no outraged shouts of protest or letters from enraged feminists." Commenting that all of the other ACC college newspapers at the time decided that women students were "old enough to make up their own minds without ... censoring ads directed at them," Drescher added that as for the *DTH*, "we're easy ... we'll take anybody's money." "This paper," Drescher concluded, "in its great tradition of equality, can only say that it eagerly awaits an ad from *Playgirl* seeking 'Guys of the ACC.'"[28]

By running his editorial only one day after the *Playboy* ad, Drescher may have been attempting to defuse any potential controversy. But women's rights advocates on campus took offense at the lighthearted approach to the subject. Four angry women stormed into his office, while others wrote letters. "We found your editorial comments as insulting as the original advertisement," a letter from Sarah Lee, a spokesperson for the Association of Women Students, read. "The ad was a blatant insult to the women of UNC and the *DTH* participated in this insult by disseminating it to the community," the letter continued; "We wonder if you would have run an ad for the KKK asking for black volunteers." Lee's letter also noted that pornography was at the time a $5 billion annual business, four times larger than the fast-food giant McDonald's, and enumerated concerns that it led to various social ills, primarily violence against women. "If not out and out contributing to the objectification of and violence against women, pornography is certainly doing nothing to stop it," Lee wrote. "We have in our country a situation in which over half the population is female and these woman are afraid to go out at night or even to be alone during the day. If nothing else, this fear will keep women from attaining their true position of equality in our society."[29]

Drescher and the *Daily Tar Heel* staff decided to handle the now burgeoning controversy firmly but sensitively. The paper's official position was that the *Playboy* ads were legal and protected under the First Amendment, and had been proven so in court. Thus the ad ran again on February 11, although for a balanced perspective a column was reprinted on the editorial page from the campus AWS paper, *SHE*, entitled "*Playboy* Ad Degrades Women." On February 14—Valentine's Day—Drescher wrote a column "Women in advertising" explaining in detail why the decision was made to run the *Playboy* ad. "The first point important to make," Drescher wrote, "is that newspapers that run advertisements for pornographic magazines are not promoting pornography any more than they are promoting alcohol or cigarettes or topless bars" (all of which were legal to advertise at the time). "It is neither proper nor practical for a newspaper to set the moral standards by which its readers should live." Dismissing the comparison of *Playboy* to the KKK, Drescher cited the 1973 court case of *Miller v. California*, establishing the legality of pornographic publications. "The second important point," the editor continued, "is that research shows pornography does not necessarily lead to violence." As evidence he noted a commission established by President Richard Nixon, some of the research for which was conducted at UNC. But Drescher was careful to be sensitive to the issue. "The heart of the problem is that much of advertising is sexist and that many consumers apparently like it or continue to tolerate it. Newspapers and magazines, which financially rely on advertising and are great believers in First Amendment rights, cannot be expected to reform the advertising business." He concluded the piece by urging readers to attend an AWS showing of "Killing Us Softly," a film about the portrayal of women in advertising.[30]

Having settled the issue regarding placement of *Playboy* ads in the *Daily Tar Heel* (at least temporarily, as it would resurface again in 1989), the paper ran another ad in March, as well as stories about both the campus visit of the magazine's photographer and the appearance of the "Girls of the ACC" issue in August, featuring three UNC women. Though John Drescher's call for a "Guys of the ACC" *Playgirl* issue never materialized, in a humorous twist to the story, the *DTH* did report in November 1983 that a Clemson student

"MRS. CONLEY, DOES MY CONTRACT SPECIFICALLY REQUIRE ME TO KISS THE HOMECOMING QUEEN?"

had created a "Men of the South" calendar, featuring five former UNC football players.[31]

The broader cultural issues of the changing status of women and traditional gender roles in American society were evident at UNC in 1975 and again in 1983, when two men won the annual election for homecoming queen. The discussion began seriously enough in the fall of 1974, when the paper reported a debate on campus, in the wake of Title IX, about whether the election should be gender-neutral and whether the title should be changed to homecoming "monarch" or "person." The following year a male ran, and won, which caused some grumbling on campus and awkwardness in the rituals. However, in 1983 another male student, wearing exaggerated female attire and running under the name "Yure Nmomma," won, causing a backlash from many students and alumni. A *DTH* editorial took the position that the man ran as a joke and was elected democratically, so the situation should be viewed with some degree of levity. The paper followed both campaigns with some bemusement, though the latter stunt halted the tradition of electing a homecoming queen for one year.[32]

While the matter of male homecoming queens may have been an amusing diversion, the growing public awareness about homosexuality, gay rights, and gender identity in the 1970s and early 1980s became a topic of much serious discussion and debate within the UNC community. In fact, the staff of the *Daily Tar Heel* had been faced with the question of covering homosexuality at least as far back as the early 1950s. Rolfe Neill, editor in 1953–54, remembered being briefed by the university's top administrators about a "big dust-up" concerning a dozen male students who were being expelled for being caught engaging in sexual activity in a basement men's restroom of Wilson Library. As a curious news reporter, he remembered going over to look at the holes cut in the walls of the toilet stalls. Though he was not asked to suppress the story, Neill decided not to print it, as homosexuality was not a subject publicly discussed in the 1950s. Apparently the clandestine Wilson Library men's restroom trysts were still going on a decade later, as two letters to the editor in early 1964 cryptically noted that doors to the stalls (which shielded the activity) were being removed, and suggested this action constituted discrimination of "minority groups." In November 1964, the paper ran an atypical wire service story on the editorial page, without comment, consisting of the text of a speech given by a minister in Baltimore who offered an enlightened view of sexual expression, including homosexuality. The timing of the sermon and the story was almost certainly the result of the scandal involving Walter Jenkins, a top advisor to President Lyndon Johnson, who had recently been arrested for "disorderly conduct" in the bathroom of a YMCA in Washington, D.C. That incident brought public conversation about sexual orientation into the open and onto the pages of the nation's largest newspapers.[33]

The *Daily Tar Heel*'s first significant attempt to cover homosexuality in a balanced manner—the April 1971 full-page "Insight" feature that led to the attempt by the North Carolina state legislature to bar the use of student fees to publish the paper—was followed by more frequent coverage of the subject. Growing sensitivity to gay rights on campus was revealed by critical letters to the editor in January 1974, following publication of a *DTH* music review that included the word "faggot." And although some opinion columns and letters continued to condemn homosexuality and to reveal deep-seated prejudice, the editorial policy of the paper from a remarkably early date denounced discrimination based on sexual orientation. For example, soon after the controversial music review containing the epithet appeared, a news story ran about the members of the American Psychiatric Association voting to remove homosexuality from its diagnostic manual of mental disorders.[34]

In September 1974, the university officially sanctioned the Carolina Gay Association (CGA) and the *Daily Tar Heel* found itself in the midst of some of the most vicious overt prejudice in UNC history. Though CGA organizers had put out flyers announcing its first meeting, precautions were taken to protect the anonymity of those attending. At a football game a few days before the meeting, however, leaflets mysteriously appeared and were distributed that reproduced the CGA flyer with the addition of the name, address, and telephone number of the dean who had approved the organization. In a front-page article about the incident, the *DTH* ran a photograph of the flyer, but it soon regret-ted the coverage. On September 17 the *Daily Tar Heel* published one of the most significant editorials in its history, entitled "A Question of Civil Rights." "The time has come for the jeering of the Carolina Gay Association to stop," the editorial began. While comparing the tactics of those who had distributed the doctored flyer at the football game to those employed by Richard Nixon, who had resigned just weeks earlier, the paper also issued a mea culpa. "The *DTH* has erred as well," the editors sheepishly admitted, as the staff's sensitivity on the issue turned to snickering, and the incident "became a media-event on our pages," which was "not only childish, but inconsistent with our previous attitudes." While stating that the *DTH* "does not endorse homosexuality," they added "we stand up for the rights of gays to meet openly and safely." The editorial continued:

> Just as in race relations there will always be the inevitable and predictable jokes, but the jeering now prevalent threatens gay rights. It will take courage for homosexuals to come out completely in the open. It will also take courage for heterosexuals to face them openly and honestly. The traditional practice of pretending gays do not exist is both expedient and demeaning. Direct confrontation will test our maturity as much as any possible social difference, but it will eliminate centuries of mindless prejudice.
>
> We must be careful in the meantime not to let the jokes turn to jeering, the humor to humiliation. For the first time since the early fifties we are asked to begin facing up to a question of civil rights. Now that it's our turn, let's do better than the generations before us.[35]

The Carolina Gay Association was founded in 1974 and soon began holding events and conferences on campus, which caused much controversy well into the 1990s. (*Yack*)

In effect—and after some soul-searching, as evident from this editorial—the *Daily Tar Heel*'s stand on gay rights was born alongside the CGA. As had been the case with civil rights, the paper became the medium through which the issue was discussed in both a cultural and political context at UNC. And although some African Americans have objected historically to the comparison between the fight for racial equality and what some view as sexual preference, the editors and staff of the *DTH* clearly saw the matter from the beginning as one of basic fairness in a democratic society, and on the campus of the nation's oldest public university.

Just as with the discourse regarding civil rights, the rhetoric surrounding homosexuality and gay rights on the pages of the *Daily Tar Heel* was not always consistent. To many with traditional religious and conservative political beliefs,

homosexuality was unnatural, abhorrent, and, at the time, illegal. Eight days after the paper's strong lead editorial appeared, Rorin Platt, the *DTH*'s resident conservative columnist, wrote a scathing rebuttal entitled "Social Rights Must Be Defended." Calling the establishment of the CGA "the glorification of perversion," Platt described homosexuality as "abnormal behavior ... patently offensive," and "perverse, base, and immoral." "If homosexuality is glorified," Platt argued, "then what is next—transvestism, bestiality, or even necrophilia?" According to Platt, "Society has the right to deny homosexuals access to its public interactions if the goals of the deviants conflict with those of society." Though stating that "legal harassment or persecution of homosexuals is not the goal," Platt declared that "the freedom of the majority must be protected," and he added gay rights to the list of what he saw as forces weakening UNC. "The advent of the public gay activity at Carolina further deteriorates the quality of a great institution which has already given in, either by its own initiative or by external pressure, to the 'demands' of the black militants, liberal students and professors, [and] the women liberationists."[36]

Daily Tar Heel coverage and editorials on gay rights during what might be termed the movement's early period at UNC—from the establishment of the CGA in 1974 to the dawning of the AIDS epidemic in the mid-1980s—primarily focused on incidents of discrimination and hate based on sexual orientation, a perennial battle over funding of the CGA by student government, and events that occurred in connection with the annual Gay Awareness Week. Despite the strong statement made in 1974, the paper still struggled with an objective approach to the issue. In October 1975, a story appeared about bartenders at He's Not Here, a popular Chapel Hill bar, asking two men not to dance with each other. The incident sparked several anti-gay letters to the editor, and the paper called for tolerance. But in January 1978, a column by a UNC exchange student describing his experiences in Toronto included a sentence about a visit he had made to a nightclub that read, "Two fags were at the next table." Several angry letters to the editor appeared soon after, objecting to the use of the derogatory word "fags," and the editor issued a rare apology: "You're right, we're wrong. The *Daily Tar Heel* normally does not change copy in a personal column but in this instance editing was justified." And following the beating death of a gay man near Durham in April 1981, the paper interviewed the chair of the CGA, Les Mullis, quoting him as saying, "Two gay people can not walk down Franklin Street without getting verbal threats or having bottles thrown at them." Mullis wrote a letter objecting to the quote, however, stating that the paper left out the words "holding hands" from his statement, which he felt was done on purpose. In a related story, the paper also reported that after the beating death some students were afraid to attend CGA meetings in the student union, and that future meetings were being moved to an undisclosed location.[37]

The attempts to end student funding of the *Daily Tar Heel* by those who did not agree with its editorial policies served as a model for similar actions against other controversial organizations, including the Association of Women Students, the Black Student Movement, and the Carolina Gay Association. Though the appropriation for the CGA was negligible during the first decade of its existence (fluctuating between

$650 and about $1,100), the *DTH* reported no fewer than five attempts in nine years to cut off student support for the organization entirely. In 1982, for example, the Campus Governing Council discussed discontinuing funding for the CGA, as well as for the AWS and the BSM, characterizing the groups as "political." The paper also reported a frequently hostile environment for student politicians who supported the CGA. One student legislator came under fire in 1975 because he voted to support funding for the association, and a cautious candidate for student-body president told a *DTH* reporter in 1978 that the group "should be funded in some way, but I don't know if it's fair for our student fees to go to something that there's no way we're going to be involved in."[38]

Aside from publishing *Lambda*, a monthly newsletter (now the longest running LGBTQ college publication in the United States), the primary public activity of the CGA in the late 1970s and early 1980s was the celebration of Gay Awareness Week, held each spring. The *Daily Tar Heel* covered the week's activities objectively and empathetically, often running front-page stories and supportive editorials. The week included events to help individuals who were "coming out" as homosexual and featured Blue Jeans Day, an opportunity for everyone on campus regardless of sexual orientation to show support for gays and lesbians by wearing jeans. But the event soon caused a backlash; in the spring of 1982, one heterosexual student took out a classified ad in the *DTH* complaining that it was an inconvenience not being able to wear jeans that day, lest he be branded as gay. A lead editorial appeared several days later, asking students to think about their reaction to this seemingly harmless event. "Across campus," the editorial reported, "thousands of people who normally would have worn jeans wore corduroys or khakis.... That kind of attitude shows hostility and fear of homosexuality." Noting that recently several gay people who had been interviewed for *DTH* stories or who had written letters to the editor asked that their names not be used—and pointing out that the current president of the CGA had also asked not to be publicly identified for fear of his safety—the paper questioned whether Chapel Hill was really the "center for progressive thinking and acceptance of various lifestyles." "The fact that gays still fear the consequences of coming out into the open shows we still have far to go in respecting personal freedoms."[39]

In fact, virtually every spring during this era the *Daily Tar Heel* published angry letters from students opposed to the public activities of Gay Awareness Week, and carried stories about acts of vandalism against related signage. Yet the level of hostility towards the CGA that appeared on the pages of the *DTH* during the 1970s and early 1980s, despite the paper's editorial pleas for tolerance, was about to get even worse. With a rightward shift in politics, and a deadly new virus closely associated with homosexuality—Acquired Immune Deficiency Syndrome, widely known as AIDS—about to cause worldwide panic, the LGBTQ community across the nation and at UNC would soon face an even darker period.[40]

PREPPIES ON CAMPUS: THE RISE OF CONSERVATISM AND THE NEW RIGHT

Opposition to feminism and gay rights activism contributed to a growing social and political conservatism in the United States during the 1970s and early 1980s. The Republican Party underwent a major realignment during this period, driven to a significant degree by the so-called New Right, which interjected strong religious beliefs into the political arena. The South, and in particular North Carolina, played a major role in the realignment, the result of the rise of Jesse Helms and his political action committee, the National Congressional Club, which helped not only keep Helms in the U.S. Senate, but also to put Ronald Reagan into the White House. Between the election cycles of 1972 and 1984, North Carolina became a viable two-party state, after three-quarters of a century of Democratic rule. College campuses in the state and across the nation also became more socially and politically conservative. And although Carolina's student body was never as monolithically liberal as critics often claimed, there was a definite movement to the right during the era that few would have predicted scarcely a decade earlier. In March 1978, a front-page story in the *Daily Tar Heel* quoted alumnus Roy Underhill (later a popular host of UNC-TV's *The Woodwright's Shop*), who was on campus demonstrating early American woodworking skills: "When I was here from '68 to '72, it was acid land. There were riots, and the police were holding people [in Lenoir Hall during the food workers' strike]. Now it has mellowed out. Everything is beach music and skateboards." In a November 1980 *DTH* interview, UNC alumnus and *New York Times* columnist Tom Wicker commented on the "cultural counter revolution of conservatism" then underway, which he argued "arose in reaction to the dramatic changes of the 1960s and 1970s." This shift also meant, generally speaking, different priorities for most students. A special December 1983 *DTH* section on political activism on campus described the 1960s as "sandwiched" between the conformity of the 1950s and the "me generation" of the late 1970s and early 1980s. The current generation of students, one article noted, were interested in political and social issues but were "not likely to act."[41]

The rise of conservatism in the late 1970s and early 1980s was as much cultural as political. The bell-bottomed jeans, "earth" shoes, peasant blouses and long unruly hair of the late 1960s through the mid-1970s gave way to khakis, topsiders and "weejuns," shirts branded with alligator and polo-pony emblems, traditional blazers, plaid skirts, and neatly styled hair—as ads in the *DTH* for "Carolina campus classics" attest. A feature story in September 1978 reported that current and former students moving to New York City to take jobs soon found that the UNC "preppy" look was out of step there and viewed as a throwback to the late 1950s and early 1960s. When the best-selling *Official Preppy Handbook* sold out in one week in Chapel Hill in December 1980, the paper covered it as a major cultural event. And it was the *DTH* that broke the story— as front-page news—that the producers of the blockbuster college movie of the preppy generation, *Animal House*, intended to film at Carolina, until their request was denied by the UNC administration.[42]

Some aspects of this new conservatism may have been superficial and lighthearted, but the deeper shifting political and cultural currents resulted in a period of soul-searching at the *Daily Tar Heel*. Having weathered extensive criticism by leading conservatives across the state and on campus for decades, as well as the dogged efforts

to end student funding, the staff of the paper found itself by the mid-1970s trying to balance increasingly polarized opinions and interests. Though the nature of journalism—and particularly college journalism at a progressive public institution like UNC—traditionally tracked to the left of center, there was a renewed effort at the *DTH* to provide a forum for all perspectives. One approach that developed during the era was increased involvement by the *DTH* board in editorial content. Where it had generally been the practice for the editor in chief (or coeditors) to be entirely responsible for the lead editorial each day, by the mid-1970s discussions were being held about the paper's stand on issues, and the unsigned lead was more frequently written by other members of the board, usually (though not always) following consensus of opinion.[43]

The effort to offer a balanced perspective was most evident in political endorsements, which proved a struggle at times. The practice of extensively covering state and national political campaigns and publishing endorsements just prior to elections only became a consistent feature of the *Daily Tar Heel* during the 1960 election cycle. By the late 1960s, political endorsements were a significant point of contention, and, according to critics, a prime example of the paper's liberal bias. Interestingly, less than three months after the *Arrington v. Taylor* lawsuit was filed in 1972, the *DTH* published its first outright endorsement of a Republican candidate, James Holshouser, in the state gubernatorial race. Citing a "time for change" in the executive mansion, the paper's praise of Holshouser was tepid, however, in comparison to sharp criticism of the other two major Republican candidates, Richard Nixon and Jesse Helms. In fact, there was more newsprint devoted to condemning Nixon and Helms than to actually endorsing their democratic opponents. The *DTH* had been printing columns and editorials critical of Nixon's first term as president for some time, and it was ahead of many other papers in its suspicions of the wider implications of the Watergate break-in. In early November an editorial entitled "Stink" appeared expressing alarm at the reported activities of CREEP (Committee to Re-Elect the President), especially by one high-ranking student operative—a twenty-two-year-old named Karl Rove, later senior adviser and White House deputy chief of staff under George W. Bush—who was rumored to have orchestrated ballot-box stuffing in mock elections on college campuses.[44]

The harshest criticism during the 1972 elections was directed towards Jesse Helms, candidate for U.S. Senate from North Carolina. Not only was Helms a leader of the more extreme wing of the Republican Party, he was a longtime critic of the University of North Carolina and had tangled with the *Daily Tar Heel* in several very public battles during the 1960s. "Strangely enough," the paper reported with tongue planted firmly in cheek in September 1972, "the *Daily Tar Heel* is currently on the Jesse Helms for Senate campaign mailing list.... Of course, all the other candidates also have the *DTH* on their mailing list, but we were not quite certain we would be on Jesse's." The paper soon dropped any pretense of amusement over Helms's candidacy, all but calling him a liar when he accused his opponent, Nick Galifianakis, of financing his campaign primarily through out-of-state contributions. Citing public financial statements showing that Helms in fact received more out-of-state money than Galifianakis, the paper charged that the Republi-

can candidate "cannot stay out of the gutter with his campaign advertisements."[45]

The *Daily Tar Heel* conducted a poll a week before the election which showed a clear student preference for the Democratic candidates at the top of the state and national tickets; Helms fared particularly poorly on the UNC campus, garnering only 11.9 percent of the student vote compared to 79.7 percent for Galifianakis. After the Republican landslide, one of the largest in American history, the paper's editorial opinion of Nixon proved more prophetic than had its polling. "We fear the basic freedoms of all Americans will continue to be ignored for political purposes," the lead editorial warned following the election. "Bugging, unwarranted subpoenas, 'neighborhood schools,' and government over-classification have marked the first four years and will probably increase in the next four. ... What a bummer." As for the election of Jesse Helms to the U.S. Senate, the official *DTH* opinion was summed up in one word: "Yuk."[46]

The *Daily Tar Heel* endorsed Democrat Jimmy Carter for president in 1976, but it read the tea leaves incorrectly five months later when an article ran declaring that the GOP was "ailing," and that a two-party system in North Carolina was "useless." The paper corrected itself in November 1979, noting a "growing conservatism" in both national and local elections. That growing conservatism, along with disappointment in the Carter presidency, led to perhaps the most hotly debated election cycle in the paper's history. The editor in chief during the 1980 campaign was George Shadroui, whose politics were something of a mixture of moderate and libertarian. While Shadroui favored fiscal conservatism and was openly critical of Carter's failures,

he was a staunch supporter of equality under the law, especially with regard to race. In April 1980, Shadroui wrote an editorial entitled "More Than a Token," applauding Chancellor Christopher Fordham for appointing a full-time affirmative action officer at UNC. Shadroui acted as he spoke; he was the first *DTH* chief to appoint African Americans to senior editorial positions. Others on the editorial board, notably associate editor Tom Jessiman, were liberals who supported the left wing of the Democratic Party, and were convinced that Carter's Republican challenger, Ronald Reagan, would take the country in the wrong direction. John Anderson, who entered as a third-party independent candidate, further complicated the presidential race.[47]

Three presidential contenders with very different perspectives created a situation on the *Daily Tar Heel* editorial page in the spring and fall of 1980 that Shadroui later described as "schizophrenic," as the unsigned lead editorials were written by various members of the board. Shadroui penned one piece entitled "A Capricious State of Mind," writing of Carter, "We are beginning to question his ability to lead this country in an effective manner, particularly in the area of foreign policy." Tom Jessiman, no fan of Ronald Reagan, wrote another entitled "Bedtime for Bonzo," a derisive reference to the former actor's less-than-stellar B-movie career. In this environment of extremes, college students across the country began to look toward John Anderson as an alternative. Anderson made a campaign stop at UNC, and even though an editorial in the paper appeared calling support for the long-shot, third-party candidate a "wrong move," it also noted that the *DTH* office had become a "room full" of Anderson backers. This situation put a good deal of pressure on Shadroui, who was responsible for the official *DTH* endorsement. Some members of the editorial board feared Shadroui would endorse Ronald Reagan, and there were rumored threats of a mass resignation if that were to occur. Following his own convictions, Shadroui endorsed Anderson, citing the independent candidate's "sound platform," and a split of the board did not happen.[48]

Along with supporting the independent John Anderson for president, the *Daily Tar Heel* also endorsed two Republican candidates for state office in 1980, presenting overall a moderate editorial page in keeping with political and social trends both nationally and at Chapel Hill. There was, however, great concern among some of the editorial staff about the New Right wing of the Republican Party, and about how religion was becoming a political weapon. "State and church are not merging," one editorial declared, but "politics and religion are." "By tying political support for political issues and candidates to moral righteousness, the New Right violates the power invested in them by their God and encourages demagoguery." Referring to the so-called Moral Majority as an "Immoral Morality" in a democratic society, another editorial warned: "On the eve of the so-called New Conservatism, it is up to every American to take a critical look at the argument and methods used by the New Right leaders. Morality is hardly moral when it is practiced selectively."[49]

Tension over the 1980 election was one factor that led the following spring to the launching of a new paper at UNC, the *Phoenix*—the first real attempt at competition with the *Daily Tar Heel* since the days of the *White and Blue* in the 1890s. Following a bitter and contested election for *DTH* editor in February 1981, associate editor Tom Jessiman, who lost the race, used family money to establish the *Phoenix*, stating that he and his new staff "feel strongly that having another editorial voice on campus is extremely important. The *DTH* has had a monopoly on this for years, and perhaps with another voice more issues will be discussed and contemplated." When Jessiman went to the Campus Governing Council requesting a large appropriation to

fund continued publication for 1981–82, a vigorous debate ensued about the need for the additional newspaper and its true mission. The *DTH* went on record officially opposing student funding, stating that the *Phoenix* "was duplicating the *Daily Tar Heel* in certain areas and, therefore, that it was not as deserving of financial support as some campus publications that have a long history at the University and are now finding it difficult to secure adequate funding." Although two former editors of the *DTH* publicly supported student funding for the *Phoenix* (including outgoing editor George Shadroui, who at times disagreed with Jessiman politically), another staffer summed up the situation as she saw it. "*The Phoenix* is not a much-needed extension of the spot news covered by the *Daily Tar Heel*— it is the extension of political loss. The paper should not be called *The Phoenix*, which arose from its ashes, but *The Sour Grapes*, which arose from the emotions of a bad loser." In the end the new paper did receive student funding, and although it never seriously threatened to overtake the *DTH*, it continued as a periodical for more than a decade, one of the longest runs in the history of UNC student publications.[50]

Once established, the *Phoenix* generally assumed the editorial role of supporting the political left on campus, reflecting the beliefs of its founder, Tom Jessiman. At the same time, some in the university community feared that the *Daily Tar Heel* was compromising its progressive heritage and becoming too moderate. In the 1982 congressional race, the paper endorsed the Republican candidate, William "Bill" Cobey, who had served as UNC's athletic director from 1976 to 1980. "In many respects, this paper's editorial philosophy is more in tune with Democratic incumbent Ike Andrews," the endorsement stated; however, "the *DTH* believes that Cobey would be a stronger, more effective leader, and would represent this district better." Under Title IX, according to the editorial, Cobey "ran the growing [athletic] department well, and supervised the expansion of women's athletics." While expressing some concern that the candidate was "so closely aligned with the National Congressional Club"—and adding pointedly that the *DTH* "would not endorse Cobey if there were a more moderate alternative to the incumbent"—the editorial staff concluded, "Cobey is not a dogmatic crusader like much of the New Right, and he does not show the relentless infatuation with the moral issues also associated with the New Right." The backhanded Cobey endorsement pleased few people. Many Republicans were offended, and some Democrats were outraged. Stirling Haig, a professor of French and UNC alumnus, wrote a searing letter to the editor:

The *DTH* I knew in my undergraduate days in the conservative 1950s, when racism, religion, and reactionary politics were the three R's of the Old South, was at least a progressive student newspaper.

The editors of those years, the Charles Kuralts ... the Ed Yoders and the Jonathan Yardleys would have recoiled with contempt at the suggestion that they endorse a Republican candidate who is the lackey of the rich and the righteous, yet [the paper has] endorsed one who has swilled at the public trough for the past few years [through tax loopholes]. By your endorsement you have turned your back

on a proud tradition of student liberalism and ... Chapel Hill's best and brightest, and sullied the *DTH* as an ally of the Jesse Helms–Moral Majority reactionaries.[51]

Even before voters went to the polls in November 1982, stories began to appear in the *Daily Tar Heel* about the upcoming 1984 elections, in which Ronald Reagan would run for reelection, and Jesse Helms would face his strongest Democratic opponent, North Carolina two-term governor Jim Hunt. Regarding the presidential race, much of the focus was on "Reaganomics," the presidential policies that sought to drastically cut domestic spending. Some of Reagan's cuts deeply affected public education and college students in particular, spurring heated debate on the editorial pages of the *DTH* on both sides of the issue. The tenor of the senatorial race was perceived as even more potentially ominous, carrying the potential to reignite social and racial antagonism in North Carolina. The first *DTH* story about the Senate race appeared in October 1982, and was followed by stories expressing concern about "racial overtones," including one entitled "a ghost of elections past," which contained a detailed discussion about the 1950 senatorial race in which former UNC President Frank Graham had been smeared as pro-integration and pro-socialism. The comparison to the 1950 race by the *DTH* was apt, as that campaign marked the first political appearance of Jesse Helms, who served as an adviser for Graham's opponent, Willis Smith.[52]

Ultimately the 1984 senatorial race proved as ugly as feared, and the *Daily Tar Heel* broke two stories that appeared to be efforts to discredit the

September 1984 cartoon by Bill Cokas lampooning U.S. senator
Jesse Helms. Helms was a favorite subject of *DTH* cartoonists
for decades. (Bill Cokas)

reputations of both UNC and university system president William Friday, who was a prominent supporter of Helms's opponent, Jim Hunt. In September 1983, an independent journalist approached the *DTH* staff with an explosive story about documents that linked Friday with the FBI, purportedly showing that the UNC president had provided the agency with inside intelligence information on campus radical groups during the 1960s and 1970s, including the Black Student Movement. Editor Kerry DeRochi ran the story on the top of the front page, under the journalist's byline, after his credentials were verified. The story caused outrage, as many felt it was politically motivated, and Friday, in a highly unusual move, refused to comment. The origins of the story were never made clear, though the Helms office had used leaked portions of FBI documents in the past, particularly to discredit Martin Luther King during the debate over

establishing a national holiday in his honor. De-Rochi later remembered that though the journalist's credentials had been checked, the decision was made not to use such sources again. Slightly more than a year later, only two weeks before the election, the *DTH* published another banner headline story involving Friday, this time regarding a pro-Helms letter that a North Carolina minister had written and sent to the president accusing him and UNC of fostering "a liberal/atheist clique," and charging that "homosexuality and Communism are of epic proportions" on campus. "As Christian taxpayers, we demand that this contingency of degradation, which festers like a cancer on the forehead of North Carolina education, be excoriated from our presence," he wrote. The Helms campaign denied any connection to the letter, and Friday, who turned the letter over to the State Bureau of Investigation, told the *DTH*, "I view this as a vile, hateful communication that is meant to induce fear on this campus."[53]

Polarization of opinion was so intense during the 1984 election, along with concern over how the *Daily Tar Heel* would ultimately cover the races, that it became the prime focus of discussion during the campaign for the paper's editor that February. At a public forum all of the candidates agreed to a "moderate" coverage-and-endorsement policy if elected, and they debated issues of political bias on the *DTH* and how to best create an environment of balanced opinions. Ultimately that November the paper endorsed Democratic challengers Walter Mondale and Jim Hunt over incumbent Republicans Ronald Reagan and Jesse Helms. "Students should say 'No' to Sen. No," the paper declared in the Helms-Hunt race, characterizing the contest as "a fight between a forward-looking representative of the progressive New South and a right-wing ideologue who resists change in any form." The paper did endorse Republican Jim Martin for governor and, in a switch from 1982, threw its support behind incumbent Democratic representative Ike Andrews over second-time challenger Bill Cobey—with the stipulation that after this term "Andrews should come home for good." Cobey won the race, and the paper's other choices also lost, with the exception of the lone Republican it endorsed, Jim Martin.[54]

Together with its efforts to provide balance in political reporting and endorsements during the 1970s and early 1980s, the *Daily Tar Heel*, as it had done for decades, continued to be a forum through which columnists and the university community could debate a range of social and cultural issues. In addition to publishing letters to the editor from readers of all perspectives, several conservative students with strong journalistic voices became regular contributors to the editorial page, notably Robert Putnam III, Rorin Platt, and Garth Dunklin. Of these, Rorin Platt was perhaps the most controversial. Possessed of strong right-wing opinions and an impressive command of the written word, Platt became both admired and reviled to an extent not seen for a *DTH* columnist since the era of Armistead Maupin a decade earlier. Along with his positions opposing the women's movement and gay rights, he took on what he considered radical black leadership and the enactment of affirmative action laws—arguing in one column that there was a "morality" to some types of discrimination. But Platt reserved his harshest language for abortion, the central religious-based cause of the Moral Majority and the New Right. Calling legalized abortion "the wholesale slaughter of unborn children," Platt charged in November 1974 that the *Roe v. Wade* Supreme Court decision "ushered in not only the destruction of human life in America, but it also ushered in a new era of judicial tyranny." Dramatically declaring that in effect following *Roe* "murder became legalized in the United States," he added with a macabre flourish: "The neo-paganists rejoiced, already working for the step-child of feticide-euthanasia." He also reported that nearly $300,000 from various Rockefeller funds had been given to UNC to test abortion-inducing drugs in a UNC clinic, observing that "this transfer of funds destined for the engineers of death should make the University lower its head in shame."[55]

Despite a demonstrated balance in political endorsements, and the amount of space given to conservative columnists on the editorial pages during the 1970s and 1980s, the *Daily Tar Heel* remained entrenched in liberal philosophy in the eyes of many. As a result, there were efforts at UNC to establish alternative publications with a more conservative focus. Two earlier efforts had been short-lived: the *Carolina Conservative*, which appeared between December 1964 and October 1965, and the Hayakawa Society's *Carolina Chronicle*, which, despite much publicity, ran for only three issues in 1969. But establishment of the *Phoenix* showed that an alternative to the *Daily Tar Heel* (albeit a liberal one) could be sustained on campus, and in February 1982 a conservative publication entitled the *Carolina Free Press* was launched. Declaring itself "unabashedly partisan," the new paper was founded with $500 from the National Congressional Club, and proudly refused to apply for student funding, which supported both the *Phoenix* and the *DTH*. "If you believe that race relations are the number one problem on campus, or that the Association of Women Students fills a vital need ... the *Free Press* may not exactly be your preferred publication," the editors announced in the inaugural edition, an obvious comment on *DTH* coverage. "But if you think ... that Jesse Helms isn't all that bad," they suggested, perhaps the *Carolina Free Press* was a better choice.[56]

Ultimately the *Carolina Free Press* only lasted nine months, but that run did give the paper the distinction of being the longest-lasting conservative campus publication up to that time. Interestingly, as the final issue was published in the fall of 1982, a second lawsuit was being prepared seeking to strip mandatory student funding from the *Daily Tar Heel*, again by students who believed their constitutional rights were being violated by the paper's editorial policies. Filed by the same plaintiff attorneys who had argued *Arrington v. Taylor* a decade earlier, the new case was titled *Kania v. Fordham*, named for one of the three student defendants and UNC Chancellor Christopher Fordham. *Kania* was brought on the relatively weak premise of a 1977 case involving members of a teacher's union in Detroit, who were being forced to pay mandatory dues even though the union might be engaged in political, social, and economic activities that the individual workers did not support. The federal court made short order of the *Kania* case, handing down a ruling only four months after it was argued, again upholding the legality of mandatory student funding of the *Daily Tar Heel* and reaffirming all of the findings of the *Arrington* case.[57]

Although the *Carolina Free Press* and the

Kania v. Fordham lawsuit were both unsuccessful, conservatives at UNC were able to establish a publication of their own in 1987 that ultimately lasted seven years. Published variously as a biweekly and a monthly periodical, the *Carolina Critic* declared in its mission statement that it was "dedicated to the discussion of individual liberty and its relationship to politics and society." Less openly confrontational than its predecessors, the *Carolina Critic* was founded and edited initially by John Hood, a journalism student who later became director of the John Locke Foundation, a conservative North Carolina think tank.[58]

THE CONTINUING RACIAL DIVIDE

Despite desegregation of the university in the 1950s and the triumphs of the civil rights movement of the 1960s, racial issues continued to plague both the UNC system and the Chapel Hill campus during the last quarter of the twentieth century. The issues stemmed from persistently low African American enrollment and faculty hiring, black students negotiating the nebulous divide between maintaining a separate cultural identity and integrating into the larger, predominantly white culture, and ongoing racial tension in the state and nation. As it had done for decades, the *Daily Tar Heel* followed these topics closely, though at times the staff found reporting and editorializing on the evolving racial landscape challenging.

In the early 1970s, on the heels of both the civil rights and Black Power movements, African Americans debated about where they fit in broader American society. At UNC that conversation centered on existing campus social organizations, such as the Greek system. A *Daily*

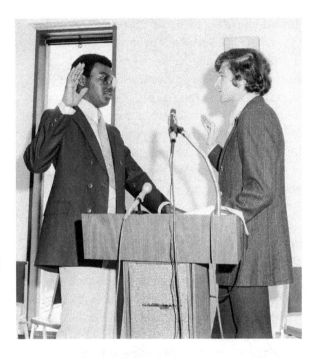

Tar Heel article in November 1970 reported that the small number of black students on campus "want to be sure they are not Greek tokens," quoting one rushee, "black identity, black pride, and black togetherness are going to have to come first." Cureton Johnson, president of the Black Student Movement, put the question into broader context in a column published in the paper:

> From a logical standpoint, brothers and sisters can sit by and suck-up Carolina's white culture, sports, education, and various resources. But is this kind of white logic what we desire? Upon arriving we saw through her liberal facade.... We are here, as DuBois would verify in his theory of the Black 10 percent, to become vanguard leadership for Black people rather than Uncle Tom forces for the racist American system.... Then our goal is Black Liberation.... America is sick and dying. For scores of years Black people have been sick and mentally asleep in the face of American racism, fighting little battles but nevertheless moving too slow.[59]

In fact, the African American presence in Carolina's traditional "white culture" did increase during the 1970s. Enrollment rose slowly but steadily, and black staff and faculty members were hired, including Hayden Renwick, who became associate dean in the College of Arts and Sciences, and Sonja Haynes Stone, a professor in Afro-American Studies. Both were outspoken about matters of race and were frequently covered in the *Daily Tar Heel*. Along with the growing number of black athletes, two African Americans were elected student-body president.

In March 1972, the paper came out in support of Richard Epps, calling him "the best man," and, significantly, it did not mention his race in the official endorsement. Epps was the best choice in part because his opponent, Paul Dickey, ran on the largely nonsensical "anti-platform" of the Blue Sky Party, which included abolishing student government and erecting a weatherproof dome over the campus. After Epps's victory, *DTH* editor Allen Mask put the election into context, noting that it "proves progress has been made in the area of human relations at this major Southern University." Mask added that a "Black student president in 1972 marks a change in attitudes at Carolina.... It proves that progress in racial attitudes is taking a positive turn." The editor was clear to point out UNC's racist history, however, and warned that with relatively low black enrollment, few black faculty, and no black coaches, it would be "a big misunderstanding" to suggest that racism was dead at Carolina.[60]

Efforts were also made to establish a black cultural identity on campus, and it was these efforts that caused the most friction with some members of the administration and a segment of the majority white student population. The Black Student Movement became an official student organization, and now bolstered by student-activity-fee funding, its existing newspaper, *Black Ink*, began regular publication in 1971 with a ten-person staff. Bruce Sampson, the first editor, told the *Daily Tar Heel* the goal was to create "a newspaper blacks can turn to for truth on any issue" and to "try to draw the community and the campus blacks together." In 1975—just as had been done with the *Daily Tar Heel*—a small group of conservative students fought to end mandatory activity-fee funding of both the BSM and *Black Ink*, arguing that only a small segment of the student body was being served, and that the organization and the paper were "political." The battle over funding of the organization and its paper resurfaced in one form or another almost perennially for more than a decade.[61]

Despite its support for African American issues that stretched back to calls for an end to segregation in the mid-1940s, the *Daily Tar Heel* regularly faced criticism by black leaders on campus from the 1970s to the early 1990s. At times the criticism seems to have been warranted, especially with regard to the very few black staff members, though at other times it seems the paper was a convenient target that broadly represented white student culture. For example, a letter to the editor in 1972 accused the paper of ignoring black students, despite a front-page photograph the previous fall showing an African American couple walking among the fallen leaves, and the fact that columns by black students ran with some regularity on the editorial page. In 1974, the president of the BSM called the *DTH* "biased and irresponsible." And though the paper consistently called for continued funding for the BSM and *Black Ink* during the numerous student government budget fights of the era, in February 1985 an angry Sherrod Banks, who was then president of the BSM, blamed the tepid endorsement of the paper for a razor-thin loss of a nonbinding student referendum to defund the organization. As late as 1990, the BSM called for improvement in the paper's coverage of minority issues.[62]

The lack of African Americans on the staff of the *Daily Tar Heel* did prove a persistent problem. Despite the efforts of George Shadroui and other editors to increase the number of black staff members, the paper remained predominately white in the late 1980s and early 1990s. Following a rumor on campus that blacks need not apply to work at the *DTH*, a 1988 editorial ran stating categorically, "Black students [are] welcome at the *DTH*, as they should be at all other student organizations." In the fall of 1989, a student legislator whose political opinions were more liberal than those expressed in the paper threatened a recall election of the editor for a variety of reasons, including his "having a poor record in hiring minorities." The problem apparently stemmed more from the lack of African American journalism students who wanted to work on the *DTH* than any overt prejudice or discrimination, as editorials continued to appear periodically calling for diversity on the paper's staff and asking for minority students to apply for positions.[63]

BLACK INK

*Freedom
Justice
Unity
POWER*

BLACK STUDENT MOVEMENT OFFICIAL NEWSPAPER
University of North Carolina, Chapel Hill, North Carolina

March, 1975

Vol. 6, No. 5

Mrs. Gaitha Lassiter, Buddy Ray, and Walter Davis at the Multi-Purpose Center.

BSM promotes community action

By Bernadine Ward
Feature writer

Cars followed each other much like a funeral procession, only this was on occasion for fun and good times, not sorrow. After parking, everyone hesitantly, but expectantly entered the Multi-Purpose Center here in Chapel Hill. This February 14 meeting was a chance for students and senior citizens to become acquainted.

Lunch hour was just coming to an end when students entered the room, cluttered here and there with dishes. After dishes were pushed aside, the get acquainted session began.

From the start humor prevailed. When Mrs. Gaither Lassiter said that the men preferred young ladies and women young men, one man clapped and said, "Mrs. Lassiter, you alright."

Buddy Ray, Off Campus Coordinator for the BSM spoke to the group saying that this would be a learning experience for all involved.

The Ebony Readers presented poetry selections.

When the senior citizens learned that the BSM Gospel Choir and Drama Group were included on the schedule for a later date, many became so enthused about hearing the choir that they asked any

members present to sing. Besides entertaining at the center, students are to call their citizen every day and visit them at least every two weeks.

"You can call me everyday," and "Give me a very young man," could be heard among peals of laughter as

Mrs. Lassiter made introductions.

One woman mistook BSM member Walter Davis for basketball star Walter Davis, but she was quickly informed,"HE AIN'T THE ONE."

(continued on page 8)

Participants in BSM program for the aged.

NCCU Law School

Accreditation may cause problems

By Ethel Johnson
Lay out editor

Accreditation could pose a problem for North Carolina Central University Law School, according to a committee report of the American Bar Association (ABA). In a February 12 confidential report, the committee told NCCU officials that it would begin proceedings to strip the law school of accreditation if a comprehensive improvement plan is not submitted by June 1. The report called for a new law building, and improvements in the instructional program and school management.

An article in the Durham Sun stated that on February 19, University of North Carolina President William C. Friday announced that an overall supplemental request which included funds for the new law building, would be submitted to the legislature. Monies for the new building and improvement of the school's library had been cut by the Advisory Budget Commission in the

original UNC budget proposal, Friday said.

Eventhough steps are being taken to maintain the law school's accreditation, many who know its history are skeptical. A fact sheet distributed by the law school, which was chartered in 1939, states that the first attempt to close the school occurred when the Supreme Court rulings abandoned the concept of "separate but equal" facilities. In 1966 an effort was made to omit support for the school by Governor Dan K. Moore's state budget. In 1969, a report of the state Board of Higher Education advocated merger of the school into the UNC school system; NCCU rejected both alternatives. The fact sheet continued that the ABA accreditation body viewed the school's facilities in March '74 and warned that accreditation may be withdrawn if additional space resources, and funds were not allocated to the school.

Dean of North Carolina Central Law School, LeMarquis Dejarmon, stated that "although the $2 million

for the new law building was our number one priority, the state Advisory Budget Commission cut it from the original UNC budget proposal." Dejarmon added that the commission's usual procedure is to give strong consideration to each of the sixteen universities first priorities and cut the least important items.

"The denial of meaningful support to our Law School by the State of North Carolina is a matter of historical record, President of NCCU Student Bar Michael Lee said. Lee said, however, what bothered him most was the ABA report inference that individual students were incompetent. "The ABA inspection team did not attempt to measure student ability, nor do their procedures exhibit any real yardstick by which they might test individual ingenuity, motivation, and desire," Lee stated.

Students at NCCU law school shared various opinions on the ABA report, but most agreed on the necessity of a new law, building. Second-year student William Dudley,

expressing concern over the state of the present building said, "How do you expect me as a student to compete when I am subject to such inadequacies. At present, this building has no "john" and there is no heat except small portable heaters." Dudley added that approximately 300 students are enrolled, but the school's reading room has only 30 chairs to accomodate them.

Another student, who asked that his name not be disclosed, stated that some of the professors at the school would rank with any in the nation; however, other professors appeared less interested because they were transient.

The only reason the school in not up to par in its instructional program in the mind of Professor of Property and Legal Writing, Ernest Fullwood, is due to lack of money. "The quality of teaching has been good and the faculty has done admirably well," Fullwood said. He added that he really wasn't sure what the ABA

(continued on page 8)

As African American students worked to establish an integrated yet independent presence on campus, a larger drama centered on race was unfolding involving the UNC system and the U.S. Department of Health, Education, and Welfare (HEW). Ultimately the struggle between UNC and HEW dragged on for more than a decade, amid a revolving carousel of federal officials and four different presidential administrations of both political parties. It began somewhat unexpectedly in 1970, when officials in the Nixon administration decided to enforce a provision of the 1964 Civil Rights Act, prohibiting federal funding of institutions that demonstrated racial discrimination. HEW officials identified public university systems in eight states, including North Carolina, which appeared to discriminate based on statistics citing minority percentages at certain campuses. The University of North Carolina was in a complicated position; President William Friday supported equal racial access and integration of minorities as much as was practicable, but he also deeply resented intrusion of the federal government into the state's public university system. Further, even though the UNC system incorporated five historically black schools during its reorganization, administrators and alumni of those schools were wary of white intervention and fought to maintain their identity. What resulted was largely de facto segregation, as the historically black schools continued to be predominately African American and the traditionally white schools remained overwhelmingly white.[64]

The *Daily Tar Heel* followed the constantly changing HEW story with moderate interest. Generally speaking, editorial opinion supported efforts to integrate more fully, while both criticizing HEW and at times chiding President Fri-

day and the system for moving too slowly. In 1977 the paper disagreed with a particular federal ruling in the ongoing saga, but it also accused Friday of moving at a "snail's pace." "So far, he has been a masterful poker player, holding his cards close to his vest. HEW will no doubt back down on its latest and most absurd demand. But sooner or later someone is going to call Friday's bluff. No one can go on promising a full house and playing an empty hand forever." Later the same year, an editorial summed up the situation: "For seven long years, the UNC system has made a big deal about its commitment to desegregation and its good faith effort to accomplish this goal. But the evidence points to the contrary. The University should recognize publicly the painful slowness of its progress and solicit funds from Raleigh and Washington to build a model program. If the funds cannot be found, then the system must tighten its belt and give desegregation high priority."[65]

The battle went back and forth throughout the late 1970s, driven largely by President Jimmy Carter's HEW secretary, Joseph Califano. "The traditional hatred against government meddling has found its way into the disputes between Joseph Califano, HEW and the 16-campus UNC system, but the rhetoric and politics cannot suppress one simple fact: UNC has been dragging its feet when it comes to desegregation," *Daily Tar Heel* editor Lou Bilionis wrote in 1978. While arguing that HEW should be a "watchdog," the paper also called certain HEW demands (including closing duplicate programs in the system) "vague, inconsistent, unpredictable, [and] overbearing." By 1979 editorials referred to the "endless battle" between the UNC system and the federal agency, though an end was soon in sight.

Following the election of Ronald Reagan, a solution was sought by federal officials to bring the matter to a quick close. As resolution neared, the *DTH* noted that there were some 1,687 black students at UNC in 1980, representing roughly 7.9 percent of the student body, a significant increase from 2.3 percent in 1970. "The increase in the percentage of blacks here from roughly 2 percent to 8 percent is indeed a positive sign at which people should not scoff," an editorial stated, adding, "Yet the final percentage figure is still far too low in a state where a quarter of the population is black."[66]

During the decade of the HEW battle, two high-profile racial confrontations in North Carolina occurred involving the Ku Klux Klan. Not only did both events unfold on the pages of the *Daily Tar Heel*, but the paper itself became embroiled in them. The first, and the more significant of the two incidents for UNC, was the campus appearance in January 1975 of David Duke in Memorial Hall. Only twenty-four years old and barely out of college himself, Duke was the national information director for the KKK and had already earned a reputation as an outspoken advocate for white supremacy. In an effort to offer a range of political opinions at UNC, the Carolina Forum had invited Duke to speak for an honorarium of $800, which was provided by student fees. What transpired at the event ultimately led to two months of anger, recriminations, and racial conflict on campus, as well as a broader conversation about the limits of free speech at the state's leading public university.[67]

The timing of the Duke appearance was complicated by months of building racial tension on campus. In late September 1974, the BSM became the defendant in a campus court suit brought by two white students who wanted to end student funding of the organization, charging that it discriminated against white students. Though the *Daily Tar Heel* vigorously supported BSM funding, the paper came under attack from the group's president, who stated that he was "upset with a previous *Daily Tar Heel* article which said we were inviting whites to join. The BSM is open to everyone; anyone can join." In November, black activist Angela Davis appeared at UNC attacking what she called the "social repression" of nonwhites, charging that a "fascist tendency is endangering the nation." And even though the *DTH* ran a lead editorial in honor of Martin Luther King's birthday in January (the second year such a piece had appeared), concern over white supremacy on campus remained high. The day before the King editorial was published, the paper reported that the BSM and leftist groups the New American Movement and the United Farm Workers of America were organizing protests for the Duke talk.[68]

On the evening of January 16, 1975, as Duke was about to speak, some 200 primarily African American protesters marched down the aisles of Memorial Hall and effectively drowned him out by loudly stomping their feet, clapping, and chanting "Power to the people" and "Go to hell Duke." Student-body president Marcus Williams—who happened to be African American—attempted unsuccessfully to defuse the situation. Telling protesters that he wasn't interested in what Duke had to say either, he urged them to let him speak, and asked the students to join him in watching the N.C. State vs. Maryland game on TV instead. Although Duke was heckled off the stage by the protesters and many in the audience, he was able to give an impromptu talk at a reception for him in the Morehead Building. The *Daily Tar Heel* covered the remarks, including Duke's comments that the KKK was not anti-black or anti-Catholic, but that "the Jews control the banks and the media," and that "white people are discriminated against … especially white males." His revealing complaint about the heat in the room betrayed his racial prejudices and may have been an unintentional pun on what had just transpired in Memorial Hall: "My ancestors came from Europe, not Zambia. It's too hot in here for me."[69]

Debate erupted on campus and at the *Daily Tar Heel* following the aborted Duke appearance, which occurred only seven years after the reviled Speaker Ban Law had been declared unconstitutional. The BSM defiantly declared that it would continue to protest white extremists, seeing its demonstrations against Duke's appearance not as an incident of preventing free speech, but of halting hate speech. But many others, including leading campus liberals, disagreed. Chancellor Ferebee Taylor condemned the protest, calling it a "transgression [against] the highest and noblest tradition of this university—that is support of the concept of freedom of expression." Dan Pollitt, an outspoken liberal faculty member and former president of the North Carolina branch of the American Civil Liberties Union, came out in support of the BSM, but he also defended Duke's right to speak. Student-body president Williams, caught very much in the middle of the controversy because of his race, summed up what many unsympathetic to Duke thought: "You can't rectify a wrong with a wrong."[70]

Four days after the incident the *Daily Tar Heel* ran a full-page "Insight" feature on the KKK, together with an editorial declaring that the dis-senters may have been successful in silencing Duke but that in effect they had "accomplished nothing." The editorial staff also decided to print in full an exasperated and somewhat rambling letter from Duke about what had transpired. Stating that he had spoken all over the country, Duke wrote that "this is the first appearance where heckling has prevented the audience from hearing me. I also know of no case in Chapel Hill's entire history when a speaker *on a podium* was prevented from speaking by hecklers." The next day two more columns about Duke appeared on the editorial page, one arguing that hate speech should not be allowed on campus, and another, by associate editor Cole Campbell, calling the whole affair "shameful" and arguing that regardless of one's opinion about Duke, he should have been allowed to speak.[71]

The *Daily Tar Heel*'s resident conservative columnist, Rorin Platt, was outraged and challenged Chancellor Taylor in print to "punish those students who prevented Mr. David Duke from presenting his lecture, pursuant to UNC policy," noting that though Duke's speech was mostly aimed at Jews, no Jewish students had protested. Taylor did not take Platt's suggestion, but an eighteen-year-old freshman from Raleigh, James Arthur "Art" Pope, did. Pope—who would later head his family's highly successful discount retail store chain and fund numerous conservative campaigns and causes—filed suit with the UNC student court, charging BSM president Algenon Marbley with violating a section of the Student Code by preventing Duke from speaking and thus "willfully disrupting a normal operation or function of the University."[72]

The ensuing trial roiled the campus into early March, keeping the controversy alive weeks after it would have likely subsided, and the *Daily Tar Heel* was in the thick of it. Student attorney general Nite Mitchell strongly objected to the presence of *DTH* reporters at the trial, citing Marbley's right to a closed hearing. Editor Campbell responded, noting that the paper had received more letters about the Duke incident than any other story that school year. "I think the students' right to know supersedes, in this case, Mitchell's objections," Campbell wrote. "We have weighed the drawbacks and have decided to print. It is an important public matter, and the whole University should know of the trial." As a result of the paper's position, jurors were instructed by the student court not to read the *DTH* so as to be "free of any prior conceptions or opinions about the trial." Marbley requested that at least four of the seven jurors be African American, and his legal team made a motion to dismiss the trial on the basis that Pope was not a legitimate accuser, characterizing his motivation as "political and unfounded." Following Marbley's acquittal in late February, one white juror told the *DTH* that the trial was "a travesty," arguing that the verdict should have been based on the actual violation of campus code, not "on moral grounds," adding that in this case the rights of students to hear David Duke had been trampled. In the aftermath of the trial, the paper's response was conflicted. Although sympathy clearly lay with Marbley, an editorial appeared after the verdict strongly supporting free speech on campus and imploring the administration to enforce that right in the future.[73]

In the end, Art Pope and David Duke had the last words on the whole affair, which were printed in the *Daily Tar Heel*. Pope wrote a letter declaring that in bringing the suit, "I was not the least bit motivated by racism." "I came to Carolina expecting the unbridled pursuit of knowledge," Pope explained. "I thought I would have the right to decide for myself if what I learned was the truth or a lie. Unfortunately these past events have shown that I was mistaken. Well, at least I tried." And for a second time the editorial staff decided to publish a lengthy letter from Duke. "Once again justice is thwarted by an arrogant minority," the KKK leader wrote. "You people who prevented my being heard are not only petty tyrants and intellectual cowards, but are also *liars*.... Klansmen and women are infinitely more honorable than you are." Addressing the "white student body," Duke asked: "How long are you going to allow yourself to be pushed around and bullied by these arrogant parasites who are sucking the life blood of academic freedom from your university body?" And with a defiant flourish he added, "I will return."[74]

Four years after the Duke incident, a conflict between the KKK, Nazi sympathizers, and a pro-Communist labor group led to a shooting in Greensboro that left five people dead. The shooting occurred at an anti-Klan rally organized by the Communist Workers Party (CWP) in a poor and predominately African American neighborhood on November 3, 1979. Those killed included marchers and one bystander sympathetic to the CWP, even though members of both sides anticipated violence and were armed. Ultimately five KKK members were brought to trial on murder charges, but with conflicting accounts of what occurred and a limited amount of hard evidence, they were acquitted by all-white juries. Tensions were highly elevated during the trial in November 1980, and the staff of the *Daily Tar Heel* decided to run a five-part series beginning

November 1986 campus protest against UNC investments in South African companies that practiced apartheid. (*Yack*)

with an article above the banner entitled "Violence Marks Shift in Race Relations." An editorial statement explained the rationale behind the series: "We consider the racial problem on campus and nationwide acute enough to warrant this kind of scrutiny. It is our hope that this series will probe minds, gently or not, and will bring into the open the problems and questions that all too often are conveniently pushed aside, and labeled quiet and subtle, until they do in fact ferment and explode." The same day the first part of the series appeared, the verdict in the trial was announced, and in response the staff of the *DTH* joined student government, the BSM, and a group of law students in staging a "Rally for Justice" in the Pit, which drew some 800 students. The sponsorship of the rally by the *DTH* was significant, as this had only happened three times previously (in 1962 in support of James Meredith; in 1966 during the Speaker Ban controversy; and in 1970 following the Kent State shootings). The day after the rally a related article ran with the headline "Racial Harmony Still an Unfulfilled Goal at UNC." George Shadroui, who was editor at the time, later regretted the paper's sponsorship of the rally, as certain groups used the event to promote other causes.[75]

The *Daily Tar Heel* became involved in another racially divisive issue during the mid-1980s, this time involving the university's investments in South Africa. As the discriminatory practice of apartheid was challenged and ultimately brought down in that country, groups around the world worked to support the black cause. In the United States one form of support involved sanctions against white-owned South African businesses that perpetuated apartheid, and American corporations that did business

with the country's government. On college campuses students organized to divest university endowments of any holdings in such companies, and at UNC the student action began in 1984 with the *Daily Tar Heel* rallying support. In September 1985, days before a planned protest against U.S. policy in South Africa at an appearance by President Ronald Reagan at N.C. State University, the *DTH* issued a strong statement. "Reagan continues blindly to support the guarantors of law and order, as if whites were the only ones who could keep it," the editorial stated, predicting that "blacks will come out on top, as their intensifying spirit and struggle indicates, [it] is only a matter of time." Another editorial called for "campus action," urging UNC students to "push for reform by lobbying for divestment of University funds from South Africa." A rally followed in the Pit in October, and the stage was set for a showdown with university trustees over the question of divestment. In November, the UNC Board of Trustees turned down a request for divestiture of university funds in South Africa, which elicited a withering editorial in the paper. When a subsequent resolution made by the Faculty Council calling for limited divestment passed ten days later, the *DTH* reported that trustee John Pope (the father of Art Pope) objected, stating "The Board of Trustees should not concern itself with foreign affairs, but with the affairs of the University," and adding that many countries were "more oppressive than South Africa."[76]

No action had been taken on the issue by the spring of 1986, and a group of students decided to put pressure on the trustees. One night in mid-March, under the cover of darkness, a "shantytown" of shacks arose on McCorkle Place, in full view of the South Building offices of the chancellor and other top university administrators. The shacks were ordered removed, but as soon as university maintenance workers took them down, students rebuilt and occupied them. The *Daily Tar Heel* dubbed them "musical shacks," and a standoff began that would last more than two weeks. At the high point of what the paper called a "violent drama," protesters staged a funeral procession that featured a black coffin draped with the flag of South Africa, disrupted by a mock police attack that left bodies strewn all over the quad. Tensions were heightened when members of the College Republicans and a newly formed conservative organization, Students for America (both of which opposed divestment and supported the South African government's opposition to Communism), taunted protesters by erecting a fifty-foot-long "Berlin Wall" of lumber, chicken wire, and white sheets to block the view of the shacks. While supporting the ultimate goal of divestiture, and opposing the reaction by conservative students, the editorial staff of the paper became increasingly concerned that the protesters were being overly dramatic and confrontational. "Instead of taking the path to violence and disruption," one editorial argued,

the protesters "would better achieve [their] goals by broadening the base of support throughout the student body. Protesters need to bring other students into the movement instead of alienating them." Imploring the students not to "blow things out of proportion" and to seek a "peaceful solution," the paper warned that recent comments and actions "point toward an escalation of debate into what might be the type of conflict that has rocked other campuses like Berkeley."[77]

In early April the shanties were torn down for a final time and five students were arrested. Although the protesters lost the battle, ultimately they won the war, and by 1987 the university was finally divested of business interests in South Africa. As an interesting footnote to the story, one of the two trustees who changed his mind and tipped the balance on the matter was Richard Jenrette, who had been editor of the *Daily Tar Heel* in 1949–50, during the first serious challenge to racial segregation at UNC. One of the more conservative editors in the paper's history, Jenrette came out against immediate desegregation in 1950 and drew considerable ire at the time from members of the university community who supported admitting African American students. Nearly four decades later, as a founder and partner of the highly successful Wall Street firm of Donaldson, Lufkin & Jenrette, he reconsidered his position on divestiture and helped effect a major change in university policy on international human rights.[78]

Of all the issues involving race that divided the UNC campus in the last quarter of the twentieth century, none was more contentious than the battle over the creation of a freestanding black cultural center. Symbols of white supremacy were literally built into the Carolina

landscape: overt examples included the 1913 Confederate Soldiers' Monument ("Silent Sam"), and Saunders Hall, named for a Civil War officer and nineteenth leader of the KKK in North Carolina. More subtle reminders could be found in the names of prominent slaveholding alumni on campus buildings and streets, and in the purposeful and pervasive twentieth century "Old South" revival-style architecture. As the number of African American students at UNC began to slowly rise in the early 1970s, and as a sense of preserving and celebrating black culture devel-

oped, the desire for a dedicated physical space on campus increased. The first such space was the Upendo Lounge ("Upendo" means "love" in Swahili), which primarily served as a safe haven for black students to gather and hold events. Originally created in Chase Dining Hall in 1972, the lounge moved twice over the ensuing thirteen years, to avoid closure by administrators who wanted to allocate the space for other purposes. Ultimately, it would take sixteen years for the dream of a freestanding center to become a reality.[79]

By 1985, the Black Student Movement was calling for a permanent African American cultural center in the Graham Student Union. A separate center for blacks, which some white students, administrators, and alumni saw as reverse segregation, was controversial from the start. The *Daily Tar Heel*, acknowledging the controversy, nevertheless backed these early efforts. Citing the need for "aggressive support" to create such a center, a 1985 editorial argued that the facility "could provide a base for black students on campus while helping to introduce non-black students to Black culture and issues facing blacks." To help the cause, the paper published a front-page story about black cultural centers on other college campuses, calling them a "hit." Tired of waiting for the administration to act, a group of BSM students officially organized the Black Cultural Center (BCC) in July 1988, which marked the beginning of a five-year period of student activism to gain official university recognition and move the project forward. From the fall of 1988 through the spring of 1991, as calls for the center grew louder, the *DTH* regularly ran editorials backing student efforts, including "Students Shaping the BCC" in November 1988 and "BCC Deserves Top Priority at UNC" in October 1989. "We hope that in the '90s, a BCC will be built," an editorial welcoming the new decade declared in January 1990, "creating a unique resource in which the University can take pride."[80]

Opponents of the BCC also voiced their opinions, many of which appeared on the pages of the *Daily Tar Heel*. "It seems to me," university trustee John Pope remarked in November 1988, "that if [African American students] are interested in a Black Cultural Center, then they should attend a black university." A *DTH* edi-

torial called Pope's statement "appalling." The paper also reported that Lieutenant Governor Jim Gardner, in a campaign for governor, had told a group of Orange County Republicans "I thought we had a wonderful cultural center—it was called the University of North Carolina," and added, if elected, "I would try to use my influence ... to stop [the BCC] and get our university trustees not to bow down to pressure." That opinion, along with remarks critical of UNC's LGBTQ student organization, caused the *Daily Tar Heel* to endorse Gardner's opponents in 1988 and 1992.[81]

The fight for the freestanding black cultural center shifted into high gear in the fall of 1991, following the death of Dr. Sonja Haynes Stone, who had been the faculty adviser to the Black Student Movement. Stone's years at UNC had been at times a struggle, including a very public battle over her tenure in 1979. The BSM decided the best way to honor Stone was to name the future BCC for her, as well as create scholarships that bore her name. Jennifer Wing, editor of the *Daily Tar Heel* at the time, wrote a column supporting the BSM's goals and called the naming of the BCC for Stone "highly appropriate." But other events regarding the BCC that followed during the 1991–92 academic year were not so clear-cut, and the *DTH* showed that while it supported creation of the center, it was not always in lock-step with the BSM or more radical proponents of the project. In one of her last editorials, Wing argued that Chancellor Paul Hardin, who agreed with the concept of naming the center for Stone, had also ruled that no large freestanding structure would be built for the BCC and that students should accept that decision. Several weeks later a column in the paper suggested that Howell Hall,

which was then being vacated by the School of Journalism (ahead of a move to Carroll Hall), would be a good location for the BCC.[82]

Pressure on Chancellor Hardin from Black Cultural Center supporters increased in 1992 and 1993. The paper criticized Hardin, saying he offered "sympathy but no solutions to demands," and it also continued to publish letters critical of the BCC, acknowledging that the university community had a "mixed reaction" to the BSM concept of the center. The paper's staff commissioned a graduate student in sociology to conduct a campus poll on the matter, which found that 45.9 percent of the student body supported construction of a free-standing BCC, and that 45.8 percent did not; the headline declared "BCC divides UNC on racial lines." The *Daily Tar Heel* was also wary of extreme rhetoric on either side of the issue. When rap artist and activist Sister Souljah appeared at UNC in March 1992—two months before her controversial comments on the Rodney King beating in Los Angeles caused presidential candidate Bill Clinton to denounce her remarks and distance himself from her—the paper labeled her speech "detrimental to race relations."[83]

In a clever public relations move, supporters of the BCC organized a rally at the Dean Dome

Cartoon by Alex De Grand showing UNC chancellor Paul Hardin assailed by supporters of a freestanding black cultural center, September 1992.

in September 1992, and invited noted filmmaker Spike Lee (who happened to be a cousin of Sonja Haynes Stone) to be the keynote speaker. Ahead of the rally, some 300 protestors marched to Chancellor Hardin's residence, demanding he act on their requests for the BCC. Two days before the rally, the *DTH* ran an editorial entitled "Do the Right Thing: Go See Spike," a pun on the title of one of Lee's best-known films. About 5,000 students attended the event, and while on campus Lee urged African American athletes to use their celebrity and financial power to back the BCC. Although most agreed that Lee's speech was effective and moderate, others who spoke that day stirred racial animosity. Noting this, the paper's lead editorial the following day was critical of the speakers and the rally, concluding there was "not much to cheer about." Another column by Eric Wagner suggested students should "support the BCC, but don't excuse the rhetoric."[84]

Despite the rally's controversial tone, support for the free standing Black Cultural Center built rapidly. Student government passed a resolution in favor of the center, and other student groups followed suit, including B-Glad (the new name of the Carolina Gay and Lesbian Association), and Sangam, which was founded in 1986 as an organization of students from the Indian subcontinent. Significantly, a university panel created to study the feasibility of the center came out in support of a free-standing structure, and as a result agreed to join with advocates of the BCC to move the project forward, a development the *Daily Tar Heel* dubbed a "ground breaking compromise." Finally, following a protest at the annual University Day proceedings, Hardin approved plans for a freestanding BCC in October

1992. Using a football analogy, the paper praised the chancellor as he "turned the corner and completed his touchdown drive." "With the declaration that 'I support a free-standing black cultural center,' Chancellor Paul Hardin conceded victory to the students struggling for a new BCC," *DTH* editor Peter Wallsten wrote in a column. "Hardin relented, and supporters celebrated. But that victory will remain only a symbolic one until the new BCC takes the shape of bricks and mortar. It will remain only a shallow one until the new BCC fulfills its mission of service to future students."[85]

THE RISE OF BASKETBALL, MULTICULTURALISM, AND AN INDEPENDENT *DAILY TAR HEEL*

The effort to create a freestanding black cultural center and the ongoing controversy surrounding it was one of the biggest stories on campus during the 1980s and early 1990s, a period of dramatic transformation at UNC. As the university approached its bicentennial in 1993—the same year the *Daily Tar Heel* would mark its centennial—other major stories included the rise of basketball as the premier varsity sport, increased diversity on campus and attendant issues of "multiculturalism," and the five-year process of the venerable student newspaper becoming an independent nonprofit entity.

The *Daily Tar Heel*, founded originally in 1893 to promote the recently organized UNC inter-collegiate football team, continued to cover that sport more extensively than any other well into the 1960s—even during the 1950s when a succession of editors questioned its more unseemly aspects and criticized its outsized role in campus life. Basketball at UNC, first played on an intercollegiate level in 1911, garnered less attention despite national championships in 1924 and 1957. Following the arrival of Dean Smith as the men's head basketball coach in 1961, however, the sport's popularity in the university community increased substantially. By the time Carolina won its next NCAA championship in 1982, basketball had become the university's premier varsity sport, and the program was on its way to becoming one of the most respected and consistently top-ranked in the nation.

Not surprisingly, *Daily Tar Heel* coverage of basketball, especially outside of the sports section, increased with the team's reputation. The rise in front-page space devoted to basketball also grew in direct proportion to the accomplishments of one of the most talented athletes to ever to play the game, Michael Jordan. For example, it was a major story in March 1982, just ahead of the ACC tournament, when Jordan was admitted to the infirmary to drain a peritonsillar abscess. Following the national championship win, the paper ran a two-page spread on the victory, featuring Jordan's winning jump shot (the issue also featured a full-page ad from Budweiser beer

congratulating the Tar Heels, at a time when the legal drinking age was eighteen). Jordan quickly became a campus legend, and large front-page photographs of the star in action, usually shot by staff photographer Scott Sharpe, appeared nearly a dozen times between 1982 and 1984. Not even football hero Charlie "Choo-Choo" Justice received that level of coverage during his heyday in the late 1940s. The importance of basketball at UNC by the early 1980s was confirmed by a particular honor; in November 1983, the *DTH* ran its first full-color, non-advertising photograph on the cover of the special basketball supplement for the upcoming season. But the Jordan era came to an end early. In September 1984 the paper announced that the star would get "bucks from Bulls," after signing a seven-year contract with the Chicago team, making him the third-highest-paid rookie in NBA history.[86]

Along with a national championship and Michael Jordan's gravity-defying jump shots, the 1980s also brought a brand-new, state-of-the-art sports facility to UNC, the primary feature of which was an indoor basketball arena with more than 21,000 seats. *Daily Tar Heel* coverage of the facility began in 1978, when the estimated cost—which quickly escalated—was to be $21 million. "The complex is still not a top priority of our institution, but it's getting there," the paper quoted athletic director Bill Cobey at the time. The project soon became a top priority of alumni and the Educational Foundation (also known as the Rams Club), however, and the *Daily Tar Heel* found itself in the position of having to defend students' interests. "Well, we knew it all along, but to have someone come out and say it is somewhat disturbing," the paper reported in September 1980. "The University

This image of an airborne Michael Jordan making the winning shot for UNC during the 1982 NCAA men's basketball championship was taken by *DTH* staff photographer Al Steele.

needs money for a new $30 million student athletic center, and it is willing to do anything, just about, to get it." The "anything" being proposed was to sell parking spots close to Kenan Stadium on football game days. This scheme required that students living near one residence hall "give up their parking spaces on Saturdays so alumni—rich alumni that is—won't get tired and sweaty as they walk to the game, where they'll probably find a seat on the 50-yard line." Pressure from the *DTH* worked, and plans to take away student parking on game days were quickly dropped.[87]

Soon another problem with the proposed arena emerged that would cause friction between students and alumni even after the facility was completed. In August 1981, the *Daily Tar Heel* ran a large front-page story about the sports complex that featured an architectural rendering of it, along with a breakdown of the how seating was to be allocated. Student seating was limited, but for donations starting at $5,000— about the price of a small new car at the time— individuals could purchase perpetual rights to two seats each basketball season. Four seats could be bought for $10,000, and $25,000 bought prime box seats. This revelation set off recriminations, protests, and heated negotiations that lasted some three years, as students fought to have access to more and better seating for games. Ultimately availability of student seating was increased, including 350 seats at half-court be-hind Coach Dean Smith and the team, but only to the point where one-third of the student body could attend a game. Even Smith, the legendary coach who led the Tar Heels for thirty-six years, expressed concern over the influence of alumni and money in college athletics at a 1982 univer-sity seminar on the subject, covered extensively in the *DTH*. With the front-page headline "Smith says Americans Overplay Value of Sports," the paper reported that the coach expressed aston-ishment at "how some universities bow down to alumni." "It's like someone snuck in the store and changed all the price tags. . . . The value given to sports is too high," Smith declared. "Take the new Student Activities Center, for example. With the economy in its present shape, to raise $30 million in two years is amazing. They say people get in the habit and pledge money to other things, like cancer research. I hope that's the case. I say if someone gives $2 million, they can tell me when to go into the Four Corners." Two days later, the paper's lead editorial praised the coach. "Smith has become a legend at UNC be-cause of his success with the basketball program . . . but it's his concern with academics and per-sonal growth that makes him the ideal basketball coach" the editorial concluded, noting a 95 per-cent graduation rate among players.[88]

The Student Activities Center, or SAC, as it was known during construction, ran over bud-get and behind schedule (at one point the *Daily Tar Heel* mocked progress by referring to it as the "Slowly Assembling Center"). When it finally opened in January 1986, costs ran to $33.8 mil-lion—some $10 million more than the recently completed new main campus library, named in honor of alumnus and trustee Walter Royal

Davis, who had given $1 million towards com-pletion of the SAC. Deeming it a "marvel," the *DTH* proclaimed the facility "beautiful and be-fitting the nation's top-ranked basketball team, no doubt about it." In front of a capacity crowd of 21,444, the Tar Heels "christened the building by banging a champagne bottle named [for UNC star player] Steve Hale over Duke's head." Before the game, at a $500-a-plate, black-tie dinner, the building was officially unveiled as the Dean E. Smith Student Activities Center, "a name," the paper declared, "that undoubtedly will continue to be shortened to the alliterative *Dean Dome*."[89]

Three years after the Dean Dome opened, the issue of student seating was again front and cen-ter, and once again the *Daily Tar Heel* led the call for action. "Money talks, it doesn't cheer," ran the headline of a January 1989 column by editor Jean Lutes. The title was a play on words, referring to the relative quiet of alumni during games in the new center, as opposed to the raucous student cheering that had been a staple in Carmichael Auditorium, the old basketball arena. "Aerial views of the Smith Center are great," Lutes wrote. "When the cameras swoop down from the Caro-lina Blue sky to photograph the huge structure, television viewers from across the nation think how lucky those UNC students are to have such a great basketball arena." In fact, as Lutes pointed out, most students' view was from the upper level of the arena, as they occupied only about 1,600 of the 8,000 lower seats. Dubbing this state of affairs "The Great Ticket Scandal," the paper quoted campus leaders who accused the Athletic Department of misleading students about which seats would be available to them. The *DTH* fol-lowed up by conducting a survey of sports arenas at eleven comparable schools, in which it found

Dean Smith standing in the nearly completed Student Athletic Center, to be named for him in January 1986. (NCC/Hugh Morton Collection)

most were funded with student or public funds. "The Smith Center," the paper reported, "because it was funded entirely by private donations, gives priority seating to patrons." Thus, another lead editorial argued, "Putting the 'S' back in SAC" should be the Athletic Department's priority. The publicity campaign worked to a limited degree, as 291 student seats were subsequently added to the lower sections.[90]

The increasing number of African Americans on varsity athletic teams in the 1980s and early 1990s reflected the growing racial and cultural diversity of UNC, though as the fight over the Black Cultural Center revealed, the place of nonmajority cultures on campus was often contested. By the early 1990s serious discussion about the concept of multiculturalism—the acceptance of all communities on equal terms—was underway, with the *Daily Tar Heel* asserting that it was "a must for UNC." One group traditionally ignored at UNC was the Native American community, even though North Carolina has a rich history of native peoples that long predates European settlement. Following the models of the women's and gay rights movements, Native American students created the Carolina Indian Circle in the mid-1970s and began sponsoring an annual weeklong celebration of their culture in part to raise awareness about their issues. As it had done with minority groups for decades, the *DTH* supported the efforts of Native American students through news coverage and editorials. Beginning in 1989, the paper repeatedly called for administrative action to increase recruitment of both Native American students and faculty (of which there were none at the time). "Understandably, many Native Americans are apprehensive about attending UNC," a September 1989

editorial stated, noting "a scant 137" enrolled students and no faculty. In November 1992, a full-page "Focus" feature brought attention to the Native American "struggle for recognition" and revealed that "UNC's smallest minority faces discrimination," including racial slurs and the absence of any class offerings about their heritage and ethnicity.[91]

Although women were no longer a minority of the student population by the last quarter of the twentieth century, and though Title IX and other policies increased gender equality, in many ways the UNC campus remained a male-dominated culture. With regard to women's issues, attention turned during the period to the systemic problem of physical and sexual violence. Periodically, sensational cases of assaults on female students captured the attention of the university community and the *Daily Tar Heel*: notable examples include the 1965 fatal stabbing of Suellen Evans in the Coker Arboretum in broad daylight; the 1985 abduction from the Morehead parking lot of Sharon Stewart, whose murdered body was later found stuffed in an oil drum; and the 1992 assault of a female student at Granville Towers, perpetrated by an assailant who climbed into the window of her second-floor room. The *DTH* first began seriously attacking the problem of rape in 1975, and did so increasingly in the 1980s and 1990s. In 1984 the paper established a policy of not publishing the names of rape victims in order to protect their privacy and hopefully to encourage more victims to report crimes. Editorials subsequently pushed for changes in administrative policy on sexual violence and harassment, including supporting efforts for the treatment of victims and the raising of awareness through initiatives such as creation of a "Rape

Free Zone" on campus in 1993. In 1986 the paper took on the problem of date rape, an issue particularly relevant on a college campus. A 1990 editorial called the crime "a life-destroying problem," and another in 1992 stated flatly: "Date rape. It's real. It's happening. And University students should be concerned."[92]

Gender issues during the late 1980s and early 1990s brought the editorial staff of the *Daily Tar Heel* into public opposition with one UNC trustee, John Pope. The wealthy businessman garnered national attention for his conservative views, which he espoused in articles in the *Washington Post* and the *New York Times*. "We've got a girl's school at Chapel Hill," Pope was quoted as saying in reference to his suggestion that male applicants be given priority admission. "Forty percent of the girls who graduate from Chapel Hill five years from now won't even be in the job market," he told the *Times*. Pope's concern, apparently, was that women wouldn't be family breadwinners in future years and that the amount of money donated by these nonworking alumni would drop. Following the national press the *Daily Tar Heel* ran a feature story dubbing Pope the "maverick trustee," as well as publishing as a guest column a letter to the editor calling for his resignation. At a trustee meeting in the fall of 1992, during a discussion of violence against women on campus, Pope declared that he had little sympathy for female students who "go home with a bunch of drunken boys at two or three o'clock in the morning and then yell rape at eight that morning." The *DTH* was shocked and appalled:

On their surface, Pope's words make a mockery of the seriousness of the crime of rape, particularly date rape. Is Pope trying to affirm the age-old absurdity that a rape victim is to blame for the crime that is committed against her, that she "asked for it?"

As if the words themselves weren't disgraceful enough, consider that they came out of the mouth of a representative of this school's governing body, a man appointed by the governor to deal with problems on campus. Not that anyone who has followed Pope's illustrious career should be surprised by his latest feat of callousness—the trustee is notorious for sexist and racist comments.

Wake up Mr. Pope. Rape is real, and right now, so is the threat of rape for every woman—and man—on this campus that you've been charged to oversee.

In a telephone interview with a *Daily Tar Heel* reporter, Pope said that his meaning was misconstrued, though he did not retract his statement. "My comment was not concerning the rapes and assaults on female students," he told the reporter, but rather "what the University was doing to protect the students." "If anybody knows John Pope," he added, "they know I'm a strong believer in law and order.... As far as I'm concerned, [for] anyone guilty of rape, the punishment cannot be too strong." But many students and members of the university community were not mollified, and letters denouncing Pope poured into the *Daily Tar Heel* for weeks following his remarks.[93]

As divisive as the rhetoric about sexual violence against women was at UNC during the period, it was not as intense as the prejudice and discrimination against the gay and lesbian community. Restricting openly gay activities and organizations on campus was the Maginot Line for many conservatives, representing the last bastion of what they saw as a traditional and moral culture. To this end, the same-sex community endured all manner of attacks by the College Republicans and two new conservative groups, Students for America (SFA) and Campus Watch. Through news coverage and editorials, the *Daily Tar Heel* did what it could to mitigate the hostility and to call for understanding and equal treatment. Since the mid-1970s, controversy had arisen each year at UNC around Gay Awareness Week in the spring, and over student activities fee support for the Campus Gay and Lesbian Association, but the advent of the AIDS epidemic and the fear it caused exacerbated the situation (the name of the CGA changed to CGLA to include women in 1985, and again in 1992 to B-GLAD, the Bisexual, Gay Men, Lesbians, and Allies for Diversity). The first two *DTH* articles about AIDS appeared in February of 1985, and the paper consistently and steadfastly championed efforts to understand the disease, counter hysteria, promote scientific research to find a cure, and support initiatives to ease the suffering of those infected. The paper proudly announced in December 1988 that anonymous AIDS tests were being given at the student health center, making UNC the "only university in North Carolina that offers this kind of testing program." In subsequent years the paper reported that the School of Pharmacy's AIDS program had won first place in a national competition sponsored by the U.S. Department of Health and Human Services, ardently supported a Student Congress resolution to place condom machines in every dorm, and editorialized on the need for a home in Chapel Hill to shelter and care for AIDS patients.[94]

The *Daily Tar Heel* also challenged discrimination based on sexual orientation at the university and beyond, as it had done with racial segregation in the 1960s. In 1989 the paper came out against the actions of a local dance bar, On the Hill, which purportedly instituted a dress code that was little more than a thinly veiled attempt to weed out homosexual patrons. Reporting that any male in "all black clothes, long hair or earrings" was being turned away at the door, the paper blasted both the assumption that such people were gay and the club's attempt to cater only to a "mainstream" clientele. In a clever turn of phrase, one editorial charged the owners of the club with "forcing homogeneity," calling the restrictions "out of place in Chapel Hill." Two years later, when Cracker Barrel announced that it did not hire homosexuals, the *DTH* called for a boycott of the national restaurant chain. Comparing Cracker Barrel's policy to racial discrimination, an editorial called it the "same monster with a different face," and added that, "unlike African Americans who are protected against discrimination by federal and state laws, homosexuals enjoy no such consideration." In 1992, the paper took a bold and somewhat risky step not taken during the civil rights era—Doug Ferguson was given a regular column where he discussed what it was like being gay at UNC, and in which he wrote about issues affecting the same-sex community. Though Ferguson was not the first openly gay *DTH* staffer (others include Frank Bruni in the early 1980s, who later became an op-ed columnist at the *New York Times*), he was the first to write frankly and sensitively about a world foreign to many students and to put a human face on the often ugly debate about sexuality and morality.[95]

This October 1988 cartoon in the *Daily Tar Heel* pokes fun at Campus Watch, a conservative organization opposed to student funding of the Carolina Gay and Lesbian Association.

The most contentious arguments about the rights of gays and lesbians on campus occurred within the political arena and represented, in microcosm, the ongoing national debate of the time. All of this also occurred within the context of the reenergizing of the political Right, which viewed homosexuality as a moral issue that resonated with its base supporters. Both of the new conservative groups that formed in the mid-1980s at UNC, the Students for America in 1984 and Campus Watch in 1988, actively advocated cutting off university funding for the CGLA, as well as restricting public activities of gays and lesbians on campus. In 1986, when pressure on members of the student congress did not yield the desired results, the SFA attempted to organize a student referendum to end CGLA funding. After the group was called homophobic, a letter ran in the *Daily Tar Heel* from an SFA member who took issue with that label. "Sex with a dead body, an animal or species of the same sex is not natural, but perverted," the student asserted, and quoting Thomas Jefferson on religious liberty the student declared: "To compel a man to furnish funds for the propagation of ideas he disbelieves and abhors is sinful and tyrannical."[96]

But not even all members of the SFA were in agreement with the group's efforts. A very public internal squabble, which played out on the pages of the *Daily Tar Heel*, pitted an executive member of the chapter against others in the group. When Brad Torgan objected to the SFA's policies on the subject, he was kicked out, causing two other executive committee members to resign in protest. "SFA is a conservative, political organization," Torgan told the paper, "although in this case, they've chosen to supplant conservatism with bigotry and prejudice." The *Daily*

Tar Heel also had its own troubles with SFA at the time. In September 1985, a quotation from nineteenth-century German philosopher Friedrich Nietzsche, "God is dead," ran in large type at the bottom of the front page, part of a new design that featured famous and provocative quotations each day. The paper received a great deal of mail, mostly in opposition to publication of the quote, which sparked debate about religious intolerance on campus. Students for America called for yet another ballot referendum to cease student funding of the paper, though this attempt proved to be the last time a conservative group tried to use that tactic to silence the *DTH*.[97]

Repeated attempts to end student funding for the Carolina Gay and Lesbian Association occurred almost yearly into the 1990s, and the paper took the position of defending the organization each time. The *Daily Tar Heel* had seen this all before; conservative groups were trying the same methods used unsuccessfully to defund the paper almost two decades earlier, in part because of its stand on homosexuality. After SFA failed to get a campus referendum to end student funding of the CGLA in 1986, Campus Watch took up the cause in 1988 and called for the state legislature to pass a bill banning financial support for such organizations at public universities. Jim Gardner, then running for lieutenant governor, backed proposals for the legislation, and UNC student leaders and the *Daily Tar Heel* cried foul. Labeling Gardner's support of the Campus Watch proposal a "foolish mistake," the paper excoriated him and endorsed his opponent. In "a calculated attempt to exploit the anti-homosexual sentiments of conservative voters," an editorial declared, "Gardner has called for legislation that would prohibit the allocation of UNC Student fees to the Carolina Gay and Lesbian Association. His support of such interference in student self-governance shows disrespect for students and a disturbing desire to meddle in University affairs." Gardner won the election and a bill was introduced, but it failed to receive widespread support. The paper followed the bill's progress in early 1989 and reported that similar measures failed in several other states, where they were found to be unconstitutional.[98]

The tensions wrought by multiculturalism at Carolina engulfed the entire campus in the fall of 1990, with the installation of a group of bronze statues in front of Davis Library entitled "The Student Body," a $65,000 gift from the class of 1985. Intended by the artist to represent the cultural diversity of the university, the figures were immediately criticized by large numbers of students as perpetuating racial, ethnic, and gender stereotypes. The group included two figures depicting African Americans: a male twirling a basketball on his finger, and a woman balancing a book on her head. Two others showed a Caucasian couple, the man with his arm around the woman, who held an apple (taken as a biblical reference to Eve tempting Adam). One of the last large-scale campus controversies to occur before the dawning of the digital information age, the debate about the statues raged on the pages of the *Daily Tar Heel*.[99]

As it turned out, the fall of 1990 witnessed a number of incidents of intolerance—if not hate—at UNC, all against the backdrop of the highly contested U.S. Senate race between incumbent Jesse Helms and Harvey Gantt, the former mayor of Charlotte. Gantt was African American, and the campaign became as much about race as about any political issues. In September, the paper reported that the racial slur "No nigger senator" and the letters "KKK" had been written on a Gantt campaign poster in Mangum Dormitory. It seemed to be open season on all minority groups: a week after the Gantt poster was vandalized, anti-homosexual signs were found on the walls of the fifth floor of Carmichael Residence Hall, followed the next week by anti-CGLA comments painted on the free-expression CUBE in the Pit. And in late October, an anti-Semitic group sent a letter to the computer center in Phillips Hall.[100]

The staff of the *Daily Tar Heel* took on the hate incidents and the ballooning controversy over the Davis Library statues as parts of the same problem, and through news coverage and editorials offered opportunities for various views to be aired. Coeditor Jessica Lanning herself called for the immediate removal of the statues, arguing that they "carry overtones of sexism and racism, and those are two isms this campus should not tolerate." Declaring that the recent "rash of hate crimes must stop," Lanning referenced the Confederate Soldiers' Monument on McCorkle Place in pointing out that "elements of this campus have strong traditional values that unfortu-

nately harbor discriminatory views." Letters from readers poured into the paper, some disagreeing with Lanning, stating that they did not find the statues offensive and suggesting that their removal was tantamount to censorship. The artist, Julia Balk, felt compelled to write a letter of explanation, which the paper ran as a guest column. "Although I believe a work of art should speak for itself," Balk wrote, "in this case, unfortunately, my voice is not being heard." Arguing that "the identity of each figure within the group is meant to be defined not primarily by race, but rather by the challenge of the unknown ... [of] who they will become," Balk stated flatly that her intent was to represent racial harmony, and that for anyone to interpret racism or sexism in the statues "is to see the sculptures with one's eyes closed."[101]

Despite the artist's explanation, students began peaceful protests to have the figures removed, including a sit-in organized in front of Davis Library that lasted nearly a month. Soon the statues were being vandalized, and after the basketball figure was knocked down and the ball stolen, the figures became targets for groups with differing agendas. "The student body in garbage bags," the paper announced when a group protesting the war in Kuwait covered the statues in plastic bags. The College Republicans, who accused those condemning the art installation of being hypocrites, hung Jesse Helms campaign signs around the necks of the figures, placed backward with slogans including "You want to hide this, yet fund homosexual filth," and "Censorship is censorship." The situation turned into such a three-ring circus that dedication of the sculpture was postponed, and an editorial entitled "A violated 'student body'" lamented the

fact that the carnival-like atmosphere "sabotaged the most serious discussion of racial tension that this campus has seen in years." During the course of the debate the *Daily Tar Heel*'s position softened somewhat, and a column by editorial board member Elizabeth Murray determined that the "problem can be corrected by *moving*— not *removing*—the sculpture to a place on campus where people can choose to view it if they wish." The paper then called for the chancellor to do something about the situation, and in mid-January 1991 it reported that a decision was made to move the entire installation to a less conspicuous area between Hamilton and Bynum Halls.[102]

Amid debates about multiculturalism and intolerance at UNC based on race, gender, ethnicity, and sexual orientation—taken as a whole, a primary editorial focus of the *Daily Tar Heel* from the mid-1980s to the early 1990s—the student newspaper was in a period of profound organizational and administrative change, ultimately leading to its separating from the university, and becoming a self-supporting nonprofit corporation by 1993. In part this transformation was indicative of changes in the industry of print

'DTH' enters computer age with $95,000 system

By JEFF HIDAY
Editor

Following a trend among college newspapers across the country, *The Daily Tar Heel* has purchased a $95,000 computer system that will allow student reporters to write and edit stories on video display terminals.

Today's paper is the first regular edition of the *DTH* produced with the new computers.

The computer system has revolutionized the *DTH*, pointing it toward financial independence and almost eliminating the need for the manual typewriters the staff depended upon for so many years.

Until late June, when the computers were installed, the University Department of Printing and Duplicating typeset and positioned all *DTH* stories and advertisements. The *DTH* paid UPD about $60,000 a year for the service.

Now, students both typeset the stories and place the copy on the pages, with the assistance of two full-time, paid production coordinators hired by the *DTH*.

Also, students assume greater responsibility in that they become entirely responsible for seeing to it that the paper makes it to press each night. As usual, the paper must be ready by 12:30 a.m. each night for delivery to Hinton Press, in Mebane.

For the *DTH*, the switch has been a somewhat painful realization of the maxim "in with the new and out with the old."

It spells doom for Horace and Mildred, the beloved Associated Press Model 20 teletype machines who have been serving the paper faithfully for decades. In their stead, via telephone lines, news dispatches will feed directly into the computer.

Besides general mourning for Horace and Mildred, a few complaints have accompanied installation of the computers.

Several *DTH* writers and reporters

See COMPUTERS on page 4

Staff writer Jim Zook types a story into new video display terminal

journalism at the dawn of the digital information age, and in part it resulted from issues unique to the *DTH*. The introduction of a national newspaper in 1982, *USA Today*, had significant ramifications. Known as the "*USA Today* effect," certain fairly radical elements introduced by that publication, such as concise front-page stories that did not "jump" to interior sections and layouts generated on computers, were soon adopted by papers nationwide. The *Daily Tar Heel* entered the computer age in August 1984 with an investment in a $95,000 system. "The computer system has revolutionized the *DTH*," the paper declared, "pointing it toward financial independence and almost eliminating the need for the manual typewriters the staff depended upon for so many years." There was a tinge of nostalgia, as the new equipment "spells doom for Horace and Mildred, the beloved Associated Press Model 20 teletype machines who have been serving the paper faithfully for decades," a story reported. Presag-

ing the World Wide Web, the article also noted that in place of the teletype machines "via telephone lines, news dispatches will feed directly into the computer." When an Apple Macintosh system was bought in 1988, the *DTH* entered the world of desktop publishing, doing away with the centuries-old system of laying out pages by hand.[103]

The most significant changes to the operation and business side of the *Daily Tar Heel* in the last quarter of the twentieth century came with the arrival of Kevin Schwartz in January 1988. A graduate of Purdue University, Schwartz had been at UNC since the fall of 1986, pursuing a master's degree in journalism. Schwartz was an alumnus of the *Exponent*, Purdue's student newspaper, and was intrigued by the contrast between its successful independent incorporated model and the less successful university-governed models of other college papers. Deciding the *DTH* would make a good case study for his thesis, he went to the paper's office where he was promptly hired as assistant business manager (non-student professionals had held business positions since the early 1970s). When the *DTH*'s first professional general manager, Anne Fulcher, left at the end of the semester, Schwartz found himself in that position, which he would hold during twenty of the next twenty-five years. Schwartz immediately set about enforcing deadlines and production schedules so that the paper would appear on time every morning, overhauling and modernizing the distribution system (which had been problematic for years), and improving various aspects of the advertising operation. In his thesis he had developed a five-year plan to create a *Daily Tar Heel* independent of student funding and university control, modeled primarily on the *Exponent*. The plan became the blueprint for the steps taken between 1988 and 1993, and it contained three principal elements: incorporation of the *DTH* as a 501(c)(3) nonprofit entity wholly separate from UNC; cessation of student-fee funding, to be decreased over the five-year period until it reached zero; and selection of the editor in chief by a committee established by the paper, rather than by annual campus-wide student election. All of these operational changes and administrative policies were made with the purpose of strengthening the paper's reputation among area businesses, in anticipation of building advertising revenue to the point that it could support the nonprofit entity without university funding.[104]

One by one, each of the three main elements was accomplished. The first was incorporation of the paper, which might have faced some opposition from the university but was helped along by good timing. The Internal Revenue Service

had begun investigating revenue-producing entities on nonprofit college campuses as a result of a 1986 change in the federal tax code, and the university was looking for ways to shed such operations. In addition, there were increasing concerns among UNC's legal advisers about the school's liability for actions of semi-autonomous groups, and incorporation was a good solution to protecting the university from lawsuits. Thus in November 1989, the student newspaper became the first entity to incorporate, as DTH Publishing Corporation. This first step was crucial to implementation of the second and third elements of the five-year plan. Cessation of student fee funding would allow the new corporation to conduct business as it saw fit, rather than under the financial rules of the Student Activities Fund Office, which were antithetical to running a newspaper (including one rule that prevented the paper from investing any surplus profits). And only by removing Student Congress as the budgetary approval authority for the paper and rewriting the Student Code could the *DTH* change its annual election process for editor.[105]

Though incorporation was a fairly smooth process, undertaking the second element of the plan was more complex and contested. Since the agreement reached in 1975, the *Daily Tar Heel* had received 16 percent of the student activities fees collected each year, which by 1988 amounted to approximately $100,000 of the paper's annual budget of over $600,000. The plan called for reduction of the amount received by 4 percent a year, to give the paper time to wean itself entirely. Ending that appropriation required a campus-wide referendum, under the terms of the student government constitution. Even though passage of the referendum would free up a comparatively large sum of money to be distributed to other campus organizations, Student Congress refused to put it on the ballot in February 1990 (when elections for the next academic year were held). The reason was apparently rooted in a desire to retain some type of control over the paper, though news and editorial content had always been determined without consideration of the wishes of campus politicians. Undeterred, the paper's staff collected more than enough signatures on a petition to put the referendum on the ballot, and it passed handily with 76.5 percent of the vote. Despite the problem with Student Congress—and the long history of fighting over *DTH* funding that stretched back to 1969 that included an earlier referendum, a bill in the state legislature, and two lawsuits—the initiative seems to have been something of foregone conclusion by early 1990. There was very little coverage of it in the paper, aside from parts of two editorials explaining why the action was being taken. By contrast, another item on the ballot received far more coverage in the paper at the time—the question of whether to allow cable television service in the dorms.[106]

Passage of the referendum meant that once the *Daily Tar Heel* stopped taking activities fees in 1993, the third and final element of the plan, changing the method of selecting a new student editor each year, could be implemented. Since 1923, when the paper became an official part of the university under the old Publications Union Board, selection of the editor had been made by campus-wide election, with votes cast the same day as for student-body president and other campus positions. Open election of the editor had proved problematic at times; some years it became a popularity contest, and the person

selected was not always the most qualified to run the paper. Occasionally other problems occurred, such as delays in changing editors as the result of a runoff or disputed returns, and the loss of seasoned staff who lost the election. Jean Lutes, editor in 1988–89, wrote an honor's thesis outlining how selection of the editor could work through a committee of students and faculty under the auspices of the new nonprofit corporation, and it was her format that was basis for the new process.[107]

During the five-year period from 1988 to 1993, as the paper underwent the process of separating from the university, it also dealt with issues regarding freedom of speech and freedom of the press. In September 1989, the *Daily Tar Heel* once again ran an advertisement for *Playboy* magazine, this time in the form of a full-color insert, and once again there were student protests. The protests were more organized than earlier ones, however, and a group circulated a petition calling for an apology and a donation of the ad fee to a nonprofit serving women. General manager Kevin Schwartz knew the ad was legal and saw the issue as a question of the paper being able to control its own advertising. After meeting with representatives from the protest group briefly during their march on the *DTH* office, the paper reported that "Schwartz said that the *DTH* does not plan at this time to run an apology and that he would not recommend to the *DTH* Board of Directors that the ad revenue be donated to a women's group." Some twenty-nine college newspapers ran the *Playboy* ad, and the *DTH* later noted that the largest protest related to it came on the UNC campus.[108]

The following year, the paper fought twice for its right to access information needed to

fully cover stories. The first incident involved the paper's ability to obtain university police records, and the second concerned allowing a female *Daily Tar Heel* sports reporter equal access to interview football players after games in the locker room. Both efforts were successful (the latter by an agreement to remove all reporters from the locker room and instead to conduct formal press post-game interviews), and laid the foundation for the paper to even more aggressively seek information from university sources in years to come.[109]

As the staff of the *Daily Tar Heel* worked toward creating an independent corporation, it also locked horns with hostile members of Student Congress. Members not only voted down the paper's request for a ballot referendum to end student-fee funding in early 1990, but they tried several times to sabotage the defunding process over the next three years. One editorial termed the actions of student congressional members "politicization," an effort to restrict the freedom of the press and to punish the paper for positions with which they did not agree. Most of

these members were acknowledged conservatives who were at the same time attempting to restrict or end the funding of certain other organizations, including the Black Student Movement and the Carolina Gay and Lesbian Association, as well as opposing campus initiatives the *Daily Tar Heel* supported (most notably creation of the freestanding Black Cultural Center). Doug Ferguson suggested in a column that the "Ringling Brothers congress" needed "a new act." But it wasn't as humorous when student representative Eric Pratt, following a close vote to continue funding of the CGLA in March 1992, blurted out, "You're all a bunch of faggots." The *DTH* and others called for Pratt to be censured for his outburst, and the Student Congress Ethics Committee voted unanimously to do so. It was also Pratt, in a last-ditch effort to kick the *DTH* on its way out of the door, who authored a bill in the spring of 1993 prohibiting the paper from utilizing university property and calling for eviction from offices in the student union. The bill passed, and an attempt was made to enforce it, but as Kevin Schwartz remembered "We just

Yi-Hsin Chang, 1993–94 editor of the *Daily Tar Heel*. Chang was the first editor chosen by the paper's staff and management, following seventy years of election by the student body. (DTH Media)

locked the door and ignored them." The matter was settled by Don Boulton, vice chancellor and dean for student affairs, who ruled that only he and the union's board of directors, not the Student Congress, had the authority evict anyone from the premises.[110]

In the year leading up to the *Daily Tar Heel*'s one-hundredth anniversary the paper mounted a campaign among alumni to raise capital funds to get the new nonprofit corporation off the ground, which netted $30,000. With private funds in hand, the paper took its last student-activities-fee appropriation in January 1993. The actual centennial, February 23, 1993, was celebrated with the publication of a regular daily edition that replicated the typeface and layout of the first 1893 issue on the front page, and a special commemorative edition that traced the history of the paper and included interviews of and articles by *DTH* alumni stretching back to the 1930s. Governor Jim Hunt issued a proclamation declaring February 23 "*Daily Tar Heel* Day" across the state. More important than the celebratory events was the selection of the new editor in April 1993, which was done without a campus-wide election for the first time in seventy years. The inaugural election revealed certain kinks in the system, and as a result it took six votes to choose Yi-Hsin Chang to replace Peter Wallsten, who held the editorship ten weeks longer because of the delay. Chang, a rising junior who had been features editor, was also the first Asian American to serve in the position.[111]

In late April 1993, with DTH Publishing Corporation now fully functioning, and with the selection of a new editor completed, Peter Wallsten wrote a lead editorial entitled "Free Press Must Prevail," in which he put the latest maneuver by the Student Congress to kick the paper's staff out of the Student Union into the context of the paper's long history, and foresaw a bright future:

The *Daily Tar Heel* celebrated its 100th birthday this year with a glimpse back at a century of editorial freedom. Looking through those dusty *DTH* annals, we found a history riddled with threats to that coveted freedom but also with stunning triumphs over would-be censors.

And as we take pride in our past, we've also looked forward with hope to a future free from threats by those tugging at the *DTH*'s purse strings. Through a mandate of the student body, the *DTH* will become financially autonomous this year.

This [recent] incident [by Student Congress] will be a mere blip on the screen of *DTH* history. If it is remembered at all, it will be held up as just another example of second-rate campus politicos trying desperately to use their last few moments in 'power' to punish this newspaper for the criticism they've received on the editorial page ... and the scrutiny they've endured in our new stories.

Pratt and his cohorts are not the first congress members to lose sight of the value of a press free from threats to editorial freedom. We are confident that they will not be the last, but we are equally as confident that the *DTH* will continue to survive such threats as it ventures into its second century, continuing to criticize when necessary and criticize when deserved.[112]

EPILOGUE

SERVING UNC STUDENTS AND THE UNIVERSITY COMMUNITY SINCE 1893

At the time the *Daily Tar Heel* became independent of student-fee funding in 1993, no one could have anticipated the challenges that lay ahead in the new millennium. The quarter century between the paper's 100th anniversary and its 125th witnessed the coming of the digital information age, and virtually all aspects of traditional print journalism were upended, almost to the point of extinction. Simply put, the way news is gathered and delivered, and the way people access and interact with it, has been revolutionized.

What resulted during the difficult transition was professional carnage, as many venerable newspapers folded and others shrank drastically in staff and print size. News, editorials, and perhaps most importantly reader response and opinion became literally instantaneous, available 24/7 on a variety of highly portable wireless devices that erased the lead time necessary to print and distribute hard copy. Though print media had faced downsizing and even obsolescence before—first with radio in the early 1920s, followed by television after World War II—it had been able to retool and find a place alongside the new technologies. But the obstacles of the digital information revolution were far more daunting.

In general, college newspapers, with very targeted and captive audiences, were able to initially weather the storm. This was particularly true for the *Daily Tar Heel*, which serves Orange County as well as the university. As late as 2011, the new nonprofit independent business model of DTH Media boasted cash reserves of some $1 million. But the recession of 2008–2009 drove down advertising revenue as businesses tightened their belts or closed altogether, at the same time that social media became a virtual platform

Sharif Durhams, first African American editor in chief of the *Daily Tar Heel*, 1998–99. Durhams has gone on to a successful career in journalism, including positions with the *Milwaukee Journal Sentinel*, the *Washington Post*, and CNN. (DTH Media/Erik Perel)

for reaching far more potential customers at a fraction of the cost of print. Soon the venerable *Daily Tar Heel* was hemorrhaging an average of $200,000 a year and financial crisis loomed, though this was not made public until 2016.[1]

Through good times and bad, the paper's student and professional staffs have worked to uphold the traditions that have made the paper a campus institution and nationally recognized publication, while simultaneously navigating the rapidly changing landscape of print journalism. Several of the major stories and issues the *DTH* covered and helped to shape during previous decades continued to develop, though the paper

now had a different organizational relationship with the university. Following nonprofit incorporation in 1989, the *DTH* had the ability to legally challenge UNC for access to information, and the paper exercised that ability several times in the ensuing years.

And though increasing numbers of young adults arriving on university campuses didn't grow up with a hard-copy newspaper as part of daily life, the campus coverage provided almost exclusively by print student publications has kept them from becoming obsolete. Interestingly, alumni and parents living outside of the circulation area of the print edition read the online version of the *Daily Tar Heel* more than do students, who still can be seen carrying paper copies around campus. The *DTH* was, in fact, one of the first newspapers of any type in the country to provide web content, though it was not initially a calculated decision. Two computer science students, who were not members of the staff, approached the general manager in 1994 with a proposal to create an online version of the paper via the campus computer network. On November 19, 1994, the *Daily Tar Heel* began offering a digital version of its news content, first posted as text-only the night after the print edition appeared.[2]

The changing nature of print journalism and how it is taught at UNC has created certain unanticipated challenges for the *Daily Tar Heel*. As the percentage of majors on a news-editorial track at UNC's School of Media and Journalism shrank from nearly 80 percent to less than 30 percent, the paper had to rely more on less-experienced freshmen and sophomores and non-journalism majors to fill its newsroom and its leadership positions, which had been the province almost exclusively of upperclassmen in the past. The lack of experience led to a decline in quality, a problem the *DTH* addressed by hiring its first-ever newsroom adviser in 2008—long after many of its peers had done so. Erica Beshears Perel, the paper's editor in 1997–98 and a veteran reporter at the *Charlotte Observer*, was the choice for the job. She characterizes her role as one of teaching and advising the students about professional journalistic standards and methods, not shaping editorial policy or news coverage, which continues to be solely driven by the student staff. According to Perel "journalism at its core is critical thinking ... [and that] is the

most important skill we can teach here." Perel argues that even in the new digital age traditional journalism "is still a worthwhile career, it is still important to democracy, there is still a public service mission to it." In addition, she sees it as a significant part of her job to instill in each new generation of students the "ethics and values of the paper, and [promote] this idea that we are to be the watchdog of the university."[3]

In the tradition of being the watchdog of the university, the *Daily Tar Heel* continued in the years after gaining its independence to cover and editorialize about major stories in the life of the UNC community. And though the student staff continues to cycle on and off the paper, there is continuity in the threads of certain central themes, particularly with regard to efforts to protect and ensure academic, speech, and press freedoms and ongoing debates about what a public university should be. The threads of these themes include questions of equality and treatment based on race, ethnicity, gender, and sexual orientation, as well as the role big-time athletics play in the life and operation of an institution of higher learning.

Following the campus uproar in 1991 over the "Student Body" statue, the debate about race and inclusion often involved physical space, focusing on symbols built into the UNC landscape. For example, once agreement was reached on the contentious issue of creating a freestanding Black Cultural Center in 1992, almost immediately the battle began over the building's location. Supporters wanted the structure built on a piece of land at the southern corner of Polk Place, a prominent location between Wilson Library and Dey Hall. The editorial page of the *DTH*, which had vacillated about the center for several years

before coming out in favor of it, strongly opposed placement of the building on Polk Place and chastised supporters for pushing so strongly. Ultimately the center was built on another parcel of land on the opposite side of South Road and opened in 2004, named in memory of African American professor and Black Student Movement adviser Sonja Haynes Stone.[4]

As fundraising and planning for the Stone Center was under way, attention focused on two longtime campus landmarks with ties to the Confederacy, and the *Daily Tar Heel* became embroiled the controversies surrounding both. In October 1999, a group of students wanting to bring attention to racism institutionalized in the university's landscape strung black ropes symbolizing nooses on trees outside Saunders Hall, and hung KKK banners on the building. Tied to the state's antebellum planter elite, UNC alumnus William Saunders had served as a Confederate officer and later as North Carolina's secretary of state. During the 1870s he was widely believed to have been one of the top leaders of the first incarnation of the Ku Klux Klan in North Carolina, though he denied this in congressional hear-

ings. In 1922, the UNC Board of Trustees named a new classroom building in his honor, having two years earlier officially cited his KKK activities among his accomplishments. The nooses and banners hung in 1999 were a silent protest not only to the honoring of Saunders on campus, but also because the historical plaque on the building glaringly omitted his Klan involvement. In fact, the first public discussion about Saunders Hall and his KKK connections had come in the form of a *DTH* opinion piece in 1975, in the wake of Klan leader David Duke's appearance on campus. The article, however, did not call for the removal Saunders's name from the building.[5]

In 2001, following publication of a column in the *DTH* by controversial conservative writer David Horowitz arguing against payment of monetary reparations to descendants of African American slaves (a topic much discussed at the time), students marched from the Pit to Saunders Hall, and then on to South Building protesting the treatment of minorities at UNC. The group's spokesperson said the naming of Saunders Hall and the *DTH*'s publication of Horowitz's column constituted examples of the "many manifestations of racism on this campus." Editor Matt Dees responded that publication of the column was "a freedom of expression" and argued that it was the paper's responsibility not to "just sweep somebody under the rug because some people think he is racist," adding that "calling [the *DTH* staff] racist for running someone's views is ludicrous." A note under the story read: "*DTH* Editor Matt Dees did not edit this story because he was quoted in it."[6]

A column in the paper in the wake of the Saunders Hall and Horowitz incidents by opinion staff member Ashley Stephenson drew a sharp line between what to do about the naming of a building for a former KKK leader and a related issue: calls to pull down the most controversial symbol of the Old South on the UNC campus, the statue nicknamed Silent Sam. Erected on McCorkle Place in 1913 as a memorial to UNC students who fought for the Confederacy, the statue became the topic of perennial debate in the late twentieth century. Acknowledging that a plaque should be placed on Saunders Hall revealing the Confederate colonel's connection to the KKK, when it came to destroying Silent Sam, Stephenson declared her opposition: "I stand my ground." She argued that the statue was a monument to the UNC soldiers who served in the war, and not a monument to slavery or racism. (Interestingly, the same controversy has not surrounded Memorial Hall, which originally was also named for UNC's Confederate dead, and displays carved stone plaques in their honor.)[7]

As the centennial anniversary of the dedication of Silent Sam approached, the debate intensified, and the paper covered efforts by historians to put the statue and its meaning into the context not of the Civil War, but of the white supremacy movement of the late nineteenth and early twentieth centuries, which brought Jim Crow segregation and political disfranchisement to North Carolina. At the same time, students became more organized and active, and the Real Silent Sam Coalition (RSSC) was formed in 2011 to protest racist elements of the UNC landscape and raise awareness of the issues involved from an African American perspective. By 2012, the opinion of student columnists at the *Daily Tar Heel* seemed to have evolved. In a column entitled "Silent Sam still matters," Zaina Alsous declared that "racial injustice is not a thing

of the past, and neither is Silent Sam." Pointing out that in a speech at the 1913 dedication, Julian Shakespeare Carr (for whom Carrboro and Carr Hall are named) triumphantly proclaimed that he had once "horse-whipped a Negro wench, until her skirts hung in shreds" for insulting a white woman on Franklin Street, Alsous argued that the statue "must be understood not only as a memorial to honor the war dead, but, just as significantly, as a symbol of the unending struggle against institutional racism in our community." "Silent Sam isn't so silent after all," Alsous concluded. "Rather, the voices he silences with his presence [are] deafening if we chose to listen."[8]

The events following the August 2014 police shooting and killing of Michael Brown, an unarmed black teenager, in Ferguson, Missouri, set off a series of nationwide protests. Out of these protests the Black Lives Matter (BLM) movement was born, which soon had a presence at UNC, as it did on college campuses across the country. At UNC the RSCC and BLM groups worked toward a variety of goals, the most high profile of which was the removal of the name of William Saunders from the classroom building. By this time, the fact that the UNC Board of Trustees listed his Klan involvement as a reason for naming the building for him in the early 1920s had been uncovered, and became the "smoking gun" that convicted him in the minds of many. After intense pressure from student groups, the Board of Trustees voted 10–3 in May of 2015 to remove Saunders's name from the building, and rename it simply "Carolina Hall." This action angered many on both sides of the issue. Some argued that Saunders had done many good things for the state, and that history should not be "whitewashed" if subsequent gen-

erations happen to hold a different view. But many of those who wanted Saunders's name removed, including RSSC and BLM activists, were angry that an innocuous name was chosen instead of that of a prominent African American historically associated with the university. In addition, the Board decreed that no other campus landmarks would be changed or renamed for sixteen years, and that a task force be impaneled to study UNC history and make recommendations for interpreting and preserving the university's past.[9]

Daily Tar Heel coverage of the renaming of Saunders Hall followed the patterns set in heated controversies of previous decades, though as with civil rights in the 1960s, the paper's coverage and editorials moved steadily in support of

student protest groups as events unfolded. In March 2017, an alternative plaque appeared on the exterior of Carolina Hall, declaring the building "Zora Neale Hurston Hall." Hurston was an African American writer who took summer school courses in Durham in the 1930s at what was then North Carolina College for Negroes (later North Carolina Central University), and tradition holds that she was invited to attend some classes at UNC taught by legendary dramatist Paul Green, even though as a black woman she could not enroll at the time. Though the story has not been verified, the RSSC pushed for the building to be named in Hurston's honor. The *DTH* quoted from a RSSC statement explaining their stand on the Trustee action: "'Carolina Hall' is a sugar-coating of Saunders Hall updated for the aesthetics of 21st-century white supremacy: color blindness and multicultural diversity … This isn't justice, it's pageantry. We named this building after Zora Neale Hurston precisely because racist and sexist admissions policies excluded her and other Black women from UNC."[10]

The discussion about race and culture also extended into the classroom during the first decade of the new century, in an intense debate over academic freedom not witnessed at UNC since the 1960s. In 2004 the John William Pope Foundation entered into talks with the university about making a large donation to the school's endowment. Though the Pope Foundation did not offer specific recommendations for the gift, UNC administrators, apparently in an effort to please the donors, suggested funding for creation of a program in Western civilization. What followed was ultimately two years of angry recriminations, mostly from UNC faculty and students, in an effort to reject any monies from this particular foundation. The problem, in the eyes of those who opposed the gift, was the politically conservative causes the foundation supported, particularly those of the John William Pope Center for Higher Education Policy, which had been critical of the increasingly multicultural curriculum at UNC. The foundation's namesake, John William Pope, and his son Art Pope, who chaired the charitable organization, had been controversial figures with regard to the university in the last quarter of the twentieth century and often found their way onto the pages of the *Daily Tar Heel*.

Despite the paper's history of criticizing the Popes, in the case of the proposed gift in 2004, news coverage and editorials sought to sort out fact from fiction in the contentious debate, and more often than not supported the Pope Foun-

dation's role in the matter. Articles pointed out that the Pope Foundation and the Pope Center for Higher Education Policy were not one and the same (though the foundation financially supported the center). In addition, the concept of a program in Western civilization had been developed by university administrators and approved by a small committee of faculty, not by the foundation or the Popes themselves. Nor did the Popes ever suggest or imply that they would have control over elements of the curriculum or faculty hires, a charge frequently leveled by opponents. A November 2004 editorial argued that "this funding proposal should be no cause for consternation," as it was "not an attempt by the foundation to buy itself a major role in University decision-making and to gain some control of the curriculum." The editorial continued by suggesting that "UNC has shown that it doesn't bend easily to outside pressure, and students and faculty should have faith that the administrators won't let any outsiders run the show." Art Pope's daughter Joyce, a UNC freshman, wrote a letter to the editor shortly afterward, stating that she was "outraged that professors would seek to deprive the very students they are here to teach by encouraging the University to refuse the money and refusing to teach courses if the donation were accepted," adding that those opposed to the gift were "encouraging the kind of closed-minded thinking and ignorance they seem to pride themselves on being above." Ultimately the proposal was scrapped, and the Pope Foundation donated $2.3 million, including a $2 million endowment to support UNC's football program and $300,000 to "fund fellowship opportunities for undergraduates studying Western cultures."[11]

Discussions about issues of race and discrimination at UNC grew to include to the treatment of Muslims and those of Middle Eastern heritage in the wake of the terrorist attacks on September 11, 2001. The *Daily Tar Heel* was involved in two incidents on this topic in 2005 and 2006 that garnered national attention, and fueled debate over free speech and the limits of a free press. In September 2005, at the time of the fourth anniversary of the 9/11 attacks, columnist Jillian Bandes wrote about airport security in the United States. "I want all Arabs to be stripped naked and cavity-searched if they get within 100 yards of an airport," Bandes wrote, adding, "I want Arabs to get sexed up like nothing else" (an oblique reference to a comment made by conservative writer Ann Coulter about extensive airport body checks being akin to sexual intimacy). Protests poured into the *DTH*, particularly from American Muslim groups. Bandes ultimately was fired from the paper because of the column, but not for the reason most people assumed. Opinion editor Chris Coletta stated the dismissal was the result of "journalistic malpractice." "I fired her because she strung together quotes out of context ... [and

misled] sources when she conducted interviews," he explained. "Not because of her opinion." Bandes briefly became a darling of the national conservative news media, which took the opportunity to accuse the *Daily Tar Heel* and college press in general of extreme liberal bias.[12]

Five months later, in February 2006, another polarizing event put the *Daily Tar Heel* in the middle of national discussion about press limitations and responsibility. Editorial cartoonist Philip McFee drew a cartoon commenting on recent violence by Muslims incited by cartoons in a Danish publication that included a physical depiction of the prophet Mohammed, something strictly forbidden in Muslim culture. McFee's cartoon showed Mohammed standing between two mosque windows, one with a view of the Danish flag, and the other depicting a man with a machete in front of a burning building. "They may get me from my bad side," the caption read, "but they show me from my worst." Once again the *DTH* was assailed by those who were offended by the cartoon, including a sit-in at the paper's office organized by the UNC Muslim Students Association. Editor Ryan Tuck defended McFee and held his ground, issuing a statement that read in part: "I apologize to anyone personally offended by the image's publication, but I will not apologize that it was printed." Following the sit-in he elaborated: "Either political cartoons, indeed all aspects of a newspaper, are used as discussion sparkplugs, a force through which to challenge belief systems and standards, or as a PC [politically correct] entertainment medium. It can't change from one to the other willy-nilly." Three weeks after publication of the cartoon, recent UNC graduate Mohammed Reza Taheri-azar drove a rented SUV into the crowded Pit on campus, injuring several people. It was later suggested that Taheri-azar, who declared his allegiance with the 9/11 terrorists and wanted to avenge the treatment of Muslims in America, might have been angry in part over recent coverage of Muslims in the *Daily Tar Heel*.[13]

Several times since the paper became independent of university funding, the staff has initiated lawsuits against the UNC administration to gain access to information for news stories. The first lawsuit used the North Carolina Open Meetings Law to successfully argue that reporters should be allowed to attend all official university meetings and hearings other than those specifically exempt in the law. The suit grew out of a closed student honor court case involving the theft of copies of UNC's conservative publication, the *Carolina Review*. In the spring of 1996, the journal ran a cartoon on its cover showing candidate for student-body president Aaron Nelson as the devil, with horns and a pointy tail, holding a pitchfork. An article inside the issue charged Nelson with promoting "anti-Christian" policies. Nelson is Jewish, and the image in particular raised the specter of centuries-old stereotypes of Jews. The cover caused a great deal of controversy on campus regarding free speech versus hate speech, and the publication's faculty adviser, who had recommended against printing the cover, resigned. About 1,500 copies of the journal were stolen prior to distribution, and the court initiated disciplinary hearings against a number of students. The *Daily Tar Heel*, covering the story, attempted to attend the hearings, but was denied access. The paper retained the firm of attorney Hugh Stevens, coeditor of the *DTH* in 1964–65, and filed suit in Orange County Superior Court charging that the university was interfering with the paper's constitutional right to freedom of the press. A judge issued a temporary restraining order enjoining the honor court proceedings until a trial could be held. Although the *DTH* did not gain access to the honor court proceeding because the federal Family Educational Rights and Privacy Act (FERPA) protected the student's right to privacy, the action did lead to the N.C. Court of Appeals declaring that dozens of university bodies that had met for years without notice or adherence to other provisions of the law would now have to comply. A *DTH* editorial noted a year later that increased access to meetings and hearings allowed the paper's staff to obtain information that led to the publication of some thirty-nine stories.[14]

A second lawsuit grew out of a series of events starting in 2010 that became part of the biggest athletic scandal to hit the University of North Carolina since the Dixie Classic era of the early 1960s. Allegations surfaced that "improper benefits" were being given to UNC football players, and the NCAA opened an investigation. Most damning among the allegations were charges of academic fraud, tutors doing much of the players' work, and the regular enrollment of athletes in virtually non-existent independent studies courses in the African and Afro-American Studies Department. When the *Daily Tar Heel* joined seven other media outlets, including the Raleigh *News and Observer* and the Associated Press, in seeking access to public records in the case, the fallout was swift and loud. The intensity of the bombardment directed at the *DTH* by some members of the university community mirrored that which the paper received following criticism of the football program in the 1950s. Public editor Evan Rose acknowl-

Turn to **page 3** for news and **page 9** for SportsMonday coverage.

To mark Sexual Assault Awareness Month,
an editorial opinion from

The Daily Tar Heel

Volume 121, Issue 20   dailytarheel.com   Monday, April 1, 2013

RAPE IS A VIOLENT CRIME.

AT UNC AND COLLEGES ACROSS THE COUNTRY, IT IS TREATED AS AN INFRACTION.

Something so fundamentally wrong demands a principled solution.
This means undertaking a complete overhaul of the way the University deals with cases of rape. And it means forgetting for a moment the problematic requirements of federal guidelines, and instead creating a system that realizes the University's responsibility to protect its students. A culture of false justice lies at the heart of a broken system, and should be replaced with a focus on:

1. Support for survivors;
2. Education for all students on the consequences of rape;
3. Deference in the pursuit of justice to trained law enforcement.

For years, universities have played an inappropriate role in the aftermath of incidents of rape involving students. At UNC, the Honor Court, a quasi-judicial board made up entirely of students, heard and adjudicated cases of sexual assault until last year. Similar models were used across the country, becoming the object of intense scrutiny as to whether they could effectively deal with such a sensitive crime.

In 2011, the U.S. Department of Education issued what is popularly referred to as the "Dear Colleague" letter. The letter included a set of guidelines for making the ways colleges dealt with sexual assault compliant with Title IX of the Education Amendments of 1972, landmark legislation aimed at preventing sex discrimination. During the last two years, UNC and the rest of the nation's universities have implemented the changes demanded by the letter: lowering the standard of proof required to determine guilt in rape cases and the hiring of an individual to oversee the processes, among others.

Yet despite the changes, the University's updated procedures remain confusing, arbitrary and disturbing in the respective burdens they place on both students who file complaints and students who stand accused. Examples abound.

The very makeup of the Student Grievance Committee — the body charged with formally resolving complaints — is baffling. One-third of its members are students whose only qualifications are that they managed to be appointed by the student body president or the Graduate and Professional Student Federation president, individuals who are not elected on the pretense of expertise in the area of sexual assault.

The policy goes on to speak only in vague terms on the level of training given to a group with so much responsibility, leaving too much room for error to a group of amateur judges.

And the committee has at its disposal a number of punishments, ranging from a written warning to expulsion.

In short, changes to the system failed to correct the same kinds of heinous flaws that a group of current and former students has used as evidence in bringing two federal investigations to UNC.

The current system functions as a stopgap answer to the demands of the "Dear Colleague" letter. And while many have praised the document as a step in the right direction, the letter largely standardizes and codifies the trappings of a broken system. By taking steps like mandating a change in burden of proof, the letter further legitimizes the quasi-judicial bodies that have long suggested the possibility of justice for survivors but failed to provide it.

But, whatever its many shortcomings, the letter carries the weight of federal law, and the University has an obligation to comply with it. And yet this does not mean the University should feel as though its hands are tied in what it can change. The "Dear Colleague" letter is a complicated document, but its broader requirements are clear, and could be satisfied by a system that is narrower in scope, but better accomplishes its mission.

For example, the Title IX coordinator could be responsible for considering complaints of sexual assault, providing both sides the opportunity to present evidence and wielding only the corrective action that is in the best interest of immediate student safety. Meanwhile, this coordinator could also be responsible for working with law enforcement to seek justice. But reorienting the roles of administrators isn't enough to fix the problem of ineffective sexual assault policy.

Indeed, such a revised system would work only as part of a multi-dimensional approach — one that stresses greater education, sustained support and deference to law enforcement. These are the proper means for the University to help fight sexual assault, and they work hand-in-hand with each other. The University can make the often intimidating criminal justice system more manageable through counseling. By educating students about the criminal — rather than institutional — consequences of rape, the University can more effectively prevent it.

But why not allow the University to provide a separate avenue for survivors of rape to pursue resolution? Proponents of this approach, in place at UNC and across the country, argue that such systems are desirable because they cater to the special needs of college students. They allow for quicker resolution, more privacy and more support than the criminal justice system can give. And it's true that the criminal justice system is not known for its sensitivity in cases of rape, which are notoriously difficult to adjudicate — in a student hearing or a court of law.

But the fact remains that it is not the University's place to suggest it can systematically provide justice for victims of rape; a system that issues rulings, features various degrees of punishment and boasts a standard of proof implicitly makes that empty claim. Gentler treatment of sexual violence — for the victims and the perpetrators — is a form of discrimination in itself, because it treats the crime less seriously than other severe crimes.

Relieving ourselves of the expectation of adjudication does not mean turning our backs on victims of rape, and it does not mean denying those accused due process. It is simply a response that is both moral and sensible — an answer to the hard question of how to handle this problem across the country.

Those most capable of changing the policies of the University — its leadership — are making an honest effort to re-evaluate this system. They should not entirely dismiss wholehearted and comprehensive reform because it doesn't stick to a conventional reading of the "Dear Colleague" letter, especially given the Department of Education's tendency to work with, rather than punish, allegedly noncompliant colleges.

South Building should not let perceived legal complications stand in the way of its moral obligation and its ability to effect large-scale change. The University is a respected institution in public higher education. It can be a leader on this issue, but only if it is willing to call a crime a crime.

| INSIDE | 3 | A community member's call to speak out and a timeline of controversy | 7 | A rationale for the format of today's issue from editor Andy Thomason | 8 | An opinion page devoted to the issue of sexual assault at UNC |

Front page, April 1, 2013. The *Daily Tar Heel* continues its tradition of confronting significant social issues, including sexual violence. In terms of gender equality and sexual identity, the paper also supported same-sex marriage and opposed the infamous 2016 North Carolina House Bill 2 (HB2), which barred transgendered people from using public bathrooms and locker rooms corresponding to their gender identity. (DTH Media)

edged the withering criticism and tried to put the situation into context. "Many of you have decided the *DTH* editors need to rein in their ego, quit resume-building and repent for their betrayal of UNC," Rose wrote. "The emotions here are understandably complex. Many of us are students. Most of us love our University. And most of us desperately want our football team to kick ass." But, as Rose explained, the *Daily Tar Heel* is a "big boy" newspaper, which did not mean the paper always got it right, but it did mean the paper operated in the same sphere as the professional media companies also involved in the suit. "What's at stake is the free flow of information from an institution that, technically, belongs to you," he wrote. "Transparency is the medium of accountability."[15]

In 2012, after the *Daily Tar Heel* suit was successful, and as the wide-ranging damage from the scandal had become more apparent, editor Andy Thomason reflected in a column on what had happened:

On October 29, 2010, Butch Davis was still UNC's head football coach, Julius Nyang'oro was still head of the African and Afro-American Studies Department, and Holden Thorp was still the long-term chancellor. Those three men all saw their jobs claimed by the inevitable trickle of information, most of which emerged against the will of the University.... I don't think it's controversial to say that the University has done everything in its power to keep information about its shortcomings from reaching the public view. Like every organization, it believes it could function better if given total control of information.[16]

The scandal continued to grow in the mid-2010s, as allegations from several former players and an athletic tutor became public. After two internal university investigations were criticized for not being thorough enough, UNC System President Tom Ross and the new chancellor, Carol Folt, engaged former federal prosecutor Kenneth Wainstein to get to the bottom of issues regarded possible academic impropriety. Released in October of 2014, the Wainstein report revealed that between 1989 and 2011 approximately 3,100 students received what the *Daily Tar Heel* characterized as "irregular instruction in the Afro and African-American studies paper classes." According to Wainstein, a disproportionate number of those students were athletes, aided by a few faculty and administrators who were named in the report. The university administration went into crisis-management mode, and those named resigned or were fired.[17]

Fallout from the athletic scandal—including controversy over departmental cancellation of a class by history professor Jay Smith in 2017, who had coauthored a book on the subject with the principal whistleblower—caused the editorial staff to take stock of the situation in light of other recent issues, from the fight over Saunders Hall to handling of sexual assault cases to the privatization of the student bookstores in 2016. In April, after forty history department faculty members condemned cancellation of the class, the *Daily Tar Heel* editorial board addressed the matter in an editorial entitled "Administrators want to silence UNC's past, but our community must discuss it." "Many thought the academic-athletic scandal would be a topic of discussion for decades, but lately it seems the scandal has been pushed under the rug. A rug made, as are

many, by interwoven dollars," the board wrote. Citing cancellation of the class as emblematic of larger problems, the editorial wove together key struggles in both the sometimes difficult history of the university and of the *Daily Tar Heel* itself; freedom of speech, academic freedom, and the role of big-time sports at an institution of higher learning:

> UNC's image, the all-important brand, would be prioritized over teaching about deceit central to our recent past. As such, the University fails in its founding principles of lux, libertas—light and liberty—by shrouding the past in darkness. History professors took a stand for light to be cast on the issues, knowing that there might be consequences. The entire UNC community—faculty, staff, students, alumni, and otherwise—could learn a great deal from this example of leadership.
>
> Ultimately, the cancellation of Smith's class is just a moment in the larger academic-athletic scandal timeline. Acknowledgement of the University's unsavory past is essential to building an informed student body.[18]

While the mission of the venerable *Daily Tar Heel* remains true to the original 1893 vision of the student founders, its business model continued to evolve as it passed its 125th birthday. In 2010 the staff moved operations from the Frank Porter Graham Student Union, its home since 1968, off campus to a leased office building on Rosemary Street in downtown Chapel Hill. "The *Daily Tar Heel* will always be a campus fixture, no matter where its writers pound the keys," Ryan Tuck, editor in 2005–06, was quoted as saying at the time. "The *DTH* may be moving to a

new address, but I'm sure the soul of the place will not be going anywhere."[19]

In 2016, after five years of behind-the-scenes financial and administrative struggles, the student-majority board of what is now called DTH Media, Inc. brought on a new general manager, Betsy O'Donovan, to help chart a new course. O'Donovan began by issuing a public statement about the state of DTH Media, and laying out conceptually a direction to make the business model successful again and viable for the twenty-first century. Noting that the newspaper was facing its 125th anniversary potentially broke, O'Donovan declared that avoiding this fate and setting a new course would require "candor, collaboration, and creativity." Though it may be more than a century old, the *DTH* was facing the future "in start-up mode." "Community journalism—the act of putting questions to power, watchdogging, and sharing a community's knowledge and stories—is a fundamental civic activity," O'Donovan wrote. "It also takes a lot of time, or a lot of money, or sometimes both." To achieve these goals, O'Donovan asked for community donations (as DTH Media is organized as a nonprofit), and broadly outlined actions and new directions for the future. The *Daily Tar Heel* would stop publishing a print edition on Tuesdays to save costs, though digital content would continue to be provided. Classified (paid) ads for engagement announcements, weddings, anniversaries, and obituaries would be added, a first in *DTH* history. Expanded services would be offered, including "a creative services agency—a group of skilled, creative students led by an experienced agency director, offering graphic design, video, photography, social media, and sponsored content creation to the business

Coverage of the 2017 UNC Men's basketball NCAA championship.
(DTH Media)

> *This could last for a lifetime. We can talk about this for the rest of our lives.*
> **Brandon Robinson,** first-year guard

SPECIAL EDITION

Serving UNC students and the University community since 1893

The Daily Tar Heel

dailytarheel.com

 71 65

AT LAST, REDEMPTION

community at a range of rates, and with DTH excellence."[20]

Through all the technological and operational changes, through all the fights over freedom of speech and the press, through all the various controversies, the experience of working on the *Daily Tar Heel* has remained remarkably consistent at its core. As she left her year in office in April 2011, Sarah Frier, like so many editors before her, reflected on her time at the paper in a column entitled "The learning curve of the *DTH*." "The job means working constant hours and making decisions that draw merciless public scrutiny," she wrote. "It means feeling, sometimes, like you're graduating from the *Daily Tar Heel* and not from UNC." When asked why she invested so much of her college experience in the paper, Frier replied: "I do it for the questions that won't get answered unless we answer them. I do it for the momentum of each night, after midnight, after the paper has been sent to the printer and my managing editors and I talk about what we can tackle tomorrow. Most of all I do it for the people—about 56,000 people—who open each day a blue newspaper box or an Internet browser and read."[21]

At the time of the paper's 120th anniversary in February 2013, an editorial noted: "In the office of the *Daily Tar Heel*, newspapers are everywhere. Stacked in hastily arranged piles, mounted on the walls, or stowed away in tiny rolls of microfilm in the back of a cluttered storage room, they represent an ever-present record that compensates for the newspaper's necessarily deficient institutional memory." After a century-and-a-quarter, after growing in circulation a hundred-fold from about 500 to some 56,000 in both print and digital formats, after multiple attempts to silence its publication by those who opposed its editorial perspective, the *Daily Tar Heel* carries on its job of printing news and raising hell.[22]

ACKNOWLEDGMENTS

This book was a very complicated project on many levels, and I am indebted to several dozen people who assisted its progress along the way. The project began in April 2011, when the book was commissioned by DTH Media. The manuscript was completed in October 2013, but did not arrive at UNC Press for another three years. In a somewhat bizarre plot twist, the book became entangled in the financial and administrative struggles at DTH Media, written about briefly in the epilogue. I am deeply grateful to all of those who worked to see this published, and who helped to keep me calm during an extremely difficult and trying process.

The book is dedicated to Bill Friday, who was critically important in the very earliest stages of this project in terms of shaping its overall themes and direction. I was privileged to know him during the last fourteen years of his life, and we worked together on several projects along the way. It was an honor to know a man of his character and historical significance to the University of North Carolina and to the state.

After Bill, the most important person to thank is Ed Yoder. His assistance was invaluable in writing portions of chapters 3 and 4, but equally important, he became an advocate of the project early on, and remained a source of steadfast support over some six years. He pushed and prodded anyone who might move the book along—at times when no one else would—and served splendidly as a cheerful and sharp-eyed critic of the manuscript. There were times I was in despair over this book, but Ed was always there to bolster my spirits and rally the troops.

UNC Press, particularly in the persons of David Perry and Mark Simpson-Vos, made this book a reality. David believed in the project early on, and was a source of great support and a wonderful sounding board in the early stages. Mark took over when David retired, and went far beyond the call of duty in terms of sticking with the project as we wound our way through several years of legal issues. It would have been much easier, and understandable, if Mark had walked away. But he did not, and for that I am eternally grateful. Mark's persistence and guidance not only resulted in publication under the UNC Press imprint but also produced a far superior book. My thanks also to those at UNC Press who were part of this project, particularly Mark's able assistant, Jessica Newman, who cheerfully guided me along in the final stages (no small task).

As noted, DTH Media originally commissioned the book. I am grateful to Erica Perel, the only staff member there through the entire course of this project, for her assistance and support along the way. Betsy O'Donovan, who took over as executive director in mid-2016, understood the value of the manuscript to the future of the *Daily Tar Heel*, as well as to its past, and worked with me to see the book in print. It is my hope that the book will both help future students who work on the *Daily Tar Heel* to understand its rich history and context, and assist DTH Media in reinventing and strengthening its business model to assure that the paper is around for another 125 years.

Several longtime colleagues and friends played important roles in the creation of this book by keeping me sane and on track over this extended process. Carolyn Elfland, retired associate vice chancellor for campus services at UNC, spent long hours on the phone with me sorting out business and legal issues, and offering advice. Katie Otis and Anne Whisnant, dear friends and gifted colleagues of some twenty years from my graduate school days, are two of the kindest souls I know. A newer friend and colleague, Richard Harrill, director of the UNC Campus Y, provided boundless support as I worked through issues with this book while simultaneously working on a history project for the Y.

My family was along for the ride; by now they know my projects can get quite involved and take over my life for years at a time. It's difficult to put into words the significance of the support of my mother, Sharon Davis, and my two brothers, Michael and Eric. Both brothers are UNC alums, as am I, though they are much more rabid sports fans. Eric, now an attorney and North Carolina's state juvenile public defender, made useful suggestions regarding the legal issues I was navigating. Michael, now chair of the Department of Religious Studies at the University of Kansas, was a vital sounding board as a fellow academic and having published his first book with UNC Press. Michael's research and mine had never really intersected before, so it's been a rewarding experience that we've had common areas of interest on this book and his current book project.

I was very fortunate to have accomplished and sharp-eyed readers on earlier versions of the manuscript. Among those were Ed Yoder; John Sanders, retired director of the UNC School of Government; Jim Leloudis, professor of history, associate dean of honors, and my graduate and dissertation advisor and supporter of my professional career for some twenty years; and Wayne Hurder, editor of the *Daily Tar Heel* in 1968–69. All of these gentlemen took a great interest in the project, and helped in various ways to move it along when it became stalled. Wayne Hurder proved to be an invaluable source of information for chapter 4, and I must recount an amusing story about locating him. At the time I was living in Boylan Heights, an early-twentieth-century neighborhood on the western edge of downtown Raleigh. I wanted to interview Wayne for the book, and set about finding him. To my great surprise, he lived only four houses away, though we'd never met. Along with his phenomenal memory about events during the seminal period he was on the paper's staff, Wayne kept a treasure trove of papers of that period which proved invaluable to my research.

The staffs of both the Park and Wilson Libraries at UNC were critical in aiding my research. Stephanie Brown, director of the Park Library in the School of Media and Journalism, was a gem. She was particularly helpful in allowing my unfettered access to their bound volumes of the *DTH*, and to bringing to my attention other resources in their collection. For some two decades, on a variety of UNC history projects, I have had the privilege of working with folks in various parts of Special Collections in Wilson Library, particularly those connected with the North Carolina Collection. Special thanks go to Bob Anthony, Linda Jacobson, Jason Tomberlin, and Keith Longiotti for their assistance with this book.

DTH Media provided several professionals along the way to help in completing the manuscript. Melody Ivins came on near the end to help me do spot research for the epilogue, Katie Haywood edited an earlier version of the manuscript, and Katie Sweeney shot a number of images from back issues of the paper.

It is important to thank the two attorneys who took on the unusual task of sorting through the legal issues to get the book into the capable hands of UNC Press. Richard Vinegar got the ball rolling, and took actions and made a number of useful suggestions that were very valuable in moving the process forward. When he had done all he felt he could do, he suggested I might try to find an attorney more closely connected to UNC. This led me to Deborah Gerhardt, a professor in the UNC School of Law and an expert in copyright and intellectual property law. She proved to be exactly the right person with the right talents to "close the deal," and bring the long period of legal limbo to an end. I am very grateful to both Richard and Deborah, who gave generously of their time and skills to assist me.

Finally, I was able to interview a number of people associated with the *Daily Tar Heel* over the years. Some of these were formal taped interviews, and some were more informal "background" conversations. All proved critical to the book. There is no question that chapters 3, 4, and 5 are stronger because I was able to talk to people who were part of the events. Several other critical potential interviewees, stretching back into the 1930s and chapter 2, passed away only a few years before I began this project, which was an opportunity lost. My thanks to: Hugh Stevens, John Drescher, Jane Ross Hammer, Rolfe Neill, Ed Yoder, John Sanders, Sory (Kuralt) Bowers, Tom Lambeth, Mike Putzel, Jonathan Yardley, Michael Yopp, Wayne Hurder, Karen Parker, Bill Amlong, Jim Wallace, Todd Cohen, Keri (Kisa) Derochi, George Shadroui, Bill Cokas, Jessica Lanning, Peter Wallsten, Erica Perel, and Kevin Schwartz.

PHOTO CREDITS

Uncredited photos are from various issues of the *Tar Heel* and the *Daily Tar Heel*. All others are provided by one of the following sources.

Bill Cokas: courtesy of Bill Cokas, former cartoonist for the *Daily Tar Heel*.

DTH Media: courtesy of DTH Media Corp., publishing company of the *Daily Tar Heel* since 1993.

Hellenian: courtesy of the *Hellenian*, yearbook of the University of North Carolina at Chapel Hill, 1890–1900.

Wayne Hurder: courtesy of Wayne Hurder, former editor of the *Daily Tar Heel*.

Jock Lauterer: courtesy of Jock Lauterer, former photographer for the *Daily Tar Heel*.

NCC: courtesy of the North Carolina Collection, Louis Round Wilson Special Collections Library, University of North Carolina at Chapel Hill.

NCSU: courtesy of North Carolina State University Libraries, Special Collections Research Center, University Archives.

Schlesinger Library: courtesy of Schlesinger Library, Radcliffe Institute, Harvard University.

Jim Wallace: photograph by Jim Wallace, © J&J Wallace LLC.

WRAL-TV: courtesy of WRAL-TV, Raleigh, North Carolina.

Yack: courtesy of *Yackety-Yack*, yearbook of the University of North Carolina at Chapel Hill since 1901.

NOTES

ABBREVIATIONS

DTH
  Daily Tar Heel (1929 forward, with exceptions as noted)
Friday interview
  Author's two-part interview with William Friday, June 9 and September 6, 2011
SOHP
  Southern Oral History Program, Center for the Study of the American South, University of North Carolina at Chapel Hill
TH
  Tar Heel (1893–1929, 1941–46, 1952–53, and certain summer editions after 1963)
WB
  White and Blue
Yack
  Yackety Yack, yearbook of the University of North Carolina at Chapel Hill since 1901
Note: all of these university-related publications are now available in digitized format online, either directly through the Wilson Library website or by a link from that site. In addition, Wilson Library now also offers a headline archive for the *Daily Tar Heel*.

INTRODUCTION

1. Friday interview.

2. The origins of this quote, like many in journalism, are murky. Philip Graham, publisher of the *Washington Post* from 1946 to 1963, used it often and is sometimes given credit for it. But its roots go back at least to 1905. See Tony Pettinato, "Newspapers: The Rough Draft of History," posted October 4, 2010, on www.readex.com /blog/newspapers-rough-draft-history.

3. The origins of this quote are even murkier, but versions of it are in popular use today. For a more complete discussion of the university's academic structure and mission after 1875, see chapter 1.

CHAPTER 1

1. For history of the university during this era, see Archibald Henderson, *The Campus of the First State University* (Chapel Hill: University of North Carolina Press, 1949); Louis Round Wilson, *The University of North Carolina, 1900–1930: The Making of a Modern University* (Chapel Hill: University of North Carolina Press, 1957); and William S. Powell, *The First State University: A Pictorial History of the University of North Carolina*, 3rd ed. (Chapel Hill: University of North Carolina Press, 1992). This number of students and faculty was listed in the March 9, 1893, edition of the *Tar Heel*.

2. Ibid; the shower baths are described in the *TH*, September 25, 1893.

3. *TH*, February 23, 1893; Walter P. Fuller, "The Old Familiar Cycle," *University Magazine*, October 1913, 9.

4. James L. Leloudis, *Schooling the New South: Pedagogy, Self, and Society in North Carolina, 1880–1920* (Chapel Hill: University of North Carolina Press, 1996), chapter 2.

5. Ibid., 67.

6. For a more detailed history of this period in North Carolina, see Paul Escott, *Many Excel-*

lent People: Power and Privilege in North Carolina, 1850–1900 (Chapel Hill: University of North Carolina Press, 1989), chapter 10; David S. Cecelski and Timothy Tyson, editors, *Democracy Betrayed* (Chapel Hill: University of North Carolina Press, 1998); and William A. Link, *North Carolina: Change and Tradition in a Southern State* (Chapel Hill: University of North Carolina Press, 2010), chapter 12.

7. There is surprisingly little written about the history of college newspapers in the United States. For more on student publications at UNC, see the online exhibit *"Tar Heel* Ink," produced in 2005 by the North Carolina Collection (https://exhibits.lib.unc.edu/exhibits/show/ink).

8. Much of this history of the university press shop comes from Thomas A. Bowers, "The Origins of Journalism Education at UNC–Chapel Hill" (Gladys Hall Coates University History Lecture, UNC School of Journalism and Mass Communication, October 15, 2009), and Wilson, *University of North Carolina*, 19–20.

9. An example of a missed issue is one that would have been published May 8, 1898. The first issue to appear under Wolfe's editorship was October 14, 1919. Special YMCA issues were published June 18, 1903, March 3, 1907, and February 4, 1909. The state newspaper convention issue was published on December 9, 1916.

10. *TH*, September 15, 1916; Fuller, "Old Familiar Cycle," 9, 14–15. The first photograph to appear was of a rendering of the new Alumni Building, on October 18, 1901.

11. *TH*, March 28, 1907; May 13, 1916; Fuller, "Old Familiar Cycle," 9.

12. *TH*, October 26, 1904; February 8, 1906; Jen Pilla, "The Ground Just Covered," *DTH* centennial edition, February 23, 1993, 3.

13. *TH*, October 4, 1906; January 31, 1907. Jen Pilla, "A Glimpse Back," *DTH* centennial edition, February 23, 1993, 5.

14. *TH*, February 23, 1918. For histories of early athletics at UNC, see Henderson, *Campus of the First State University*, 250–55; Wilson, *University of North Carolina*, 26–28 and 147–52; and Pamela Grundy, *Learning to Win: Sports, Education, and Social Change in Twentieth-Century North Carolina* (Chapel Hill, University of North Carolina Press, 2001), 13–23.

15. Ibid.

16. *TH*, November 9, 1897.

17. Leloudis, *Schooling the New South*, 67–68; Grundy, *Learning to Win*, 4–7 and 12–18; Patrick Miller, "The Manly, the Moral and the Proficient: College Sport in the New South," in Patrick Miller, editor, *The Sporting World of the Modern South* (Urbana: University of Illinois Press, 2002), 17–51. For a detailed study of muscular Christianity and the YMCA, see Clifford Putney, *Muscular Christianity: Manhood and Sports in Protestant America, 1880–1920* (Cambridge: Harvard University Press, 2001).

18. "The Discoverer of Carolinium: Dr. Baskerville the Only American Who Ever Found an Element," *New York Times*, May 22, 1904; Wilson, *University of North Carolina*, 27–28.

19. *TH*, March 30, 1893; Wilson, *University of North Carolina*, 27 and 147–48.

20. *TH*, September 25, 1893.

21. *TH*, September 27, 1894; March 14,1895; February 22, April 18, May 2, and September 19, 1896.

22. *TH*, September 19, 1896.

23. According to Bob Quincy, *They Made the Bell Tower Chime* (Chapel Hill: Published by Orville Campbell, 1973), football legend John Heisman credited Carolina with the first use of

the forward pass in 1895. Apparently Heisman, who was head coach at what is now Auburn University in Alabama, was in attendance at the game. It was not a legal play at the time. Wilson, *University of North Carolina*, 147.

24. *TH*, October 4, 1902; September 29 and November 30, 1905; Wilson, *University of North Carolina*, 147–48. On Roosevelt and football, see John J. Miller, *The Big Scrum: How Teddy Roosevelt Saved Football* (New York: Harper Collins, 2011).

25. *TH*, February 1, 1906.

26. *TH*, November 19, 1908; November 27, 1909; Wilson, *University of North Carolina*, 148–50.

27. *TH*, December 18, 1912; February 21, 1919.

28. *WB*, March 8, 1894.

29. On the Dialectic and Philanthropic Societies during this period, see Albert Coates and Gladys Hall Coates, *The Story of Student Government in the University of North Carolina at Chapel Hill* (Chapel Hill: Albert Coates and Gladys Hall Coates, 1985), 105–15; and Leloudis, *Schooling the New South*, 66–67.

30. *TH*, March 2, 1894; *WB*, March 8, 1894. See also Fuller, "Old Familiar Cycle," 11–14; and Wilson, *University of North Carolina*, 25.

31. Wilson, *University of North Carolina*, 21–25; Leloudis, *Schooling the New South*, 60; *WB*, May 25, 1894.

32. *WB*, March 15, 1894.

33. Fuller, "Old Familiar Cycle," 13; *WB*, September 14 and 21, 1894.

34. *WB*, January 19, 1895.

35. *TH*, March 2, 1894.

36. *TH*, February 6, 1908.

37. *TH*, June 18, 1903; March 7, 1907; January 14, 1909.

38. See note 17; Henderson, *Campus of the First State University*, 250–52; Wilson, *University of North Carolina*, 161.

39. *TH*, January 11, 1898; Wilson, *University of North Carolina*, 28. For more on the early history of basketball at UNC, see Adam Powell, *University of North Carolina Basketball* (Charleston, S.C.: Arcadia Publishing, 2005); and Adam Lucas, *Carolina Basketball: A Century of Excellence* (Chapel Hill: University of North Carolina Press, 2010).

40. *TH*, April 25 and September 9, 1896; *Hellenian*, 1898, 152 and 165; "Louisvillian had starring role in basketball's birth," *Louisville Courier-Journal*, November 30, 2006; *The Alumni Review* 29, no. 7 (April 1941): 224. According to the 2006 article, Mechling moved to Louisville to complete his medical training at the Hospital College of Medicine, and also served as director of physical education at the Louisville YMCA.

41. *TH*, November 1 and 16, 1898; February 8, 1899; December 5, 1901; January 24 and February 14, 1903; Wilson, *University of North Carolina*, 28.

42. *TH*, February 25, 1904; January 8, 1905; Kenneth Joel Zogry, "The Forgettable Memorial," *Carolina Alumni Review* 102, no. 1 (January/February 2013): 36–45.

43. *TH*, January 30 and October 15, 1908.

44. *TH*, February 25, 1904; October 11, 1906. The first article about hazing actually appeared in 1896, when the paper ran a front-page story reprinting verbatim the text of an anti-hazing resolution passed by the sophomore class. But the story ran without commentary, and the real editorial campaign against the practice didn't begin in earnest until 1904.

45. *TH*, September 27, October 4 and 11, 1906.

46. *TH*, October 15, 1910; Coates and Coates, *Story of Student Government*, 106.

47. *TH*, September 26, October 10, and November 17, 1907; April 2, 1908.

48. *TH*, April 26 and 30, 1908; March 2, 1910. This 1908 incident is puzzling. All other sources agree that the election of editors was conducted only within the membership of the Athletic Association until the establishment of the Publications Union Board in 1923, which made the *Tar Heel* an official student and university publication.

49. *TH*, March 13, 1912.

50. *TH*, September 18, October 3, 10, and 16, 1912; March 20, 1913.

51. Ed Yoder, who was a student of Russell's and would himself become editor of the *DTH* in 1955–56, recounts the story of Russell's meeting with Venable in a 1963 newspaper column reprinted in his book, *The Night of the Old South Ball, and Other Essays and Fables* (Oxford, Miss.: Yoknapatawpha Press, 1984), 47.

52. *TH*, April 9 and 16, 1910. For a more complete account of the establishment of student government at UNC, see Coates and Coates, *Story of Student Government*, chapter 4.

53. *TH*, May 11, 1893; April 6, 1894.

54. *TH*, December 18, 1909; October 4 and 6, 1910.

55. *TH*, September 17, 1914; Albert Coates, *Edward Kidder Graham, Harry Woodburn Chase, Frank Porter Graham: Three Men in the Transition of the University of North Carolina at Chapel Hill from a Small College to a Great University* (Chapel Hill: Albert Coates, 1988), 1–27.

56. *TH*, January 21, 1909; February 12, March 25, and November 18, 1915.

57. *TH*, October 9, 1913; Wilson, *University of North Carolina*, 220–21, 464.

58. *TH*, February 16, 1914.

59. *TH*, October 16 and November 13, 1913; October 1 and 15, 1914; Daniel Joseph Singal, *The War Within: From Victorian to Modernist Thought in the South, 1919–1945* (Chapel Hill: University of North Carolina Press, 1982), 120.

60. Singal, *War Within*, 120; *TH*, October 2, 1913. The work of Eugene Branson has not yet been thoroughly studied, and contemporary academics are dismissive of his views on race, suggesting he fits into the paternalistic mold of white supremacists of the era. Daniel Singal characterizes him as "a gentle soul who kept clear of controversy and paid careful obeisance to southern tradition," and quotes Howard Odum as describing him as "a fine stimulator and progressive spirit . . . but withal an unreconstructed southerner of noble mien." Branson was involved with the Committee on Interracial Cooperation, formed after World War I, the work of which historian Charles Holden notes "appears cautious to us now," yet "broke new ground" in certain respects regarding race. See Charles J. Holden, *The New Southern University: Academic Freedom and Liberals at UNC* (Lexington: University Press of Kentucky, 2012), 28–29.

Certainly Branson has suffered historically in comparison to those that followed him at UNC starting in the 1920s, including Howard Odum, who challenged the boundaries of race in the South in various ways (discussed in chapter 2). However, the coverage he received in the *Tar Heel*, the conference he organized on lynching, and the clear effect he had on students at the campus YMCA—who began sanitation surveys in African American communities and started the Negro Night Schools—suggests there is more to be uncovered and understood. Notably the re-search for this book suggests that Branson was a major influence on the young Frank Porter Graham's views on race, which were to be called radical beginning in the late 1920s. We need not broadly brush Branson himself as either entirely paternalistic or radical on this issue; it does seem evident, however, that he served as something of a bridge in the evolution of white southern atti-tudes on race, certainly at the university.

61. *TH*, February 7, 1897; Anna Griffin, "Women and the *Tar Heel*: From Discrimination to Equality," *DTH* centennial edition, 6.

62. *TH*, March 14, 1923; Wilson, *University of North Carolina*, 379–80.

63. *TH*, March 20, 1923; Wilson, *University of North Carolina*, 380–81.

64. *TH*, October 2, 1893.

65. *TH*, November 8, 1894; March 7, 1895; Feb-ruary 7, 1899; November 5, 1910.

66. *TH*, February 22, 1896; April 1, 1911; Octo-ber 25, 1921.

67. *TH*, February 12, 1916.

68. *TH*, October 14, 1916; October 6, 1917; Holden, *New Southern University*, 29–30; Warren Ashby, *Frank Porter Graham: A Southern Liberal* (Chapel Hill: University of North Carolina Press, 1980), 36.

69. Glenn Hutchinson, "Carolina Goes to War," *Carolina Magazine* 67, no. 3 (December 1937): 3–4.

70. *TH*, February 3 and April 16, 1917.

71. *TH*, April 6 and 21, 1917; October 9, 1918; Hutchinson, "Carolina Goes to War," 5.

72. Hutchinson, "Carolina Goes to War," 5, 6.

73. Ibid.; *TH*, October 9, 16, and 23, 1918; Jen Pilla, "*Tar Heel* Editors," *DTH* centennial edi-tion, February 23, 1993, 10. For more on UNC and World War I, see David Brown, "The Darkness Over There," *Carolina Alumni Review* 104, no. 1 (January/February 2015): 38–47.

74. *TH*, October 30, 1918.

75. *TH*, September 30, 1898; see note 47.

76. *TH*, March 2, 1910; April 10, 1913.

77. Pilla, "*Tar Heel* Editors," 10.

78. *TH*, March 23, 1918; February 4, 1919. For a bibliography of books and articles by and about Thomas Wolfe, see www.nchistoricsites.org /wolfe/bibliography.htm.

79. *TH*, May 30, June 14, and November 18, 1919; March 13 and April 16, 1920.

80. *TH*, December 13, 1919.

81. Henderson, *Campus of the First State Uni-versity*, 368–69; Catherine W. Bishir et al., *Archi-tects and Builders in North Carolina: A History of the Practice of Building* (Chapel Hill: Univer-sity of North Carolina Press, 1990), 237, 299. See epilogue for a discussion of the criticism of the names of these buildings in the late 20th and early 21st centuries.

82. *TH*, January 23, 1920.

83. Richard Walser, "Editor Who Threw Out the Ads," *The State*, no. 39 (January 1, 1972), 13–14.

84. *TH*, September 25, October 5 and 20, 1920; January 7 and 18, and December 13, 1921.

CHAPTER 2

1. For more on the administration establishing control over athletics in the early twentieth cen-tury, see Louis Round Wilson, *The University of North Carolina, 1900–1930: The Making of a Mod-ern University* (Chapel Hill: University of North Carolina Press, 1957), 147–52.

2. *TH*, December 13, 1921; May 4, 11, 15, and June 13, 1923; January 8 and October 15, 1924.

3. *TH*, March 2, 1894, December 9, 1916; November 8, 1931. For more on Edward Kidder Graham's promotion of journalism and the Preston Cup, see Tom Bowers, *Making News: One Hundred Years of Journalism & Mass Communication at Carolina* (Chapel Hill: UNC School of Journalism and Mass Communications, 2009), 1–12.

4. *TH*, December 2 and 9, 1916; Bowers, *Making News*, 15–17.

5. *TH*, January 18 and February 8, 1921.

6. *TH*, January 20, 1922; Bowers, *Making News*, 10, 22.

7. *TH*, September 25, 1923.

8. Tom Bowers covers the careers of Coffin, Phillips, and Spearman in the School of Journalism fairly extensively in various sections of *Making News*.

9. Much of the information on Chase in this section comes from Albert Coates, *Edward Kidder Graham, Harry Woodburn Chase, Frank Porter Graham: Three Men in the Transition of The University of North Carolina at Chapel Hill from a Small College to a Great University* (Chapel Hill: Albert Coates, 1988), 25–51; Charles Holden, *The New Southern University: Academic Freedom and Liberalism at UNC* (Lexington: University Press of Kentucky, 2012), 1–72; and Kenneth Joel Zogry and David Brown, "Harry Who?," *Carolina Alumni Review* 103, no. 5 (September/October 2014): 20–33.

10. See note 9. Chase received surprisingly little coverage in the *Tar Heel* until 1922, and the first editorial supporting his actions as president did not appear until March 25, 1924.

11. *TH*, October 5, 1920.

12. Coates, *Edward Kidder Graham, Harry Woodburn Chase, Frank Porter Graham*, 36–37; Wilson, *University of North Carolina, 1900–1930*, 378–82; *TH*, January 24, 1922.

13. *DTH*, March 30, 1929.

14. *TH*, January 24, 1919; September 19, 1923; October 13 and 18, 1927; March 31, April 3, and 5, 1928; *DTH*, December 10, 11, and 15, 1929; January 10, 28, 29 and February 2, 1930; Kenneth Joel Zogry, "The Forgettable Memorial," *Carolina Alumni Review* 102, no. 1 (January/February 2013): 36–45.

15. *TH*, March 28, 1924; William A. Link, *North Carolina: Change and Tradition in a Southern State* (Chapel Hill: University of North Carolina Press, 2010), 342.

16. Daniel Singal, *The War Within: From Victorian to Modernist Thought in the South, 1919–1945* (Chapel Hill: University of North Carolina Press: 1982), 115–52; Holden, *New Southern University*, 1–72; Zogry and Brown, "Harry Who?," 20–33.

17. Singal, *War Within*, 119, 265–338.

18. *TH*, September 20, 1924.

19. Willard B. Gatewood Jr., "Professors, Fundamentalists, and the Legislature," in *The North Carolina Experience: An Interpretive and Documentary History*, ed. Lindley S. Butler and Alan D. Watson (Chapel Hill: University of North Carolina Press, 1984), 356–74; Holden, *New Southern University*, 8–12.

20. *TH*, February 14, 1925.

21. *TH*, February 21, 1925. Poole introduced an even more extreme version of his bill in 1927, which forbade the teaching of any theory that was anti-Biblical in the state's public schools, but it was defeated in committee. For a more complete history of the antievolution controversy in

North Carolina during the 1920s, see Willard B. Gatewood Jr., *Preachers, Pedagogues, and Politicians: The Evolution Debate in North Carolina, 1920–1927* (Chapel Hill: University of North Carolina Press, 1966); and John W. Wertheimer, *Law and Society in the South: A History of North Carolina Court Cases* (Lexington: University Press of Kentucky, 2009), chapter 4.

22. *TH*, September 26, 1922; May 13, 1924.

23. *TH*, October 24, 1923; February 29, March 1 and 29, April 19, October 25 and 27, and November 8, 1928.

24. See note 8; *DTH*, October 4, 1927; October 30, 1928.

25. *TH*, January 3 and 11, 1929.

26. *TH*, December 8, 1928; January 15, 17, and 22, and February 5, 7, and 9, 1929.

27. "Style Book of the *Daily Tar Heel*: University of North Carolina" (1932). A copy of the pamphlet is in the collection of Park Library, UNC School of Journalism and Mass Communication, Chapel Hill.

28. Ibid., 1–2, 4.

29. *DTH*, October 2 and 27, and November 20, 1932.

30. 1938 *Yack*, 197.

31. *TH*, October 4, 1928.

32. Ibid.

33. Holden, *New Southern University*, 52; Bart Dredge, "Defending White Supremacy: David Clark and the *Southern Textile Bulletin*, 1911 to 1955," *North Carolina Historical Review* 89, no. 1 (January 2012): 59–91; Hugh D. Hindman, "Child Labor in American Textiles," in *The World of Child Labor: An Historical and Regional Study*, ed. Hugh D. Hindman (Armonk, NY: M. E. Sharpe, 2009), 475.

34. Holden, *New South University*, 49–56.

35. *DTH*, April 20, 23, and 30, 1929.

36. *DTH*, May 14, 1929; the story is also recounted in "Digging Up Naughty Nostalgia," *DTH*, January 17, 1974.

37. *DTH*, May 16 and 18, 1929.

38. *DTH*, November 6, 1929.

39. *DTH*, December 13, 1929.

40. *DTH*, November 5, 1929.

41. *DTH*, December 11 and 12, 1929; January 25, 1930.

42. *DTH*, January 10, 1930; David Clark and Charles W. Eagles, "David Clark," *Dictionary of North Carolina Biography*, ed. William S. Powell (Chapel Hill: University of North Carolina Press, 1979), vol. 1, A–C, 373; Holden, *New South University*, 72; Dredge, "Defending White Supremacy," 74.

43. *DTH*, January 18, 1930.

44. *DTH*, January 17, 1930.

45. *DTH*, January 26, 1930.

46. *DTH*, October 12, 20, and 30, and November 3, 1929.

47. *DTH*, January 12 and February 21, 1930; Holden, *New Southern University*, 54–72.

48. *DTH*, March 4 and 11, 1930; November 11, 1931; Holden, *The New South University*, 75–85.

49. For biographies of Frank Porter Graham, see Warren Ashby, *Frank Porter Graham, a Southern Liberal* (Winston-Salem, N.C.: J. F. Blair, 1980); John Ehle, *Dr. Frank: Life with Frank Porter Graham* (Chapel Hill: Franklin Street Books, 1994); and Coates, *Edward Kidder Graham, Harry Woodburn Chase, Frank Porter Graham*, 53–73.

50. Transcription of interview with Philip Hammer, conducted by Bruce Kalk, June 7, 1991, L-55, SOHP, 7–8, 52, 53.

51. *DTH*, January 27, March 18 and 19, 1933.

52. *DTH*, November 5 and 6, 1932. For more on the Tatum petition, see Holden, *New South University*, 126–28.

53. *DTH*, November 13, 1933; Don Shoemaker, "A Look into Davie Clark's Locker: The Era of Ruck-Making," *Carolina Magazine*, vol. 63, no. 4 (November 19, 1933): 4–5.

54. 1936 *Yack*, 361–65. For more on the Graham Plan, see Pamela Grundy, *Learning to Win: Sports, Education, and Social Change in Twentieth-Century North Carolina* (Chapel Hill, University of North Carolina Press, 2001), 107–18.

55. *DTH*, February 4, 1936.

56. 1936 *Yack*, 366; *DTH*, October 27, and November 3, 1937; Charles A. Poe, "Kick Graham Out! Nominating the Logical Man to Succeed Him," *Carolina Magazine* 65, no. 6 (March 1936): 3.

57. For more on the expansion of campus as a result of PWA projects, see Archibald Henderson, *The Campus of the First State University* (Chapel Hill: University of North Carolina Press, 1949), 292–94. A map of the expansion appeared in the *DTH* on January 15, 1939.

58. *DTH*, October 29, 1931; September 23, 1932.

59. *DTH*, September 24, 1932.

60. *DTH*, March 1, 1933.

61. *DTH*, May 7, 11, 13, 16, and 24, 1935; Holden, *New South University*, 134–35; Dredge, "Defending White Supremacy," 73–75.

62. *DTH*, September 19 and October 10, 1937; Charles J. Holden, "'A Various Course and a Wide Meaning': Academic Freedom and the Carolina Political Union, 1936–1941," *North Carolina Historical Review* 76, no. 3 (July 1999): 294–96.

63. *DTH*, December 4 and 5, 1938.

64. Langston Hughes, "Christ in Alabama," *Contempo*, December 1, 1931; *DTH*, November 21, 1931; Holden, *New Southern University*, 122–25; Dredge, "Defending White Supremacy," 81–88.

65. *DTH*, December 2, 1931; Hammer interview, SOHP, 28.

66. *DTH*, March 30, 1932.

67. *DTH*, October 23, 1932; February 11 and March 17, 1933.

68. *DTH*, December 10, 1929; March 2 and 15, 1933; 1935 *Yack*.

69. *DTH*, November 2, 1932; March 28, 1933; February 20, 1936; Hammer interview, SOHP, 27.

70. *DTH*, March 18, 23, and 28, 1933. For more in-depth analysis of efforts to desegregate the university, see Neal Cheek, "An Historical Study of the Administrative Actions in the Racial Desegregation of the University of North Carolina at Chapel Hill, 1930–1955" (Ph.D. diss., University of North Carolina at Chapel Hill, 1973); and John K. (Yonni) Chapman, "Black Freedom and the University of North Carolina, 1793–1960" (Ph.D. diss., University of North Carolina at Chapel Hill, 2006).

71. *DTH*, October 30, 1932. For more on the history of Jews at UNC, see online exhibit "The Carolina Story: A Virtual Museum of University History," www.museum.unc.edu/exhibits/jewish life/.

72. *DTH*, October 30, 1932; September 30, 1933.

73. *DTH*, September 30, 1933. For more on Krasny and Manning, see the online exhibits: "The Carolina Story," www.museum.unc.edu /exhibits/jewishlife/morris-krasny; and "Down Home: Jewish Life in North Carolina," www.sites .duke.edu/downhome/obstacles-to-learning-3/.

74. *DTH*, January 5, 1939. Holden, *New Southern University*, 108–12. For a bibliography of Pauli Murray's writings, as well as historical writing

about her, see the website of the Pauli Murray Project, www.paulimurrayproject.org.

75. *DTH*, January 5, 6, 8, and 10, 1939.

76. *DTH*, January 5 and 11, 1939.

77. Kenneth Mack, *Representing the Race: The Creation of the Civil Rights Lawyer* (Cambridge, Mass.: Harvard University Press, 2012), 217–19.

78. Hammer interview, SOHP, 27–28; *DTH*, February 12, 1935.

79. Hammer interview, SOHP, 38; 1936 *Yack*, 356.

80. 1936 *Yack*, 175 and 356–59.

81. Hammer interview, SOHP, 41–44. *DTH*, February 1, 1936.

82. Ibid.

83. *DTH*, February 1, 1936; 1936 *Yack*, 361–62.

84. Hammer interview, SOHP, 39; *DTH*, February 1, 1936.

85. *DTH*, February 2, 1936.

86. *DTH*, February 4, 1936; 1936 *Yack*, 175.

87. "Honor in Carolina," *Time* magazine, February 10, 1936, 38; 1936 *Yack*, 362 and 365.

88. 1936 *Yack*, 366; Hammer interview, SOHP, 48.

89. *TH*, January 17, 1925. For more on the history of humor magazines at UNC, see the humor section of the NCC's online exhibit, *Tar Heel Ink* (2005), http://www.lib.unc.edu/ncc/thi/humor .html.

90. *TH*, October 23 and January 26, 1923; February 8, 1924.

91. *TH*, February 11, 1926; November 24, 1928.

92. Hammer Interview, SOHP; *DTH*, January 15, 1932, and December 23, 1934. The 1934 article notes the name is Arabic, meaning "small coffee cup without a handle."

93. *DTH*, November 9, 1939.

94. *DTH*, November 11, 1939.

95. Ibid.

96. *DTH*, November 12, 1939.

97. *DTH*, November 14, 1939.

98. *DTH*, November 15, 1939; 1940 *Yack*, 211.

99. *DTH*, September 27 and October 4, 1940; January 13, 1942; *Tar Heel Ink* (2005), http://www .lib.unc.edu/ncc/thi/humor.html.

100. *DTH*, January 21, 1928; November 23, 1932.

101. *DTH*, January 9, 1930. For more on the antiwar movement at UNC, see Charles J. Holden, "'Patriotism Does Not Mean Stupidity': Student Antiwar Activism at UNC in the 1930s," *North Carolina Historical Review* 75, no. 1 (January 2008): 29–56. For a more detailed discussion of the ASU and the Communist Party, see Robert Cohen, *When the Old Left Was Young: Student Radicals and America's First Mass Student Movement, 1929–1941* (New York: Oxford University Press, 1993).

102. Holden, "'Patriotism Does Not Mean Stupidity,'" 38; 1936 *Yack*, 336.

103. *DTH*, September 22, 1939.

104. *DTH*, May 17 to 22, 1940.

105. *DTH*, May 23 and 25, 1940; Holden, "'Patriotism Does Not Mean Stupidity,'" 51–52.

106. *DTH*, September 28, October 15 to 17, 1940; Holden, "'Patriotism Does Not Mean Stupidity,'" 54.

107. *DTH*, November 2, 1940; 1941 *Yack*, 206.

108. Dick Friedman, "Pollster Lou Harris Feels the Adrenaline Flowing as the Campaign Tests His Predictions Again," *People*, February 2, 1976, retrieved online at www.people.com/archive /pollster-lou-harris-feels-the-adrenaline -flowing-as-the-campaign-tests-his-predictions -again-vol-5-no-4/.

CHAPTER 3

1. *DTH*, December 7, 1947.

2. *DTH*, January 14, 1942.

3. *TH*, May 30, 1944.

4. Tom Bowers, *Making News: One Hundred Years of Journalism & Mass Communication at Carolina* (Chapel Hill: UNC School of Journalism and Mass Communications, 2009), 42.

5. A photograph of the Roosevelt letter appeared in the paper on June 24, 1944, and again on August 14, 1945.

6. *DTH*, February 3 and 28, and April 7 and 8, 1942. For more on the Navy Pre-Flight School and UNC during World War II, see Mary Layne Baker, "The Sky's the Limit: The University of North Carolina and the Chapel Hill Communities' Response to the Establishment of the U.S. Naval Pre-Flight School During World War II" (M.A. thesis, Department of History, University of North Carolina at Chapel Hill, 1980); and David E. Brown, "The War Years," *Carolina Alumni Review* 84, no. 5 (September/October 1995): 65–101.

7. *DTH*, January 22, 1942.

8. *DTH*, May 14 to 18, 1943.

9. *DTH*, May 12, 1943; *TH*, May 20, 1943; September 3, 1944; February 5, 1946; 1943 *Yack*, 186.

10. *DTH*, July 14, 1942.

11. Roland Parker to Bob Hoke, July 20, 1942, copy, Frank Porter Graham President's Records, Consolidated UNC Campus Files (UNC-CH: Student Affairs), University Archives, Wilson Library, University of North Carolina at Chapel Hill.

12. Katherine Hill to Robert House, October 23, 1942, Robert Burton House Records, Student Organizations and Activities: *Daily Tar Heel* 1933–1955 file, University Archives, Wilson Library, University of North Carolina at Chapel Hill.

13. *TH*, April 1, 1942.

14. 1944 *Yack*, 138–39.

15. John Thomas Kerr III to Publications Union Board, July 11, 1944, copy, Robert House *DTH* files.

16. 1945 *Yack*, 134–35.

17. *DTH*, January 13, 1952; Brown, "The War Years," 97–101.

18. *DTH*, September 25, 1947; 1947 *Yack*, 198–99; 1948 *Yack*, 321–22.

19. *DTH*, October 17, 1947.

20. Author's three-part interview with Rolfe Neill, July 25 and 31, and August 17, 2012.

21. *DTH*, October 24, 1952; Neill interview.

22. *DTH*, November 6 and 13, 1949; 1950 *Yack*, 439.

23. *DTH*, September 21 and October 13, 1950; March 21, 29, and April 3 to 11, 1951; Neill interview.

24. *DTH*, April 12 and 27, and May 1, 1951.

25. Charles Kuralt, *A Life on the Road* (New York: Putman, 1990), 1–2; Neill interview.

26. Kuralt, *Life on the Road*, 15; author's interview with Sory (Kuralt) Bowers, August 10, 2012.

27. *DTH*, April 3, 1955.

28. 1955 *Yack*, 80–81.

29. *DTH*, November 12, 1949.

30. *DTH*, May 11, 1940; Gregory S. Taylor, *The History of the North Carolina Communist Party* (Columbia: University of South Carolina Press, 2009), 132–34, 157.

31. *DTH*, October 31 and November 1, 1947; Taylor, *North Carolina Communist Party*, 129–30. For a more complete biography of Scales, see Junius Scales and Richard Nickson, *Cause at Heart: A Former Communist Remembers* (Athens, Ga.: University of Georgia Press, 1987).

32. *DTH*, November 2, 1947.

33. *DTH*, November 20, 1954; November 5 and December 17, 1958; January 17, 1962; January 5, 1963; Taylor, *North Carolina Communist Party*, 199–201.

34. Taylor, *North Carolina Communist Party*, 173–80.

35. *DTH*, May 12, 1949.

36. Ibid.

37. *DTH*, May 14, 1949.

38. *DTH*, December 3, 1949; Taylor, *North Carolina Communist Party*, 181.

39. *DTH*, May 24 and 25, 1949; Taylor, *North Carolina Communist Party*, 182–83; Robert Justin Goldstein *Political Repression in Modern America: From 1870 to 1976* (Urbana: University of Illinois Press, 2001), 318; Paul Green, *A Southern Life: Letters of Paul Green, 1916–1981*, ed. Laurence G. Avery (Chapel Hill: University of North Carolina Press, 1994), 495–96.

40. *DTH*, January 11 and 12, 1949.

41. *DTH*, January 13, 1949; Taylor, *North Carolina Communist Party*, 168–69.

42. *DTH*, October 27, November 3, 20, and 30, and December 4, 1948; January 13, 1949.

43. *DTH*, December 4, 8, and 12, 1948.

44. *DTH*, April 19 and May 13, 1950.

45. Much has been written about this election. The most in-depth analysis can be found in Julian M. Pleasants and Augustus M. Burns III, *Frank Porter Graham and the 1950 Senate Race in North Carolina* (Chapel Hill: University of North Carolina Press, 1990).

46. *DTH*, May 17, 18, and 25, 1950.

47. William A. Link, *William Friday: Power, Purpose, & American Higher Education* (Chapel Hill: University of North Carolina Press, 1995), 73–75; author's two-part interview with Edwin M. Yoder, July 9 and 22, 2012.

48. *DTH*, December 10, 1950; April 21, 1954; Link, *William Friday*, 79; Neill interview; Yoder interview.

49. *DTH*, February 12, 1952.

50. *DTH*, February 14 and 22, 1952.

51. *DTH*, May 8, 11, 12, and 19, 1954.

52. *DTH*, April 1, 1954.

53. Neill interview; Yoder interview; Jon Elliston, "Charles Kuralt's FBI File," *Creative Loafing Charlotte* website, December 5, 2002: www .clclt.com/charlotte/charles-kuralts-fbi-fle /Content?oid=2350156.

54. *DTH*, November 20, 1954; March 4 to 6, 1955.

55. *DTH*, March 5 and 7, 1955.

56. *DTH*, October 29, November 5, and December 18 to 19, 1958; January 6, 1959; *Letters of Paul Green*, 495–96.

57. *TH*, June 2, 1945; July 31, 1945.

58. *TH*, November 3, 1945.

59. *TH*, December 1, 1945.

60. Ibid.

61. *TH*, December 4 and 11, 1945.

62. *TH*, December 8, 1945.

63. *DTH*, October 19, 26 and 27, 1949.

64. *DTH*, October 29 and November 4, 1949.

65. *DTH*, March 25, 1950. Interestingly, Hazel Scott had performed in Memorial Hall in October 1948 without incident. It is not clear if the audience was all white, or if her tolerance of segregated audiences had changed by the time of her second appearance on campus. See *DTH*, October 28, 1948.

66. *DTH*, October 22 and 25, 1950.

67. *DTH*, October 28, 1950.

68. *DTH*, March 28, April 5, July 20 and September 23, 1951. For more in-depth analysis of efforts to desegregate the university, see Neal

Cheek, "An Historical Study of the Administrative Actions in the Racial Desegregation of the University of North Carolina at Chapel Hill, 1930–1955" (Ph.D. diss., University of North Carolina at Chapel Hill, 1973); and John K. (Yonni) Chapman, "Black Freedom and the University of North Carolina, 1793–1960" (Ph.D. diss., University of North Carolina at Chapel Hill, 2006).

69. *DTH*, September 27, 1951.

70. *DTH*, September 27 and 29, 1951.

71. *DTH*, September 28 and 29, 1951; Barry Farber, "Desegregating Kenan Stadium on Chapel Hill," in *American Students Organize: Founding the National Student Association after World War II*, ed. Eugene Schwartz (New York: American Council on Education/Praeger, 2006), 440–43.

72. Typescript copies of the letters, along with other materials, were bound together by the *Daily Tar Heel* staff in a small booklet dated March 20, 1952 and deposited in Wilson Library (now in the North Carolina Collection).

73. *DTH*, February 14 and 29, 1952.

74. *DTH*, March 1, 1952.

75. Ibid.

76. *DTH*, May 18 and October 5, 1954.

77. *DTH*, November 19 and 23, 1954.

78. *DTH*, February 24, 1955.

79. *DTH*, March 2, 1955.

80. *DTH*, February 26, 1955.

81. *DTH*, March 31, 1955; Bart Dredge, "Defending White Supremacy: David Clark and the *Southern Textile Bulletin*, 1911 to 1955," *North Carolina Historical Review* 89, no. 1 (January 2012): 59.

82. *DTH*, October 11 and November 28, 1956; February 6, September 21 and 24, 1957; October 2, 3, 4, and 8, 1958.

83. *DTH*, November 6, 1945; November 23, 1946. For popular histories of UNC football during this era, see Ken Rappoport, *Tar Heel: North Carolina Football* (Huntsville, Ala.: Strode Publishing, 1976); and Adam Powell, *University of North Carolina Football* (Charleston, S.C.: Arcadia Publishing, 2006).

84. Kenneth Joel Zogry, "William D. Carmichael III," in *The North Carolina Century: Tar Heels Who Made a Difference, 1900–2000*, ed. Howard Covington Jr. and Marion A. Ellis, 214–16 (Charlotte: Levine Museum of the New South/University of North Carolina Press, 2002); Link, *William Friday*, 66–71.

85. Zogry, "William D. Carmichael III," 214–16; Link, *William Friday*, 66–71.

86. 1948 *Yack*, 318, 323; 1949 *Yack*, 426; 1950 *Yack* 434, 439; Neill interview.

87. *DTH*, November 12 and 13, 1949.

88. *DTH*, November 12 and 15, 1949.

89. *DTH*, November 6, 1953.

90. *DTH*, November 7 and 13, 1953.

91. Yoder interview.

92. Yoder interview; *DTH*, February 23, 1968.

93. Ibid.

94. *DTH*, February 23, 1968; *Time Magazine*, August 3, 1959; Friday interview.

95. *DTH*, January 10, 1956.

96. Yoder interview, *DTH*, February 23, 1968.

97. Ibid.

98. Link, *William Friday*, chapters 1–3.

99. *DTH*, October 19, 1956; September 12 and 20, and October 13, 1957; Friday interview; Neill interview.

100. *DTH*, November 18, 30, and December 1 to 18, 1956; Link, *William Friday*, 98–102.

101. *DTH*, November 1, December 8 and 18, 1956.

102. *DTH*, December 14, 1956.

103. *DTH*, December 18, 1956.

104. *DTH*, January 16, 1957.

105. *DTH*, January 17, 1957.

106. *DTH*, February 14, 17, and 26, 1957; Fred Powledge to Robert House, February 15, 1957, and copy of Robert House reply to Fred Powledge, February 18, 1957, Robert House *DTH* files.

107. *DTH*, February 8, March 2, 3, 23, 24, and 26, and November 24, 1957. For more on the 1957 championship team, see Adam Lucas, *The Best Game Ever: How Frank McGuire's '57 Tar Heels Beat Wilt and Revolutionized College Basketball* (Guilford, Conn.: Lyons Press, 2011).

108. *DTH*, September 26, October 9, 10, 11, 15 to 23, 26, 27, and November 20, 1957.

109. *DTH*, October 29, November 1 and 20, 1957; author's interview with Jonathan Yardley, October 9, 2012; author's interview with Tom Lambeth, August 11, 2012. This was not the first time Bass was involved in a campus controversy. See "Bass involved in mess at his dorm, of which he was president," *DTH*, January 18, 1957.

110. *DTH*, November 1, 2, 5, and 14, 1957.

111. *DTH*, November 19, 23, and 24, 1957.

112. *DTH*, November 19 and 20, 1957. A copy of the leaflet is in the Student Organizations: *Daily Tar Heel* 1957–1962 file, Office of the Chancellor, William Brantley Aycock Records, University Archives, Wilson Library, University of North Carolina at Chapel Hill.

113. *DTH*, December 3, 1957.

CHAPTER 4

1. *DTH*, September 24, 1959; April 2, 1960.

2. *DTH*, April 2 and 22, September 16 and 20, October 2 and 7, and November 9 and 10, 1960; author's interview with Jonathan Yardley, October 9, 2012.

3. *DTH*, October 14, 1960; September 28 and October 13, 1961.

4. *DTH*, October 13, 1961; "Former UNC President William Friday Dies," October 12, 2012, WRAL.com, www.wral.com/former-unc -president-william-friday-dies/3281443.

5. *DTH*, January 18, 1957; Pamela Grundy, *Learning to Win: Sports, Education, and Social Change in Twentieth-Century North Carolina* (Chapel Hill, University of North Carolina Press, 2001), 196–97, 200, 204; William A. Link, *William Friday: Power, Purpose, and American Higher Education* (Chapel Hill: University of North Carolina Press, 1995), 105.

6. *DTH*, January 10 and 11, February 15, March 19, and April 28 to 30, 1961; Link, *William Friday*, 102–3.

7. *DTH*, April 29, May 5 and 6, 1961.

8. *DTH*, May 9, 1961.

9. *DTH*, May 4 and 18, 1961; Link, *William Friday*, 103–4.

10. *DTH*, September 19, 1961; Link, *William Friday*, 102, 104–5; Grundy, *Learning to Win*, 224–25.

11. *DTH*, September 30, 1961; November 13, 1962; May 1, 1963.

12. For more on the civil rights movement in Chapel Hill and at UNC, see "I Raise My Hand to Volunteer, Student Protests in 1960s Chapel Hill," part 1: Integration Sit-ins, online exhibit, www2 .lib.unc.edu/mss/exhibits/protests/sitins.html. An excellent source of images of civil right protests in Chapel Hill during the first half of the 1960s is Jim Wallace and Paul Dickson, *Courage in the Moment: The Civil Rights Struggle, 1961– 1964* (Mineola, N.Y.: Dover Publications, 2010).

13. *DTH*, February 9, 1960.

14. *DTH*, March 3, 6, 12, and April 27, 1960.

15. *DTH*, April 6 and 23, 1960.

16. *DTH*, May 5, 6, 7, and 18, 1960.

17. *DTH*, May 10 and 11, 1960.

18. *DTH*, January 7, 8, and February 7, 1961.

19. *DTH*, May 16, 1961.

20. Ibid.

21. Wallace and Dickson, *Courage in the Moment*, xvii.

22. *DTH*, October 21 and 27, November 18 and 19, and December 1 and 10, 1961.

23. *DTH*, March 15, 1962.

24. *DTH*, September 21 and 22, 1962; March 8, 1963; author's two-part interview with Wayne Hurder, November 29, 2012, and March 1, 2013.

25. *DTH*, September 27, 1962.

26. *DTH*, September 29, October 3, 5, and 6, 1962; email from Mike Putzel to Erica Perel, May 7, 2011; author's interview with Mike Putzel, February 28, 2014.

27. *DTH*, October 3, 6, 9, and December 2 and 4, 1962.

28. *DTH*, October 30, November 15 and 30, December 4, 5, and 6, 1962.

29. *DTH*, April 28, 1963.

30. *DTH*, May 1 and 2, 1963; William J. Billingsley, *Communists on Campus: Race Politics, and the Public University in Sixties North Carolina* (Athens: University of Georgia Press, 1999), 54–55.

31. Putzel interview; https://web.cn.edu/kwheeler/documents/Letter_Birmingham_Jail.pdf.

32. *DTH*, May 7 to 10 and 17 to 19, 1963.

33. *DTH*, April 30 and September 9, 1963.

34. *DTH*, June 20 and August 8, 1963.

35. *DTH*, July 4 and 18, 1963.

36. *DTH*, July 18, 1963.

37. *DTH*, August 8, 1963.

38. *DTH*, September 22 and November 23 to 27, 1963; author's interview with Jim Wallace, August 12, 2011.

39. *DTH*, December 17, 1963; January 7 and March 14, 1964.

40. *DTH*, January 7 and 12, February 8, 11, 20, and 28, 1964.

41. *DTH*, March 18 to 22, 1964.

42. Author's interview with Michael Yopp, November 27, 2012.

43. *DTH*, March 10, 1965.

44. *DTH*, October 14, 1960; February 8, September 23 and 25, 1961; October 24, December 5 and 12, 1962; April 26 and May 19, 1963; February 25, 1964.

Efforts of the editors to provide all perspectives in the early 1960s generally met with student approval, though clearly the paper was mostly left of the political center. In April 1963 an editorial noted with some relish that a conservative student had come into the *Daily Tar Heel* office to praise the staff for publishing a "fair, balanced newspaper." Later that year, student government conducted a poll to ascertain student opinion about the *DTH*. Approximately half of the respondents (48 percent) identified themselves as "moderately liberal," providing a snapshot of campus political leanings. Regarding the editorial policy of the paper, 57 percent indicated that the paper's views were more liberal than their own, 23 percent agreed with the paper's policy, and 6 percent replied that their own views were more liberal (apparently 14 percent had no opinion).

45. *DTH*, October 11, 18 to 23, and 27, 1962; May 19, 1963.

46. *DTH*, December 4, 9, and 12, 1962; January 5, 1963.

47. *DTH*, March 12, 1960; November 4, 1961;

January 7, October 4 and 10, 1962; November 8, 1963.

48. *DTH*, October 12 and December 14, 1962; January 9 and October 2, 1963; William A. Link, *Righteous Warrior: Jesse Helms and the Rise of Modern Conservatism* (New York: St. Martin's Press, 2008), 70–71.

49. *DTH*, October 12, 1962; October 1, 1963; October 14 and December 12, 1965; September 20, 1966.

50. *DTH*, April 25, 1963; February 6, 1964.

51. *DTH*, May 5 and 8, 1963; February 16 and 22, 1964; October 21, 1965; Link, *Righteous Warrior*, 344–66; Andy Trincia, "More Tales Yet to Tell," *Carolina Alumni Review*, 102, no. 2 (March/April 2013): 54–55.

52. "Former UNC President William Friday Dies," www.wral.com/former-unc-president -william-friday-dies/3281443.

53. *DTH*, February 14, 1952; Friday interview; Link, *William Friday*, 108–27. The most complete treatment of the fear of Communists and the Speaker Ban law can be found in Billingsley, *Communists on Campus*.

54. *DTH*, June 27, 1963.

55. *DTH*, June 27, July 11, and August 23, 1963.

56. *DTH*, June 27, July 4, August 1, and October 12, 1963.

57. *DTH*, September 21 and 28, October 8, and 13, 1963; January 16 and February 4, 1964.

58. *DTH*, September 24, October 4, 5, 6, 12, 13, 15, 23, and 29, and November 10 and 16, 1963.

59. *DTH*, August 22 and November 10, 1963.

60. Link, *William Friday*, 120.

61. *DTH*, February 9, 1965.

62. *DTH*, March 31, 1962; October 3, 1963; February 17, 19, and 20, 1965.

In 1962 McKissick was included on a panel sponsored by the School of Journalism entitled "Today's Revolutions," which also featured noted historian Crane Briton, *New York Times* reporter James "Scotty" Reston, and two prominent former *DTH* editors—J. McNeill Smith, an attorney from Greensboro active in civil rights, and Walter Spearman, who was on the faculty of the School of Journalism. He was known as an effective advocate for the movement; a 1963 *Daily Tar Heel* feature story labeled him "Civil Rights Firebrand In Lawyer's Suit."

63. *DTH*, March 17, 1965.

64. *DTH*, February 21, 1964; February 23, April 3, and September 17, 1965.

65. *DTH*, May 8, 1964; May 11, 14, 18, 19, and 21, and October 26, 1965.

66. *DTH*, September 17, 18 and 23, 1965.

67. *DTH*, September 22 and 30, 1965; Link, *Righteous Warrior*, 88.

68. *DTH*, September 21, 22, and 23, October 3, 8, 19, and 28, and November 4, 1965.

69. *DTH*, November 6, 1965; Link, *William Friday*, 122–27.

70. *DTH*, February 2, 4, 5, 13 and 16, 1966.

71. *DTH*, December 5, 1965; Link, *William Friday*, 139; Friday interview; author's two-part interview with Edwin M. Yoder, July 9 and 22, 2012; Lydia Wilson, "Putting Ideas in Their Heads," *Carolina Alumni Review* 100, no. 6 (November/December 2011): 26.

72. *DTH*, February 8 and 20, 1966.

73. *DTH*, April 1 and September 13, 1966; September 12, 1967; February 20, 1968.

74. *DTH*, September 24, October 1, 2, 3, 8, and 9, and December 15, 1970.

75. Link, *William Friday*, 159–85.

76. *DTH*, February 18, 1971.

77. *DTH*, December 16, 1970; February 17, 20,

21, 22, and 23, March 26, September 3, and October 5, 1971.

78. *DTH*, October 25, 1963.

79. *DTH*, November 14, 1964. Built in 1922, Saunders Hall was originally named for William Saunders, Confederate officer and later North Carolina Secretary of State. He is also widely believed to have been one of the leaders of the original Ku Klux Klan in the state during the 1870s. In 2015, following student protests, the UNC Board of Trustees voted to change the name of the building to Carolina Hall. See epilogue.

80. Hurder interview.

81. *DTH*, February 23, 1963; January 10, 1964; December 10, 1965; September 13, 15, and 18, 1966; October 10, 1967; October 18, 1970; March 2, 5, and September 2, 1971.

The subject of recreational drug use on campus first appeared in the *Daily Tar Heel* in late 1965, and had to do with LSD, which the paper noted could "produce weird dreams" and was being sold in Chapel Hill. An ad for a recording of LSD guru Timothy Leary talking about the wonders of the hallucinogen ran in the paper several times in the fall of 1966. Also that fall, the paper carried several articles about the growing problem of the stimulant Dexedrine on campus, which was a pep pill that helped students stay up late and cram for exams, as well as accelerate weight loss. A crackdown on illicit sales of the drug resulted in the suspension of six students. In October 1967, a front-page feature story appeared titled "Drugs Killing Hippies— Doctor Says Flower Children Bring Own Ruin," about a psychiatrist at North Carolina Memorial Hospital who had gone to San Francisco during the so-called Summer of Love and observed the "happenings" of the counterculture group known as hippies. "Outlined by a flickering strobe light," the article dramatically reported, "the psychiatrist perched on a tall stool, looked out across the candle-lit Crossroads Cafe, and began to talk about the end of the hippie movement." In an apparent warning to students, the doctor described the hippies as "terribly, terribly innocent," and said they were "defeated by the introduction of drugs."

By the fall of 1970, marijuana had become the subject of much discussion at UNC, and the *Daily Tar Heel* ran two full-page feature stories about it that academic year. For the second feature the paper conducted a poll, finding that 43 percent of the student body admitted to smoking marijuana. Accompanying the story was a photo with a caption that read: "Two UNC students engage in what has become a common pastime in Chapel Hill. They are smoking finely ground marijuana through a special pipe. Both the marijuana and the pipe are easily accessible in Chapel Hill." A cartoon several days later declared, "Legalize Grass." But changes in editorship often meant changes in opinion, and in September 1971 an editorial ran entitled "Marijuana: Assassin of Youth."

82. *DTH*, May 18, 1950.

83. *DTH*, March 30, 1963; May 12, 1965.

84. *DTH*, November 2, 1965; Link, *Righteous Warrior*, 88.

85. *DTH*, March 27 and May 4, 1963; September 22, 1970.

86. *DTH*, May 5, 1971.

87. Link, *Righteous Warrior*, 89–98.

88. *DTH*, October 19, 20, and 21, 1966.

89. *DTH*, October 26 and 27, and November

10 and 11, 1966; "The Coy Mistress Caper," *Life*, November 11, 1966, 99–102; Link, *Righteous Warrior*, 90.

90. *DTH*, October 22 and 23, 1966.

91. *DTH*, November 4, 1966.

92. *DTH*, February 3, 1967.

93. *DTH*, December 7 and 14, 1970.

94. *DTH*, March 6 and April 7, 1971.

95. For more on the rise of Black Power at American colleges, see Martha Biondi, *The Black Revolution on Campus* (Berkeley: University of California Press, 2012).

96. *DTH*, September 24, 25, and November 13, 1964; May 6, October 2, and November 19, 1966; September 24, 1967; November 4, 1970.

97. *DTH*, September 27 and October 12, 1967; February 22, 1968.

98. *DTH*, September 22, 26, and 29, October 7, November 16, and February 17, 1968.

99. *DTH*, April 6, 1963; October 2, 1965; November 12 and 17, 1967; author's interview with Bill Amlong, December 15, 2012.

100. *DTH*, October 19 and November 21, 1968; Hurder interview.

101. *DTH*, April 10, October 12 and 18, 1968; "I Raise My Hand to Volunteer, Student Protests in 1960s Chapel Hill," part 3: The BSM and the Foodworkers' Strike, online exhibit, www2.lib .unc.edu/mss/exhibits/protests/strike.html.

102. *Carolina Alumni Review* 57, no. 6 (March 1969): 25; Hurder interview.

103. Hurder interview.

104. *DTH*, September 29 1968; March 6, 1969; Link, *William Friday*, 141–50.

105. *DTH*, March 9, 1968; Link, *William Friday*, 144. For more on Charlie Scott, see Gregory J. Kaliss, *Men's College Athletics and Politics of Racial Equality: Five Pioneer Stories of Black Manliness, White Citizenship, and American Democracy* (Philadelphia: Temple University Press, 2012); and Art Chansky, *Game Changers: Dean Smith, Charlie Scott, and the Era That Transformed a Southern College Town* (Chapel Hill: University of North Carolina Press, 2016).

106. *DTH*, May 19, September 24 and October 10, 1963.

107. *DTH*, May 1, October 17 and 24, 1965; November 10 and 12, 1967.

108. *DTH*, September 14, October 7, 10, 12, 21 and 22, 1967.

109. *DTH*, December 5 and 12, 1967; November 3, 1968.

110. *DTH*, January 4, 5, and 31, and February 1 and 2, 1967; Hurder interview.

111. *DTH*, March 25, April 12, and May 1 to 9, 1970.

112. *TH*, masthead, summer editions, 1966. Various sources claim authorship of the phrase, but the earliest documented is Wilbur E. Storey. See Justin E. Walsh, *To Print the News and Raise Hell! A Biography of Wilbur F. Storey* (Chapel Hill: University of North Carolina Press, 1986); Ed Yoder, in his interview with the author, noted Walter Spearman's use of the phrase.

113. Link, *Righteous Warrior*, 112–16, 223, 229–31, 232–34.

114. "'Moderate Students' Organize Hayakawa Society in Chapel Hill" (February 6, 1969), "Hayakawa Society Officers Meet with Chancellor at Chapel Hill" (February 10, 1969), "Six UNC Faculty Members Become Advisors to New Hayakawa Society at UNC in Chapel Hill" (February 13, 1969): UNC News Bureau press releases; Jesse Helms, "Viewpoint" #2031, February 12, 1969.

Photocopies of all of these documents from the files of Wayne Hurder.

115. "[Hayakawa Society] to Start Newspaper to Compete with *Daily Tar Heel*" (February 7, 1969), UNC News Bureau press release, Hurder files; Hurder interview.

116. "Newspaper to be Published by Hayakawa Society in Chapel Hill" (February 28, 1969), UNC News Bureau press release, Hurder files; Hurder interview.

117. *DTH*, May 9 and 14, 1969.

118. Jesse Helms, "Viewpoint" #2097, May 21, 1969; and #2104, May 30, 1969, Hurder files.

119. *DTH*, November 23, 1969; Jesse Helms, "Viewpoint" #2127, September 18, 1969, Hurder files.

120. *DTH*, January 9, February 11 and 19, March 15 and 19, 1970.

121. *DTH*, February 13 and March 19, 1970.

122. *DTH*, April 23 and August 31, 1971.

123. *DTH*, August 31, 1971.

CHAPTER 5

1. *DTH*, August 29, 1972; Student Organizations and Activities: *Daily Tar Heel*: Arrington v. Taylor Case, 1972–73 files, Office of Chancellor, Nelson Ferebee Taylor Records, 1972–1980, University Archives, Wilson Library, University of North Carolina at Chapel Hill.

2. The decision in the case was handed down on August 24, 1974. See www.leagle.com/decision/19741728380FSupp1348_11552.

3. *DTH*, September 1, 4, 5, and 22, October 3, 6, 9, 23, 27, and 30, and December 6, 1972.

4. *DTH*, September 6, 20, and November 3, 1973; Arrington v. Taylor ruling; "Another Proud Student History Minute—From the History Files of the NCCU, www.nccueagles.yuku.com

/another-proud-student-history-minute-from-the-hist-t5280.html.

5. www.leagle.com/decision/19741728380FSupp1348_11552.

6. *DTH*, September 3, 1974.

7. *DTH*, October 10 and 16, 1972; January 24, February 1, 6, and 8, 1973.

8. *DTH*, August 25, 1975.

9. Ibid., and *DTH*, September 3, 1975.

10. *DTH*, September 29, 1972; September 5, 1975.

11. *DTH*, September 3 and 4, 1975.

12. *DTH*, September 5, 1975.

13. *Technician*, September 8, 1975; *DTH*, September 9, 1975.

14. *DTH*, September 9, 1975.

15. *DTH*, September 10, 18, 19, 23, and 25, October 16, and December 5, 1975; March 30, 1976; February 1 and 7, 1977; August 30, 1978. Author's interview with Kevin Schwartz, January 11, 2013.

16. *DTH*, March 12 and 13, 1964; February 19, 22, and March 8, 1971; November 20, 1972; January 12 and November 16, 1973.

17. *DTH*, March 27 and October 9, 1973.

18. *DTH*, October 5 and November 20, 1973.

19. *DTH*, January 18, October 23, and November 20, 1973; August 28, 1975.

20. *DTH*, October 24, 25, 26, and 29, 1973.

21. *DTH*, October 26 and 29, 1973; August 26 and November 26, 1974; April 17, 1975.

22. *DTH*, November 20, 1973; January 17, 1974.

23. *DTH*, August 29 and November 20, 1972; February 21, 28, March 6, April 2, and November 16, 1973; April 17, 1975; August 27 and October 19, 1976; February 16 and October 24, 1979; September 8, 1980; January 22 and February 10, 11, and 12, 1981; author's interview with George Shadroui, December 17, 2012.

24. *DTH*, November 7, 1974; August 28, 1975.

25. *DTH*, October 13 and 17, December 2 and 4, 1975; November 15, 1977; January 31, 1979.

26. *DTH*, September 26 and 27, 1978; February 8, 1979; August 25, 1980; November 22, 1982; October 9, 19, and 29, 1984.

27. *DTH*, September 14 and 23, 1976; April 7 and 18, 1978.

28. *DTH*, February 8 and 9, 1983; Jennifer Talhelm and Thanassis Cambanis, "*Tar Heel* History Colored with Attempts to Censor Content, Ads," *DTH* centennial edition, February 23, 1993, 10.

29. *DTH*, February 10 and 11, 1983.

30. *DTH*, February 10, 11, 14, and 16, 1983.

31. *DTH*, March 15, 17, August 29, and November 16, 1983.

32. *DTH*, November 22, 1974; October 21, 1975; September 26 and 28, 1983; October 30, 1984.

33. *DTH*, February 27, March 6, and November 19, 1964; author's three-part interview with Rolfe Neill, July 25, 31, and August 17, 2012.

34. *DTH*, January 22 and April 9, 1974.

35. *DTH*, September 13, 17, and 18, 1974. For more information on the early years of the LGBTQ community at UNC, see T. Evan Falkenbury and Aaron Hayworth, "The Carolina Gay Association, Oral History, and Coming Out at the University of North Carolina," *Oral History Review* 43, no. 1 (Spring 2016): 115–37; "LBGT Identities, Communities, and Resistance in North Carolina, 1945–2012," at Outhistory.org (www.outhistory.org/exhibits/show/nc-lgbt/campus-activism/queer-student-orgs); and Layla Quran, "The Fall '13 Internship Project: The Carolina Gay Association and the Sexual Revolution at UNC," in the Southern Oral History Program newsletter, October 16, 2013 (www.sohp.org/2013/10/16/the-fall13-internship-project-the-carolina

-gay-association-and-the-sexual-revolution-at-unc/).

36. *DTH*, September 25, 1974.

37. *DTH*, October 20, 1975; January 23, 1976; January 31 and February 2,1978; April 24, 27, 28, and 29, 1981.

38. *DTH*, October 3, 1975; November 22, 1976; January 31, 1978, April 9 and 16, 1982.

39. *DTH*, March 13, 1978; April 4, 1979; April 2, 1982.

40. *DTH*, March 25, 1983; November 28, 29, and 30, 1984.

41. *DTH*, March 22, 1978; November 19, 1980; December 7, 1983.

42. *DTH*, September 27 and November 14, 1978; January 26, 29, August 30, and September 14, 1979; December 2, 1980.

43. Shadroui interview.

44. *DTH*, September 16, October 16, 25, and November 3, 1972.

45. *DTH*, September 19 and October 31, 1972.

46. *DTH*, November 3 and 9, 1972.

47. *DTH*, October 28, 1976; March 22, 1977; November 9, 1979; April 21, 1980; Shadroui interview; author's interview with John Drescher, May 9, 2011.

48. *DTH*, March 11, April 16 and 24, September 2, and October 1 and 31, 1980; Shadroui interview; Drescher interview.

49. *DTH*, October 9, 29, and 30, and November 11, 1980.

50. *DTH*, March 20, April 13 and 14, 1981.

51. *DTH*, October 28, 29 and November 1, 1982. The paper also endorsed Cobey in his first political campaign for lieutenant governor in 1980, which he lost.

52. *DTH*, April 20, 23 and October 22, 1982; November 28, 1983; September 6, 1984.

53. *DTH*, September 16, 1983; October 19, 1984; Link, *William Friday*, 373.

54. *DTH*, February 13, 15, October 30 and 31, and November 1, 1984.

55. *DTH*, October 10, November 8 and 20, and December 6, 1974.

56. *DTH*, March 15, 22, and 21, and October 26, 1982. For a brief description of the *Carolina Conservative*, see the online exhibit, "*Tar Heel* Ink": www.lib.unc.edu/ncc/thi/politic.html.

57. For the decision in the lawsuit, see: www.leagle.com/decision/19831177702F2d475_11079.

58. *Carolina Critic*, October 12, 1987.

59. *DTH*, October 20 and November 3, 1970.

60. *DTH*, February 28, March 2 and 3, September 16, and October 14, 1972.

61. *DTH*, August 31, 1971; August 25 and September 18, 1975; April 4 and 5, 1978: April 19 and 26, 1979; April 9 and 19, 1982.

62. *DTH*, October 11, 1972; February 13, 1974; November 3, 1982; February 7 and 13, 1985; February 8, 1990.

63. *DTH*, September 2, 1988; October 3 and 4, 1989; August 31, 1992.

64. William Link, *William Friday: Power, Purpose, and American Higher Education* (Chapel Hill: University of North Carolina Press, 1995), chapters 9–12.

65. *DTH*, March 3, 1973; February 1 and December 6, 1977.

66. *DTH*, February 2 and March 28, 1978; February 26 and April 25, 1979; October 22 and November 25, 1980.

67. *DTH*, January 16 and 20, 1975; Tyler Bridges, *The Rise of David Duke* (Jackson: University of Mississippi Press, 1994), 51–52.

68. *DTH*, September 27 and November 20, 1974; January 14 and 15, 1975.

69. *DTH*, January 17, 1975.

70. *DTH*, January 20, 21, and 23, 1975.

71. *DTH*, January 20 and 21, 1975.

72. *DTH*, January 24, 1975.

73. *DTH*, February 18, 19, 20, and 26, and March 3,1975.

74. *DTH*, February 28 and March 23, 1975.

75. *DTH*, November 17, 18, 19, and 21, 1980.

76. *DTH*, November 13, 1984; August 26, September 6 and 9, October 11 and 15, November 15 and 25, 1985.

77. *DTH*, March 19, 24, 25, and 26, April 1, 2, and 4, 1986.

78. *DTH*, April 5, 1986; "University of North Carolina students win divestment from apartheid South Africa, 1986–1987," Global Nonviolent Action Database: nvdatabase.swarthmore.edu/content/university-north-carolina-students-win-divestment-apartheid-south-africa-1986-1987.

79. *DTH*, October 20, 1976; February 16, 1978; October 12 and December 2, 1983; January 27 and February 10, 1984; September 19, 1985. The name of William Saunders was removed in 2015, and the building was renamed Carolina Hall (see epilogue).

80. *DTH*, October 2 and 3, 1985; September 29, October 6, and November 11 and 26, 1988; October 31, 1989; January 12 and February 2, 1990.

81. *DTH*, November 4 and 26, 1988; October 27, 1992.

82. *DTH*, April 20 and August 27, 1979; February 14 and March 9, 1989; August 27, and September 3, 4, and 11, 1991; February 27 and March 19, 1992.

83. *DTH*, March 12, 18, 23, April 2, August 27, September 2, and November 2, 1992.

84. *DTH*, September 4, 11, 14, 16, 18, 21 and 22, 1992.

85. *DTH*, September 2, 22, October 2, 13, 16, and 22, 1992.

86. *DTH*, March 2, 15, 29, and 30, and December 1, 1982; January 13 and 24, February 11, and November 28 and 29, 1983; January 26, February 20, March 16, and September 13, 1984.

87. *DTH*, November 6, 1978; September 17 and 18, 1980.

88. *DTH*, August 28, 1981; February 26, August 23, November 3 and 5, 1982; January 20, 1983; January 6, 1985.

89. *DTH*, August 30, 1983; August 28, 1984; August 22, 1985; January 17 and 20, 1986.

90. *DTH*, January 18, 19, 20, and 24, and August 31, 1989.

91. *DTH*, April 4, 1978; April 20, 1982; December 2, 1988; March 7 and 31, September 19 and 26, and December 5, 1989; February 19, March 21, April 12, and September 4 and 19, 1990; March 17 and 31, September 17, and November 11 and 18, 1992.

92. *DTH*, August 25, 1975; March 21 and April 5, 1984; August 26 and September 3, 1985; April 9 and 10, 1986; February 3 and 6, April 13 and 19, and September 11, 1989; January 29 and March 5, 1990; April 1, 2, and 24, May 18, August 31, and September 1, 8, and 23, 1992; February 15 and 24, March 2, 25, 26, 29, and 31, and April 1, 1993.

93. *DTH*, October 25, 1989; September 29 and 30, October 1 and 14, 1992.

94. *DTH*, February 11 and September 11, 1985; September 22, 1986; November 4 and December 1, 1988; January 17, February 1, April 14, 19, 20, and 25, August 31, September 5, 6, and 12, November 14, and December 1 and 4, 1989; December 3, 1990; April 1, 1991; April 15 and September 22, 1992.

95. *DTH*, October 4, 5, 12, and 13, November 9, and December 4, 1989; March 18 and 27, April 2, and September 12, 1991.

96. *DTH*, September 4, 10, and 16, 1986.

97. *DTH*, April 9, August 19, September 5, 12, 18, and 24, and October 1, 1985.

98. *DTH*, October 12, 17, 25, and 27, and November 4, 1988.

99. *DTH*, October 25, 26, and 29, 1990.

100. *DTH*, September 25 and 27, and October 3, 15, 18, 23, and 26, 1990.

101. *DTH*, October 25, 26, and 29, 1990.

102. *DTH*, November 9, 12, 15 and 29, 1990; January 14 and 15, 1991.

103. *DTH*, August 27, 1984; September 1, 1988, Schwartz interview; author's interviews with Kerry DeRochi Kisa, May 6, 2013; and Peter Wallsten, May 7, 2013.

104. Schwartz interview.

105. *DTH*, September 8, 1989; Schwartz interview.

106. *DTH*, February 16, 19, and 21, 1990.

107. Schwartz interview.

108. *DTH*, February 23, March 22, 23 and 24, 1993; Schwartz interview.

109. *DTH*, September 5, 12, 13, 14, and 25, 1989; Schwartz interview.

110. *DTH*, January 24, August 27, September 24, and October 2, 1990; March 20, 1991.

111. *DTH*, March 20 and 27, 1992; February 15 and 17, 1993.

112. *DTH*, April 23, 1993.

EPILOGUE

1. Author's interview with Kevin Schwartz, January 11, 2013. Betsy O'Donovan, "Necessity, Invention and the *Daily Tar Heel*," Medium.com, August 23, 2016, www.medium.com/now-what

-next/necessity-invention-and-the-daily-tar
-heel-65d1c306c188.

2. Schwartz interview.

3. Author's interview with Erica Beshears Perel, June 13, 2013.

4. *DTH*, February 9, March 25, April 14, 15, and 16, 1993.

5. *DTH*, October 7, 8, and 9, 1999. For the original record the naming of the building in 1920, see UNC Board of Trustees minutes, volume 12 (January 1917–January 18, 1924), 234. The name was authorized in 1920 in anticipation of construction of two buildings. However funds were exhausted for the construction of Steele Building and other repair projects. As a result, Saunders's name was given to the next campus building completed, behind Steele, in 1922. For the first article about the name Saunders Hall, see the *DTH*, March 19, 1975.

6. *DTH*, April 3 and 4, 2001.

7. *DTH*, April 9, 2001.

8. *DTH*, October 28, 2012.

9. *DTH*, June 4, August 27, and September 18, 2015; March 28, 2017.

10. *DTH*, March 28, 2017.

11. *DTH*, November 16 and 19, 2004; September 12, 2006.

12. *DTH*, September 11, 2005; "UNC student fired for 'malpractice' in column on Arabs," *USA Today*, September 16, 2005: usatoday30 .usatoday.com/news/education/2005-09-16-UNC -columnist_x.htm.

13. *DTH*, September 15, 2005; February 9, 2006; tarheelcon.blogspot.com/2006/02/cartoon -jihad-at-unc.html.

14. Schwartz interview.

15. *DTH*, November 4, 2010; July 26, 2012.

16. *DTH*, October 28, 2012.

17. *DTH*, October 22, 2014; for more on the Wainstein report and its fallout, see "The Waiting," *Carolina Alumni Review* 104, no. 1 (January/ February 2015): 16–27.

18. *DTH*, April 26, 2017.

19. *DTH*, June 24, 2010.

20. O'Donovan, "Necessity, Invention and the *Daily Tar Heel*."

21. *DTH*, April 26, 2011.

22. *DTH*, February 21, 2013.

INDEX

Page numbers appearing in *italics* refer to illustrations.